Although his investigation necessarily touches upon mystical experience, it is not directly concerned with mysticism in the strict sense but with the broader, more universal experience of the ordinary sincere religious life. The specific concern of the book is with the problem of Christian experience in the Catholic Church, but since the Church's mediation is only a way of transmitting the mediation performed by Christ, the whole experience described is an experience in Christ.

THE CHRISTIAN EXPERIENCE

THE CHRISTIAN EXPERIENCE

An Introduction to a Theology

BY JEAN MOUROUX

TRANSLATED BY GEORGE LAMB

Sheed and Ward · New York · 1954

Library of Congress Catalog Card Number 54-11143

NIHIL OBSTAT

Thomas J. McHugh
Censor Librorum

IMPRIMATUR

✠ Jerome D. Hannan
Bishop of Scranton

Scranton
October 26, 1954

Manufactured in the United States of America
By The Haddon Craftsmen, Inc., Scranton, Pa.

Acknowledgments

We wish to thank The Newman Press for the use of the excerpts from *The Complete Works of St. John of the Cross,* translated by E. Allison Peers, contained in this book; and Benziger Brothers, Inc., publisher and copyright owners of the translation by the Fathers of the English Dominican province of the *Summa Theologica* of St. Thomas Aquinas, with whose kind permission passages from this work are reprinted.

Preface

THE problem of the Christian experience necessarily arises in any philosophy of religion, or any theology. It is a cardinal problem for the religious person whose one wish is to enter into contact with God—to see him, touch him, feel him. In the hope of finding God, he feels about with his hands like a blind man (Acts xvii, 27), and thus the problem of the experience of God arises inevitably in any practice of religion, or any religious thought.

But it may be true to say that it arises in a more acute form in the Christian consciousness. In the first place, the Christian believes in an incarnate God who assumed a human body and a human soul, and gave himself the appearance of a man, so that he might be seen, heard, and handled (I John i, 1). Further, the Christian lives in faith; he hopes for eternal life—i.e., he hopes to see God face to face—but he knows that God cannot be seen here on earth, and so for him faith is the beginning of eternal life—without the seeing. The result is that he finds himself faced with the most formidable of mysteries, the most unheard-of paradoxes, and the constant possibility of scandal; and all these things make it hard for him to be faithful to the end, hard to live by pure faith and not to give way to temptation and the snares of experience. Whenever men succumb to these things there arise those movements in Christianity that put far too much emphasis on feeling and end by opposing experience to the faith, and so force the Church to make a vigorous effort to throw off all this disastrous "experiencing." The Protestant crisis with its "experience" of justification, the Jansenist crisis with its "experience" of predestination, the Quietist crisis with its "experience" of spiritual purity, the Traditionalist crisis with its move to set up "experience against reason," the Modernist crisis with its "heart versus head" experience—these are all so many regrettable stages in the recent history of Catholicism. But this endless resurgence of the same demand is sufficient proof of the reality of the problem, endlessly arising only to be endlessly destroyed.

The contemporary consciousness, moreover, is such as to make this problem more urgent than ever. Today, experience is all-important, for we live in an age of experiences. The transformation of the material world, the control of life, the cynical grinding down of human material, the revolutionary artistic activity, the new efforts in all the realms of the spirit, violent, anarchic, perverted—all these things mean that we are plunged into a chaos of experiences. And when the modern man turns towards Christianity, the question he asks is, "What worthwhile experience can you give me?"

Before we tackle the problem of the Christian experience in the Catholic Church, we must first be quite clear about what this book is not.

The word "experience," which has many meanings,[1] denotes at least two different kinds of problem, the first of which is necessarily excluded here by the very nature of the Christian experience. On the one hand, in fact, experience can be regarded as a search for truth. This kind of experience is governed by and directed towards discovery, proof, verification, and it involves a series of steps which, as a result of an inquiry conducted at different levels, end in the apprehension, formulation, and proof of a new truth. The beginning is inquiry, the end possession, and the journey from one to the other, in all its varied complexity, provides the actual experience. In this book we are not concerned with this first meaning of the word "experience," because our point of view is taken from within the Christian experience itself: we are not studying this "search for truth"—or for salvation—which is the movement from unbelief to faith, for its own sake.

But "experience" can also denote the grasp of a reality. In this sense

[1] Cf. the very interesting note by F. GRÉGOIRE, "*Sur les termes intuition et expérience*," in *Rev. Phil.* (Louvain, 1946), pp. 411-415. The author gives the word four different meanings—verification, knowledge drawn from life, experimentation, habitual knowledge. "The common element" is "an immediate knowledge of concrete things," and "ultimately, the word *experience* suggests concrete knowledge and knowledge united to life."

every experience is something that is received. It is the consciousness of a given reality; not a search for truth, but the experienced presence of a reality; not a journey, but possession. This kind of experience lies at the very heart of a particular order of realities or values. And when the reality in question is spiritual, and necessarily complex, experience means the possession, the consciousness of, the deepening insight into, a structured reality. It can then be defined as the act or series of acts involved in apprehending an object or realizing a presence, the consciousness of an experienced structure. In short, it is in the first place an activity involving contact and, ultimately, communion. It is this kind of problem that we have endeavoured to tackle in this book.

Obviously, of course, any sort of integral experience involves a certain amount of inquiry. But this presupposes an experience of a given reality, and it prepares the way for a deeper understanding of it; and this rhythm, made up of the experience that means inquiry and the experience that means a grasp of reality, takes place within a given structure which becomes clearer and fuller as it grows and develops.

It follows that the inquiry undertaken in this book does not proceed at the psychological level. In the sense that we have just defined, experience transcends any purely psychological investigation—if such is possible—at all points. I have therefore made no attempt to describe any states of the soul, or to inquire into any of the various forms which the life of faith may take. In particular, I have had no intention whatsoever of basing any of this work on those feelings and impressions and emotions which are all too often taken for the religious experience itself. For (as I shall endeavour to explain in detail) all such "psychologism" is bound to be superficial, mistaken, and dangerous. Spiritual experience is a highly complex, coherent structure, like the person itself, and only a genuinely philosophical or theological inquiry can give a proper account of it.

But this book does not aim so high as to present an integral theology of the Christian experience, and for three very good reasons at least: in the first place, because such a study would mean speaking from the very centre of this experience, seeing into its very depths, seeing its fundamental forms of expression and the way these complement or contrast with each other; second, because any such investigation would involve a whole series of historical inquiries—on the grand scale, and in detail—which have not so far been made, and also a detailed theological account of the Church's decisions when faced with dogmatic crises, and the spiritual problems raised by such crises; and third, because it would mean entering into a discussion of the mystical experience, at least in its main outlines and classic forms. Such a vast labour—need I say?—I have not endeavoured to perform.

My aim has been less ambitious. Leaving aside any direct treatment of the mystical experience in the strict sense of the word,[2] I have confined my attentions to a more humble, more fundamental, more universal experience, that of the ordinary sincere religious life; and I have aimed to supply the materials for the theology of this experience by examining a few of what seem to me to be the essential points. The first three chapters are concerned with problems antecedent to the experience proper; these are introduced to explain what our actual inquiry is to be, and the direction it must take. The first necessity is to give a precise meaning to the "idea of religious experience" (Ch. I), and to disentangle this from empirical notions that falsify it and render it useless from the Catholic point of view. Next (Ch. II) it has to be made quite clear that there is indeed a "possibility of Christian experience," and this I have attempted to do by, on the one hand, giving some account of the decisions reached by the Council of Trent as against various Protestant positions, and, on the other, by showing the difference between the Christian experience and the mystical experience. Then, because this religious experience takes place entirely within the confines of the faith, I have endeavoured, on the basis of passages drawn from the liturgy and the canon, from the writings of the Fathers and succeeding theologians, to show what consciousness a Christian may have of his faith (Ch. III). The three chapters that follow describe some of the main scriptural themes that raise the problem of religious experience and give some sort of outline of the experience itself—themes which run concurrently, if haphazardly, in St. Matthew's Gospel (Ch. IV), in St. Paul's experience of the Holy Spirit (Ch. V), and in the extremely

[2] Those interested in this subject may consult a work that appeared after my own book had been completed: Rev. Fr. Truhlar, *De Experientia mystica* (Rome, Gregorian, 1951).

solid structure of the Christian experience which is to be found in the First Epistle of St. John (Ch. VI).

The remaining chapters attempt to show some of the essential lines of this structure, lines which, so to speak, supply the standard data for the experience. In the first place, it is an experience that takes place within the Church (Ch. VII), and this gives it some of its most characteristic features. But because the Church's mediation is only a way of transmitting the mediation performed by Christ, the whole experience is an experience in Christ (Ch. VIII). Furthermore, since the Christian experience is not an affective experience, but the integration of an affective experience, I have tried to explain my own view of this highly difficult and dangerous point: Chapter IX repeats a few general facts which are all too often forgotten, and Chapter X endeavours to put "spiritual feelings" in their proper place. A note about St. John of the Cross continues these observations on to the plane of the mystical life. Finally, since the main principle of the experience is the "faith that works through charity," the last chapter (XI) is an attempt to explore this complex structure and to make clear both our knowledge and our ignorance of charity; whilst the ultimate limits and scope of the Christian experience are brought out in a few concluding pages.

This book is thus a kind of introduction to a theology of the Christian experience, and, humble though it is, I hope that it may prove useful. May God grant that it will at least enable the power and fecundity of Catholic principles to be realized a little more clearly, and encourage younger minds to continue the work here embarked upon.

Dijon. 25 March, 1952.

CONTENTS

PART I
Problems

CHAPTER ONE

The Idea of Religious Experience

There are few more deeply human problems than the problem of religious experience. One would therefore expect this problem and the idea on which it centres to have been studied frequently, at length, and in systematic detail. But it has not. Even the assumptions that necessarily condition the problem have not always been clearly brought out—the problem is often settled in advance without any reference to them, and even, it seems, without any realization that they exist. For though there may be no greater topic of discussion than the essence of religion, nothing is more difficult to understand, more obscure, in spite of custom and appearances, than the idea of experience. People talk about it as though it were a simple fact that could be defined without any difficulty. But the truth is that it raises a whole host of problems, and there has to be some sort of metaphysical decision about it before it can be used legitimately. It will be convenient, in an endeavour to show how necessary some sort of radical criticism is in these matters, and before going on to explain my own view, to turn to the old but still highly instructive book by William James, *The Varieties of Religious Experience*.[1]

1

It is a remarkable fact that this religious experience, which is regarded as a pure fact of immediate experience, can only be reached after a threefold eliminating process has taken place. To begin with, the social or institutional element has to be eliminated, for there

[1] New York, Longmans, 1952. The references that follow are taken from this edition.

has to be a drastic separation between inner religion and socialized religion, the latter being simply a later accretion, artificially added on and petrified—any kind of orthodoxy ends inevitably in a mere external observance. In this view, any genuine religious experience has to be a strictly individualistic affair. Then, within this inner religion, the intellectual element has to be eliminated, as being obviously secondary and derivative. Intellectual imagery is fundamentally nothing more than the development—invariably, to a great extent, artificial, and containing a strong tinge of the social element—of a deeper reality; hence the enormous number of divergent and often contradictory variations to which it has been subject throughout the whole field of religious experience.

Finally, any sort of clear and definite relationship with God has to be eliminated—for any such relationship would demand clear and definite ideas about God (even if only negative ones), some sort of affirmation about him. James dismisses this as an impossibility, because he abstracts the intellectual element from the hard core of religion, and hence cannot admit that religion has its own clearly outlined specific field: "As there thus seems to be no one elementary religious emotion . . . so there might conceivably also prove to be no one specific and essential kind of religious object, and no one specific and essential kind of religious act."[2] Consequently, again, God himself becomes merely secondary in religious experience. He is reduced to the stature of an unknown quantity who exists solely that we may live: we do not serve him, we make use of him, James says, repeating a phrase of Leuba's—and the really interesting and typical element in religious experience is to be found in the power which is attributed to God and which flows from him into us. This deliberately utilitarian conception—the utter negation of any genuine God of religion—ends in the most unmitigated anthropocentricism; and ultimately our relationship with God, which is an essential part of religion, becomes for James a movement that takes all its meaning and reality from below—from the state of exaltation which it induces in human beings. Here is James's own definition: "Religion, therefore . . . shall mean for us the feelings, acts, and experiences of individual men in their solitude, *so far as they apprehend themselves to stand in relation to whatever they may consider the divine*.[3] Here

[2] P. 29.
[3] Pp. 31-32.

the words italicized denote no more than something that is useful practically for the purposes of diagnosis and clarification; there is no question of its being an essential, integral part of the experience itself. It may be said without exaggeration that what interests James in the state of exalted communion which is the most typical feature of religious experience is not the communion, which may be an absolute illusion, but the exaltation, which he regards as the one really true and beneficent element in religion.

What then remains as the hard core of religious experience? A "dynamogenic" feeling—the consciousness of a power that gives life by giving a new savour to existence, a feeling of incomparable security in the soul, a power of which the will knows nothing.[4] We enter this world as the result of "a vivid sense of the reality of things unseen."[5] We advance further through a consciousness of having passed from anxiety to deliverance. We reach consummation when "religious aims form the habitual centre of [our] energy";[6] but this centre always remains the "infinitely pleasant feeling of the presence of God," the essential part of which, of course, is the pleasant feeling that is experienced—or, in the words that James uses to describe the Christian religion, but which are valid for all religions, the centre is always "the excitement of a higher kind of emotion, in the presence of which no exertion of volition is required."[7] Thus the essence of religion is this feeling which is to be found everywhere, and religion is fundamentally the actual experience of this joy and strength that transfigure human life.[8]

[4] A history of this reduction of religion to feeling would prove highly instructive. As far as modern thought is concerned, it would mean beginning with the revolution started by Luther, of course—faith becoming a matter of emotional intuition and expressing itself in a powerful affective experience (cf. H. Strohl, *La Pensée de la Réforme* [Neuchâtel-Paris, 1951], pp. 31-32). Luther once wrote: "Fundamentally, love and faith are the same." Strohl, quoting these words (p. 35) sees Lutheran faith as "the experience of the love of a God holy, just and always active" (p. 92). For A. Nygren, Lutheran faith is a pure opening-out to God's love, through which man—like a canal (a "pipe")—receives agape from above and gives it back below (*Agape and Eros*, II, 2). A whole line of irrational mysticism was to arise out of Luther's ambivalent faith, leading by way of Schleiermacher's *Second Discourse on Religion* to the sentimental empiricism of Liberal Protestantism and one section of Modernism.

[5] P. 421.

[6] P. 193.

[7] P. 46.

[8] P. 48.

Essentially, therefore, James's point of view seems to mean reducing religion to the level of the immediate experience of the repercussions of a particular attitude, and thus to the level of a purely empirical experience. But is it not clear that a number of strictly philosophical assumptions are involved here? that behind the generous—sometimes over-generous—good nature of his highly accommodating psychology there lies hidden an entire positive metaphysic of religion and experience? The social aspect of religion is rejected because society is held to be an entirely external affair compared with the person's private life. The intellectual element is rejected because any real knowledge about the transcendent world is considered impossible. The actual relationship with God himself is rejected in favour of a biological relationship because it is believed that biological functions are the only genuine realities . . . the result being that this vast book, which starts from the assumption that religious experience can be accepted as a pure fact, appears from beginning to end as a highly personal creation. It is perhaps the misfortune of any kind of empiricism that it is always obliged to create, when it claims merely to be stating facts. We shall therefore have to reject this imaginary disinterestedness, this pseudo-evidence, this mutilated essence, and consider the whole problem from the beginning again. As has been so well said by Boutroux: "Fundamentally, what is this special experience that is described as religious experience? Is it no more than a purely subjective state, or is it a genuine communication with a being different and distinct from the conscious subject himself? Does it not rather seem that, just as Locke and Kant introduced the criticism of sense experience, so it is legitimate and indeed necessary for philosophy to proceed to the criticism of religious experience?"[9] Without embarking on such an ambitious project here, I should at least like to try in this chapter to "place" the actual idea of religious experience correctly, as seen from the philosophical point of view.

2. *Religion*

First let me explain what is meant by religion—as far at least as is necessary for the purposes of this inquiry. Religion is a relationship to the Sacred Being, and it is established by the interaction of two

[9] Preface to the French translation of *The Varieties of Religious Experience*, p. xviii. See also *Science et Religion* (Paris, 1908), pp. 332-338.

essential components. The Sacred Being is in the first place an object of adoration—and therefore someone on whom all beings depend—because he is absolutely transcendent over man, because he is the absolute fullness in which all other beings merely participate, and because he demands absolute submission and absolute homage. He is also an object of love—and therefore someone to whom all beings must call—because he is the archetype, the model and end for man made in his image; because he is the fullness in whose possession lies all blessedness, and because he demands of us the perfect gift of self which institutes—as far as possible—perfect communion between man and God. These two necessary kinds of relationship need to be qualified from within by a fact which is not essential but which is involved in the human condition—the fact of sin. As a result of this, between man and God there is not simply an infinite metaphysical distance of the kind that separates creature from Creator, but also an infinite moral distance between the Holy One and the sinner. As a result of this, again, love cannot simply be a joyful movement from the being who is called to the Being who calls: the creature needs pardon and purification before his soul can be raised to God. Thus, a movement of penitential sorrow, ardent supplication, and humble hope—which can only find its fulfilment in a religion that is literally *revealed*—is added to the essential relationship of adoration and love. Nevertheless, despite this addition, religion still remains essentially an indissoluble relationship of adoration and love—the two attitudes being mutually involved in each other, impregnating each other and together producing the act which lies at the heart of all religion—prayer; ebbing and flowing together in a movement that makes up the life and happiness of the religious soul.

Religion is thus, fundamentally, a personal relationship to God. It is the spirit itself, at its highest or deepest point, brought into a living relationship with the infinite Spirit; it is the created person entering at the highest point of his energy into contact with the Person with whom is all adoration and all bliss. It is thus the highest act the human being can perform, the act through which, through homage and self-giving, he fulfils himself—by recognizing that God alone can fulfil him. But because the *person* is involved here, this relationship will not merely have an individual aspect, it is of necessity bound to involve a social or communal aspect. The person cannot cut himself off from others, even when he withdraws into solitude. He can only approach God as he is—i.e., bound up with all other persons—and therefore by integrating himself with others, by uniting himself with them, by deliberately immersing himself in the human community which he must serve, because from it he draws his very life and because its essential bond is its relationship with God, the Source, Archetype and End of all human beings. It is therefore in union with his fellow men that the person submits and offers himself to God the Father of all. The religious relationship is a profoundly individual affair, but it can never be individualistic. The religious soul, being open to the world of divine things, is necessarily open to the world of human things too. And true religion must be a power that increases the communion between men and develops brotherly feelings between them, so that in both respects—as self-subsistent, and as open to others—the whole person may be fulfilled in God.

This personal relationship is, moreover, an integral relationship between man and God. The whole person is involved in the religious act. All his thought is involved, because God is the highest intelligence and the highest of intellectual things, the archetype of truth, the source of all intellectual light; and by means of images, thoughts, formulas, a certain idea of God determines the movement of the mind and increases its hold on intellectual things. All his spiritual movement is involved, because man finds God alone to be the only being he can love and adore infinitely, and therefore the only object who can adequately respond to his appeals. All his freedom is involved, because in the religious act man wagers his destiny, acts according to his vocation, and fulfils himself in time by giving himself an eternal meaning. His whole body and all his activity are involved, because moral and social action and religious worship are so many essential ways in which religion must become embodied in life, a genuine service of God—are, in short, the real truth of any real religion.

If there are any spiritual instincts in man, they are all involved and integrated in this highest of all acts by which he attains to the personal, living, infinite source of all truth, goodness and beauty; more precisely still, by which he attains to this source in its genuinely religious form of infinite holiness and infinite love—because truth, goodness, and beauty culminate, and reveal themselves in all their purity, in the being who is the living God, the God of holiness, the God of love.

This integral, personal relationship thus appears as the supremely unifying relationship in human life, that which tends more than anything else to realize the living vocation for which the human person is made, from the beginning to the end of his life—in short, as the relationship that inaugurates the highest form of communion with Being and all lesser beings.

3. *Experience*

If there is any such thing as religious experience, it will be the experience of this highest of all activities, with all that it involves. But the idea of religious experience is always in danger of being doubly falsified. On the one hand, it may be based on false conceptions of religion. We have just said that religion is the most unifying and integrating activity in which the human being can take part. But the elements which it integrates are ultimately dissociable, and they can always be dissociated in fact. When this dissociation takes place, the result is a mutilation of religion, either because the "religion of the heart" is separated from the social aspect of religion, or because this inner religion is given an intellectualist, or voluntarist, or sentimental, or aesthetic form. But this mutilation of religion leads to a corresponding mutilation of experience, which in its turn becomes a matter of mere intellect, or will, or sentiment. Such kinds of religious experience will necessarily, therefore, be falsifications, because whereas they present themselves as integral experiences, they are in fact only partial.

Moreover, this mutilation is made all the easier as a result of errors bearing directly on the matter of experience itself. Certainly there is nothing more difficult to define than experience. Philosophers give us either a chaos of conflicting definitions or no definition at all—which is more significant still. It must be said that contemporary writers have tried to bring some sort of order into this chaos, and there are some forthright pages by Le Senne and a remarkable essay by Lenoble which are very well worth reading,[10] but, confining myself to our own immediate problem, I should say that the main error tends to be the depersonalizing of experience. Because it is treated as though it could be defined outside the personal relationship upon which it is based and within which it is realized, it gives rise to two opposing

[10] R. Le Senne, *Obstacle et Valeur* (Paris, 1934), ch. i, "*Expérience et philosophie*"; R. Lenoble, *Essai sur la notion d'expérience* (Paris, 1943).

kinds of error, which may be described as follows. On the one hand, there is an empirical conception of experience, as though there was no experience except of "things," and as though an out-and-out subjective passivity was the absolute criterion of experience. This kind of conception turns religious experience into a matter of "sentiment," in which impressions, emotions, feelings, all that is undergone, or endured, or felt in a merely passive way, becomes the essential thing, becomes, so to speak, the pure, primitive fact. If, for example, one turns to the article by Fr. Pinard,[11] one finds religious experience defined in these words: "Any impression experienced in the course of acts or states usually described as religious," and again: "The sensations, emotions, illuminations, comforts, which provide the experimental data of religious practice." And these definitions are perfectly just, since the errors against which they are aimed all involve them.[12] But what I intend to do here, in the name of a healthy philosophy of the spirit, is to reject all these empirical definitions, which must inevitably fail to grasp the essential nature of religious experience.

At the other end of the scale we find an idealist definition, according to which experience is a purely mental construct of a special kind, manifesting the mind's omnipotence and producing the only genuine kind of truth. There are no "things" here, of course; experience is simply the expression of the immanent activity of the mind, which is independent and absolute. A conception of this kind turns religious experience into a purely rationalistic affair, in which the essential thing is the positing activity of the mind: religion is entirely emptied of meaning and replaced by its contrary, the absolute autonomy of the ego. But both these conceptions are equally unfaithful to the person, the first tending to regard him as a thing, and the second as a self-enclosed, impersonal activity. Consequently they mutilate religious experience, which is the experience of the person in contact with a personal God.

I suggest, therefore, that there is experience when the person is aware of himself in relationship to the world, himself, or God. More

[11] *Expérience religieuse*, in the *Dictionnaire de théologie catholique*. The words quoted appear in col. 1787.

[12] Cf. the remark by G. van der Leeuwen in *La Religion dans son Essence et ses Manifestations* (Paris, Payot, 1948), p. 450: "In the spiritual life of the present day religion as a matter of living experience has been pretty well discredited. Why? Because it has been wrongly reduced to the level of mere feeling, its value being estimated by the intensity of the feeling."

precisely, experience is the act through which the person becomes aware of himself in relation to the world, himself, or God. When I say that the person "becomes aware of himself," I am intentionally using a vague term which can include every possible mode of experience, whereas in the current (empirical) conception there is an undue emphasis on feeling. Undoubtedly experience is always something that is undergone and lived through:[13] hence its living, irreplaceable character, which comes from the fact that it is a personal thing. But the very idea of what is meant by "being undergone," or "felt," or "grasped," needs to be closely examined.

In the first place, then, and in spite of all attempts at "detotalization,"[14] every mode of psychological life can include something that is experienced—experienced as a perception, or a thought, or a desire, or a feeling, or an action; because experience means something "immediately recognized by the consciousness," and there is no reason to single out feeling at the expense of the rest.

Next, rejecting every conception of experience as pure passivity, I suggest that what is experienced can be a matter of acts as well as states. For if experience means a direct awareness, an act of thought is just as much a matter of awareness as a state of physical well-being, and an act of will is just as much a matter of awareness as a state of apathy. Indeed, acts are more present to consciousness than states, for acts are the result of our own positing, and therefore infinitely more our own than states. The awareness of an act is as different from the awareness of a state as being aware that something exists in my consciousness because I put it there is different from being aware of it because I receive it. The awareness of a state is undoubtedly an inferior form of experience.[15] Thus, however it may appear at first sight, the active element in experience is more certain than the passive element, the willed more certain than the endured, the posited more certain than the felt. This assertion may be verified by reference to the free act, which is the highest of all posited things: I only have

[13] Cf. the definition in the *Vocabulaire technique et critique de la Philosophie* (Lalande,) 5th ed. (Paris, 1947), pp. 309-310: "Experience: the fact of undergoing something, to the extent that this fact is regarded not only as a transitory phenomenon but as an enlargement or enrichment of thought."

[14] Cf. R. Le Senne, *Obstacle et Valeur*, pp. 24-41.

[15] Cf. L. Lavelle, *De l'Acte* (Paris, 1937), p. 24 (on states as "the passive, individual part of myself," as opposed to acts, which are the highest, most efficacious, most transparent part of myself).

the experience of freedom because I can see, will, and choose. Indeed, I cannot even experience this freedom except in the act I posit—to be perfectly precise, I never have any experience of freedom in itself: it is a mode which I cannot experience in a pure state but only in the act to which it gives meaning. On the other hand, in this activity the "posited essence" is bound up with a whole series of antecedent or concomitant events which are felt: affective elements are always involved in any free act, which thus appears as a complex experience involving both active and passive elements.

Finally, I must deplore what is to my mind a very serious matter—the confusion that exists between two different kinds of passivity. A state may be experienced as something that is passively endured. This kind of passivity is material; it is, if I may be allowed the phrase, a passive kind of passivity; it involves something that cannot be resisted, or rejected, or ignored, something by which one is literally invaded[16] —no matter whether this comes from outside (as in the case of emotion), from within (as in the case of ideas, feelings, impulses, which spring out of the unconscious or from some profound complex), or from the sphere of the transcendent, which is the governing force in the deepest centre of the spirit. But on the other hand—and this is a very different matter—a state may be experienced as something that one willingly accepts. In this case the passivity is spiritual, and—if I may be allowed the phrase for the sake of symmetry—it is an active kind of passivity. In this case the spiritual part of the soul is involved, and it introduces into the very heart of the experience an element of expectation and appeal, of acceptance and consent, that brings our deepest powers into play. This kind of passivity is to be found in the highest human experiences—in love, in artistic creation, in religious ecstasy; and this is an extremely important fact—because it proves that the person is ontologically open to all the riches of the world, of other people, and of God.

Thus at least three meanings must be given to the verb "to experience."

Experience may take the form of an act, and this kind of experience is active and personal, because the person posits the actual reality of the experience.

[16] I leave open, of course, the question whether anything can exist in consciousness which is entirely a matter of passive endurance. Cf. MADINIER, *Conscience et Mouvement* (Paris, 1938), p. iv, n. 2.

Then again it may take the form of a state that is merely endured, and this kind of experience is passive, unfree, undifferentiated, and as little personal as anything can be.

Thirdly, it may take the form of a state that is received with welcome, and this kind of experience is still passive, but it is enveloped within a magnificent act of freedom.

It would be a mistake, of course, to separate these three meanings, as though they usually referred to three distinct forms of experience. In reality, the things they describe are usually interconnected. The result is that there is a structure of experience, and different kinds of experience, according to the relationships that are established between these three forms of experience. To take simply one example: we are experiencing other people every day, and yet this highly familiar experience is terribly difficult to describe. Nevertheless, it does not take long to see that all three components are involved in it. There is the active experience—I know, I perceive, I comprehend, someone other than myself; I react positively to him by way of love or hatred; I seek him out or avoid him. Then there is the experience that is purely passive: this other person is something resistant, an obstacle, someone who gives me a bump—physically, mentally, morally—which I cannot avoid. Then there is the experience that is received gladly: I open out to this other person and accept him; I allow myself to be penetrated and enriched—or I refuse to give myself, I remain "reserved," merely lend myself out without really giving; and this is simply the negative aspect of acceptance. Any attempt to describe the main lines of this structure, with all its subtle ramifications, would involve the whole problem of the communion between human beings;[17] but we may say that any experience inevitably has some sort of structure; that it is a tissue of relationships; that it is always inserted into the movement by which we achieve our own self-realization—if it is not the movement itself; and that on every level of reality one needs to make a detailed analysis of this structure, these relationships, this movement.

But this structured experience inevitably escapes from any kind of empiricism or idealism. It escapes from the former, because the moment one puts spiritual acts, and the relationships that these establish beween us and reality as a whole, at the centre of experience,

[17] Cf. M. Nedoncelle, *La Réciprocité des consciences* (Paris, 1942), esp. Part I.

empiricism has been left behind. Acts are not things, but the positing activity itself communicating itself and finding its fulfilment, and they can only be grasped in the movement that posits them. Experience thus has a structure—and this certainly needs to be defined—but this structure can only be properly grasped through some kind of metaphysical thought. On the other hand, as soon as experience is seen to involve a passivity that is proper to the mind, one has got beyond idealism. For then it includes not only the *shock*, and the passively endured—that mysterious and highly objectionable element which idealism is itself obliged to endure, if not to integrate—but also, and above all, that active kind of passivity, the activity involving willing acceptance, which characterizes one of the essential aspects of the spirit—in so far as the spirit is open to communion; and which, when it comes to the furthest point—contact with God—describes the deepest and most radical attitude that can be adopted by the created being.

If I may be allowed one final distinction, then, I suggest that it is necessary to distinguish between three possible levels of experience. First, there is the empirical level, i.e. all experience that remains uncriticized, which is endured but not brought out into the open, which becomes arrested or solidified almost immediately, and is therefore partial, superficial—the elements of experience rather than experience proper. Next there is the experimental, i.e. conscious, intentional level, which also relates to particular elements of experience, the elements that can be measured—these are aroused, and manipulated, and co-ordinated, and ultimately constructed into the world of science. Finally, there is the experiential level, at which an experience is understood in its personal totality, with all its structural elements and all its motivating principles; built up and grasped in a clear consciousness that is in full possession of itself, and in generous, self-giving love—in short, a personal experience in the fullest sense of the word. In this sense—and it is as such that I shall take it here—every genuinely spiritual experience is experiential in type.[18] The empiric, from this point of view, can be no more than a possible starting-point, to be criticized and transcended; the experimental, simply one stage, one

[18] Cf. the very true remark by H. Gouhier, about reflective philosophers for whom the phrase "metaphysical experience" has meaning "only if there is not the slightest suspicion of empiricism in the experience" (in *La Vie Intellectuelle*, 10th June, 1939, p. 275).

partial passing moment to be given its proper place and integrated. The experiential is the proper ground of this kind of experience, because here alone can the spirit give itself wholly, realize itself wholly, and thus discover and recognize itself wholly.

4. *Religious Experience*

In this perspective religious experience can be defined as the act—or group of acts—through which man becomes aware of himself in relation to God. It is therefore the most personal kind of experience that can take place, since it involves the meeting of the created person with the creative person, and by this very fact concerns the spirit in its total reality; and though it must be described according to the nature of the religious relationship, it must never be taken out of the personal context without which it could not exist.

In the first place, then, religious experience is usually an integrating experience. This means that all the main aspects of the person are involved and are integrated hierarchically. In this awareness of the relationship with God there is an intellectual element. It is necessarily a certain idea of God that determines the attitude and specifies the relationship. God is in fact Truth, and a religion that renounced truth would renounce God himself—whatever forms or means it used to attain to the truth about God. In the religious act I become aware of my situation with respect to God, I take up an attitude towards him; by making an act of affirmation with my intellect, I adhere to the truth of God and the truth of my being in relation to him. Adoration, humility, and love are necessarily involved in this act in its profoundest depths.

The experience also includes a voluntary element. It is necessarily an act of freedom—to be more precise, an act of generosity—that founds and posits the relationship. I accept my position as a creature, I gladly accept and submit to the greatness and holiness of God, I wager my whole destiny and vocation, I abandon myself to God so that I may serve him. For God is love, and the only way I can respond to the gift which he has made me of my being, and of himself through my being, is by the gift of myself in return.

To this must be added an affective element. For the act in which I wager my destiny, and in which I fulfil my being by giving it to God, is bound to have repercussions in my innermost depths and to arouse within me an overflowing joy and praise and adoration which remain unknown to me until I meet with the infinite. Thus I feel myself and know myself to be "prevented," surrounded, called. The consciousness and acceptance of this vocation unfold in a profound feeling of adoration, a sense of grace, supplication, inspiring humility—in a vibration of my whole being, which is penetrated to its inmost depths by the God who so infinitely transcends it.

But here below nothing ever comes to an end in true religion, and there is thus an active element in the experience, because it is a commitment which, if it is not to be unreal, is meant to inspire my whole life, to control my concrete activity and manifest itself in particular actions. In the genuinely religious person all acts become inspired or consecrated: the longing for God and the service of God know no limits or closed circles. At this level the philosopher may repeat the words of St. Paul: "Whether you eat or drink or whatsoever you do, do all to the glory of God."

Finally—and despite a prejudice that is still far too prevalent—religious experience necessarily includes a social element: because in God's eyes man is always a member of one great family; because the first motion of any true religion is "Our Father, who art in heaven"; because the person can only seek and find God on condition that he helps others to seek and find him too; because, the more he penetrates into the mystery of his God, the more he realizes that there is a mysterious appeal addressed to others, to all others, just as necessarily and as personally as to himself; because his own freedom can only be consecrated to God if it is consecrated to the search for his Kingdom and the establishment of his rule amongst men.

Hence, in the light of all these elements, religious experience manifests itself as the supremely structured experience. It is in fact the awareness of a relationship that is known, willed, felt, applied to life, and introduced into human society. More precisely, it is the grasp of a relationship in which all these elements are integrated in the simplicity of an act that contains them all virtually, separates them from one another as occasion demands, but unifies and transcends them, because it is the act of the person delivering himself up to God, who is calling him. Religious experience is the consciousness of this response, the awareness of this contact through self-giving, the discovery of God's presence at the heart of the affirmation which introduces us into it, and consequently the consciousness of the unification—in an inchoate form—of being and life at the hands of God.

Thus religious experience is an integrating force—and therefore an integral thing—or it is nothing. All attempts to reduce it to any single one of these elements are vain, for they lead to the disappearance of their very object. Anything partial is here either an aspect that has become outstanding but which was originally experienced as part of a whole, or a foretaste of or summons to some whole, a beginning which only has meaning because it is directed towards something that will complete it; or a mutilation and deformation, a mere residue of the authentic experience. And it is because it is in the highest degree personal, because it is a dialogue between the created "I" and the creative "Thou," that religious experience is the only kind of experience that can and must be "totalitarian."

Next, religious experience is the experience of the Sacred. This word has not yet found any satisfactory definition in the language of philosophy.[19] And not without reason. Apart from any philosophical categories to which it might be reduced, to me it signifies God regarded purely as God—that is to say, in the first place, in a mystery that can never be properly fathomed. A "clearly conceived" God could never be anything more than an idea, and therefore a nothingness, whereas the end of the religious relationship is necessarily mysterious by its very nature (whatever the truth may be about the means of attaining to this end, which we shall be concerned with later). Any experience of a person is bound to be mysterious, and it is this that gives it its charm, its value, its depth; but a person exists on the same level as ourselves, and in any relationship with him we remain on a horizontal level of experience. With God, the entire meaning of the experience is changed, God is entirely Other, and at the same time the absolute Archetype of all being; contact with him necessarily means contact with a kind of abyss. Man, it is true, is made in God's image, and is his son, but even more profoundly he is a creature—dust and ashes. Only when this absolute nothingness is realized can religious experience take place. All that we may say or feel about our resemblance to God, our family likeness to

[19] It is always worth while to turn to the book by R. Otto on this point: *Le Sacré*, trans. A. Jundt (Paris, 1929). But the inquiry should be pursued further and the book itself revised. Otto himself recognized that his categories were Lutheran. And it is not necessary—far from it—to be an irrationalist to recognize and appreciate mystery.

him, our nearness to him, needs to be understood in the light of an infinite difference, an infinite otherness, an infinite distance. We cannot connect the two terms positively from within; we can only affirm their existence in a context in which the absolute distance between them will never be done away with. To become aware of this abyss, this mystery, is to posit and live the religious reality. Religious reality is "abysmal" by definition.[20]

The next point is that this mysterious end is understood as something that is at once transcendent and immanent. I use the classical terminology, although it is regarded as out of date by some people and as unreal by others, because it emphasizes the essential paradox of religious experience. What this experience presupposes is in fact the reality of creation, i.e. the presence of the transcendent within the human being as the cause of his existence and the object of his deepest desires. From this it follows that the inevitable, fundamental movement of the created being is towards God; it involves the creature's whole being and it has a relationship with God as its end. When we say that God is present to us as our creative cause, we mean that he is, so to speak, its "constituent" reality, the original impulse behind a vocation and a demand that involve our whole human substance. Consciousness of this demand and this appeal, followed by a free acceptance of them and thus a perfect submission to God—that is the essence of religious experience.[21]

More precisely, the rhythm of religious experience is made up of an act of awareness and a positing which are interconnected—an awareness of the given relationship, which comes from creation itself, from God's pure generosity towards us and within us, but which is no more than a preliminary sketch of the reality, because

[20] The Catholic Church is often accused of emptying this mystery of meaning by its theory of the knowledge of God. Nevertheless the Church itself declares (Lateran Council, IV, *Denz. Bannw.*, 432): "Between the Creator and the creature, there is not so much likeness to be seen; the unlikeness between them is greater."

[21] It is a remarkable fact that in his reflections on the *Meaning of Being*, A. Forest should be led to describe not just religious experience but metaphysical experience too as the sense of a presence and an appeal. He writes: "The task facing philosophy is the unification of these two ideas of presence and appeal; to enable us to discover being everywhere without our being limited to what is merely given, and to reveal to us in every essence a relationship with absolute being . . . This implication of a presence and an appeal thus leads one to sense some kind of analogy between metaphysical experience and mystical experience."—*Consentement et Creation* (Paris, Aubier, 1943, p. 27).

it is an appeal to our liberty; and a positing of this relationship, which is personally accepted with gratitude, and then willed, and hence renewed, deepened, and transposed to a different level—for it raises us from the ontological level to the spiritual level, and leads to our communion, not as a merely natural being but as a personal being, with God. Such positing is therefore itself creative: I have been posited by the creative Thou; henceforth I myself in return freely posit the creative Thou, and I reach to the truth of my being by submitting myself to God. The second feature of the experience of the Sacred is thus the interiorization and personalization of the relationship with God.

But it is precisely because God is transcendent and immanent that his presence can thus be accepted and posited. God the Creator is absolutely primary; and when I realize the I-God relationship it is always as a relationship between myself and someone who knows me, chooses me, gives me being and calls me to himself. Hence the impossibility of escaping from this prevenience in knowledge, choice, and appeal. I cannot do any other than become aware of myself as someone utterly involved in this prevenience as something ever-present to me and surrounding me on all sides. In this sense, and as a result of this absolute priority of God within me, religious experience is an entrance into eternity. But this mysterious entrance takes place within a kind of return; and this needs to be emphasized. The act that posits the relationship is also an act that receives it. I posit something, but I myself am someone who is posited. I give myself to God, but I am also someone who is given to himself by God. And it is in the religious act itself that this return takes place, for in it I descend to my Source and approach towards my End. When I believe in God, love him and serve him, I grasp him, but he envelops me, because I grasp him as the adorable Person in whom is all beatitude. There is thus a dialectical return to self, and a propulsion towards God; a retirement within oneself and a decentralization towards God: in the religious act my centre becomes God, and this is the essential paradox of religious experience.

Finally, this experience emerges as the relationship between two acts, God's and mine. But a vast abyss separates them. In so far as my own act is concerned, I have a direct awareness of it, because it is I who posit it. But so far as God's is concerned, I experience it to the extent that I think it or ratify it, and in the measure that I experience its presence through its effects within me. This extent is always secondary and provisional, but it is always present, because any thought about God or acceptance of him must involve a certain minimum of feeling—even if it is only the "creaturely feeling" without which there is no religion. Only, because God always remains transcendent, he always remains beyond pure affective experience. The sense of the relationship is experienced much more clearly than its end: I cannot experience the act by which God posits me, but I experience the fact that I am posited by God. I discover my own ego in his mystery "as a Thou posited by creative Love."[22] I thus experience the divine truth that gives me my being.

It is from the fact that it is both transcendent and immanent that religious experience gets its particular form: what gives it its content is the fact that its end is God as the object of adoration and love. There is no need to go into this in detail, but we must take care not to oversimplify the matter. As God is the first cause and the ultimate end, one might be tempted to say that God is an object of adoration from the fact that he is the creative cause, and an object of love from being our end, bringing us to beatitude. And this would be true enough if our aim was merely a formal analysis. But in experience the two aspects of God are both given and grasped at the same time, and if God is an object of adoration, it is because he is both cause and end and is both of these absolutely, transcendently, and therefore in each case absolutely "separate" from man. Neither aspect has any common denominator with man: we are plunged into the same darkness both by our origin and by our beatitude, and both will always escape us here below; and that is why a holy fear seizes the religious person when he finds himself faced by this dual abyss—the nothingness from which he was created and the destiny to which

[22] G. Madinier, *Conscience et amour* (Paris, P.U.F., 1938), p. 101. This may be clarified in the light of the profound observations by J. Maritain in "Une nouvelle approche de Dieu" (*Raison et raisons* [Paris, Luf, 1947]) on the subject of the intuition of existence and the knowledge of God that is its "natural fruit." Maritain shows that the primordial motion of the reason towards God is neither "a pure intuition" nor a "philosophic process of reasoning of a technical kind," but that "in its primordial vitality, the motion of the human reason towards God is a natural reasoning, i. e. intuitive, irresistibly supported and vivified from end to end by the intellectual light of the intuition of existence" (p. 174). But in human existence infinite Existence and Love are implied, and "finally, the discovery of the value of existence does not only mean the rediscovery of God, it also means the rediscovery of Love" (p. 176).

he is called. Again, God is an object of love because he is both cause and end, with the same intimacy in both cases and in an equally personal and unifying sense. For if his absolute finality calls to man for possession and union in knowledge and love, his creative efficiency communicates being through pure goodness and forms the basis of his natural fatherhood. Religious experience can thus be defined as the relationship between these two lines of activity, which both envelop and are enveloped by each other. Adoration causes love to bow down in absolute submission, and love raises adoration in a hymn of jubilation, in a constant ebb and flow, religious experience beating to the rhythm of the creative action and thus realizing the living communion between the created being and his God.

Religious experience is, finally, a mediated experience. The presence and grasp of God which it involves are both realized through the mediation of a sign, or series of signs.[23] The presence of God cannot be a direct presence, if "direct" is taken to mean a naked contact between essence and essence, between one spiritual person and another. Neither I myself, nor others, nor—a fortiori—God, are given in this way to my consciousness; they are only present by way of a kind of mediation, which needs to be analyzed and defined in each separate case, but which must always exclude any actual face-to-face experience here below. Nor is God's presence anything indirect, if by that one means an experience coming by way of something else, referring to something else from which one might deduce a presence—which would mean an absence of real personal contact and therefore a suppression of genuine experience.

It is a presence by way of signs—a presence which from different points of view may be my own presence to myself, the presence of other consciousnesses to my own, or the presence of God to my soul in religious experience. Borrowing a phrase from Madinier,[24] one may say that God is not given in experience but grasped in it. And the sign by which God is grasped is the religious act itself—the whole act, of course, with its essential characteristic of being both received and posited, and with all its principles both objective and

[23] One of GABRIEL MARCEL's main efforts has been to discover the mysterious reality of this presence, with all its implications. On this point cf. R. TROISFONTAINES, "*La notion de Présence chez G. Marcel,*" in *Existentialisme chrétien* (Paris, Plon, 1947), pp. 222 *et seq.* Cf. also in *Le Mystère de l'Être*, I (Paris, Aubier, 1951), "*La présence comme Mystère,*" pp. 213 *et seq.*

[24] G. MADINIER, *Conscience et amour*, p. 5.

subjective—the flash of intelligence and the Being who is thought, the act of will and the Being who is chosen, the ardour of affectivity and the Being who is loved, the act of generosity and the Being who is served. . . . This act, with all its many components, is what mediates the presence; and religious experience is precisely the consciousness of the mediation realized in this act, the consciousness of the relationship it establishes between man and God, and hence the consciousness of God as the posited and positing end of the relationship. Thoughts, spiritual attitudes, feelings, religious actions[25] —through all these things God is grasped, and religious experience can thus take place.

It will be seen that I do not admit the kind of metaphysical empiricism that considers us as being capable of an intuition of God. God is reached in experience—which is, so to speak, the appropriate medium—like a refracted ray of light returning to its source. He is reached by experience as a means of knowledge taking the knower beyond himself. In this sense one goes through the experience to get to God, who is the basis of the experience, who gives it its meaning and ensures its value. In the very immanence in which God gives himself, he is reached in all his transcendence. For at the moment when I posit him, because I posit him as someone transcendent, I am posited by him, and I am more posited than positing: I am taken out of myself, and being thus delivered over to God, in this very action God himself is delivered over to me.

Because this presence can only be grasped in the act that posits it by accepting it, the subject is always both passive and active in the experience: the presence is not a thing or condition that can be possessed, but a relationship that freedom alone can maintain by its response to God: it is lived without ever being possessed. Because there is always an abyss between the sign and the thing that the sign enables one to grasp, and this abyss is here carried to its absolute limit, the experience is all the more deeply religious, the more one becomes aware of the terrible inadequacy of the thing that does the signifying compared with the thing signified, and the more that sorrow for sin and the offering of one's wretchedness surround one's

[25] A highly interesting analysis of these subtleties of religious experience, seen from the Lutheran point of view, will be found in K. Girgensohn, *La Structure spirituelle de l'expérience religieuse* (Gutersloh, 1930). See the account by M. Rabeau, *La Vie Spirituelle, Supplément*, July-Sept. 1933, pp. 51-64, 108-125.

ardour, love, praise, and service; so that God becomes more than ever "the utterly transcendent One," the One who penetrates into our inmost being more deeply than we do ourselves, and subsists in a plenitude ever beyond our reach. "More intimate than the most intimate part of myself; higher than my highest": how could Brunschvicg, who was always so ready to fasten on any illusions drawn from space, fail to see that this means an entire rejection of spatiality? For the religious experience is determined by the relationship between two abysses; fundamentally, what is involved is Pascal's "between two infinities"—once again, the experience is rooted in the mystery of a dual abyss—the abyss that is man and the abyss that is God—and can only grow to completion in the dialogue between these two abysses—"deep calls to deep."[26]

Finally, religious experience is dynamic in essence. In the first place, because the act that posits it and maintains it in being is an act of unfolding, of self-giving, of longing, propelling man towards the infinite being. Now, when one has given oneself to God by fully accepting him and consecrating oneself to him, the riches that are to be found in this self-giving are endless, and endless too the demands that are made upon one. For the willed will can never equal the willing will that actually calls us, the will by which God draws us to communion with him. Not all our thoughts and wishes, feelings and actions, can ever manage to satisfy this infinite aspiration. And the moment that man, by the religious act, abandons himself explicitly and absolutely to the appeal that is made to him, he is inevitably led on by the aspiration into which he has introduced himself from zeal to zeal, from sacrifice to sacrifice, from joy to joy; and the movement upon which he is raised is never exhausted; his inner act bears fruit in actions that endeavour to embody the infinite nature of his desires, his service and his abandonment.

Furthermore, the distance that separates man from God is infinite too, and the religious soul cannot avoid trying to lessen this distance by an effort of inner growth and assimilation to God. The soul is made in the image of God, and this resemblance is given in creation itself, but it is only given so that it may be developed by our freedom. It is in fact our real power of knowing and loving God, and far from being mere sterile wealth, to be regarded from a respect-

[26] Cf. St. Augustine, *Enarrationes in Psalmos*, 41, n. 13.

ful distance, it is a thing to be fostered and developed unceasingly as a living force—all the more so since at every instant evil and sin lie in wait for us, and we are unfaithful to ourselves as well as to God, or so feeble in our faithfulness that we produce little more than a caricature of the features we have inherited from him.

Therefore we are obliged to remake this image every day, and, since it is a case of imitating God, our work will have no end here on earth and we shall never bring to perfection the countenance we are to have in eternity. There is thus a dialectic in connection with this image too—hurling us from the infinite we are to the Infinite we long for.

Lastly, and as a result of this, the presence and possession of God which are realized in religious experience can never be anything more than a preliminary sketch, a seed, a hope. God is never *discovered*, in the strict sense of the word; and the more we enter into the mystery of him, the more we know him as someone essentially unknown, and each day, by the power of that negative affirmation which alone can give us being here below, we are taken further and further beyond all that is clear and distinct and consciously perceived.[27] God is never *possessed*, in the strict sense of the word, because he is not grasped in himself, and consequently the more nearly he is approached the more he is taken hold of as somebody absent, a presence that is always slipping away, a "beyond" sustaining the whole experience but never to be identified with it. Thus the presence of God is a hope, not a reality given to us in full; and religious experience is a continual search for God's presence at the heart of communion. "You would not be looking for me if you had not found me": that is the law. For the only result of any finding is more seeking—in this highest of all regions, in which possession only gives birth to further desire, and meeting is the motive force of more self-giving.

Here we must end these remarks. They have in fact remained largely theoretical, without descending into details of concrete experience; the reason being that at this latter level there are only experiences, variously structured. And in any case it is impossible to

[27] This is already true from the purely metaphysical point of view. See on this point, L. B. Geiger, *La Participation dans la philosophie de saint Thomas d'Aquin* (Paris, 1942), p. 318 & n. 1.

develop any theology of religious experience today without coming up against Kierkegaard. But Kierkegaard only represents one particular form of Christian experience, and he himself needs to be placed within this experience if he is to be understood and—if you like—judged. These pages have a more modest aim: since some idea of at least a hidden and unconscious kind invariably governs this kind of research, they were intended to present an explicit idea of religious experience, based on the analogy of creation.

If what we have said seems reasonable, it appears that religious experience is situated beyond the realms of the empiric and the experimental and entirely in the field of the experiential. It is made up of a tissue of relationships whose main lines we have tried to show—the relationship in which the whole human being is involved, body and soul; the relationship whose end is the whole divine Being in the adorable, beatific mystery of his immanence and his transcendence; the relationship formed by the mediation of the human act welcoming and continuing the act of creation; the relationship that is an endless source of aspiration, desire and self-giving. Again, if for philosophy the cardinal problem centring on the person concerns his freedom, and hence his vocation, and if religion is the free act whereby he realizes his vocation, religious experience becomes the experience of the discovery and fulfilment of this vocation. So nothing human is outside its scope; and the highest activities, those leading to science, art and morality, all form part of this single vocation and have to be given their proper place in this integral experience.

Thus, both by the vocational relationship which it institutes with the highest activities, and by the tissue of relationships which it is in itself, the religious experience manifests itself as the supremely structured experience, and it is impossible to speak of it as of a simple, elementary datum. In particular, it is impossible to confine it within the order of feeling. A centuries-old tradition—in the West—has restricted religious experience to this field, and undoubtedly the Protestant Reformation—based on Luther's experience—has been the decisive factor in this.[28] But we must not be bound by this

[28] On this point it is worth while reading the brief but highly illuminating essay by the Rev. Fr. Pinard, "*La Théorie de l'Expérience religieuse de Luther à James*," in *Revue d'Histoire ecclésiastique* (1921), pp. 63 *et seq.*, 306 *et seq.*, 547 *et seq.*

tradition. On the contrary, we must reject this spiritual empiricism, which falsifies the experience and hinders our search. Our first job is not to argue with our separated brethren about the place that religious experience as they understand it can have in Christianity; our first job is to recover a sound idea of religious experience as something integral and open. After which, perhaps, the way will be clear for a discussion of the problem of the Christian experience according to the sound data supplied by Scripture and Tradition.

CHAPTER TWO

The Possibility of a Christian Experience

ANYONE who tries to discuss the problem of the Christian experience immediately finds himself confronted by considerable difficulties. The Christian "experience" can in fact be used to mean some sort of religious feeling—consolation or desolation, temptation, or inspiration—but such experiences need to be very closely examined: they are of secondary importance and cannot possibly be taken to include the whole or the essence of the Christian life. Christian experience can also mean an experience of grace; but when it is understood in this sense, and regarded as the central fact of Christianity, it is, properly speaking, a Protestant conception, and as such was condemned by the Council of Trent. Lastly—this list is by no means complete—it can also mean mystical experience, but this kind of experience is more highly specialized than any other: it does not commonly fall to the lot of Christians as a whole (whatever the reason for this may be): by definition it is something out of the ordinary, compared with the ordinary devout religious life.

In all these cases the Christian experience seems to be subject to certain reservations, and before we can even ask ourselves what it is, we are obliged to ask whether it is possible, and whether the phrase can have any meaning for a Catholic. We shall try to show that the phrase has a meaning, that the Christian experience is not condemned either by the Council of Trent or by theology, and that the mystical experience itself, far from doing away with it, presupposes it.

1

This problem of the Christian experience was not forbidden either by the Council of Trent or by the theologians of the time, because it was never explicitly raised. Their problem concerned the certainty of the state of grace. The Lutheran revolution had raised this problem in the harshest fashion by asserting the necessity for a clear, compulsive experience of justification and by making "experimental knowledge" a necessary "phenomenon" of faith.[1] The theologians were in entire agreement in condemning the need for such a faith, but they were extremely divided—as we shall show later—on the question of how to formulate some positive doctrine regarding the root of this problem. They therefore decided to be satisfied with condemning the Protestant error. In order that the Council's teaching may be understood in its proper context, it may be worth while to refer briefly to the main lines of a doctrine far less crude in its form than Luther's and also far more highly developed, i.e. Calvin's.[2]

Calvin's position may be clarified by a glance at three of his major theses.

In the first place, there are the Scriptures.[3] Undoubtedly, says Calvin, there are human reasons capable of demonstrating the value of the Scriptures—their age, the miracles, the prophecies, the conversion of the Apostles, their approval by the Church. But these are all simply so many helps and means, on the one hand polemic, for the purpose of combating the enemies of Christianity, and on the other preparatory, for the sake of helping people who are on the

[1] At an earlier stage of his thought, Luther asserted the uncertainty of faith itself: "For although we may be certain that we believe in Christ, nevertheless we are not certain that we believe in all the things that appertain to him. And therefore what we actually believe is uncertain" (*in Rom.*, 3, 22). As early as 1518 he asserted its certainty, however: "I have said that no one can be justified except by faith and by not doubting in any way what will follow from grace. For if he doubts and is uncertain, he is not justified but vomits forth grace" (*Acta Aug.*, Weimar II, 13). These passages are quoted by J. Rivière, *Justification* (*Dict. théol. cathol.*, 2147-8). But what perhaps needs to be emphasized most of all is that in this case, as in so many others, his position becomes literally *paradoxical*, anguish and certitude being linked together indissolubly: "We have most help and comfort from the operation of the Holy Spirit and he is most present to us when we are most impotent and nearest to desperation" (*in Gal*, Weimer, XL, i, 585; quoted in A. Stakemaier [*op. cit. infra*, n. 11], p. 61, n. 20).

[2] On the connection between the two doctrines, cf. Fr. Wendel, *"Calvin," Sources et évolution de la pensée religieuse* (Paris, 1950), pp. 97 *et seq.*

[3] *Institutes*, I, chs. vii & xiii.

road to conversion. Fundamentally their function is apologetic, and they are incapable of giving that kind of experimental certainty which alone can convince one of the divine nature of the Scriptures. They are "secondary helps and means" compared with "the principal and sovereign witness of the Holy Spirit."

High above them, and in a completely different order, there is, then, an experience—in the order of faith—which is the witness of the Holy Spirit. This experience is the consciousness of an attraction, a light, an influence, so strong, so efficacious, and so sovereignly powerful, that it carries its own conviction. There seem to be two elements in this experience—an incomparable emotion ("a power to move") and a direct spiritual perception. Calvin says that "the efficacy of such a feeling" reveals the Godhead, that "this feeling is as perceptible and infallible" as the perception of a colour or a smell, and is of such a nature "that it cannot come into being except through a revelation from heaven."[4] We thus have an experience of an empirical type—a clear, compulsive, infallible feeling of the presence of the Spirit; furthermore, we have the supernatural witness of the Spirit identified with this psychological experience. Where the Catholic would say, this is an experience of the Spirit which is to be inserted within the Church's experience and ratified by it, Calvin says, here is an experience of the Spirit which is sufficient to itself, which dispenses with any relationship, an experience to which the Church itself refers as the immediate foundation of its own security, and which is a normal experience for all Christians: "I say nothing but what every believer experiences within himself."[5]

Secondly, there is faith.[6] And in the first place, so that we may "place" this faith, let us say that it is not a knowledge of an intellectual kind but a saving knowledge of God the Redeemer, connected not with the Church but with God and Christ (without it one forfeits one's intelligence and becomes capable of believing "the very worst errors"); a knowledge founded upon the Word of God and enabling us to know his will—not for vengeance but for mercy (nos. 2, 3; 6, 8). This leads to a definition of faith (no. 7) as a firm and certain knowledge of God's good will, based on his free

[4] *Ibid.*, ch. viii, no. 1; ch. vii, nos. 2 and 5.

[5] *Institutes*, III, ch. ii. Cf. T. Preiss, *Le Témoignage intérieur du Saint-Esprit* (Neuchâtel-Paris, 1946), ch. i.

[6] *Ibid.*, III, ch. ii.

promise in Jesus Christ, "revealed to our understanding and sealed in our hearts by the Holy Spirit." But there are various degrees of this experience, and it is this that distinguishes the faith of the damned from that of the elect (nos. 11-13). The damned have a faint, confused, transitory feeling of the grace of God, because they only experience a "lower operation" of the Holy Spirit; whereas the elect have a strong, solid, efficacious, lasting, and indestructible feeling of grace, ending in complete trust, and in the revelation of personal salvation which is the special seal of the Holy Spirit. Thus the faith of the first is not properly rooted; it is no more than a seeming, illusory reality; whereas the faith of the latter is deep and true.

As regards this experience—the trust felt by the faithful—it has the following main features. It is an unshakeable trust in God rather than any intellectual grasp of him, and it ends in a certainty whose sweetness can be felt and experienced (nos. 14-15). It gives a sense of peace at the thought of the Day of Judgment: without it the mind is troubled and distraught at the thought of God's fearful holiness; whereas with it come purity, repose, and gladness, from the knowledge that one is supported by the promises of God, which have become one's own (no. 16, and cf. 29, 32). This trust is not a settled, stagnant peace, however, but a sense of security in the midst of battle (nos. 16-22): the faithful are still divided between the Spirit and the flesh—hence all the temptations and anguish, the storms, the periods of darkness. But faith proves stronger than all these; it gives us a clear knowledge of the merciful will of God, it shows us his benign countenance shining down upon us, and enables us to contemplate him in all his glory—one single ray of whose light can banish all darkness. If there comes a time of trouble and torment, the soul arms itself with the Word of God, brandishes it in the face of all temptations, and emerges from the fight with increased certainty and trust. And the reason for this is that the assaults all come from without, whereas within all is confidence; thus the inner experience of God's mercy in Christ resists all attacks.

Lastly, this confidence is not a matter of "moral conjecture"—any conjecture being self-evidently "against faith"—but a matter of absolute certainty (no. 38). This does not mean any meddling in the incomprehensible will of God, it simply means accepting his Word "by affirming the certainty of what it has revealed to us" (no. 39), i.e. the presence—and consciousness—of the Holy Spirit within us. All the passages referring to an experience of the Spirit or an experience of Christ (e.g., I Cor. ii, 12: Rom. viii, 11, 14, 16; II Cor. xiii, 5, 6) Calvin interprets as a self-sufficient experience supplying its own evidence.[7] Hebrews xi, 1, again, in his view presents faith as a "certain and infallible possession of the things that God has promised us," as "evidence of what has not appeared, the seeing of what is not to be seen, a clear view of things that are dark, a presence of things absent, a demonstration of things hidden" (no. 41). The conclusion is always the same: so far as the genuinely faithful are concerned, "there is no doubt that (God) in a special way seals within their

[7] Calvin quotes (no. 41) St. Bernard and sets him up against the Doctors of the Sorbonne. He takes a passage from the *Sermo I Annunciat.*, nos. 1-3 (P. L., 183, 383-384), and writes:—"I believe, says (St. Bernard), that the testimony of our conscience, which St. Paul describes as the glory of the faithful (II Cor. i, 12) concerns three points. For in the first place, and above all else, you are required to believe that you cannot have remission of sins except by the free gift of God; secondly, that you cannot perform any good work unless he enables you to do so; thirdly, that you cannot merit eternal life by works unless it is also given to you freely. A little later he adds, These things are no more than a beginning . . . meanwhile, we must be resolved that he has remitted (our sins), until we are persuaded by the witness of the Holy Spirit that our salvation is indeed assured."

What in fact do we find in St. Bernard? We find a dual affirmation that both contrasts with and complements itself. On the one hand, he asserts the gratuitousness and absolute transcendence of the gift of God, going so far that with regard to eternal life (no. 2) he observes that all the sufferings of the world bear no comparison to it, that no amount of merit, which is a gift from God, can bear any proportion to such a great glory, and that the holiest of men—even though acknowledged as such by God—should always be afraid of affronting God. On the other hand, once this has been firmly established ("a certain beginning and foundation of faith"), he asserts that we must believe on the word of the Holy Spirit that we have been granted the threefold grace—forgiveness, merit, and the promise of eternal life. Faith involves both transcendence and inwardness, God's absolute sovereignty and his free mercy, the inaccessibility and the closest intimacy of the gifts.

St. Bernard simply asserts that there is this paradoxical connection, in one and the same attitude, between two convictions which both support and limit each other. He does not say that we must reach the point of being "persuaded by the witness of the Holy Spirit that our salvation is indeed assured." So little does he go towards this that, when he wants to show (*ibid.*, 4) why "these proofs are so highly credible to me," he does not base this "credibility" on any inner experience but on the objective facts of the faith: the proof of the remission of sins is our Lord's Passion; the proof of good works is the Resurrection; the proof of the hope of Paradise is the Ascension. Here once again we come across the partial coincidence of affirmations, within two fundamentally different lines of thought, which makes any comparison of the Catholic and Protestant points of view so difficult.

hearts the certainty of his grace, so that it shall be fully ratified within them" (no. 11).

These same themes are to be found in his study of justification.[8] Here there are two things to be considered—that the glory of God should be safeguarded, and that our consciences should feel easy. Now according to Calvin peace of mind is only to be found through trusting in the gratuity of justification, i.e. in God's gratuitous goodness, and in mercy joined to truth—because God keeps his promises. It cannot have any sort of connection with our consciousness of having obeyed the law, or performed good works, or having been purified from our sins; because we remain sinners, and know it. Therefore we must always come back to "faith alone, grounded in God's promise" —faith in the sacrifice of Christ who is "our peace," in the sense that by his sacrifice he calms our disturbed consciences;[9] the faith that means a sincere and heartfelt trust. We are calmed when we are "persuaded that we are acceptable to God," according as "the charity of God is spread abroad in our hearts by the Holy Spirit"; and this feeling of confidence is the condition of the efficacy of God's promises, Scripture itself declaring "that if there is doubt or uncertainty in the heart, they are rendered vain." The foundation of peace of mind is therefore the experience of this "firm heartfelt trust"; and Calvin adds, conversely, that it is doubly erroneous to count on remaining faithful after having been regenerated: objectively, because regeneration is always imperfect, and there are therefore always reasons for doubting; and subjectively, because it shows that we have not yet come into contact with God, that we have no more idea how to pray "than Turks or any other Pagans," and have "never tasted the sweetness of this grace"—i.e., free forgiveness in Christ. Only the kind of confidence defined here can enable us to "retain our peace of mind before the thought of the Judgment of God."

The last theme is predestination.[10] This doctrine is not a frightening one, but "sweet-smelling and sweet to the taste by reason of the fruit which it bears" (21, 1)—"a journey . . . safe, and peaceful, and even joyful" (24, 4). The Holy Spirit, in fact, communicates to the

[8] *Institutes*, III, ch. xiii.

[9] It will be noticed, of course, how Calvin gives a subjective experimental sense to an ontological and objective affirmation.

[10] *Institutes*, III, chs. xxi & xxiv. On this point cf. Fr. Wendel, *op. cit.*, pp. 208-215.

elect their certainty of adoption, and "God teaches his elect effectively and brings them to faith" (24, 1). Thus the "inner vocation is a warrant of salvation that can never mislead" (24, 2); and it is faith that gives the consciousness of election. There are, however, a certain number of signs (24, 4 *et seq.*) that can help us, chief among these being the contemplation of our election in Christ the Saviour. Here again, the passages in St. John's Gospel which say that what is in Christ's hand will never be snatched out of it (John vi, 37, 40; x, 27; I John ii, 19) are interpreted in the sense that, once we are convinced of our vocation with an absolute conviction, our salvation is assured (24, 6-9). This conviction is the result within us of the special vocation which is given only to the elect (8), and we must reject the separation between vocation and election suggested, for example, by St. Gregory (9). St. Gregory says that we can indeed be certain of our vocation but not of our election, only he bases election on the merit of works, not on trust in God. In the end, therefore, we always have to come back to faith.

Faith alone in fact can resolve the Christian paradox (16). God offers his grace to all, but he only predestines a few: how then can we be certain of salvation? The answer is, by faith. For with respect to God, faith is the fruit of election: God chooses, enlightens; causes himself to be sought for and found. On man's side, faith is the sign that one has been elected, because receiving God's promises by faith means knowing that they are valid for oneself; because having faith means "experiencing the sure and certain truth of the promises," and therefore undergoing the profound experience that distinguishes temporary believers from permanent ones (7-8); because God names all men so as to calm the consciences of the good and to remind them that all sinners are capable of being saved by faith. The connection is thus perfectly clear: election, enlightenment (by God), faith (in the individual man), and, as a result of this, the felt efficacy of the Gospel: "As therefore the mercy of God is offered to all men by the Gospel, there is only faith, i.e. enlightenment from God, that can distinguish the faithful from the unbelievers; the former feeling this illumination of their eternal election by God to be their rule" (16). Predestination, faith, certainty of salvation—all hang together: from election to experience the line is unbroken and necessary. Anyone who undergoes a profound experience of faith thereby has proof of his own election; anyone who does not have this experience is at most a temporary believer and will be cast into the fire. Clearly, in Calvin's view it is always an experience of an empirical kind—no matter how high it may be—that lies at the heart of the genuine Christian life.

2

If we now turn to the relevant texts produced at the Council of Trent,[11] we find a rejection and a directive: a threefold negation regarding the inner assurance (*fiducia*) of personal justification, and an indication of the spiritual attitude that is normal for Catholics.

In the first place, an inner assurance of being personally justified is not a sufficient sign that one has in fact entered into justification.[12] One may in fact have this assurance, voice it aloud (*jactanti*), claim it as a sufficient proof of justification ("in it alone being at peace"), and yet be in error. The proof of this, for the Council, lies in the governing bond with the Church: it is impossible to break voluntarily with the Church and at the same time be justified in the eyes of God. Now this assurance is to be found in heretics and schismatics, and in fact the heretics who are living at the time of the Council profess this doctrine and use it to make violent attacks upon the Catholic Church. No inner feeling can outweigh such patent schism and revolt. Therefore, their assurance has no real foundation—it is "ungrounded confidence," and, being brandished against the Church like a weapon, it is an offence against God—"a confidence remote from all piety." The first conclusion is, therefore: a rejection of inner experience as decisive proof of justification, and an appeal to the criterion of the Church as the governing criterion.

A feeling of assurance is not necessarily a sign that one is or remains justified.[13] The heretics say that the Christian has a personal

[11] The (highly complex) history of the Council's discussions on this point has recently been described in detail by A. Stakemaier in his book *Das Konzil von Trient über die Heilsgewiszheit* (Heidelberg, 1947). For the meaning of the final decree cf. ch. ix, pp. 178-189. The above pages were written before I saw this book; they agreed in advance with Stakemaier's conclusions.

[12] The list of errors to be condemned, proposed by the legates on 20th June, 1646, included this proposition: (7) "Before charity, we are justified by faith alone, by which we believe or trust or feel our sins to be taken away," etc. Ehses, *Conc. Trid.*, V, 281, quoted in A. Michel, *Les décrets du Concile de Trente* (Hefele-Leclercq, X, p. 68).

[13] In the same list of errors to be condemned: (9) "The man who is justified must believe that he is in a state of grace, that sins are not imputed to him, and that he is predestined" (Ehses, V, p. 282, quoted *ibid.*, p. 69).

obligation to believe in his own justification. The Council rejects this requirement: there is no straight line between the reality of justification and any consciousness we may have of it. In the first place, we are not under any obligation to establish the kind of certainty in which there is not a shadow of a doubt (*absque ulla omnino dubitatione*); next, there is no necessity for us to believe absolutely that we are forgiven before we can be forgiven; lastly, there is no reason why this faith *alone* should have the privilege of realizing fully (*perfici*) forgiveness and justification—without it we can still have a genuine belief in God's promises, and in the value of Christ's death and resurrection. Thus the second conclusion is: an absolute rejection of the need for any sort of compulsive experience before we can be—and remain—really justified.

The ultimate reason for all this is given at the end of the section: "as no one is able to know with the certainty of faith, in which there can be no possibility of error, that he has been given the grace of God." As regards the expression "certainty of faith" the theologians are known to have been unable to agree.[14] The Thomists accepted it because they took it to refer to infused faith as such, which is necessarily infallible; the Scotists rejected it as being too strong, because they were thinking of the "particular," individual faith, which in their meaning could lead to error. As the majority of the Council refused to settle this theological argument and confined themselves to condemning the heretics, some other way had to be found of settling the issue. But throughout hard and interminable discussions the theologians continued to oppose each other. There was a moment when they thought of dropping the problem. Finally, someone proposed the insertion, "the certainty of faith, in which there can be no possibility of error," which satisfied everybody but which itself needs to be properly understood: absolutely infallible certainty of faith was thereby excluded, while the way was left open for the possibility of a faith that might accidentally lead to error. The inserted phrase, therefore, did not refer to any property of supernatural faith in general—"faith, which, as we know, can never lead to error"—but described a particular kind of faith—"a special faith that does not lead to error."[15] The ultimate ground of the Council's

[14] A. Stakemaier, *op. cit.*, pp. 167-170.

[15] R. Aubert, *Le Problème de l'acte de foi* (Louvain, 1945), pp. 83-84. "This expression had been chosen to allow room for the Scotists' certainty of faith, which related to acquired faith, into which some possibility of error might slip."—A. Stakemaier, *op. cit.*, p. 176.

refusal is therefore this, that a compulsive experience of justification is an impossibility.

If we were asked to summarize the essence of this teaching, we should say that the Council rejects any direct, self-evident and compulsive proof of justification. It will not admit that the secret of any forgiven soul can be revealed fully to the eyes of faith. It will not admit that it is necessary, in the words of Canon XIII, to believe in one's justification "without any hesitation on account of one's own infirmity and disorder." It therefore refuses to allow that any empirical experience of grace can have any value in itself, or its value be measured by the intensity of the spiritual feeling that lies behind it. But as it rejected the necessity, the self-sufficiency, and ultimately the very possibility, of any absolute experimental certainty, by this very fact the Council was obliged to transpose the problem, and to look for a solution at another level: from the level of direct apprehension and an apparently simple experience, it makes us pass to the level of a complex spiritual attitude: from the empirical level we are transported to the experiential.

"Just as no religious man *is obliged to* doubt God's mercy, Christ's merit, or the strength and efficacy of the sacraments, similarly, when any individual considers his own soul, and his own weakness, and the faultiness of his disposition, he *may* experience fear and trepidation as regards his own grace, since no one can know, with the certainty of faith that is incompatible with error, that he has obtained the grace of God." The Christian attitude as thus described is therefore a "bi-polar relationship": it includes both looking at God and looking at oneself. When we look at God we become aware of three aspects to the reality of faith—God's merciful will, which is the beginning of salvation; the manifestation and realization of this will in Christ, who died and was resurrected for us and thus merited the grace of our redemption; the continuation and direct application of this redemptive power in the Church by means of the sacraments. This gives three levels of objective reality which faith must affirm, in which it participates by its very affirmation, and which establish it in a confidence based entirely on the Word of God and its visible manifestations, and not at all on any experience which we may be able to have of these things. This is the first and fundamental line of the Council's thought, and it reveals an unmitigated theocentricism.

On the other hand, when man looks into his own soul, he finds himself confronted by a mystery of weakness and misery. He has experienced, he experiences daily, his own sins, his lack of faith, his spiritual impurity. However alive his faith may be, when he finds himself in the presence of this "weakness," through which he is always liable to fall, and this "indisposition," which always makes him more or less disobedient to God, and knowing that an absolute certainty of grace is impossible, he cannot settle down into the security of an unshakeable trust—he may always go in fear and trembling about his own grace. It is not said that he must do this, but that the way always remains open to a humble fear on the part of the redeemed sinner.

The total Christian attitude is made up of this dual movement—absolute trust in God the Redeemer, who comes to us in Christ by way of the sacraments, and a humble fear of ourselves, because of our continual wretchedness. The trust comes first, it is an essential element in faith—as such it is in fact a duty. The fear comes second: it springs, not from the thought of God inclining towards me, but of myself as I appear before God—and, as such, this fear is a normal and inescapable manifestation of the possibility of wretchedness. But as the wretchedness only appears in the light of God, and God is mercy, the fear is swallowed up in trust—so that trust and distrust, fear and hope, make up an inextricable whole, and determine the bi-polar relationship upon which the Christian experience is built.

The Catholic attitude is thus not something closed and turned in upon itself, something certain of fulfilment, knowing the inner warmth and clarity of an absolute and undisturbed assurance. It is open—and this in two ways. In the first place, it is supported by the life of the Church, nourished by the faithfulness of the whole Body and by its recourse to the sacraments; it takes its meaning and value from its insertion within the normative, vitalizing structures of the Church. In the second place, as it is in itself, it takes us out of ourselves towards the transcendent God. The condemned attitude is tied down by a compulsive certainty. The Catholic attitude is not tied down; it rises up and only comes to an end in the very mystery of God—which means to say that there is no end to it. If we pass to the problem of predestination—which is a continuation of the problem of justification—we find the same schema (chs. xii and xiii), i.e. no certain experience of predestination, but a holy fear of being separated from God, the efforts of prayer, penance, fidelity, all enveloped in an absolute hope in God's help. Thus the Christian experience is not static and simple, like the experience of a mere feeling; it is dynamic and structured, and it can only be described as a kind of rhythm between hope and fear, each mutually supporting and generating the other. From the—impossible—experience of grace we find ourselves thrown back upon the—normal—experience of the Christian life.

3

At the Council of Trent the question was, can the Christian know that he is in a state of grace? Our question is: can the Christian be aware of himself as being in a definite relationship with God? These two problems differ in the first place as a partial problem differs from a total problem—on the one side it is grace that is involved, on the other the life of grace. The first is concerned with justification and the possession of grace—can we be sure of our justification? can we have a certain experience of personal grace? The second is concerned with the Christian life as a whole in its total structure and concrete movement: is there a normal experience of the Christian life? of the life of grace in its activity, its development, its concrete existence? On the one side the question is, can we know that we have grace? and on the other, can we know that we are Christians?

The first problem is about an element, an extract or abstract from the Christian life as a whole. For grace is not a being, a substance, a "thing"; it is a mode of being, an accident, a quality and a relationship all at once. It is not, properly speaking, a created reality, but a reality that has been "concreated"; by it the soul is transformed, deified, "graced"; to borrow an excellent saying from Suarez, "essentially what we have is not grace but a graced being."[16] Now in this case it is the "grace" itself which is sought after, for the "graced being" is not able to provide the required certainty—it is only a supernaturalized being, and what is wanted here is a knowledge, a grasp, an experience, of the modality, the transformation, the quality, in short, of grace and the supernatural in themselves. Even supposing that the aim is to study the state of grace, the inquiry immediately

[16] *De gratia*, VIII, ch. ii, 13 (Vivès, IX, 317).

tends towards its formal principle, i.e. grace itself. This is what we mean when we say that the problem is an abstract one, for it concerns an element that is required to be isolated and grasped in its absolute purity. This sort of investigation is in fact, of course, absolutely endless, even when carried on along these lines, for it is a question of grasping an accident, and this accident is a supernatural accident, and it affects the actual substance of the soul. We are immediately driven to look for the effects or signs of grace—and as the effects are always dubious and the signs always ambiguous it remains quite impossible to find any principle of unity or intelligibility.

The problem of the Christian experience, on the other hand, is a problem that involves a concrete totality. It embraces the being and life of the Christian in their full integral reality. It includes the whole complex of acts, organically connected and normally quite clearly defined, that realize, manifest, and develop Christian existence. Here it is not grace itself that is in question, but the new creature, the being who has been totally re-created in newness of life—a life that involves, integrates, and directs all the active elements and personal aspects of the human being. It is not a problem about an extract that is necessarily abstract, it is a problem about a particular organic whole. And what it leads to is not a search for the purely supernatural, but an investigation into the typical structure of a supernaturalized life. If life itself escapes me, and any definitions I may try to make of it, on the biological level, the living thing as it appears to me in its activity does not escape me: it can be seized and described and to a great extent explained. Similarly, Christian experience is, strictly speaking, the experience not of a life but of a living being. Thus the perspectives are reversed, and as the concrete active structure is in the foreground there is no need to attempt to concentrate on one particular element—which in any case can never be grasped—and then go on to study its manifestations; one is immediately installed at the heart of the essential activities that express—and are—the actual movement of a deified being, a man living in communion with God. And this is only possible because this life has been revealed, and because it is lived in faith and in the Church: all the theologian has to do is to scrutinize his faith and then tackle his problem and—if he can—solve it.

The two problems differ, further, as a static problem differs from a dynamic problem, and consequently as an empirical problem differs from an experiential problem. In the first case it is a question of grace as a possessed reality, and therefore of a state to be grasped in itself. If it is a case of charity, in which the state of grace finds its essential expression, an act is indeed involved, but this act is always regarded as an element that can be separated and pinned down in consciousness. St. Thomas shows clearly[17] that the act of charity can never be discerned, either by its species, or by its mode, or by its meritorious effect—in fact by none of its intrinsic characteristics. To the question, can grace or charity be grasped statically and empirically as possessed elements, the Catholic reply is no. And it refers one to the *signs*—which are precisely those elements, separate but interconnected and organic, that give grace and charity their proper place in an integral and structured experience.[18]

There could only be a direct, positive solution of this problem along the lines of a kind of spiritual empiricism or intuitionism in the things of grace that is in fact rejected by Catholic tradition—for rather different reasons, moreover, by St. Bonaventure and St. Thomas. This line of "spiritual feeling" has always been a temptation to any number of imprudent, unpurified, illuminated folk, who end up by "suffering shipwreck in the faith," falling from orthodoxy by centring the spiritual problem on an "empiricist" experience of the supernatural, or of grace, or of God. It is sufficient to recall Messalianism, which maintained that the spiritual person had to "seize his participation in the Holy Spirit in full consciousness and with perfect certainty";[19] and of course there are even more forthright passages than this. Then there was Lutheranism, which regarded justification as something realized in a direct, shattering but blissful apprehension of Christ as one's personal Saviour, and the Christian life as an endless struggle to preserve this certainty. There was Quietism, at least in so far as it attributed "the privileges of infused contemplation, the operation of God in the soul . . . to purely psychological states of simplification or inactivity,"[20] and therefore identified the psychological with the supernatural.

[17] *I Sent.*, XVII, i, 4.

[18] *IV Sent.*, IX, i, 3, 2^{m}; & *S. Th.*, I. II, 112, 5.

[19] Proposition 7 of the Catalogue of St. John Damascene (cf. 8, 9, 10, 12, 17, P. G., 94, 729). On this subject may be read in a well-authenticated text the *Cent Chapitres sur la Perfection spirituelle de Diadoque de Photicé* in the edition by Fr. E. Des places (*Sources chrétiennes*), Paris, 1943.

[20] J. Maréchal, *Psychologie des mystiques* (Paris, 1937), Vol. II, p. 12.

The problem of the Christian experience, on the other hand, is a dynamic and experiential problem, i.e. something going utterly beyond experience in the empirical sense of the word. Its aim is to describe a structured movement—a movement whose directing force (grace) and pole of attraction (God the Trinity) are entirely spiritual and supernatural; a movement that takes the whole being to God, with all his activities and all his passivities—the more spiritual first, and the most sensual, too, if necessary; a movement which begins and develops in faith in Christ, at the heart of the community of the Church, involving all those *de jure* and *de facto* relationships by which the Catholic is a specific member of a body, and by which his experience is conditioned, nourished, and structured. Even an empiricism of a spiritual kind has no meaning here; but in its place there arise the outlines of an experience which is only lived to the extent that it is built up dynamically and supernaturally. The activating principle behind this construction is the total effort of a being who abandons himself entirely to God by taking his place within the visible and invisible structures of the world of faith, in the mysterious and holy community of the children of God. This kind of experience is utterly transcendent to any kind of feeling, because in it feeling is included as a merely secondary aspect—which it integrates and goes beyond—of the communion with God in faith which is the veritable Christian life itself.

Seen along these lines, the problem of the certainty of the state of grace becomes simply one aspect of a much larger problem. If we attempt to turn it into a separate problem, either we are immediately thrown back upon the whole problem of the Christian experience—and that is the Catholic solution—or else we are brought up sharply against the purely psychological aspect of the matter, and sidetracked towards the kind of "spiritual feeling" that has always given birth to the most dangerous illusions. The problem of the Christian experience, on the other hand, because it is something integrating, does not merely, or primarily, concern itself with psychological phenomena, but primarily and pre-eminently with the whole mass of data about the faith that defines and realizes the Christian life.

To put this inquiry into its right context, let us say then that we are not concerned with the problem raised by the old theologians, but rather with the problem implicit in their answers when they enumerated—rather than constructed—the signs of the state of grace;

and this problem we shall attempt to explore as an integral whole. Again, we shall not be concerned with the problem of the experience of salvation, as this was raised and rejected at the Council of Trent, because not only is this a kind of problem to which there is no solution, but there is even a lack of the relevant facts; we shall therefore consider the problem to which the Council refers when it presents the Christian attitude as a relationship between fear and trust, both equally implied in any truly religious life. Thus, leaving aside any psychological exploration of mere pseudo-facts, we shall be led to investigate the theology of a particular structure.

4

Catholic dogma, then, allows one to raise the question of the Christian experience. It does more: it recognizes the existence of a specific kind of experience known as the mystical experience, and it is impossible to set the former in its right context if its relationship with the latter is not made clear. This becomes all the more necessary from the fact that there is a fairly widespread idea that the mystical experience is the only kind of experience that has any value in Christian teaching, and that consequently the mystical experience is synonymous with the Christian experience. This belief makes it necessary for us to proceed to a new distinction—this time from above—between the mystical experience and the Christian experience.

If I were obliged to take sides on the matter of the essence of the mystical experience, I should find myself faced with a singularly complicated task. But since my concern is merely to put the Christian experience in its right context, I can begin—as a working hypothesis, and so as to come straight up against the difficulty—with the widely accepted belief that mysticism means some kind of experience of the supernatural. Fr. Bainvel gives an excellent description of this in the following words: "The mystics . . . have a certain experience of the supernatural realities that are in us by grace and by the virtues that accompany grace, an experience of the ineffable love of the three Divine Persons, and of their special presence in the soul that is in a state of grace; and it is apparently in just such an experience of the supernatural that mystical states consist." "But none of this sense of the supernatural, this taste of virtue, this sort of contact with

God present in the soul, this experience of God's action within us and with us, is usually to be found in the Christian life. The usual things are inward touches, consolations, longings for heaven, a sensible increase of faith, hope and love . . . but none of this is experienced as anything supernatural. At the most the supernatural may be conjectured or deduced from it."[21] Thus the experience of grace which we denied to the "just man" here appears as the kind of experience that is typical of the mystic. The question then becomes, how does the Christian experience stand with regard to the mystical experience as thus defined?

In the first place, the Christian experience is something integral, which the mystical experience is not. The former embraces the entire Christian life; it is co-extensive with the Christian's whole behaviour in all its aspects: spiritual and incarnated; sensible and detached; active and passive; private and communal. All this is involved in the idea of the Christian experience. Mystical experience, on the other hand, does not embrace the mystic's whole life; it relates to certain moments in his life. Even supposing that it gradually extends to, and ends by penetrating and governing, his whole life, this is simply an extreme point, which is normally preceded by years of genuine mystical experience that has nevertheless been discontinuous, partial, and progressive. Thus moments of mystical experience rise out of the general current of the Christian experience. If by mystical life one means the life of a Christian who has entered deeply into mystical experience, we must say that mystical experience is an element in the mystical life, whereas Christian experience is by its nature co-extensive with Christian life in its totality. It follows that in the two expressions the word "experience" has not, strictly speaking, the same meaning in both cases: in the case of mysticism the

[21] J. V. Bainvel, *Nature et surnaturel*, pp. 63 & 307. Cf. *Introduction aux Grâces d'oraison* by A. Poulain, no. 12, p. xxx; similarly, M. de la Taille, *Oraison contemplative*, pp. 20 *et seq.* and *Théories mystiques* (*Rech. Sc. relig.*, 1928), pp. 297 *et seq.*; also J. de Guibert, *Études de Théologie mystique*, pp. 78-90. Its experimental character is always emphasized even in the most highly theological definitions of mysticism: See e.g. R. Garrigou-Lagrange, *L'Amour de Dieu et la Croix de Jésus*, I, pp. 183 *et seq.*; A. Gardeil, *La Structure de l'âme et l'Expérience mystique*, II, pp. 328 *et seq.*; J. Maritain, *The Degrees of Knowledge*. Cf. also the article by F. Cayre, in which this experimental character is in fact taken as the methodological starting-point of the inquiry, *Année théologique*, 1944, II, pp. 248 *et seq.*

meaning is "empirical," in the case of the Christian life it is "experiential."

Psychologically, in fact, the former means a consciousness of the supernatural. When Fr. Bainvel writes "a genuine experience of the supernatural," "a sense of the supernatural," "an experience of God's action within us and with us," these expressions all denote a kind of immediate datum that is the radically new element of mystical experience, the element that gives the mystic the impression of entering an unfamiliar world. Consequently, conscious passivity is an essential aspect of this experience. Supernatural love and knowledge are not only infused, but grasped as such—consciously infused, as Fr. de la Taille says. The soul that is conscious of receiving the gifts of God in this way is not, of course, inert; it is passive, but with the kind of passivity that means a welcome, and includes the consent, the abandonment, and the collaboration that are the highest acts of the spirit. But the consciousness of the *pati divina* is, so to speak, the form of the mystical experience.

In the Christian experience, however, there is nothing like this—no experience of the supernatural as such, no conscious passivity. Faith and charity are infused, but without being recognized for what they are. And in this case the activity is quite different; it is not any kind of abandonment, but a choice made by the will; not any kind of (infinitely pure) spiritual activity, but the action of an active, dynamic freedom. The Christian believes that God is active within him and with him, but he does not experience this, he knows it by faith; he acts and comes to decisions as though he were psychologically alone. There is a saying of St. Paul's which is relevant here: "I have laboured more abundantly than all they"—an intense apostolic activity is the thing that he is aware of; "yet not I, but the grace of God with me" (I Cor. xv, 10)—the profound action of God is something he knows by faith. Mystical experience, on the other hand, as conscious spiritual passivity, means the highest act of experience in the empirical sense of the word: this "suffering" presents itself on its own level as an immediate fact, it is the sense-perceived revelation of a presence, the consciousness of a direct communion with God. There is nothing of this in the Christian experience.

If we pass from psychology to theology the differences remain considerable. The Christian experience covers the whole of the normal sincere life of faith, including on the one hand all that is involved in the activity of prayer, and on the other all that is involved in practical action. Mystical experience is the realization of a certain state of faith, a faith that is enlightened, glowing, transfigured—*fe illustradisima*—a faith without concepts or speech, whose light streams forth into the soul and whose new characteristics can be legitimately ascribed to the gifts of the Holy Spirit, especially as regards their characteristics of lucidity and certainty; so that there is a "pneumatization" of faith by the divine *Pneuma*—in short, faith in its perfect state, bringing fully before the eyes of the spirit that element of communion which had been in it ever since it was born, and doing this is an experience that gives a foretaste of bliss, but which always leaves the person who experiences it hungry for more, because it is transitory and imperfect.

But if the mystic is within the faith, if faith is the fundamental principle of both kinds of experience, and if this is necessarily so because faith is the axis of the spiritual life, we must emphasize the continuity of the two experiences. Faith appears in two different states of purity, strength and fervour—in one case as a living faith and in the other as a lively faith—but in each case the faith is the same, and therefore throughout the discontinuity, which may be very deeply felt, there must run an extremely profound continuity, a radical homogeneity in the aspiration towards God, a similarity of life in the two different growths. Therefore the mystical life is not a sudden flowering that is foreign to the soul (if not an aberration), something absolutely unprepared for; it cannot even be an experience that follows upon an absence of experience, appearing as a kind of life absolutely new in its principles (the gifts), its objects (God, as someone seen and felt) and its acts (intuition or experimental knowledge). On the contrary, it appears as an experience that is a continuation of another experience—a supreme experience that deepens and purifies, clarifies, transcends, and crowns a fundamental experience of a more humble nature manifesting itself in a diversity of ways. For firstly, there are already some mystical elements in the Christian life—faith, the principle of that life, is a thing that involves mysticism and communion from the moment that it is born—and secondly, there are moments of ordinary Christian life in the genuinely mystical life, because Christian behaviour is one, the essential virtues never change, the principle and object of faith are the same in both cases, and (leaving aside, perhaps, the spiritual marriage) mystical experience is neither continuous, nor everlasting, nor unbroken, nor irrevocably separated from the ordinary devout Christian's way of living and loving. Thus in its own interests it is necessary to explain how the mystical experience is, if not inaugurated, at least prepared for by the integral Christian experience—indeed this is the only way of showing that it is not something misleading; and in the interests of the Christian experience, it is important to show that this is not something absolutely separate from the mystical experience—otherwise there is a danger of undervaluing the ordinary life of the serious believer and giving undue emphasis to the mystical experience.

This, it seems to me, is a problem of absolutely fundamental importance. The Christian experience has not been studied sufficiently for its own sake—despite the Scriptures and the tradition of the Fathers—because it has been implicitly held to be identical with the mystical experience, and because there has always been an attempt to discover (as the heretics claim to do) or deny (as Catholics do) an experience of a mystical type or form in the ordinary Christian life. But this supposed identity must be denied, and, once this is done, the way is open to a proper investigation of the facts. For if there is no experience that is not mystical, one of two things must happen.

The first possibility is that all experience of the Christian life will be excluded on principle, and this is impossible, since a place must be found for this experience. This way leads inevitably to a re-discussion of old problems that are, strictly speaking, irrelevant—the discernment of spirits, the discernment of vocations, the part played by experience in the theology of faith or grace (one has only to read the theologians of the sixteenth and seventeenth centuries to see how frequently appeal was made in this matter to the experience of the faithful); and then one finds oneself ending up with some vague, unrealized, empirical notion, in a kind of spiritual casuistry—as in another field there is a moral casuistry. Such kinds of casuistry may be necessary, but they are dangerous if they are not based upon solid theological foundations that have been seriously considered in the full light of consciousness, if they become too proliferous and all-invading, and are treated as though valid in themselves.

The other way is to regard the Christian life itself as an experience of a mystical kind, but one that can be had on the cheap. Then there will be a search into the most rudimentary faith of the ordinary believer for those elements of conscious passivity, consciousness of God, conscious illumination and inspiration, that characterize the highest mystical experience, with the result that the Christian life and the Christian experience, which do not in the first place contain any of these elements in any great degree, are falsified. The whole part of feeling in the spiritual life, and indeed in the mystical life too, comes to be overemphasized, and from that it is a short step to all those illusions, aberrations, and perversions from which the Church has at times had to suffer so much.

In the first case the genuine experience is rejected, and one is restricted to the domain of the empirical with all its insufficiencies and dangers; in the second case certain secondary or inappropriate elements in the Christian experience are transposed and overestimated, and the experimental is gradually introduced into a field to which it does not properly apply. In both cases the real problem, which is the problem of a structured experience, and therefore one that involves the experiential, is neglected. I believe that some important points regarding mysticism—its ultimate nature, for instance, its lower limits, its true value—will not be properly solved until we are quite clear about their substructure—that is to say, the integral Christian experience; which is at once continuous and discontinuous with mysticism; which is an experience of a definite type; and which must be analyzed for what it is in itself.

CHAPTER THREE

The Consciousness of Faith

"THESE are written, that you may believe that Jesus is the Christ, the Son of God; and that believing, you may have life in his name" (John xx, 31). A Christian is therefore in the first place someone who believes in Christ. But can the Christian know that he has faith? This question may seem surprising at first sight, and yet it is a well-known fact that it is raised and answered differently by the different Christian confessions, and that Catholic theologians are far from being of one mind on the subject.

I should like here to gather together some of the elements of the problem, indicate some of the ways in which theological thought has dealt with them, and finally make some modest attempt to suggest the lines along which a solution might be reached.

1. *The Evidence from the Liturgy and the Canon*

Before baptizing a convert, the Church asks him to profess his faith and say "I believe" three times. Today, according to present discipline, three questions are asked about the Creed at the doors of the church; the Creed and the Our Father are recited on entry into the church; and in the baptistery immediately before the actual baptism there is a repetition of the three questions about the Apostles' Creed. These must be looked upon as simplified and compressed survivals of the old rites of the catechumenate and baptism. When the catechumen became an *electus*, a *competens*, an *illuminandus*, he was taught the Apostles' Creed and the Our Father; he had to learn about his faith and adhere to it, know and believe it, and make a public profession of it twice—once well before baptism, at the time of the *redditio Symboli*, and again at the actual baptism itself, when he "professed," "I believe," in reply to the three questions about the faith of the Trinity, received the three purifying ablutions, and was thus baptized in the name of the Father, the Son, and the Holy Ghost. There are innumerable references to this;[1] let us look at a few of them.

St. Justin writes: "When our disciples admit that what we have taught them is true, and adhere to it by faith, when they have agreed to live in conformity with our doctrine," we make them pray and fast, and baptize them.[2] Tertullian (*De Praescript.*, 36), summarizing the essentials of the faith, declares: the Church recognizes God and Christ; she accepts the law and the prophets and also the writings of the New Testament; "whence she gives the soul faith to drink, signs it with water, clothes it in the Holy Ghost, feeds it on the Eucharist, exhorts it to martyrdom; and therefore against this institution she receives no one." D. de Puniet, who quotes this passage, comments, "It is therefore a *perfectly instructed* faith that is *consecrated* and *sealed* by baptism."[3] St. Augustine in a well-known passage says: "Such are all catechumens: they already believe in the name of Christ, but Christ has not yet given himself to them . . . If we say to a catechumen, 'Do you believe in Christ?' he answers, 'I believe,' and makes the sign of the cross: he already bears the cross of Christ on his forehead and he is not ashamed of the cross of his Lord. Thus he believes in His name."[4] Finally, St. Jerome, commenting on the baptismal formula, writes, "For it may not be that the body of him who is to be baptized may receive the sacrament unless his soul has previously accepted the truth of faith."[5]

There is a much fuller piece of evidence in the Catechisms of St. Cyril of Jerusalem,[6] all the more interesting as it appears as a sort of leitmotiv running throughout the course of the instruction. The *illuminandi* are believers who are nearing the perfection of their

[1] The main passages will be found collected together, for instance, by D. de Puniet, arts. *Catéchuménat* and *Baptême*, in D. A. C. L.

[2] *Apol.*, I, 61. Trans. by de Puniet, who gives his own slight emphasis here and there (*Catech.*, 2585).

[3] *Catech.*, 2586 & 2587 (my italics).

[4] *Tract. in Jo.*, X, 3 (P. L., 35, 1476). This passage was to pass into the explanations of the liturgy: thus Ildefonsus of Toledo, *De cognitione fidei*, c. 30: "*Catechumenus et Competens jam credunt in Christum* . . ." (P. L. 96, 125, C).

[5] *IV in Matt.* (28-19), P. L., 26, 218 B.

[6] The fact that these Catechisms are being increasingly attributed to John of Jerusalem is irrelevant here.

faith. They are already under the influence of the Holy Spirit, fanned by its temperate breath,[7] inhabited to some extent by the Spirit;[8] this explains how it is that they have faith and are already to be numbered amongst the faithful: "What a great dignity the Lord confers upon you by transferring you from the ranks of the catechumens to the ranks of the faithful."[9] "You who have so recently lit the lamp of faith, take care to keep it properly alight in your hand."[10] They are to learn more about the faith, profess it, grow in it—in utter sincerity[11]—and then they will receive the fullness of the Spirit and the faith: "Make ready the vessel of your soul to become a son of God . . . but you must approach God by way of the faith and finally achieve a faith that is perfect."[12] "If you remain solidly faithful, you will be happy; if only today you have fallen into unbelief, get rid of your unbelief at once and believe fully."[13] "What is asked of you is that each of you shall be found faithful according to your conscience . . . Not that you are to reveal your conscience to me (for you are not to be judged by any human tribunal), but so that you may show the sincerity of your faith to God, who proves the reins and the hearts and knows the thoughts of men."[14] "And if you believe sincerely, is it not true that you will draw great profit from it? But perhaps you were without faith or with only a little faith? The Lord is the friend of men and leans over you when you are on the road to conversion. All you have to say, to be wise, is, 'I believe, Lord, help thou mine unbelief.' But if you believe yourself to be faithful, nevertheless your faith is still not perfect and you need to say with the Apostle, 'Lord, increase our faith.' "[15] Finally, "By the resemblance of faith we arrive at sonship with Abraham. And then, after we have received the faith, like him we receive the spiritual seal and are circumcized by the Holy Spirit in baptism."[16] From imperfect faith to perfect faith, by way of baptism—that is the way to be followed by the catechumen; loyally, humbly and perseveringly.

[7] *Procat.*, P.G., 33, 352.
[8] *Ibid.*, P.G., 33, 343.
[9] *Catech.*, V, P.G., 33, 506; cf. *Catech.*, I, P.G., 33, 374.
[10] *Catech.*, I, P.G., 33, 371.
[11] *Ibid.*, III, P.G., 33, 426.
[12] *Ibid.*, XV, P. G., 33, 446.
[13] *Ibid.*, XVII, P.G., 33, 1010.
[14] *Ibid.*, V, P.G., 33, 505.
[15] *Ibid.*, IX, P.G., 33, 516.
[16] *Ibid.*, VI, P.G., 33, 514; cf. *Catech.*, XVII, P.G., 33, 1010.

The passages that come more directly from the liturgy are similar in tone. We know that at the very heart of the act of baptism occurred the *Confessio Trinitatis.* This was so important that there could be no baptism without it; unless it was professed in true faith there could indeed be a kind of baptism but not the kind that could save the soul—"Even baptism itself—in the case of an adult who does not believe and confess—is of no effect towards salvation";[17] and a historian has even been able to write, "Baptismal immersion and the profession of the Apostles' Creed are two inseparable elements in a single rite; in one of the passages mentioned below (*Ep.*, 67, 7: 'Novatian . . . baptizes with the same Creed as we'), St. Cyprian can say that 'we baptize by way of the Apostles' Creed, and all this together forms the sacrament of faith.' "[18] Later forms of the Western liturgy have simply developed and clarified this theme. In articles as penetrating as they are erudite, Chavasse has again and again drawn attention to this point. In his article on *La Bénédiction du chrême en Gaule avant l'adoption intégrale de la liturgie romaine,*[19] he reproduces this passage from the Liturgy for Holy Saturday:[20] "*Fides populi firmatur Symbolo . . . ,*" which he translates as, "The faith of the people is proved by the Apostles' Creed," and goes on to comment, "The *redditio Symboli* appears spontaneously, not only as a check on the catechumen's knowledge of the actual words of the Apostles' Creed, but, even more importantly, as a public attestation of the reality and exactitude of his faith. In fact, so far as Gaul is concerned, the *Expositio Symboli* of the *Gal. vet.*[21] presents the Apostles' Creed as that which provides the firm foundation for perfect faith: 'the Creed strengthening all by the perfection of belief.' In Spain, Ildefonsus of Toledo regards the *redditio Symboli* as 'evidence' that 'proves' the catechumen's faith: 'On the fifth feria before Easter the candidates say and repeat this Creed to the priest, that those whose faith has been proved may arrive by merit at the sacrament of the Lord's Resurrection.'[22] What remains of the

[17] Fulgentius of Ruspe, P.L., 65, 385 & 388 (in DE PUNIET, *Baptême*, in D.A.C.L., 318).

[18] Rev. Fr. LEBRETON, *Origines du Dogme de la Trinité*, II, p. 144.

[19] *Revue du Moyen-Âge latin*, April-June 1945, pp. 109 *et seq.*

[20] 2nd Letter of the Pseudo-Germain of Paris, P.L., 72, 96 A.

[21] *Vet. Missale Gallican.*, P.L., 72, 355 D (the Creed is "*plenitudo credendi in eo, qui docetur ac discitur*").

[22] *De cognit. baptismi*, P.L., 96, 127 A.

old *redditio Symboli* in the private rite of baptism that appears in a Mozarabic ritual of 1039 (Rit. A. de Ferotin) entirely supports our exegesis of the expression: "Then he affirms the creed, saying this prayer: May this Creed be to you a confirmation of your faith. May this true and holy belief abide in you to the remission of all your sins, to the possession of the first-fruits of eternal life.' "[23] In another essay, on the evidence provided by John the Deacon (sixth century), Chavasse writes:[24] John "regards the scrutiny as an 'examination' . . . The means employed is described as *per fidem,* and this must be understood as meaning the faith manifested by the chosen one in the solemn profession which he makes when he repeats the Apostles' Creed at the time of his 'election.' The rest of the passage gives no room for doubt. This profession is used as a means to knowing exactly what the chosen person's faith is with respect to three essential points taught him by tradition. The things that are verified are (1) whether they have fixed the sacred words in their minds . . . (2) whether they understand about the grace [i.e., baptism] which they are about to receive . . . (3) whether they acknowledge a belief in God the Father Almighty . . . Their reply makes manifest the content of their faith, for, as St. Paul says, oral 'confession' gives expression to the inward faith." To these very clear passages we may add in conclusion the magnificent prayer that occurs in the *Ordo Gallicanus I:* "Open [to thy servants] all the avenues of faith, that they may be enclosed within the walls of belief.[25] And deign to reveal more fully unto them the way of truth, that they may know how to avoid the ways of error. May they recognize the things appertaining to salvation . . . , may they understand the treasures of life . . . , may they lay aside all that they still retain of the things of darkness, and

[23] Ed. FEROTIN, *Lib. Ordinum,* col. 28, no. 1.

[24] *Deux rituels dans le Sacramentaire gélasien, in Études de critique et d'hist. relig.* (Lyons, 1948), pp. 87-88, note. The actual text runs: "For we inquire into their (i.e., the elect's) hearts by faith, to see whether after renouncing the devil they have fixed the holy words in their minds; whether they have acknowledged the future grace of the Redeemer; whether they confess that they believe in God the Father almighty. And when by their replies has been made clear that which is written: 'For, with the heart, we believe unto justice; but, with the mouth confession is made unto salvation,' their ears . . . are anointed . . . for by the ears faith enters into the mind" (P.L., 59, 402 C).

[25] *Credulitatis muri.* For the meaning of *credulitas,* cf. Ildefonsus of TOLEDO, *De cognit. fidei,* c. 36: "What does 'I believe' mean? I make an act of belief, i.e. I confess those things to be true which I do not know of myself but hear" (P.L., 96, 127 C).

receive the illumination of the full light; may the stains of the world altogether depart from them, that they may be worthily prepared for the sanctification of baptism. . . . Christ Jesus, thou who openest all doors and revealest the way to salvation, deign to embrace thy servants who come to the knowledge of thy Name, that these thy servants may desire to follow thee in their thoughts, O thou whom they have begun to confess with their mouths."[26]

The conclusion that is to be drawn from these passages is clear: before the catechumen can be baptized, and in order that he may be baptized, he must have faith—a faith that is necessarily imperfect but nevertheless instructed, sincere, and genuine—and he must profess his faith in public. What is demanded of the catechumen is that he shall be loyal to the Church and to God, and therefore that he shall affirm his faith, thereby acknowledging that he has a full intention of adhering clearly, sincerely, and firmly to all that the Church has taught him.[27]

Canonical passages, again, show the same line of thought. If we jump several centuries and open the book of Canon Law we shall find that an adult is not to be baptized unless he is "properly instructed" (Can. 752, 1); that if he is likely to die and cannot be instructed, it will be sufficient "if by any means he shows that he assents to them" (*ibid.*, 2). The passages taken from the Holy Office that are quoted in the *Fontes* leave no room for doubt about the need for faith, and a faith that is outwardly acknowledged, since it is a matter in which a decision of the Canon Law is concerned. Hence

[26] Martene, *De Antiquis Ecclesiae Ritibus, Ordo Gall.*, I, xiii, *Praemissiones ad scrutamen*, 91-92.

[27] We are speaking of baptism. It would be quite a different matter if we were discussing the death of a Christian. The passages in the liturgy supply one further proof of the different way in which the Church treats faith and hope on the one hand and charity on the other. The Church never says anything about the charity of a dying or dead person—its existence is known only to God. Faith and hope, on the other hand, are manifested in acts that do not deceive. Hence, for example, the three following statements—in the *Ordo Commendat. Animae*: "For although he has sinned, yet has he not denied God and the Son and the Holy Spirit, but has believed and had the love of God in him and faithfully worshipped God who made all things"; in the Apostolic Benediction: "Look down upon Thy people, who are commended to Thee by true faith and Christian hope"; in prayers for the dead: "That because they have hoped and believed in Thee they may have eternal life," or else: "That with him in whom they have hoped and believed they may have everlasting fellowship," or again: "that they may advance into eternal life because they have hoped and believed in Thee."

the two following replies, which are explicitly concerned with the question of sincerity in a "savage's" affirmation of faith. Reply of May 10th, 1703:[28] "It is not permitted [to baptize] if the missionary is morally certain that a savage in a state of illness has not understood, as well as his degree of intelligence allows him to, the mysteries of the Christian religion that have been explained to him, or does not believe them sufficiently, and is only promising to keep the commandments of the Christian religion from fear of seeming to contradict. But if the missionary seriously believes that when the sick savage says '*Credo et faciam*,' he really believes sufficiently and is making a serious promise to obey, he should be baptized." Again, in the reply given on August 1st, 1860,[29] it is said that the adult must have three dispositions before he can be baptized—faith, penitence, and the right intention. And "the faith that is necessary is that which proves the adult to be sufficiently instructed (according to his degree of intelligence) in the mysteries of the Christian religion, and firmly to believe them (*ea firmiter credere*)." (The reply then goes on to reproduce the passage quoted above.) These passages, therefore, demand not only instruction, as though it were sufficient for the catechumen to know the truths; they also demand an assent to the truth of the mysteries and a promise to observe the commandments—in other words a minimum of true faith, with the normal visible signs, and of a sufficient degree to convince a prudent missionary. But if the catechist is to be able to perceive the sincerity of the affirmation, this can only be by way of the sincerity with which it is expressed by the catechumen. Now this sincerity assumes that he has a clear awareness of his own mind and will, and the will to express them. Therefore, the catechumen must be conscious of what he is doing: when he says, "*credo et faciam*" he must be clearly aware[30] that he is promising an adherence. And it is to the extent that the Church regards him as being sincere, i.e. as fully conscious and decided, that she allows him to be baptized.

The conclusion to which all these remarks tend is always the same: canonical discipline and liturgical act both assume that the faith that is necessary for baptism is a personal reality that can be directly grasped by the consciousness that lives and affirms it, and having

[28] *Fontes juris canonici*, IV, pp. 42-43.
[29] *Ibid.*, pp. 235-236.
[30] I do not say "reflectively aware."

signs which enable it to be grasped by the person authorized to demand it before he can administer the sacrament.

2. *St. Augustine and St. Thomas*

Western theology is to a great extent dependent upon St. Augustine for its analysis of faith. His psychology and dialectic have supplied an immense mass of material in this field, and this is still far from being thoroughly worked out. I shall confine myself here to two passages that seem to be particularly relevant.

The first is one of the classic passages of mediaeval theology—*De Trinitate*, lib. XIII, cap. I, no. 3.[31] Here St. Augustine is glossing the Prologue to the Fourth Gospel, and he asks how we can know what faith we possess. The Gospel mentions John the Baptist and his witness, and through this passage we get our first knowledge of the Precursor. But "the actual faith that everyone knows to exist in his own heart, if he believes, and not to exist, if he does not believe, we know in quite a different way." Augustine then goes on to eliminate three kinds of knowledge—the knowledge of bodies which we can see with our bodily eyes and remember; the knowledge of imagined objects, which we can also remember; and the knowledge of living men, whom we can see with our eyes but whose souls we can only conjecture from our own. Now "the faith that is in the heart is not known in this way by the person who possesses it, but it is grasped by a very certain kind of knowledge and is cried aloud by conscience . . . And so, although we are told to believe (because we cannot see what we are told to believe), nevertheless when the faith itself is in us we can see it, because there is a present faith of things that are absent, a faith within of things that are without, a faith that can be seen of the things that cannot be seen; and this faith is realized in the order of time in the hearts of men, and if they change from being believers to being unbelievers it disappears from them. . . ."

A little further on (cap. 2, no. 5), Augustine goes on to insist that the Christian faith is a *fides ex auditu*, but that it is not attained either by hearing or by any other of the senses of the body because "this reality belongs to the heart, not to the body; it is not outside us but within our very innermost being; and no man can see it in

[31] P.L., 42, 1014, 10.

any other man, but every man can see it within himself. Finally, it can be feigned by simulation, and imagined to exist in a person who does not possess it. Thus, therefore, everyone sees his own faith within himself, but he believes it to exist in others, he cannot see it; and he believes this all the more firmly, the more he sees of the results that faith normally produces through love. . . ." The faith held by Christians is undoubtedly common to them all, but in what sense? "In very truth we say that as it comes from a single doctrine, the faith held by believers is impressed upon the heart of each of those who believe this single doctrine, but the objects that are believed are one thing, the faith that believes them another. These objects are in realities which we say exist or did exist or are to exist, but faith is in the soul of the believer and is only visible to the person possessing it; though it is in others too it is not the same but similar . . . The faith held by people who believe the same things is called 'a single faith' (Eph. iv, 5), as the will of people who will the same things is a single will. But when men will the same thing, their own will is visible to each one of them, but the wills of all the others are hidden, although they all want the same thing; and though the will makes itself manifest by signs, it is believed rather than seen. But a man who is conscious of his own mind does not *believe* that his will is his own, for he can see it perfectly clearly."

To sum up: St. Augustine draws a distinction between two kinds of knowledge, which he opposes to each other—the knowledge of self, and the knowledge of all that is not self. The knowledge of self is direct—it is something seen, an intuition. When a man wills, he is conscious of his will, he can see it. When a man believes, he is conscious of his faith, he can see it. The object does not matter: whether it is absent or external or invisible it is grasped by a faith that is a reality of the soul and the heart, and the soul has a clear awareness of this faith, it can see it within itself. The faith of others can only be believed; one's own faith can only be seen. Thus the believer has a direct experience of his faith.

So speaks St. Augustine in a technical treatise. But he says the same thing again in his popular sermons. I need only mention one particular passage, which is in fact a magnificent one. It occurs in *Enarrationes in Psalmos* (Ps. 32, En. 2, sermo i).[32] Augustine is commenting on the words: "*Exsultate, justi, in Domino, rectos decet*

[32] P.L., 36, 277 *et seq.*

laudatio." The *recti corde*—as he is always so delighted to explain—are people who rule their hearts according to the will of God, preferring God's will to their own like Christ their Head. Therefore, "you, the *justi recti,* rejoice in God, because praise is fitting for you. Let no one say, how can I be just, or, when shall I be just? Do not despise yourselves and do not despair of yourselves. You are men made in the image of God, and he who made you men became man for you. If you find yourselves worthless because of your worldly weakness, value yourselves by what you have cost . . . You must not think again that you have become strangers to all justice. But I do not want to question you about your justice; perhaps, in fact, not a single one of you would dare to answer, 'I am just.' But I question you about your faith. Just as not one of you would dare to say, 'I am just,' similarly not one of you would dare to say, 'I am not a believer' (*fidelis*). I do not ask you yet what your life is, but what you believe. You will answer that you believe in Christ. Do you not know the words of the Apostle, 'The just shall live by faith'? Your faith is your justice, because, if you believe, you watch over yourselves; if you watch over yourselves, you make an effort; and God knows the effort you make, and sees your will, and sees your struggling against the flesh, and calls upon you to go on fighting, and helps you to win, and watches you fighting, and helps you when you fail, and crowns you when you emerge victorious. Therefore, the words 'Rejoice in the Lord, O ye righteous,' I translate as, 'Rejoice in the Lord, O ye faithful,' because the just man lives by faith."

Thus, in Augustine's view the Christian ought not to live in any state of anxiety or discouragement or desolation. He may not know that he is just, but he does know, must know, that he has faith. And from this certainty he must draw confidence, courage, and joy in the Lord. The principle that underlies this exhortation is clear—it is the principle that Augustine has explained in the *De Trinitate:* the man who has faith is conscious of it, he can see it in himself. So let him depend upon it, and work like a good soldier of Christ. In this doctrine the consciousness of faith is a normal requirement both of psychology and of noetics, a first datum of Christian consciousness and one of the essential forces in all spiritual growth.

As we know, St. Thomas was always absolutely faithful to St. Augustine's deepest inspirations, and always utterly different from him in his intellectual equipment. As Gilson has written: "It can be said, taking things all in all, that St. Thomas's theological Augustinianism, which is a real thing, is a compound of St. Augustine's Augustinianism and the technique of Aristotle, as Malebranche's Augustinianism—which is no less real—is a compound of St. Augustine's Augustinianism and the technique of Descartes."[33] What will this lead to, as regards our present problem? Let us take a few characteristic passages.

St. Thomas refers to a passage from Augustine (*De Trin.*, 9, 3) in the *De Veritate*, Q. 8, A. 3, Obj. 7: "Because faith is present by its essence in the soul, it is seen in the soul by its essence." Reply: "Faith is known by its essence, to the extent that its essence is joined to the intellect as an intelligible form, and not in any other way." We know that in St. Thomas's view the intelligible form could be understood in two ways:[34] either as the principle or as the end of the act of thought (*De Ver.*, 3, 2). Which is it here, consciousness of the act, or consciousness of the object? Assuming it to be the object ("the intellectual form is the object grasped by the intellect," *De Pot.*, 8, 1, c.), this becomes, then: faith is known by the objects which it makes us affirm.

St. Thomas twice takes an objection from passages from Augustine. The first is the one already mentioned, *De Trinitate*, 13, 1, 3; and in the *De Veritate*, 10, 9, 8, the reply is: "Faith is a habit of the intellectual faculty; whence from the very fact that it is in the mind it inclines the mind to the intellectual act in which faith makes itself seen; it is otherwise with those other habits which exist in the affective faculty." This is an application of a doctrine that is constantly appearing in St. Thomas: a *habitus* is perceived by its acts. And therefore consciousness of the act of faith means consciousness of faith itself. In the *Summa* (I, 87, 2, 1^{m}) the reply is more precise: "And if faith may not be known by exterior movements of the body, yet it is perceived by that in which it is, by the interior act of the heart. No one knows that he has faith, save in that he is aware that he believes." Thus I perceive my act of believing, my spiritual act, directly, and through this perception I know that I have faith.[35]

[33] E. Gilson, *Note conjointe . . . sur l'étude de saint Augustin*, in *Année théologique*, 1944, II, pp. 324-325.

[34] Cf. the passages grouped together with a commentary by Rabeau, *Species. Verbum. L'activité intellectuelle élémentaire selon saint Thomas d'Aquin* (Paris, 1938), ch. iii, pp. 36 *et seq.*

[35] Cf. II. II, 4, 5, 4^{m}.

In his treatise on grace, discussing the consciousness of grace (I. II, 112, 5, 2^m), St. Thomas raises the objection: "Whoever receives knowledge from God knows that he has knowledge . . . Hence, with equal reason, whoever receives grace from God, knows that he has grace." Reply: "It belongs to knowledge that a man have certitude of the things whereof he has knowledge; and similarly it belongs to faith that a man have certitude of the things whereof he has faith; and this especially because certitude pertains to the perfection of the intellect, in which the gifts in question exist. Thus, whoever has either knowledge or faith is certain he has it. It is not at all the same with grace and charity and other things of the sort, which perfect the appetitive faculty." This passage emphasizes the objective aspects of consciousness. Certainty is a perfection of the mind, knowledge and faith are realities of the mind, and it is therefore essential for them to have certainty about the objects which they affirm. In this sense, "he who possesses knowledge or faith is certain that he has them."

In the Commentary on II Cor. xii, 12 (Lect. I) we first come upon a general statement: "Being in Christ can be understood in two ways: firstly, through faith and the sacrament of faith, according to Gal. iii, 27, 'For as many of you as have been baptized in Christ have put on Christ,' i.e. by faith and the sacrament of faith; and in this way the apostle knows that he is in Christ." There is another passage, much more precise, on II Cor. xiii, 5: "Know you not your own selves, that Christ Jesus is in you, unless perhaps you be reprobates?" Commentary: "In themselves, they can discover two things by examination, for (1) either they will know that they hold the faith and so can discover and know that Christ is in them. Which is as much as to say, because where faith in Christ is, there Christ is; (2) or they will know that they do not hold the faith, so they may discover that they are reprobate. And therefore it is said 'unless . . .' i.e. you will discover indeed that you have Christ, unless perhaps you have lost the faith and are reprobate from that which you first had by faith." Does it follow then that we know that we have charity because we have Christ? No, because there is no parity between the act of the intelligence and the act of the will, and Christ can be within us either *quantum ad intellectum* or *quantum ad affectum*. In the second case there is no certainty, but only conjecture; whereas in the first, if it is a case of Christ being in us *quantam ad intellectum*, "then he dwells in us by faith (as distinct from charity); and in this mode nothing prevents us from knowing with certainty that Christ dwells in us, i.e. when we know that we hold the faith that the Catholic Church teaches and holds." We can therefore know with certainty that we have faith, and that Christ is within us, when we "hold the faith," when we have not "rejected" it, more precisely, when we hold in full consciousness the faith taught and held by the Catholic Church. St. Thomas affirms both the consciousness of the act ("we may know that we hold") and the consciousness of the object ("the faith that the Catholic Church holds and teaches"). About supernatural faith, as distinct from charity, he does not hesitate: we can know with certainty that we possess it.

Cajetan, commenting on one of these passages (I, II, 112, 5, 2^{m}), is known to have come down heavily on the side of a knowledge of personal faith that even shares the certainty of infused faith: "Whoever knows with certainty that he has the gift of infused faith knows it with the certainty of faith. And this is the difference between an experimental certainty of faith and grace; for however much from the actions of grace a man may think himself to be in grace, nevertheless he stands in fear of the opposite; but from the actions of faith a man may believe without any fear of the opposite that he has faith, just as he believes the other things he believes, viz., Christ's Incarnation. . . ." It will be noticed that in this passage Cajetan describes the concrete perception of faith in various ways—"to know with certainty," "experimental certainty," "believe without any fear of the opposite": this difficulty of language—if it is not in fact a difficulty of thought (is it a knowledge or a belief?)—reflects the difficulty of the problem.

3. *Suarez and Others*

With Suarez we enter into quite a different kind of problem and reach some very different conclusions.

Suarez maintains that there are two opinions on this subject, and his own very clear presentation of these opinions is in itself highly instructive.[36] On the one hand there are all the people who believe that it is possible to have a strict certainty about the act of faith: "As regards the act of faith, many learned theologians have taught that any particular believer can and should believe with a sure faith not

[36] *De Gratia*, I, IX, c. 12 (Vivès, IX, pp. 553 *et seq.*).

only the direct object of belief but also its reflex act, if he attends to this reflection, i.e. by believing the act by which he believes to be an act of supernatural faith." And he goes on to divide these people into three groups, according to the immediate principle which they adduce for this certain knowledge—infused faith itself (Cajetan, Medina, Soto); the clear experience of a direct perception (Vasquez, Lorca, etc., based on St. Augustine and St. Thomas); and a kind of synthesis of faith and experience (St. Bonaventure). Against these people Suarez does not hesitate to set up a second opinion ("*seu quartus modus verus*"), according to which the only possible kind of certainty of faith is a moral one (Durand, Richard, Scotus, Ayala, etc.). Fundamentally this means that the ancients are on one side and the moderns on the other. How does Suarez establish his own opinion?

First of all he bases his argument on the existence—established elsewhere—of a natural or acquired faith. St. Thomas had "tried to eliminate this natural acquired faith from supernatural faith,"[37] but this had persisted, and it now appears in a more flourishing state than ever. In Suarez's view, in fact, there are two kinds of faith in the soul of the believer—the kind that comes from the sheer grace of God, and another kind that comes from long personal effort. This theological couple, the "acquired-infused," was to play a considerable part in theological debate and theory.

These two kinds of faith, says Suarez, are radically distinct from each other. They can exist together, but even when united they maintain their own specific nature. They can also be separated, and then, particularly in the heretic, the acquired kind may dominate the infused. Now—and this is the point—there is no sign enabling anyone to make a sharp distinction between the infused kind and the acquired kind. The fact is that in the Christian the acquired kind is always there, mixed in with the infused. In the modern sense of the word, it is a solid, tenacious, profoundly personal *habit*. It is a sort of "double" of the infused kind, and inserts itself within it and reinforces it: it clothes it in the eyes of consciousness with all the psychological elements (i.e., tendencies and thoughts) that integrate it. It being established that the believer can always perform acts of acquired faith (he only needs to will them—"it depends on his freedom and actual condition"); that he can perform just as many and

[37] R. Aubert, *Le Problème de l'acte de foi* (Louvain, 1945), p. 69 & n. 76.

perhaps more of them than he can of acts of infused faith; that these acts can relate to all that is revealed ("in the Catholic, acquired faith can be given to all things which he believes by infused faith")[38] —assuming this possibility, this frequency, this universality of acquired faith, it is impossible to dissociate it from infused faith and to grasp the infused faith with any certainty.[39] It should be noted that this series of affirmations implies no kind of internal unity of component principles between the two kinds of faith, but only a factual unity between the psychological and the supernatural. Consequently any certainty about the infused faith implies an equal certainty about the supernaturalness of faith[40]—and it will be understood that Suarez firmly rejects any direct apprehension of the supernatural mode of faith.

And here we touch upon another profound reason for Suarez's rejection. At this point the actual line of argument seems to have changed, so that the upshot of all the critical precision introduced by his more explicit and more constructive kind of theology is that the very object of the problem seems to have altered. For in the first place the problem was how to account for a particular act; now it has become a case of how to account for a mode of the act. Let me try to explain. According to Suarez, there exists an infused faith, made up of three relationships (*habitudines*)—rationality, freedom, and the supernatural.[41] The first two of these belong to both acquired faith and infused faith; the third alone is proper to the infused kind —it makes the believer believe "as is necessary" and confers the "mode of supernaturality."[42] Suarez has already expressed his mind very clearly on this mode.[43] He distinguishes two possible meanings of the "substance-mode" couple. According to the first meaning, the substance

[38] *De Gratia*, I, II, c. 10, n. 22 (Vivès, VII, p. 626). Saurez explicitly refers to this passage to prove that the believer cannot have evidence of belief *sicut oportet*, I, IX, c. 12, n. 11 (Vivès IX, 557).

[39] Suarez is haunted by the problem of the heretic, and he finds experimental proof of his affirmations in the heretic who, having lost infused faith, keeps an acquired faith and even an inner impulse to believe what he has in fact already rejected (*ibid.*).

[40] Cf. the following highly revealing passage: "As in these actions, both natural and supernatural motives always occur together in some manner . . . no man can ever discern clearly enough whether he is moved by purely supernatural reason . . ." *De Gratia*, II, XI, no. 35 (Vivès, VII, p. 639).

[41] *De Gratia*, I, IX, c. 12, no. 7 (Vivès, IX, 555 *et seq.*).

[42] *Ibid.*, nos. 10-11.

[43] *Ibid.*, I, II, c. 4, nos. 1-4 (Vivès, VII, 598).

denotes the generic character of an act, and the mode its specific difference: the substance of charity is to be found in the fact that it is a kind of love, and its mode in the fact that it is a supernatural kind of love. According to the second meaning, the substance denotes the total reality of an act, and the mode an accident: the substance of charity lies in the fact that it is a supernatural act, and its mode in the fact that it has such and such a degree of intensity. As regards our own problem, it is the first sense that is involved, and what it leads to is this: Envisaged in its substance, a spiritual act—believing or loving—is in itself neither natural nor supernatural—it prescinds from either of these;[44] it becomes the one or the other according to its mode, i.e. according to the difference that contracts and modifies the genus. Thus an act of acquired faith is identical with an act of infused faith in its substance; it is specified from it by its mode. Knowing with certainty that we can posit an act of infused faith would imply that we can grasp the supernatural mode of the act directly. Now this is impossible. It is even impossible for us "to know with evidence whether our assent is true or infallible or based upon God's authority alone: for these are extremely hidden properties which cannot be manifested with evidence by experience."[45] Faith, in fact, is an obscure thing, as is proved by the case of the heretic, who believes he has faith when he has only opinion—"which would be quite impossible if he knew the nature of his assent, and its motive, clearly and intuitively. A fortiori, the proper mode of supernatural faith is too elevated and too hidden ever to be known by clear experience."[46] The conclusion is inevitable: it is impossible for the Christian to have a certain knowledge of his faith.

Lastly, a final line of reasoning—drawn from psychology—is used to support this conclusion. St. Thomas had based his different treatments of faith and charity on their difference in origin—the one springing from the intelligence and the other from the will—and the different conditions supplied to consciousness by the two faculties and hence by their habits. Suarez will have absolutely none of this,[47] and he denies energetically that there is any disparity between them: the act of intelligence is not a whit more evident than

[44] *Ibid.*, no. 3.
[45] *Ibid.*, I, IX, c. 12, no. 19 (Vivès, IX, 512).
[46] *Ibid.*, *loc. cit.*
[47] *Ibid.*, no. 13 (IX, 558 *et seq.*).

the act of will, for three reasons at least—because the intellect does not know itself or its act any better than the will does; because intelligence and will may not be separate powers, and if this is so, then the act of knowing does not apply to the intellect any more than the act of loving, and the "condition" of the one is no more evident than the "condition" of the other; finally, because if the reflective consciousness demands a *species* of the act, this will be needed for love too, whereas if it is not required for the act of knowledge it will not be required for the act of love either, for it too is spiritual, intelligible, and interior to the spirit. Thus there is absolutely no foundation for any sharp discrimination between the evident knowledge of an intellectual act and the conjectural knowledge of an act of will. A fortiori, in this matter of faith any special grasp of the supernaturalness of an intellectual assent is, once again, quite impossible.

It will be seen what a revolution has been performed by this vigorous criticism. On the psychological level Suarez rejects the Thomist conception of the intelligence and the will, as two separate principles formally opposed to each other but structurally implicated in each other. By substituting a much looser distinction (if indeed he leaves any at all), by refusing the act of thought any special privilege over the act of love, Suarez destroys at its root the very possibility of any difference in treatment between faith and charity. Conversely, on the theological level he splits up the concrete unity —which is a complex matter, but primary and indestructible—of the act of faith, breaks it up into elements, and reduces the possibility of any consciousness of faith to the possibility of a grasp of its pure supernaturalness. Theology is thus driven back to a merely negative solution of the problem. Lastly, at a level that is both theological and psychological, Suarez posits the normal and continuous co-existence, in the spiritual activity of any Christian, of an infused faith and an acquired faith, each radically distinct from the other and formally separable from it. Since the acquired faith penetrates and embraces the infused faith, this means that any certain grasp of supernatural faith is more impossible than ever. And that is why Suarez cannot but assert against the position maintained by the ancients—the *prima opinio* in its three forms—that only a moral certainty is possible in the knowledge of faith.

We are by now in a completely different world. The field of faith, like the field of grace and charity, has become a prey to this all-devouring "moral certainty" that rules the spiritual world with a rod of iron. And the number of Suarez's followers was to be endless—but there is no need to go into all that here. However, they were always to find themselves faced by another line of thinkers, who also could never be exterminated—people who refused to bring the intelligence down to the level of the will, refused to distinguish between the various aspects of the acts of faith to the extent of separating them entirely, and refused to "double" infused faith with an acquired faith without ever managing to integrate them. We shall content ourselves with examining one or two of the more important examples.

First, there was Lugo's vigorous counteroffensive.[48] Lugo defended with considerable decision the principle that there is an experience—a perception and a memory—of supernatural acts, and that to say that only natural acts can be perceived is "*singulare et contra mentem theologorum omnium et Patrum*" (no. 183): it is contrary to Scripture, which affirms the experience of good will towards God, and contrary to normal experience, "which religious men have every day" when they offer their good desires and prayers to God and ask God to reward them for them. "To say that we are not in this case speaking of prayers or pious desires that we can perceive or remember, but of others which we are unable to remember and have never perceived, is absolutely foreign to the mind and spirit of all the faithful. Who indeed among the faithful will believe that the acts of penance, contrition, and burning charity which St. Francis experienced his whole life long, were of no account towards his salvation or merit, and that he only merited by other hidden acts which took place in him without his knowing it and which he could therefore never remember?" (no. 186).

Moreover, such a position doubly endangers the Christian life. In the first place, as regards all acts that are expressed in outward actions—like the case of a virtual intention (a priest celebrating Mass, for instance). This intention (no. 187) originates in a particular act of the will that is preserved by memory. If there is no memory of the supernatural will born of faith, but only of the natural act of acquired faith, there cannot be any supernatural intention or act of merit. This becomes more serious still in the case of an act of supernatural faith. We can indeed endeavour to perform such supernatural acts on the basis of the testimony of God the Revealer, but we cannot

[48] *De Fide*, disp. I, sect. 9, nos. 186-191 (Vivès, I, 67-70).

know whether we really posit them; we even know by experience that we cannot do so, and that in spite of all our efforts we are always performing natural acts of faith whose stability is weak and inferior. "And since men are indeed led by experience, the result is that unless we are idiots we shall stop trying" (no. 189).

But in any case, it will be said, it is impossible to perceive these acts because they are supernatural (no. 191). Here we reach the heart of the problem, and Lugo's answer is curiously unconvincing. Briefly, he says that the knowledge of these acts is not supernatural *simpliciter*, because the acts themselves are not purely supernatural (like grace and the infused habits); it is supernatural *praesuppositive*, and moreover confused. For assuming the existence of these supernatural acts, the intelligence must know them by direct reflection, because it is a property of a reasonable nature to know its own operations, whatever these may be. And therefore this reflective knowledge does not require any infused habit—the natural powers suffice; it is natural. "Reflective knowledge of its own act is due to our nature itself, which in so far as it is intellectual demands to know what it wills and what it does not will; therefore this knowledge does not go beyond the demands or the powers of nature, save *praesuppositive*, in so far as it supposes something exceeding the powers of nature." We may find this solution disappointing. If the principle that the intellectual nature must know its own acts seems difficult to argue against, nevertheless it seems doubtful whether this natural reflective consciousness is indeed the best way of solving the problem. Here, undoubtedly, Lugo allowed himself to be slightly affected by the spirit—and the argumentation—of the doctrines which he otherwise combated so energetically.

Now let us turn to two passages from Thomistic theologians. The theologians of Salamanca explain the classic passage in St. Thomas (I. II, 112, 5, 2^{m}): "Whoever has knowledge or faith is certain that he has them," by distinguishing between three different meanings that the phrase "to be certain of one's faith"[49] may have. It may refer either to the object that is believed, and then the Catholic has the infallible certitude of his faith; or to the strict supernaturalness of the act, and then one cannot have the infallible certainty of one's faith—for it is not revealed that I perform an act of supernatural faith, and there is no "proper species" of the super-

[49] *De Gratia*, disp. 9, dub. 1, nos. 16-17 (Vivès, X, 294 *et seq.*).

natural—or, finally, it may refer to the act of believing. But here the Salmanticenses refuse to consider the concrete, existential problem of the act of faith and restrict themselves to an abstract point of view about the act—its essence as an act of belief. And they write that if we consider "the act of belief and its principle, abstracting the character, supernatural or otherwise, of the act and its principle,"[50] then "the believer has the infallible certainty of his faith, because by evident experience he knows that he believes and submits to the doctrine of the Catholic Church; just as he who knows, knows clearly that he knows, and he who doubts, sees clearly that he doubts; this characteristic being common to all the acts of the intellect."

St. Thomas therefore means that "the believer, in the very act of believing, has an evident experience that he believes"—without more ado; because, unlike grace, "faith abstracts from the natural and the supernatural and by this very abstraction produces this effect—the act of believing" (no. 17). Thus as the quality of the act always remains unknown, the only things one can be certain about are the object, and an unqualified assent. This is a curious example of how Suarez's line of argument can be followed even while remaining faithful to St. Thomas.

Gonet takes the same passage from St. Thomas and adopts an attitude directly opposed to that of Suarez.[51] After noting that the latter's assertion, that it is impossible to be any more certain about faith than about grace, is contrary to St. Thomas's teaching, he goes on (no. 30): "It is better to answer, I concede the antecedent" (i.e., one can have an infallible certainty about faith), "but deny the consequent and the similarity" (i.e., and therefore also be certain of one's grace and charity); and this for two reasons. The first is the fact that faith is intellectual in character: "Faith is a certain habit existing in the intellect, which can reflect upon itself perfectly: for every form informing a subject confers upon it its formal effect; therefore, the faith that informs the intelligence gives it (1) an infallible certainty about its proper object and (2) secondarily, by reflection, an infallible certainty about itself." This is not true of

[50] There remains the "genus," and here we find that the position that is adopted is the same as the one adopted by Suarez, for whom the genus of an act of knowledge or of love itself prescinds from its natural or supernatural character (*De Gratia*, II, 4, no. 3.—Vivès, VII, 598).

[51] *De Gratia*, disp. 5, art. 2, nos. 28-30.

the will, which is not a knowing faculty, or of charity, which does not have certainty as its formal object.

The second reason is drawn from the Church's regulation of faith (no. 31). "Faith has an extrinsic rule which is certain and infallible, and which we can and should know infallibly—the propositions made by the Church." For though the formal rule of faith is divine revelation, "*quoad nos*, its motive, or rather the application of its motive, is the actual authority of the Church, which proposes something to us as having been certainly revealed. And that is why, when we are through faith certain that the Church in which we now exist is the true and lawful Church, we can also be certain that when we give our assent to the truths which she proposes to us as now revealed, we can have faith about these truths."[52]

Finally, to avoid making too long a list, let us jump a few centuries and turn to the solution—whose precision has always been a matter of debate amongst theologians—proposed by Canon Didiot.[53] Canon Didiot notes in the first place that though there may be a deep, internal, and necessary action of God at the root of faith, we are not conscious of this action: all we know is that we are assisted in a general way. He goes on: "Nevertheless, faithful Catholics have a very sure and simple way of knowing whether such and such an act of faith is genuinely supernatural and that God contributes to it in a way beyond all doubt." For faith relates to truths proposed by the Church, and God wills us to believe them supernaturally (i.e., in the way of salvation). Therefore, "if we respond with a sincere belief to the faith proposed by the Church, we are absolutely certain that the grace of God is with us in our belief, as it is present in the Church in the proposition itself. Thus, finally, we have irrefutable proof of (1) God's supernatural participation in our act of faith and (2) the complete objectivity of this act of knowledge."[54]

In a note he adds: "Though I can thus be sure of the supernaturalness and hence the absolute truth of my acts of faith when they are

[52] In Suarez's view, this characteristic, which is "the best sign of believing as one should," does not always give rise to anything more than moral certainty, because it is only probable that faith in everything taught by the Church is not entirely acquired (*De Gratia*, IX, 12, n. 15; Vivès, IX, 559-560). Billuart's reply (*De Gratia*, disp. 6, art. 4, 2^{m}; Palme, III, 170) is modelled exactly on Gonet's.

[53] *Logique surnaturelle objective*, I, pp. 623 *et seq.*

[54] P. 626, no. 870.

made in response to infallible propositions by the Church, I cannot have the same degree of certainty about my other religious acts. The fundamental reason for this difference is that the assimilation of my soul to the Redeemer really begins with my supernatural faith, and if I was refused grace for the act of faith this would be equivalent to refusing me access to this same divine Redeemer at the very moment when I beg for him in all humility and sincerity; it would also mean that in spite of my will to believe in Revelation, I am refused the ability to believe in it as God ordains that I should—i.e., supernaturally."

Having thus stated a metaphysical distinction (the difference between intellect and will), a theological analysis (the part played by the proposition of truths by the Church) and a dogmatic requirement (the personal call to supernatural faith), Canon Didiot ends: "Fidelity to the true, definitive teaching of the Church is thus the highest and most precise guarantee that God gives us here below of the perfect truth of our acts of faith, not only in a general sense but with regard to each one in particular."[55]

4. *Suggestions for a Conclusion*

These brief remarks on the consciousness of faith should be sufficient to show that this difficult problem is still open to further investigation, that theology has certainly not yet taken full account of some very clear indications to be found in the practice of the Church and in Patristic thought; and that in this matter philosophical considerations have deeply marked—and affected—the answers given so far by theologians. Perhaps by way of conclusion I may be allowed to suggest, not a complete solution, but a few pointers towards a solution of the problem, following in the footsteps of St. Thomas.

The act of faith is a supernatural affirmation. If we are conscious of it, it is usually the consciousness of the affirmation that enlightens us, and thus a noetic element is necessarily involved. Let us turn to St. Thomas's teaching on this point.[56]

When I posit an act of thought—when I affirm an object—I am

[55] P. 628.

[56] The essential passages are well known and have often been discussed. An excellent discussion of the problem will be found in J. de Finance, *Cogito cartésien et Réflexion thomiste* (Paris, 1946).

directly aware of my act. But thinking means thinking something; it means making an object exist in oneself intelligibly; it means forming a mental image—an idea or a judgment—by means of which one grasps a reality. The mental image is an immanent, constructed object, the product of my intellect's reaction to the reality; it is a whole complex, formed by the intelligible determinations posited by the act of thought; and it is therefore inseparable from this act—the thought thought only exists in and through the thinking thought. And the act of thought is immanent in the image which it engenders, maintains in being and relates to the living principles of all intelligibles—the First Truth—by affirming it to be true: it is the esse *intelligibile* of the mental image. And since the image is entirely orientated to the reality as its end, by way of the thought thought and the thinking thought, the intellect aims at, attains and affirms the reality. It is by the mediation of the thought object that I enter into the intelligible world and affirm the truth.

What consciousness can I have of this act? According to St. Thomas it seems necessary to say: I am conscious of my act of thought because I cause it, because it is the product of my intellect and is completed in accordance with my intellect as an intellectual power. But since the act only exists as the principle of an object, I am directly aware both of the affirmed object and of the affirming act. The awareness is spontaneous, of course:[57] when I think an object, I am directly—clearly and distinctly—aware of the thought object, and also directly—but implicitly and obscurely—aware of my act of thought. For it is a property of the mind that it cannot be absolutely obscure to itself, but is always open to itself, even in thoughts about a reality that is as external to itself as can possibly be: "By one same operation, I understand the particular matter and know that I understand it."[58] There can also be a reflective consciousness of the same act. Here the direction

[57] Cf. the converging reflections by R. VANCOURT, in *Mélanges de Science relig.* (Lille, 1945), II, pp. 301 *et seq.* Also, J. MARITAIN, *Salut de l'Homme*, pp. 16-17: ". . . the highest functions of the human mind, particularly those connected with the judgment, take place within a kind of vital and spontaneous view of consciousness, which accompanies every act of intellection that is achieved or accomplished." This spontaneous view of consciousness "only expresses the auto-interiority, the auto-implication proper to the human mind; it is simply the diffused light of reflectivity—a reflectivity lived and applied (*in actu exercito*) but not conceptualized (*in actu signato*)—within which all spiritual labour takes place in the human soul. . . ."

[58] *I Sent.*, d. l, q.2, a. l, 2^m^. Quoted in J. DE FINANCE, *op. cit.*, 38, n.5.

of the thought is changed; the intellect fixes upon the subjective conditions and the intelligible existence of the object, on the positing activity and the mental image. The immediate object then becomes the direct act itself, maintained by the thought. For "the reflective act is no other thing than the direct act which has become transparent to itself."[59] And reflection grasps the thinking thought and the thought thought, the act and the image it engenders, directly, in their unity. It can penetrate to various depths and orientate itself towards either the esse or the essence of the image. Reflection is involved here, since there is a "backward look" at the act and the image, but this reflection takes place through a "perception," a "view," an "intuition."

Furthermore, as regards this act that springs from my intellect and posits an object, I do not grasp it in its pure emergence but in its connection with the object. I only grasp it in fact as something that makes the object exist, something utterly involved in the existential position of the image, something only to be explained through the intelligible determinations of the object. Since I cannot have any pure, direct intuition of my soul or my intellect or my spiritual activity, I cannot get to the source of my act as it emerges, unconnected with the thinking power; I can only get to it in so far as it is effective intelligibly, and that means not as something determining my substance ontologically but as the determining power of the intelligible object.[60] In so far as the inner experience and the awareness of the act are concerned, the essential thing is the mediation of the mental image and the connection with the object.

May we—making the necessary adjustments—apply these views to the awareness of the act of faith? This St. Thomas seems to do without any hesitation. Affirming God in faith means making him exist as an intelligible object in a supernaturalized intellect. Speaking of the object of charity, St. Thomas says that it is God as an "intelligible good" (II. II, 24, 1, 1^m), more precisely still a "good of the intellect"—God as a good that is thought (II. II, 24, 1, c, and 8, 4, c). Now the act that makes God exist in us as an intelligible object —"good of the intellect"—is the act of faith. And there is no ambiguity about the meaning of the first phrase: "First and chiefly the interior concept of the mind is called the word" (I, 34, 1, c). The

[59] *Ibid.*, p. 42.
[60] *Ibid.*, p. 82, n. 1; p. 112, n. 2.

formation of a mental image, or the formation of enuntiables (II. II, 1, 2, 2^m^) through which the divine reality is affirmed—such is the act of faith in so far as it is an intellectual act. Let us try to enlarge upon this assertion.

In faith, the Word of God is addressed to me: it is the manifestation of God's thought, a *Verbum exterius* expressing the *Verbum interius* of God. Receiving this Word of God means forming an immanent object from this word within myself through the grace of the Holy Spirit, who transforms my intellect into something supernatural. I make an idea—for instance, of the Trinity—or a judgment —for instance, that Christ is the Son of God—exist within me, and through this mental image I aim at, grasp, and affirm the divine reality. Through the mediation of the mental image I enter into communion with the divine thought. Thus everything depends upon the thought object: the more pure and rich and in conformity with the Word of God it is, the more fully and authentically God will be thought and affirmed.

Now for this object of thought to be valid, a source and a rule are necessary. The source, as we have already said, is the light given by the Holy Spirit: this is necessary from the very earliest stages of faith, to connaturalize the intellect to the active thought of God, and during the succeeding stages to increase this connaturality and allow an ever-deepening penetration into the thought of God. The rule, on the other hand, is external: it is the proposition of the Word by the Church. For this proposition is the only thing that can supply us with the intelligible data which can help us to form a human thought that is in conformity with the divine thought. Thus, the internal guarantee of the authenticity of faith in its intelligible formulation is the will to conform to the Word of God as transmitted by Holy Church. This function of the Church as, in Cajetan's words, a *ministra objecti* is absolutely necessary for any valid development of a genuine act of faith. When it is remembered that, on the supernatural level even more than on the natural level, the thought thought can never exhaust the thinking thought, that incorrect or erroneous elements naturally slip into our ideas about God, that the thinking thought itself can at times be weak, confused, embryonic, evanescent, it will be seen what an important part—with respect to the object—is played by the Church's proposition and—with respect to the subject—by the will to conform to it.

It may be worth while to refer here to a passage written by a doctor of the Church who can never be suspected of any watering-down of doctrine, and who also—in full conformity, indeed, with a long tradition—shows himself to be fairly pessimistic in the matter: I mean St. Robert Bellarmine.[61] He quotes St. Augustine: "If Christ was only born for people who can have full intelligence of these (truths), it is almost in vain that we work in the Church";[62] and he goes on: "That this is indeed true is proved by experience, considering that most of the faithful, as a result either of their age (children), or of their sex (women), or of their lack of intelligence, or of their lack of culture (nearly all the *rustici*, for instance), not only cannot understand the mysteries of the Trinity and the Incarnation, and other truths of the same kind necessary for salvation, but even have a certain amount of difficulty in conceiving anything more in their minds than the sound of the words; and yet all these are rightly counted as being of the faithful, because they profess to believe that God is the Father, the Son and the Holy Spirit in the sense meant by Holy Church." We will leave the reasons for this to the Holy Doctor, but it can be seen that in these difficult cases the act of faith remains genuine in his eyes because it is linked with the Church's proposition. And that is the point in connection with our present problem: the Holy Spirit gives the power to affirm, but he does not—usually—supply the enuntiables except through the mediation of the Church. It is the authentic teaching of the Church that presents the Word of God as an object of thought and therefore determines the construction and validity of the mental image. Thus, the formation of enuntiables in conformity with the teaching of the Church means a genuine affirmation of this human word as a Word of God, an affirmation of it by way of the Church because of Christ and God; it means the positing of the supernatural act of faith.

Henceforward, the problem of the awareness of faith appears in the following terms. As I do not grasp my acts of thought in the act of springing from their source, I shall never grasp my act of faith in the act of springing from my mind, and therefore even more certainly I shall never grasp it as it springs from my supernaturalized intellect—in this latter case the source escapes me twice over. But

[61] *De Justificatione*, I, 7 (*De Controversiis* [Ingolstadt, 1659], Vol. IV, col. 948 B).

[62] Ep. 102 *ad Evodium* = Ep. 169, no. 4, P.L., 33, 744.

on the other hand, in the act of faith I am directly—clearly and distinctly—aware of the object affirmed, and at the same time—in a concealed way and obscurely—aware of the act of affirmation. Moreover I can reflect upon this act, make it transparent to my intellect, perceive it as positing its object and its immediate condition. Let us take the case of an adult convert to whom the priest says, when he is baptizing him, "Do you believe in God the Father?" and who replies, "I believe." This affirmation is perfectly clear and conscious; it comes at the end of a long process of intellectual and moral preparation; it implies an absolute, definitive commitment to the truth of its object. The person who is being baptized can reflect upon it: by a single act of reflection he can grasp what lies at the very heart of the affirmation, i.e. the object of thought and its proposition by the Church, and also his will to affirm it as proposed by the Church. This means an awareness of faith, and this awareness is immediate, clear, and certain.

And here of course we come right up against the objection raised by Suarez: how are we to know that it is not a purely acquired faith that makes us believe? But we are not concerned with the same kind of problem as Suarez was. In the first place, we do not believe that there is in the Christian a natural faith, distinct—and separable—from infused faith and able to "double" or supplant the latter. It is the actual grace of faith that enables us to posit the act of faith by transforming our minds, and so long as the mind is concerned with the Word of God as taught by the Church, the Christian adheres to it in a single movement whose sources are the grace of Christ and its own transfigured power working in conjunction with each other. The efforts he has made, the frequency, depth, and upright courage of his acts of faith, far from producing any distinct *habitus*, are simply the results of his freedom superelevated by grace, and they have simply ploughed up and deepened and purified his spirit so that it may be capable of being taken over ever more deeply, more sovereignly, more transformingly, by the Spirit of God. Consequently his spirit is more of a unity than ever, more like the Spirit of God, more docile to its all-powerful action. The human elements are purified, controlled, and integrated more than ever by the impulse of grace. His thought and will are more than ever a sharing in the thought and will of God. There is no room here for any surreptitious human activity independent of the Spirit of God, silently escaping his action, calmly turning itself into an autonomous reality and so falsifying the whole activity of faith in a blacked-out consciousness.

Again, any reference to the heretic's experience seems to be highly irrelevant. It can only concern the formal heretic who has lost his faith by a direct personal sin against it. Now the point is that this heretic is a heretic! That means to say that he has of his own accord broken the bond with the Word of God as taught by the Church, and hence the bond with the Spirit. In doing so, he has put himself into an utterly different situation from that of the believer. He has lost both the source and the objective rule of faith. And if he is unaware of his connection with the Spirit, he cannot be unaware that he has broken the bond with the Church. He is outside, abandoned, alone. All that remains to him of his faith, as St. Thomas would say, is a *habitus* on the way to corruption. Mental habits, affective polarities, psychological reactions, remnants of the faith—all these may remain, perhaps; but the essential thing is not there—the bond of submission, adherence to and communion with the Church of God, by which the bond with the Spirit of Christ was ensured. You may say that he still has acquired faith, if you like. My answer is that it is a bad expression, for in fact it refers to the *reliquiae fidei*. But I shall not argue about this. The only thing is, that whatever the psychological appearances may be, this reality is utterly different from the faith of the believer, and the heretic cannot but know that on the level of free acts he has chosen against his original faith, against the rule that ensured it, for the sake of a truth different from the truth proposed by the Church, a truth which he has manufactured for himself by a fearful decision of his own freedom. The two experiences are in this respect contradictory, like their principles. And theology can gain nothing from the case of the formal heretic that can help it to explain the faith of the believer; unless perhaps it be this proof *a contrario*, that where the rule of faith is different, faith and the experience of faith are different too.

Finally, we are not trying to isolate the supernatural mode of the act of faith, but on the contrary to grasp this act in its existential totality. For this act, with all its constituent relationships, is the only object of direct experience, and hence arouses the only problem. The more one attempts to split it up into its component parts, the more it becomes a series of abstract relationships and the further one gets from the real problem of the awareness of faith. On the other hand, the more one attempts to grasp it as a complex of synthetically posited relationships, the more chance there will be of coming up against the real problem and of finding an acceptable solution to it.[63]

The way is thus open, and we can go on. In so far as, by means of the image I form in my mind, I have the will to affirm the divine reality as expressed in the Word of God and proposed by the Church, and in so far as I am aware of what I am doing—to that extent I am aware that I am positing an act of supernatural faith, because I am aware that I am submitting myself to all its objective determinations. Just as it is through the determinations of the object that I grasp my thought in act, so it is with the objective determinations of supernatural faith. As in the case of natural knowledge, the determination by the object is primary and normative here too. I do not (leaving aside the question of mystical knowledge) grasp the supernatural root of my act; I grasp its supernatural objective determinations. And if the Church requires the adult convert to profess the Catholic *Credo* and the Catholic belief about the Trinity externally, this is because the *verbum exterius* is the sign and pledge of a *verbum interius* conforming to the thought of God transmitted by the magisterium of the Church and therefore supernatural.

No doubt there is more in it than this; no doubt we could go on to discuss the *credulitatis affectus* of the Council of Orange[64] and St. Thomas's *instinctus interior;* and no doubt we should try to integrate this awareness of the object with the awareness of a call and a duty.[65] All this would reinforce our present conclusions, but it would raise another aspect of the problem. It is also quite clear that the question can be enlarged to include not only the problem of the act of faith but the problem of the whole life of faith, which St. Augustine, for

[63] And here, of course, we come up against two different metaphysics: a metaphysic of esse, like St. Thomas's, is equipped to grasp or at least cope with the acts themselves; a metaphysic of essence, like Suarez's, naturally tends towards the analysis of the notional components in the activity. On this point, besides the venerable and still very solid work by Fr. A. Marc (*L'idée de l'Être: Archives de Philo.*, Vol. X, Bk. I), see the recent book by E. Gilson, *L'Être et l'Essence* (Paris, 1948), esp. chs. iii & v.

[64] For the historical meaning of this expression, cf. J. Chéné, *Rech. de Sc. rel.*, Paris, Dec. 1948, pp. 566 *et seq.*

[65] Cf. L. Malevez, *Théologie dialectique et Théologie naturelle* in *Rev. Sc. rel.*, 1937, pp. 531 *et seq.;* also my *Sens chrétien de l'homme* (Paris, 1945), pp. 164 *et seq.*

instance, deals with in the passage we have quoted from the *Enarrationes in Psalmos*. Nevertheless, it still remains true that one can consider the restricted problem of the act of faith, and that without having recourse to any (normal) consciousness of inner illumination or attraction—that is to say, confining one's attentions to the act of faith in its connection with the object—it is possible, keeping to his own line of thought, to give clear proof of the truth of St. Thomas's statements: "Whoever has knowledge or faith is certain he has it," and "Faith is perceived by him in whom it is by an interior movement of the heart." With these it is possible to prove St. Augustine's words: "Everyone can see his own faith." Lastly, it is possible to explain, without any minimization, the Church's practice of requiring the baptized adult to have faith and an awareness of his faith, and to affirm it before God and man.

Additional Note

In a critical note on the preceding chapter[66] (*Rev. Thom.*, 1951, 11, 479-481), Fr. Corvez says something that I find very gratifying: "If I have infused faith, I know with certainty by an intuitive knowledge that I have it, because the reality of the faith implies this reflection upon itself." This implies "a supernatural knowledge experienced in consciousness." A little further on he says, "My certainty that I possess infused faith is of the experimental order: this experience is necessarily based upon the presence of a gift from God and is clothed in its light." With these statements I am in entire agreement. My whole argument has been based on the same conviction. It is therefore only about the implications of this experience that we disagree. Now:

1. Fr. Corvez maintains that this supernatural knowledge "cannot be transported on to the rational plane so that I can distinguish the *supernatural character* of the faith within me" (my italics). But I never said—quite the opposite—that the believer can grasp the "supernatural character" of his faith directly: I said that he could grasp its necessary conditions—which is quite a different thing.

2. Fr. Corvez maintains that it is quite possible to know "with certainty," by an "intuitive knowledge" that one possesses infused

[66] The preceding chapter was published separately.

faith, without being able to give "any rational account of it." I will grant him this, but it is not quite the point. The point is whether we can be certain by "intuitive" or "experimental" knowledge, "experienced in consciousness," that we have faith, and at the same time doubt this same consciousness and experience; whether we can have a certainty of the experimental order that we possess infused faith, through an experience "clothed in the light of a gift from God," and at the same time be absolutely without any certainty that we possess this same faith. The question whether we can transpose this experience on to the rational level is quite different from the question whether we can give a rational account of it: everyone knows that having and formulating, being conscious of and transmitting, are very different and perfectly distinct operations. But to be certain without knowing it, to have an experience of infused faith without knowing the meaning of this experience, seems to me, I must confess, rather difficult to imagine.

3. Now Fr. Corvez is only led to say this because of something else—because of his theory of natural faith, which in his view lies at the root of the problem. But:

(1) I must confess that I am very much surprised to find him describing the theological opinion that rejects natural faith as a "very bold" one. For not only is this an open question on which freedom of opinion is allowed, but it is surely up to the people who believe in this natural faith to prove their position. There is no need to recall the theological and in fact dogmatic difficulties of the position, which is not to be found in Scripture or Church teaching or the Fathers; it will be enough to remember that recognition of a natural credibility has nothing to do with any recognition of a natural faith, for the former ends in this, that I can and must believe in Revelation, whereas the latter states categorically, I believe. Fr. Corvez must surely know that many theologians—including some Dominicans—admit the first and reject the second. As for our Reverend Father's categorical statement that "the Devil's faith is not impossible to man," I should say that this is a sin of angelism at least, and that it is rather a "bold" thing to do, to compare any human faith with the faith of a pure—and ultimately damned—spirit.

(2) In any case, my chapter does not contain any discussion of natural faith as such: all I have done is to reject any permanent

co-existence of the two—natural and supernatural—habits of faith in the baptized believer. Whether a natural faith can exist in the person who is progressing towards the faith, or in the person who has lost infused faith, is something that can be argued about; but I made no attempt to discuss it; and my remarks on these two points did not even touch upon it. I was concerned with the co-existence of the two faiths, and all I was discussing was "the proper way of confronting the divine revelation." Here again, to admit a natural faith as a preliminary step to supernatural faith (which does not seem to me to be psychologically impossible, if it does not lead to anything, or dogmatically dangerous if it helps towards salvation), or as a remnant of supernatural faith, does not by any means mean admitting ipso facto the persistence of an acquired *habitus*, formally distinct from the infused *habitus*, in a soul living by supernatural faith.

(3) Again, amongst the "objective determinations" of the act of faith, there is one that Fr. Corvez does not mention, and which nevertheless I emphasized particularly, and consider essential. I did not in fact speak only of "the connection that [the act of faith] has with its object, without any further consideration"; I said that a person being baptized grasped "the object of thought and its proposition by the Church, and also his will to affirm it as proposed by the Church," that "the inward guarantee of the authenticity of faith is the will to conform to the Word of God as transmitted by the Church." This is in my view one of the essential objective determinations of the act of supernatural faith. And it is part of that "loyalty" which Fr. Corvez will not allow the Church to judge, and which nevertheless—as the passages I have quoted show—it asks to be judged.

To admit that a baptized person can profess the whole of the Catholic *Credo*, can wish to believe it as proposed by the Church, and yet might do this only by an act of natural faith that puts him outside supernatural truth, deceives him about his own reality as a "Christian," and turns his whole spiritual activity into an illusion—this seems to me to be a very grave matter indeed. On this hypothesis, it is impossible to see, in fact, how there can be any—objective—realization of the concrete economy of Christian salvation, according to which God does not refuse his grace to anyone who does what he can; nor is it any easier to see how any Christian soul can—

subjectively—live in the peace promised by Christ. For there has been introduced into the very heart of the Christian life not only a new element of uncertainty, but a fundamental principle raising doubts about the whole matter of the life of faith. Thus it becomes impossible to speak of any "moral certainty," as Fr. Corvez does. And if one has a logical mind and is thoroughly aware of what one is doing, one is bound to introduce into the Christian consciousness the reign of anguish—whilst at the same time, presumably, losing the essential Catholic balance.

How much more reasonable appear these lines by Fr. Garrigou-Lagrange. Replying to the objection, "If one admits the possibility of an acquired natural faith, it is impossible to distinguish it from infused faith," Fr. Garrigou-Lagrange writes: "To this difficulty it must be replied that the soul with good will, who believes unrestrictedly *propter auctoritatem Dei revelantis*, performs the act of supernatural faith required for salvation: *Facienti quod in se est, Deus non denegat gratiam*. I believe that the natural faith mentioned in the objection is a very rare thing, *if it exists at all* [my italics]" (in *Le Réalisme du Principe de Finalité*, Paris, 1932, p. 330). And cf. the important note (*ibid.*, n. 1): ". . . Anyone who is not conscious of such a sin [i.e., against faith], and adheres with complete conviction to the Christian dogmas, need not doubt the essentially supernatural character of his own faith." Cf. this note by Mgr. Journet (*L'Église du Verbe Incarné*, II, p. 346, n. 1): "In the eyes of Catholic theology, it is impossible to have a complete certainty that one is predestined except through an extraordinary revelation or a fatal illusion . . . But it is quite possible to have a practical, experimental knowledge that one is in a state of grace . . . *And it is still easier to be certain that one belongs to the Church* through baptism or *theological faith* [my italics]. . . . Cajetan was not afraid to say that every Christian can have a certain faith that he has faith."

PART II

The Christian Experience in the Scriptures

CHAPTER FOUR

Themes of the Christian Experience in St. Matthew

The Call

EVERYTHING begins with a call. Nothing in Christian experience has its first origin in man: everything springs from an eternal call by the all-merciful Father revealed in Christ in the world of time.

This call is heard through the Word of God. It was with a solemn Word—a *kerugma*—that Christ instituted his ministry: "Do penance, for the kingdom of heaven is at hand" (iv, 17). His essential task was to ensure that the call should be heard by all souls, because all are sinful: "For I am not come to call the just but sinners" (ix, 13). To be saved, to be a Christian, means "hearing" the Word of God and "keeping" it. The first aim of this Word therefore is to save us from our ignorance of ourselves and of God, from our sins, our damnation—and this it does by revealing to us that we are called to salvation by the Father and by Christ, our Messias and his Son. The mediation of the Word is thus an essential dimension of the Christian experience.

But words were only one of the signs used by the Word. There were also all the things that in Christ revealed his redemptive will—his attitude, his deeds, his silences, his tenderness and power, the miracles set like a halo round his head. All these things were included in the Word, and through all these things sounds the call. And because the words were surrounded by this ineffable atmosphere of divine signs, this "glory," when Christ spoke it was a unique event: he taught, not like the scribes and Pharisees, but "as one having power" (vii, 29), the power of God himself.

Consequently this Word had the power of the divine will itself.

It could cure the body and transform the heart, cast out devils and deliver men from their tyranny, save from sin and give life in God. It was both a judgment and a transfiguration. In short, it was the grace of God, and therefore it was not something that simply came from without, it was a mysterious virtue operating within. Through the Word came the call, and, if the soul opened in response, the Word brought salvation. We have an example of this in the miracle of the man sick of the palsy (ix, 1-11). He had already heard the Word, and had welcomed it, and it was faith—conviction, repentance, and hope—that took him to the feet of Christ. Then the Word was addressed to him personally, judging him with a judgment that was also an approbation: "Be of good heart"; transfiguring him spiritually: "Thy sins are forgiven thee"; curing him as a sign of the spiritual power of the Son of Man: "Arise, take up thy bed, and go into thy house." A revelation of Love, a manifestation of Power, the inauguration of the Kingdom—such is the Word that calls and saves.

This is the first essential fact, from which all the rest takes its meaning. With the Church we are in the world of the Word. Everything begins from contact with the Word—in other words, the Christian experience begins and ends in Faith. And the Word is inseparable from Christ. It comes from God, but it is *his* Word. *His* are the words that we have to hear and understand and keep—they are so divine that they will never pass away. The world of the Word is thus the world of Christ too—so that it comes as no surprise when St. Paul and St. John reveal that Christ is himself the Word of God. Already we can say that the Christian experience begins and ends in Christ.

There is no need to say any more about this here, because all that follows will simply be a development of this first affirmation. I will merely add that if this is so, then the Word must sound without and within for ever, for every human generation until the end of time—so that when Christ disappeared, it was necessary for his followers—his chosen ones—to continue his mission—and thus it was that the Church emerged in response to the requirements of the Word, and in its turn appeared as an essential element in the Christian experience.

Conversion

The beginning of the Word is: "Do penance, for the kingdom of heaven is at hand" (iv, 17); and these had been John the Baptist's words. God's call is a call to conversion.[1] In the light of the Word, man is a sinful being who must change his life, change his soul, change his being. He must turn right round, if he is to escape from self and give himself to God. Thus at the root of the movement there is an act of faith in the judgment of the Word—as St. Mark said: "Repent, and believe the gospel" (Mark i, 15). Since the Gospel is an announcement of forgiveness, this act of faith implies repentance and penance, hope and joy, the gift of self to God, and this is the way one turns round and enters the Kingdom as a new man. All the sorrow and isolation in this action are undergone for the sake of sharing in the divine goods, the life with God which is his Kingdom. The conversion is done for the sake of life, the renunciation for the sake of joy; and thus we have the first appearance of that synthesis of contraries that makes up the Christian mystery.

Moreover, this conversion needs to continue throughout life, and at the other end of the Gospel (xxi, 29-33) the short parable about the two sons whom the Father sent into his vineyard emphasizes this forcibly: "And he answering said, I will not. But afterwards, being moved with repentance, he went. And coming to the other he said in like manner. And he answering, said: I go, Sir. And he went not. Which of the two did the father's will? They say to him: The first. Jesus saith to them: Amen I say to you, that the publicans and the harlots shall go into the kingdom of God before you. For John came to you in the way of justice: and you did not believe him. But the publicans and the harlots believed him: but you, seeing it, did not even afterwards repent, that you might believe him." The Word has thus not been spoken once and for all: the call and the reply to it make up the whole drama of existence. If we have refused it, it remains for us to "afterwards repent," and return to this faith which demands repentance and obedience. Conversion and belief form a single act of giving by which we enter into the Kingdom.

[1] "The best translation of the Hebrew and Greek words seems to be, not 'Do penance and repent,' which do not literally mean anything more than regret, but 'Be converted,' which includes the change of conduct that follows upon repentance."—D. Buzy, *Évangile selon saint Matthieu* in *La Sainte Bible* by L. Pirot (Paris, 1935), Vol. IX, p. 26.

Moreover, even when we have entered the Kingdom, the need for conversion still remains. Man is always tending to pride, and this ever-recurring obstacle has to be continually broken down. When the disciples were trying to discover who was to be first in the Kingdom, Jesus said to them, "Unless you be converted and become as little children, you shall not enter into the kingdom of heaven" (xviii, 3). This means that we have to change the direction of our desires, "be converted," and this means becoming a child again, like the little child in the parable, who was not interested in being first. The child is detached because of his ignorance and indifference, his still unawakened innocence: we have to become detached voluntarily through renunciation and self-abasement. We may go even further; for if it is true that our entry into the Kingdom is never ultimately ensured here on earth, that God's will calls us daily and we are always being tempted to refuse to respond to it, then the *metanoia* appears not only as the act that gives life, or restores it in moments of crisis, but as the Christian's permanent attitude. Thus the conversion theme is continued, and resolves itself into the theme of choice.

No one, in fact, can serve two masters (vi, 24-34): love of the one will mean contempt for the other. For life has a meaning; it is a matter of choice; it implies that something is loved and served above all other things, and that around this one thing everything else revolves. Man finds himself in fact between two masters, God and life—life in the sense of eating and drinking and being clothed, and the money that is the means to all these things. It is demanding and imperious, and the attraction of created things tends to silence the call from on high and make it ineffective. We therefore have to choose, and the choice faces us anew every day. The Christian must choose God, seek the Kingdom of heaven and its justice, i.e. have his soul faced towards spiritual goods; and then the Father who knows all our needs will provide for them. Therefore the search for the Kingdom must come first. This means a fundamental detachment from all that is merely vital, and hence all that is created: the search takes place amidst all the temptations of the visible and the tangible, through a daily struggle, a continual choice, an endlessly repeated conversion. Every morning brings a return of anxiety, the worry of how to live, the fear of what the next day will bring, but these must be suffused and transcended by trust in God and fidelity to God.

The Christian life is thus a hierarchy energetically—and painfully—re-established each day, so that what is spiritual and eternal, the soul and God, may be dominant within us. There must be no anxiety about how to live, for the Father knows; no fear about what the next day may bring, for it will be a new day in which the difficulties will melt under the warmth of the Father's regard. Instead, there must be faith—faith that gives confidence and is ever forward-looking, that can see even in created things the delicate, considerate, royal goodness of the Father who is in heaven, faith that banishes anxiety and substitutes a joyous seeking after God. There is thus a hierarchy between the vital and the spiritual—a hierarchy needing to be incessantly maintained through conflict, and the conflict springing from an incessantly renewed choice. "Seek ye first the kingdom of God" (Luke xii, 31).

This explains the need for detachment, which is simply one aspect —the visible, costing, negative aspect—of the search. The Kingdom is the hidden treasure, the precious pearl (xiii, 44-46). All "having" is as nothing compared to it: we must sell all that we have to buy it, and do this joyfully because we have discovered the true riches. It will be understood, too, how much deeper and more detailed this theme becomes when instead of the Kingdom it is Christ himself who has to be sought. The essential thing, in fact, is to follow Christ (xvi, 24-28). To become his disciple and share his life we must deny ourselves and take up his cross. We have to die to ourselves in order to live, lose our souls to gain them, sacrifice the whole world in order to save our souls, and to be rewarded by the Son when he comes in the glory of the Father. These words spell tragedy; but they do not imply any contempt for this world, which reflects God's glory and is the setting of our human drama; what they mean is that the world is incommensurable with the soul, that the possession of the whole world at the risk of losing one's soul is a temptation towards nothingness, and that we must breathe and love and live in an atmosphere far beyond that of the material world in which we are so deeply enmeshed.

The hierarchy is established on earth by sacrifice, and this sacrifice refers particularly to a certain way of possessing ourselves and the world, a way that is egoistic and fleshly, a way that comes naturally to us but is opposed to the way of God. It therefore involves the kind of inner poverty which comes from detachment from both inner and outer goods, and from self through them, a poverty that is fully realized in the Cross, in the uprooting of the ego that is made up of earth and time, and which is prepared to sacrifice the body itself—feet, hands, or eyes—whenever it should tempt us and lead us into sin; a poverty that is thus the first demand made by choice and conversion, and consequently the fundamental condition of life and salvation. To sacrifice all in order to follow Christ and possess the heavenly treasure is such a tremendous demand that man himself would find it quite impossible; it is only possible to God, and to those to whom God gives his strength. But the strength is always there for us to take, for the Father's love never ceases to call us, to work upon us, obliging us to make the choice. And although the word is not mentioned here, the strength that responds is also love, the love that chooses, and renounces, and gives itself; and that is why conversion prolonged into choice has such a compelling power to separate us from our adherence to created things and unite us with the Father who is in heaven.

The choice is made more tragic still because we are not alone against God: the Tempter is also active amongst us. No doubt Satan first appears as a mysterious being who takes men by force, a leader who opposes another Leader in personal conflict. But Satan also works upon the hearts of men. He sows tares amongst men. He is at the root of all evil, and therefore evildoers belong to him (xiii, 39). He lords it over the soul, and when he has been cast out he tries with ungovernable energy to get back into it (xii, 43-45). He can thus destroy the body and the soul in Gehenna (xvi, 28). He is so closely involved in the mysteries of the human heart that a man can cast out devils in the name of Christ and yet belong to him and ultimately be condemned with him (vii, 22, 23). His frightening mastery over bodies thus appears as an expression and manifestation of his fearful power over souls. It is therefore not surprising that Christ should say, on the one hand, in connection with the lunatic, "This kind is not cast out but by prayer and fasting" (xvii, 20), and on the other hand, to the disciples who fell asleep during his agony, "Watch ye and pray that ye enter not into temptation" (xxvi, 41). Man cannot serve two masters. And now we find two masters appearing in person—not only God and the world, but God and Satan. Man is under these two masters, and at the Last Judgment he will find himself under one of them for ever (xxv, 34-41). These two masters are very unequal, no doubt, for Christ is King, Lord, Victor, whereas the devil is damned; but they face each other in the heart of man, and the choice is made all the more tragic by the fact that the composite soul of man is attracted to both, and can only purchase its deliverance from the Evil One, and its fidelity to its Lord, by ceaseless prayer and penance.

Inwardness

This is implicit in all that has been said, for the act of conversion and choice is necessarily spiritual. But the religion of an incarnate spirit is bound to be made incarnate in life. And because of the danger of "formalism" Christ lays strong emphasis on the need for inwardness, which alone can give meaning and value to religious activity.

He asserts this in the first place against the Pharisees, and the first value that he sets up against legalistic pride is purity of intention: for a life built up on a mass of external regulations he substitutes a life animated by the impulse of love. The Pharisee, in fact, is an "outsider." Religion is a matter of love and service, both of which need to be embodied in act. The Pharisee lacks love, and his soul, devoid, so to speak, of any inner sap, slowly degenerates into mere outward observance. His attitude is no longer an attitude adopted before God, the attitude of a servant who knows himself unworthy and helpless and in his master's debt, and so humbly knows his place; it becomes an attitude adopted before men, the attitude of a "great I am" who is only concerned with his own glory, the honours accorded to his position, the obedience given to his authority. Consequently he is only concerned with the outside of the religious act, and he degrades the religious relationship into a soulless ritualism (xv, 1-20). There can be no true religion without purity, and God has willed that Israel shall be a pure people amongst the nations. The Pharisees have allowed purity of heart to be swallowed up by legal purification. Hence the inevitable conflict: "Why do thy disciples transgress the tradition of the ancients? For they wash not their hands when they eat bread." The first thing Christ does is to re-establish the true order by giving homage its true value: the commandment of God comes before all human traditions—if it is not honoured above everything else, the human tradition becomes worthless, and if it is altered by the tradition, the result is hypocrisy and the dishonouring of God. Then he makes everything centre on the inward condition: there is only one kind of impurity, and it is not a matter of dirty hands but of the corrupt heart that produces impure acts. Washing, feeding—all such outward affairs are valueless in themselves; the essential thing is to be found in the movement of the heart, in being faithful to conscience and the commandment of God—in such a simple duty, for example (and one so often violated), as showing respect and love to one's parents.

As the Pharisees falsify the object of the religious act, so they falsify its fundamental intention, and doubly so. In the first place, they act so as to be seen (vi, 1-18). They pray, they fast, they give alms, all for the sake of being seen by men, all for the sake of seeming to be ascetic, so that men will look up to them. They turn the religious act into a means of personal glorification. This is the corruption of pride, that acts for men. Our Lord reverses the order, and says that everything should be done for the sake of the Father who sees and rewards. Prayer and fasting and alms-giving are simply so many means of giving oneself to God, and this self-giving needs to be protected against pride if it is to remain pure. Hence the need for absolute secrecy, to safeguard the purity of the giving. When everything is hidden from the eyes of men, we share a secret with the Father that is wholly suffused by God, utterly open to him and entirely inhabited by his love—the secret of faith. The choice is between being seen by men, and being seen by God. The Father is invisible, and he can only be reached invisibly. Being seen by men has to be avoided rigorously, for as a motive, it is a very powerful temptation: good works are meant to be seen, they are meant to give testimony, but they will never be to the glory of the Father if they are not in the first place pure, religious, buried in secret with God—like seed that must sprout in the earth before it can appear above ground and bear fruit.

Second, the Pharisees' aim in all their actions is domination. They are the teachers of the Word of God (xxiii, 1-12), but they have corrupted it because they have forgotten that its teaching is love. They transmit it, but they do not practise it; they treat it as a value obligatory for others but not for themselves; and the fact that the Word thus remains absolutely outside their own consciousness is the first reason for their hypocrisy. This is all the worse because they increase the harshness of the legal regulations, "but with a finger of their own they will not move them," because what they are really interested in are the crude material advantages of spiritual power—being seen and respected and flattered by men. Thus they usurp the name of Rabbi, Master, Father; but there is only one Master and Father—God, and Christ whom he has sent. They should be servants of their fellow men, should humble themselves in the thought of God's sovereignty and the value of the souls of the little ones entrusted to them, the awe-inspiring greatness of their mission. By doing this they would be "exalted," i.e. would become truly, in the clear humility of adoration, the fathers and spiritual teachers of their people. Outward show, "vanity," hypocrisy, on the one hand; inwardness, reality, integrity, on the other: these things are opposed to each other, but they hang together. One understands Christ's malediction upon them: "Woe to you, scribes and Pharisees!" (xxiii, 16-18). They are slaves of the visible and tangible, forgetting that the inside of the cup is more important than its outside, the heart more important than the outward action, and that therefore the commandments relating to the main spiritual acts—justice, compassion, good faith—come before observances in themselves and apart from the inward intention meaningless, like paying tithes of mint and anise and cummin. They are formalists, spiritually inverted, bad shepherds who tomorrow—like their fathers—will be murderers of the prophets. "Woe to you, scribes and Pharisees!" Inevitably there comes to mind St. Paul, expressing the same theme in his own vigorous way, in words so reminiscent of the words of the Gospel: "For it is not he is a Jew who is so outwardly: nor is that circumcision which is outwardly in the flesh. But he is a Jew that is one inwardly; and the circumcision is that of the heart . . . whose praise is not of men but of God" (Rom. ii, 28-29).

The Christian is therefore the inward man, whose heart and intention are centred on God and whose life is entirely devoted to the search for God. He lives in the mystery of this personal relationship with God, and carries it with him wherever he goes. He lives on earth, and his visible actions enter into human history; but his true home is invisible because it is spiritual: "For where thy treasure is there is thy heart also" (vi, 21)—and the "treasure" is a thing to be chosen. The Christian has chosen God, and through his love he is already in heaven. Consequently he is in the light: by seeking God first, he has purified his sight, and his eye, having become single (vi, 22-23), can discern the Father's will, can see the way, however narrow it may be, along which God is calling him, and recognize his presence around him, in his life and in his soul. The inwardness demanded by Our Lord is thus not any kind of self-centredness; it is the grasp of a relationship to God in the orientation of a freedom towards God, and hence, when man enters into himself, it is not to indulge in sterile self-regard, but to discover God's call and judge himself before God.

Nothing, indeed, is demanded more urgently than a spiritual awareness of oneself. The Christian's inwardness being entirely open to the eyes of God, entering into oneself means becoming aware of oneself as a being who is seen and judged, and consequently it should end, in spite of all the temptations to exteriority and pride, in that judgment of oneself which is the result of genuine sincerity and the condition of genuine clarity of vision. This is the lesson taught by the little parable of the mote and the beam (vii, 1-5). We naturally tend to criticize other people, but we must resist this tendency, because any such judgment implies an utter self-ignorance, it makes us act unjustly and leads to our own condemnation. Instead, we must enter into ourselves, and recognize the beam that is in our own eye. This is necessary if our attitude is to be true—and it is relatively easy, if we judge by the difference between a mote and a beam. We are culpable—hypocrites—not to see the beam, because we cannot "be aware of the state of our own conscience."[2] The awareness of one's own wretchedness, as a reaction against the movement of pride, here appears as one of the essential elements of the Christian attitude. Later, we may try to get rid of the mote . . . and perhaps once will be enough.

It is not only other human beings who can see us, there is also God. More precisely, there is his Word, which calls each one of us and judges each one of us personally. Now Christ thought it necessary to describe the state of souls, as they appear before the Word, in the parable of the sower (xiii, 1-9, 18-23). Souls may be closed, or shallow, or mixed, or deep: we ought to be able to recognize ourselves as one or other of these types, and so become spiritually aware of ourselves. The soul that is closed hears the Word without understanding it; the shallow soul and the mixed soul hear it and under-

[2] M. J. Lagrange, *Évangile selon saint Matthieu* (Paris, 1923), p. 146.

stand it but reject it or allow it to be choked; the deep soul accepts it, understands it and makes it bear fruit within itself—a transforming comparison takes place. This brings a new demand as well as a new effectiveness: the Word reveals the depths of the soul, it makes us enter into ourselves and judge ourselves, it obliges us to take sides—separating, penetrating beyond all our easy complacent ideas of ourselves as far as the division of the soul and the spirit. But, clearly, before we can enter into ourselves in this way and judge ourselves before God, both light from God and humility are needed. Only the grace of God can enable us to receive and understand the Word. "To you it is given to know the mysteries of the kingdom of heaven" (xiii, 11); and the fallen soul that has heard the call and has to be diagnosed forms part of these mysteries. Now this light is only given to the humble, and this is one of the essential aspects of God's scheme of things, the Father's "good pleasure": he has "hid these things from the wise and prudent and . . . revealed them to little ones" (xi, 25-26), i.e. hearts that are simple and upright, with no pride of caste, hearts conscious of their insignificance and unworthiness.[3] Humility thus appears as the only true awareness of ourselves before God, because it "situates" us exactly—puts us in our proper place, makes us aware of our real dimensions, and, in contrast to pride, which apparently exalts us, brings us down and shows us what we are in hidden reality—tiny children before God. Inwardness thus appears as what it really is—our means of entry into our own mystery, which is the mystery of our being before God, and consequently the mystery of God's sovereign "good pleasure" and his redemptive call within us.

It can be seen, then, that this inwardness is never-ending; it means an unceasing effort towards interiorization; it is difficult, and endlessly being put to the proof. This is a fact so strongly brought out by St. Mark—the disciples' failure to understand the Word because they were people of little faith, not sufficiently detached from themselves, not poor enough or humble enough, not sufficiently converted. The fundamental inwardness that we have been discussing is one of the lasting demands—and one of the essential products—of *metanoia*.

[3] On simplicity, cf. C. Spicq, *La Vertu de Simplicité dans l'Ancien et le Nouveau Testament*, in *Rev. Sc. phil. et théol.*, 1933, pp. 5-26.

Homage

Man's greatest task is to pay homage to God, and that is why the heart of religion is prayer, in which man speaks to God, and gives himself up to God, in the deepest part of his spirit, in adoration and love.

The first example of this attitude is given at the beginning of the Gospel, in Christ's temptation (iv, 1-11). This was a trial, and Christ's attitude to it was to determine the subsequent attitude of all Christians. After his long fast he was hungry, and Satan seized upon his biological requirement for food as a means to destroying his spiritual life. The two suggested miracles—the stones to be turned into bread, and the falling unharmed from the temple—and the offer of "all the kingdoms of the world," were all temptations to pride; to which Christ's reply was absolute homage to God, expressed in worship. His reply to each temptation was made by referring to the Word of God as expressing God's actual orders to his creatures, demanding their obedience in faith and hence a fundamental humility and submissiveness. The spiritual life, thus brought up against temptation, is shown to mean acceptance, "mastication" of the Word of God,[4] absolute respect for God, worship and service of God alone. Faced with the prospects of hunger, or glory, or absolute human power, our sole duty is to be found in serving God; everything else has to be left behind, despised and rejected if necessary, so that we may remain creatures who worship the Lord. This affirmation, and the attitude it implies, are a direct continuation of the Old Testament teaching: Christ came not to destroy but to fulfill. And thus the worshipping in spirit and in truth that is so strongly inculcated throughout the Bible is given its proper—i.e., first—place at the very beginning of the Gospels, and integrated once and for all into the Christian attitude.

This attitude of worship involves a holy respect for everything that concerns God. There are, for instance, words that refer so exclusively to God that they have no right to be used in connection with human beings. When the rich young man called Our Lord "good master,"

[4] On this passage, cf. F. PRAT, *Jésus-Christ*, I (Paris, 1933), p. 165, n.1. For the "exemplary" significance of the temptation of Christ, cf. A. FEUILLET, *Richesses du Christ, Serviteur de l'Eternel*, in *Recherches de Science religieuse*, 1948, p. 434 and n.2.

the answer was not slow in coming: "One is good, God" (xix, 17). It was an affirmation of God's infinite fullness and transcendence. Nothing on earth—not even the man Jesus Christ—is good, except by reflection and participation. Every good has its source in the infinite, the *bonitas fontalis,* and man must never lose the sense of the abyss that separates the creature from the Creator. One only is truly Good, as one only is Master and one only Father (xxiii, 8-9).

Contrariwise, anything that has any connection with God is sacred and must be treated with religious respect. The man who tries to forswear himself can find nothing on earth that belongs to him (v, 33-37): everything is marked with God's seal and escapes his grasp—heaven, earth, Jerusalem, even our own heads are God's, not our own, and we have no right to do whatever we like with them. We are paupers in the midst of God's riches, creatures amongst other creatures like ourselves; like everything else, we belong to God; we must not take what does not belong to us for our own personal profit: we must respect God. More than anything else, of course, the temple is sacred. It is the house of prayer, the place where God is present and where people render homage to him in detachment and adoration, where they must leave behind their selfish desires, where it is sacrilege to serve the mammon of iniquity—the master who sets himself up against God (xxi, 12-13). Lastly, children and the poor and the unfortunate are sacred above all things. God is their father in a special way. He loves them and reveals his mystery to them. He wants them to be served out of love of him. Defenceless little children manifest one of the highest values on earth: people who can see things properly can see something of the glory of heaven reflected in their eyes: "Their angels in heaven always see the face of my Father who is in heaven" (xviii, 11), and woe to anyone who scandalizes them! Thus the whole world is sacred, sacramental: it testifies to the sovereignty and holiness of God. It is a place for worship.

Nevertheless, only the Father's own mystery reveals the full depths of worship. "Our Father who art in heaven": all God's transcendence, sovereignty, and infinite inaccessibility are denoted by these few words. Our Lord says them with his usual simplicity, without any dramatic emphasis, but with great force. There is the parable of the labourers in the vineyard (xx, 1-19). This is concerned with man's eternal destiny. God gives eternal life to all the elect, and he does this with perfect freedom. Eternal life belongs to him alone, it is "his own good," and it is only gained as a result of a call from him: it is he who does the hiring and promises the just reward. What he gives is infinite, but he gives it with infinite independence. Consequently he is the sole master of his decisions—infinitely just ("I do thee no wrong"), infinitely good ("Is thy eye evil because I am good?"), but Sovereign Lord—"Is it not lawful for me to do what I will?" There can be no asking God his reasons. We must simply submit to his sovereign, loving will, which alone decides what is good; when we do not understand it, we must worship it more deeply still. God is the Lord.

Whenever the mystery of the redemptive will is mentioned, Our Lord's reply is the same: he always refuses to attenuate the mystery, refuses to give any enlightenment, refuses to answer. We can only enter into this mystery through absolute worship. If it is a matter, for instance, of our place in the Kingdom (xx, 23), the Father alone can decide: "To sit on my right or my left hand"—it is Christ himself who is speaking—"is not mine to give to you, but to them for whom it is prepared by my Father." If it is a matter of the Day of Judgment (xxiv, 36), that day when the blessed shall be solemnly separated from the damned and we shall each of us go either to the Kingdom or the fire: "Of that day and hour no one knoweth, no, not the angels of heaven, but the Father alone." If it is a case, as reported by St. Luke (Acts i, 7), of the restoration of the Kingdom of Israel: "It is not for you to know the times or moments, which the Father hath put in his own power." The Father is entirely enveloped in a secret not here to be revealed. The restoration of the Kingdom, the day and hour of the glorious Judgment, our rank amongst the blessed—all these things have been fixed for ever, but they are all beyond our knowledge, hidden in the bosom of the Father. Absolute homage, in holy awe—we are to watch and pray; in filial trust—it is the Father's will that determines all things; in worship—it is a lasting mystery: this is the Christian attitude; and it is from the heart of such homage that we must think of our eternal salvation, supplicate the Father and say, "Thy kingdom come, thy will be done."

But precisely because it is a *Father* with whom we are concerned, our worship can never go without love. Here we find the other main line running through the Old Testament being taken up by Our Lord, but developed and deepened to a remarkable degree. The great commandment has not changed, and cannot change: "Thou shalt love the Lord thy God, with thy whole heart and with thy whole soul, and with thy whole mind. This is the greatest and the first commandment" (xxii, 37-38).

One of the clearest forms taken by this love is trust; not a vague feeling of well-being but a movement in the depths of the soul, a reliance on God's infinite affection and power—the miracle of a love that believes in this power as something that is at the service of affection. The Father gives us our all, whether we are amongst the justified, or sinners. Life (v, 44-48), and the whole physical reality into which we are plunged and which we need for our existence, is simply the result of our Father's immense regard for us. There are no anonymous events in the world of the Gospel; it is a personal world, in which we are always embraced by the Father's will. The sun and the rain, the feeding of birds, the dress of the lily, the life of the sparrow (v, 44-48; vi, 23-34; x, 29-30) are something more than mere atmospheric or biological phenomena, or objects of knowledge or aesthetic contemplation; they are gifts—endlessly repeated, wonderfully generous gifts—of the Father's love. As such they are a sign that his charity is always close at hand, and a continuous call to us to have trust in him. Because the Father gives us our existence in this world, he knows our needs (vi, 32) even before we ask him (vi, 8). He watches over today and he will watch over tomorrow (vi, 34), for the days too are the medium and means of his Fatherhood.

But all this is wrapped in endless mystery. The Father's presence is not an object that can be observed, or a rational conclusion; it is infinitely above our human vision, for this can only see the unfolding of a life or the process of history; it is the mystery of supernatural creation itself, and it can only be reached in a sphere beyond all human understanding—in the act of faith. The Father is not to be found on any of our terrestrial roads, because he is in heaven, and it is only in mystery, through the dolorous and crucifying aspect of the world, that we can find his love. That is why the trust that is demanded of us is not indolence or easy indifference or unintelligent passivity before life; it is an act full of vigour and purity that is an outrage to our earthly eyes, the magnificent homage of a faith that turns appearances upside down and penetrates beyond them—they are pretty solid!—and believes in the unfailing presence of an invisible Love.

Naturally, the Father hears our prayers. In this world which is a personal world, not a world governed by laws, it is persons who count; the fact that they have been called counts, and the only real events are their spiritual acts. The Father who sees in secret listens in secret too, and he hears the cries of his children (vii, 9-11)—in his own way, which remains mysterious, for it is the child of God that he hears in us, and in his own time, which can never be foreseen, because time is an instrument of salvation in his hands; and that is why intensity and persistence are normal features of prayer, turning it into a constant supplication: "Ask and it shall be given you: seek and you shall find: knock, and it shall be opened to you." As the Father is infinitely good, prayer is not only a matter of asking, it is also a form of praise; and as Christ has given us an example of worship, so he gives us an example of exultation. The infinite mystery that we should adore in the consciousness of our own nothingness is also a mystery of love, and, when this aspect comes before the eyes of faith, gratitude, praise and exultation should burst forth from our lips, as they burst forth from Christ: "I confess to thee, O Father, Lord of heaven and earth, because thou hast hid these things from the wise and prudent, and hast revealed them to little ones. Yea, Father; for so hath it seemed good in thy sight" (xi, 25): an adoration and love that make us adhere joyfully to the Father's sovereign, blessed will.

I have been speaking of the Father because the Father is at the heart of things. But our trust must be directed equally to the Son and the Holy Spirit. Only very infrequently, however, is the latter mentioned in the Gospel, and this makes it all the more necessary to emphasize the Trinitarian passage (x, 19-33), which gives "three excellent reasons for having trust, which bring out without any parade of metaphysics the attributes of the Father, the Son, and the Holy Spirit."[5] The world is for Christians a place of persecution, but they will never be forsaken: the Father watches over his creation, over a mere sparrow—how much more, then, over the very hairs of his children's heads! If they are dragged before cunning judges—a grim prospect for those far from subtle Galileans!—they must have no fear: the Spirit of the Father will inspire them and speak through their mouths. If they are persecuted, they will have an advocate in heaven—the Son, who will confess them before the Father. Thus

[5] M. J. Lagrange, *L'Évangile de Jésus-Christ* (Paris, 1928), p. 339.

the whole Christian adventure is enveloped in the love of the Trinity.

Moreover, every act of homage has value in the eyes of the Father. Prayer, alms-giving, fasting (ch. vi) bring their own reward. When they are the secret overflowing of the soul in the secrecy of God, they become a gift to God which he will return; for he will not allow himself to be outdone in generosity. Here again it is not a matter of calculation, but of trust in faith. It is only through a lived, concrete renunciation of any immediate, tangible, human recompense that there can be any growth of this humble, detached hope of a hidden, unknown reward, later, from the "Father who is in secret." Again the paradox: God rewards absolute purity and utter detachment. Secretly I pray, fast, give alms; the Father may make what he likes of all this, glory and beatitude—everything is in his hands. . . . Furthermore, his demands are sacred, and any deliberate violation of them means that I take my place amongst the damned. The Father wills us to serve him with purified hearts, and since we are always sinning and always needing to be forgiven, he requires us to forgive others so that we may be forgiven ourselves. If we fail to observe this commandment, our homage is vitiated: God will not forgive our offences (vi, 14-15) but will chastise us severely (xviii, 23-35). A justice all the more to be feared in that it is born of love, and for which, because of man's sin, there are not only "blessed" ones but "accursed" ones too.

It is not difficult, to bring our discussion of this point to an end, to see that the whole attitude of homage is summed up in the *Pater:* adoration, because the creature and the child of God are created for the glory of God, and supplication, because they need to be nourished, forgiven, and delivered from evil; the whole expressing a love infinitely simple and trusting (speaking to a Father) and infinitely humble and worshipping (speaking to a Father who is in heaven).

This homage would be incomplete if it did not become incarnate in act and in life. Its inwardness is not that of feeling or self-enjoyment, but the inwardness of giving and self-commitment. That is why receiving the Word means enabling it to bear fruit (xiii, 23). Homage culminates in faithfulness.

The highest homage that we can pay to God is to do his will—in the secrecy of our hearts, so that our homage may be genuine, and in the full daylight of our lives, so that it may be genuine from beginning to end. It is not flesh and blood that bring us into intimate contact with God and glorify him: "For whosoever shall do the will of my Father that is in heaven, he is my brother, and sister, and mother" (xii, 46-50). Faithfully keeping God's commandments, or, as St. Luke's says more succinctly (viii, 21), to "hear the word of God, and do it," is the way to become brother to Christ and a son of God. It is so tempting for a being as divided as man to perpetuate the division within himself, that Our Lord insists on this point. To hear the Word without doing it is sheer folly. We congratulate ourselves on having heard the Word, we rather like it—and there we stop; and the torrent of our instincts and lusts and actions goes on following the same old course. We are houses built on sand and will fall. Wisdom is only to be found in hearing the Word and doing it: then, the spiritual life becomes established in a profound unity of thought and action, on the unshakeable foundation of faithfulness—it becomes a house built on rock (vii, 24-28).

The analogy of the good and bad trees (vii, 15-20) explains that this concrete faithfulness is a matter of purity of spirit and purity of act. Good sap produces good fruit, and the quality of the sap can only be judged by the taste of the fruit. The same is true of the "prophets," and, through them, of all Christians: they are not to be judged either by their words or their "appearance" but by the spiritual value of their acts, their habitual faithfulness to the Word. For every life involves at its root a fundamental choice that gives it its meaning and value, and this is revealed in the general tendency of its acts, for or against the Father's will, which reveal whether it is endeavouring to enter into the Kingdom or is turning its back upon it. In this sense, "every good tree bringeth forth good fruit, and the evil tree bringeth forth evil fruit." But we must understand what exactly this fruit is that Our Lord is speaking of. The comparison emphasizes the inner bond that joins the fruit to the tree and gives it its quality, and the revelation of the quality that is provided by the fruit. The same is true of the acts that spring from a life and reflect its quality.

This introduces into the Gospel a view of words which needs to be carefully weighed. Whether they concern ourselves or other people, human words are ambiguous in religious matters, and the Gospel divides them into three main types. First there is the voluntary, considered word, which manifests a deliberate intention and is always an act in the strongest sense. Between it and the spontaneous unfolding of life there is always a certain distance, the result of the conscious mediation of thought. But this word can become a calculated thing, veiling the soul's real impulse and fundamental choice and inevitably ending up by being palpably untrue to life: it is then judged and condemned by life—it is hypocrisy—and so we get the false prophets. Sometimes the word is one of commitment; it is introduced into the gift that leads to life, and manifests the being's true orientation and his will to absolute faithfulness: it is then a testimony—we shall return to it later. There is the lived word, which derives from man's deepest tendencies, adheres closely to the actual movement of life, and springs spontaneously from the soul. This always reflects—and betrays—our inmost being. In this sense, "out of the abundance of the heart the mouth speaketh" (xii, 33-37), and "a good man out of a good treasure bringeth forth good things; and an evil man out of an evil treasure bringeth forth evil things"—as an involuntary testimony to his holiness or wickedness. Lastly, there is the word, ambiguous by definition, which simply expresses a movement of affectivity. It is a sign not of activity but of feeling: in itself it says nothing about the deeper parts of the soul, pays no kind of homage, nor is it introduced into the truth of life (vii, 21, 23); and the affective movement that produces it is to be judged by one standard only—whether the will of God is accomplished or not. And therefore, "Not every one that saith unto me, Lord, Lord, shall enter into the kingdom of heaven, but he that doeth the will of my Father who is in heaven, he shall enter into the kingdom of heaven." This constitutes a radical criticism of feeling which must never be forgotten: faithfulness to the Word, obedience to the Father's will and conformity to its demands, are the things that give everything else its religious value.[6]

This is true to such an extent that at the other extreme, when it is a case not of the Word but of the charisma and miracles, the law remains the same. Prophesying, casting out devils, performing miracles, are the very works of Christ; they testify to his mission (xx, 1) and prove their Word to be authentic; they are the works of God and

[6] I follow Buzy rather than Lagrange, who takes this to refer to orthodoxy. Buzy says, moreover (*op. cit.*, p. 96), primacy of action over words; I would add, taking it a little more deeply (words being only a sign), primacy of activity over feeling.

the friends of God. And yet even here the same distinction applies: God can use the spirit when the heart has been refused him; people can have been traversed by the divine power and yet "commit iniquity." Thenceforward, they are neither friends of God nor disciples of Christ; they are lost and will be damned: "I never knew you, go far away from me." Even St. Paul did not go further than this in his criticism of the charisma: only one thing counts, says Our Lord—faithfulness, which means purity of intention, obedience, and love.

Serving the Neighbour

Service of the neighbour follows naturally upon homage to God, and the attitude of brotherly love is simply a way of making explicit our faithfulness to God. Never throughout the Gospel does the soul's connection with God mean any weakening of its connection with other men; on the contrary, the movement towards God demands and leads to the gift of oneself to one's fellow men. For the Christian is in the world as someone who is called upon to work in it for God. The parables about the Kingdom (ch. xiii) show Christians as being inevitably involved with evildoers, persecuted by them, sorrowing over them, raising the level of human society like yeast within the dough, working for a visible and extraordinary growth of the Kingdom in the world. Thus the Kingdom is on the move, it is a pilgrimage, its consummation is not yet; and the life of Christians is a life hidden in the deepest depths of the human mass, a life of service, struggle, suffering, defeat, and victory, until the day of the ultimate separation of the good from the evil and the reign with Christ for ever.

The name of this attitude to our fellow men is love. It is a highly complex attitude, and the Gospel does not explain it specifically. But two main features need to be noted from the beginning. First, love is a commandment—the second commandment that is like to the first (xxii, 39). Israel had already taken the words in Leviticus—"Thou shalt love thy neighbour as thyself"—from their context, and connected them up with the first commandment: they are quoted by the scribe who questions Our Lord (Luke x, 27). But Christ repeats this. He raises the words to the level of an absolute commandment. He links the second commandment sovereignly and indissolubly with the first, makes it into an essentially religious duty, and introduces it into the matter of homage as an extension, a "function," and a sign of the love of God. With incomparable force he proclaims a mysterious unity between himself and those who are his: "He that receiveth you, receiveth me: and he that receiveth me, receiveth him that sent me" (x, 40-42). In a very special sense, all who through their powerlessness and poverty are more particularly at the mercy of others—the destitute, displaced persons, the poor, the sick, prisoners (xxv, 31-46)—are brothers of Christ the Servant who humbled himself and made himself as nothing for us. Serving these "lowliest of brothers" means serving him, and rejecting them means rejecting him. But here again this mysterious bond can only be established by faith. The people before one's very eyes one must be able to see (x, 40-42) as prophets, just men, disciples, and they must be received "in the name of a prophet . . . a just man . . . a disciple," i.e. because of their connection with God. And in the same way, whenever our neighbour has need of us, he takes on a mysterious likeness to Christ and must be recognized as having within him the hidden presence of Christ. Thus the eyes of faith see God or something of God in each of our neighbours; they transform the service of our fellow men into a form of religious homage paid to beings who are sacred, and turn the love of our fellow men into a form of the love of God.

This charity is primarily, in the strict sense of the word, service. The progress from the old law to the new (v, 17-45) is described in terms of an inter-personal experience as limitless charity. Not only must we not kill, but we must practise gentleness, reconciliation, and agreement with our enemies (21-27); not only not commit adultery, but respect our neighbour by keeping our hearts pure and sacrificing ourselves (27-30); not only not swear, but not swear by any of the things of God, and speak always quite simply and frankly (31-37); we must not follow the principle of an eye for an eye, but show an utter, heroic detachment from our own personal interests (38-42); not love our neighbours and hate our enemies, but love even our enemies (43-48). No doubt there are some things here that seem to be a kind of "reaching for the stars," but the main point is clear: we must serve our neighbour intentionally in a disinterested, religious way, and so imitate the Father (48) and become his sons (45). The unlimited charity of our Father who is in heaven is the only model to be followed by sons of God living amongst their fellow men. Apostolic workers especially should become the servants of their fellow men, in the same way as Christ himself became the servant of all (xx, 25-28).

Next, the Christian must forgive, and this is one of the most extraordinary acts that is demanded of us. The greatest manifestation of God's charity, and the greatest revelation in the Gospel, is the fact that the Father can forgive sinners like ourselves. But he requires us to imitate him, so that we can say to him, "Forgive us our debts, as we also forgive our debtors" (vi, 12). Forgiving our neighbour is therefore a strictly religious act, whose roots go down into our dual awareness of our own sinfulness and God's mercy. When a Christian has been offended in any way, he should remember that he is a sinner in the eyes of God, a being who has had his own sin washed away by the absolute Mercy without any right or merit of his own; a being who today and tomorrow and the next day will commit some offence against God and need to be cleansed anew by pure charity; a being who has wounded the infinite holiness and love within himself, whose act of sin goes down into the deepest depths of his being; a being in whom absolute mercy, with all its splendour and all its obligations, and the need for purification, which is always so acute and so urgent, must be increasingly manifest in holy fear and joyful gratitude. The more he is forgiven, the more he knows that he needs to be forgiven. Past forgiveness stirs up his awareness of his misery, his weakness, his imperfection, and thus awakens a need and a desire to be forgiven even more.

Only the man who lives thus encompassed within the miracle of forgiveness can forgive as Our Lord wants him to forgive. His consciousness of the infinite extent of his own sin flows back upon any offence that is done against him; he realizes what an abyss there is between offences done against him and any offence against God—he himself is not infinitely holy! He realizes that any debts owing to him are as nothing compared with his debt to God—no more than a hundred pence as against ten thousand talents (xviii, 21-25). He knows that he has already been forgiven by the unwearying Mercy again and again. Then, in one great movement of obedience, gratitude and hope, he cancels the debt, he forgives, he behaves as though the offence had never been committed. And at the thought of his innumerable sins and the immeasurable Mercy, he forgives not once but always and without measure—till seventy times seven times (xviii, 21-22).

It is clear what is implied in this wonderful thing called charity: a vivid sense of our own condition as redeemed sinners, a victory over the dreadful reactions of wounded pride, a change of heart towards those who offend us—faith, abnegation, faithfulness; in short, conversion, repeated again and again. Forgiveness of sins thus appears in its true light—not as the indifference of the unaware, or the wise calculation of the well-meaning philanthropist, not even as the impulse of a good heart, but as homage, which may be tragic but is always magnificent, paid to our Father who forgives us, and whom we do our best to imitate.

Lastly, this love of the neighbour means bearing witness. Being a Christian means serving as Christ served, and with Christ. Christ's essential service is the bringing of truth, salvation, joy. The Christian must take part in this service, and this he does by bearing witness. There are two images that express one aspect of this Christian function. First, "You are the salt of the earth" (v, 13). Like salt, the Christian acts by contact. The power of purity and faithfulness and charity that is in him elevates his life, saves it from egoism, and gradually delivers it up into God's hands; it gives a spiritual savour to all his actions and makes him an agent of purification and preservation. Then, "You are the light of the world" (v, 14). Like light, the Christian acts by presence. The light of faith, which produces every kind of good work, dissipates prejudices, lightens the way, leads to God. It comes and awakens that power of desire and admiration and "graceful" action that slumbers in every Christian soul, and thus, by its mere presence, it causes us to glorify God. This Gospel affirmation is complementary to another. We must never act so as to be noticed by men, but only to please God. The purer the intention, the deeper the inwardness of our acts, the more direct and detached will be our search for God and his Kingdom—and the more our light will shine before men. For light does not try to be seen: it only has to exist, and then it is bound to shine; the more purely it is itself, the more brilliantly it shines. So for the Christian: the more he forgets himself for God, the more he becomes transparent to the divine light, the more he is bound to spread God around him. Purity of intention, and "candle power," are one and the same thing: it is love for the Father that attracts others to the Father and gives glory to God. *Caritas aedificat.*

But the witness given is usually very far from being as simple as salt and as tranquil as light. Christ was the enemy of sin, and the world, enslaved to sin, treated him as its enemy. It accused him, it persecuted him, it put him to death; and Christians will be treated in the same way, and hated on account of his name (x, 16-40). Arrest, ill-treatment, condemnation, death; to be regarded with a kind of religious execration, as Christ was, and on his account: such is the prospect that faces the Christian. In this acute form it is a state of things existing in the remote distance, no doubt; nevertheless, it describes a normal dimension of the Christian experience: in a veiled or violent, brutal or subtle form, persecution is promised to all Christians. Here more than ever, then, charity consists in bearing witness.

This will be done prudently and humbly, of course, for Christians are weak in the face of evil, and sometimes, instead of facing the conflict, they will have to take refuge in flight. But let them be unafraid! They will never be alone; they will always have their Father's protective arms around them. The Father watches over them, and they must abandon themselves to his power and goodness. When they face their judges, he will give them his spirit, which will act as the living principle of their fearlessness in mind and body. If they must die, their souls will be in God's hands, beyond all blows, safe in the conviction that Christ will confess them before his Father, at peace before their persecutors, whose labour is vain. A fearless confidence, a straight answer to all the questions put by those in authority, an absolute simple truthfulness in proclaiming the Christian message, unbroken loyalty in the face of every kind of suffering —such is the Christian witness. Through these things more than through any others will Christians be the light of the world, and through these things too they will be recognized as the sons by God. Faced by such a tragic task, they may, of course, give way, take to flight and deny Christ, but then they will be denied before their Father who is in heaven. Always they must have a fundamental determination to put God before self and their own lives. Perseverance to the end (22) means confessing Christ before men: witness and salvation are the same thing, for the Christian is faced with the choice between confession and denial.

Since this tragic need to bear witness is imposed upon the Christian from the very fact that he is a Christian—*propter nomen meum*—it follows that it is part of Christ's will for men. Undoubtedly he loves us, and came for the sake of peace; but when we refuse to hear his Word, this becomes a sword that cuts and separates; and Christ wants absolute faithfulness at the cost of no matter what sacrifice. Bearing witness may in the end necessitate the ultimate rending apart. "He that loveth father or mother more than me, is not worthy of me." This unchanging order of things, this fundamental choice that is demanded of us, this faithfulness unto death—this is all a way of loving God and Christ above all things: bearing witness is a function of the first commandment.

Joy

The Gospel is the Good News of salvation, and the first words of the Sermon on the Mount are the Beatitudes. Christianity therefore means joy, and it means joy because it brings us into contact with Christ. The Beatitudes, of course, are Messianic, and the reason why St. Matthew puts them at the beginning of this great speech is so that their light may illuminate all that follows. But before we study them in themselves, perhaps it may be wise to take note of a few particulars that may help us to get a better understanding of them.

The first of these takes us straight into the sphere of mysticism. It is the theme of the Bridegroom (ix, 14-17): "Can the children of the bridegroom mourn, as long as the bridegroom is with them? But the days will come when the bridegroom shall be taken away from them. . . ." The essential point here, from our present point of view, is not the sad news of a forthcoming separation, but the heart of the reply: that Christ amongst those who are his is like a bridegroom amongst the companions of his nuptial happiness. The theme of Jahweh's espousals with his people had been part of the classic tradition, and the Canticle of Canticles had voiced it supremely in a form more passionate than ever before. John the Baptist, continuing the theme, had likened himself to the friend of the bridegroom, a bridegroom henceforth united with his bride (John iii, 29). Our Lord takes up this image. He is the Bridegroom who has arrived for his mysterious espousals; he brings with him a new nuptial joy, and the disciples are now to live by it. It is an imperfect joy, a joy enveloped in mystery, a provisional joy, a joy that will only be consummated on the last day, when the souls who are prepared for it—the wise virgins—enter with the Bridegroom into the eternal marriage (xxv, 1-13). Nothing detailed is said, but we are given a restatement of the profoundest theme in Jewish mysticism: Christ once again takes the place of Jehovah in his relationship with souls, and the joy of a shared love, an ineffable union, is put at the centre of the Christian mystery. We have to wait for St. Paul and the Apocalypse before the theme that here makes such a brief appearance reappears and reaches its culmination.

In a completely different line of thought—here we see Christ in contact with suffering; not only as someone who gives a meaning to suffering and integrates it into the Redemption, but as the person who can get "purchase" on it, who has the power to transform it and can teach and help others how to bear it. "Come to me, all you that labour and are burdened, and I will refresh you" (xi, 28-30)—go to him by faith, become the disciple of one who is gentle and humble of heart. And suffering, the yoke and the burden—the commandments, with the sacrifices they call for, all the crosses—will come under the shadow of the benediction of his presence, his contact, the intimate, warm, tender-hearted teaching that is his alone. Christ is thus the Comforter, standing at the heart of human distress, giving the strength to bear it and enabling it to be seen as the appeal made by a marvellous love. Ultimately this suffering which is thrown upon Christ becomes itself a Beatitude: "Blessed are they that mourn: for they shall be comforted." Tears are not done away with; they are transfigured.

Lastly, Christ is the realization of God's promise amongst men, and blessed are those who come to him by faith: "Blessed are your eyes because they see, and your ears because they hear. For, amen I say to you, many prophets and just men have desired to see the things that you see . . . and to hear the things that you hear" (xiii, 16-17). Christ is thus the fulfilment of the Messianic hope: by his word, his miracles, his life, he is the revelation of the grace of God and the presence of salvation. In him it is given to understand the mystery and to enter into the Kingdom. Seeing him, hearing him, and understanding him are beatitudes, becauses they mean being taken from death, they mean healing and life. But there is a grace of absolute renewal to be acquired, and for this it is necessary to overcome the scandal of a man who was the son of a carpenter, and whose mother, brothers, and sisters were quite commonly known, putting himself forward as the Messias and Lord. Hence the reply, to the people sent by John the Baptist: "Go and relate to John what you have heard and seen . . . And blessed is he that shall not be scandalized in me" (xxi, 4-6). Always there is this opportunity of entering into the beatitude of union with the Lord; and if the conversion is not complete, the choice not adhered to, the death to self not accepted, then comes the scandal—and with eyes closed, ears stopped up, the heart in darkness, it becomes impossible to be converted and saved (xxiii, 13-15). Beatitude or scandal, salvation or damnation: these are the alternatives that Christ always offers us. It remains to be said that he is himself beatitude and salvation, and that it is in him that the soul of the humble believer will find its joy.

If we now turn to the Beatitudes (v, 1-12) of the Sermon on the Mount, we can say that the beatitude of contact with Christ here finds its full expression. Their first proclamation is that God's happiness has been given to men. They hold out no promise of anything appertaining to this world of flesh and time: what they offer is the mysterious reward that will ultimately be given in the possession of the Kingdom and the divine goods. This possession has in fact already begun, for the Beatitudes are Messianic, and the Messias is here to announce them and give them actuality. Next, they proclaim that happiness is to be found at the heart of the most radical human detachment. They are divine, far above man and the world he lives in, so that the disciple has to get away from the world and himself before he can attain to them. He has to be detached from concupiscence, poor, gentle, pure; detached from unbroken joy and comfortable tranquillity, afflicted and persecuted; detached from self-concern, showing mercy and bringing peace; detached from all that he has and is, and hungry for justice—and then he will be one of the blessed ones of God. Every kind of mortification and all human suffering and tragedy are enveloped in the immense benediction of the Father who is in heaven. The Beatitudes are Christological as well as Messianic: they are realized in Christ and in union with Christ.[7] We are blessed when we resemble Christ. He is the apotheosis of the "poor of Israel" —the poor man with nowhere to lay his head; the humble, gentle

[7] Cf. L. Pirot, *Béatitudes*, in *Suppl. au Dict. de la Bible*, Vol. I, col. 928.

Saviour who will not bruise the fretted reed; the man who weeps over the crowd without a leader, over faithless Jerusalem and the frightful unleashing of sin, who hungers and thirsts for justice, and whose soul burns with such zeal that he comes to set fire to the earth. He is the man of mercy who cares for the sick and the afflicted, the sinners; he is pure of heart, and in him is no sin, but perfect love for the Father and his sons; he is the man of peace who can give others peace with God and men; the man who is persecuted for justice and dies for justice. But in the midst of all his earthly trials he is the blessed one of God, and beatitude means entering into communion with him and God. The theme is always the same: carrying one's cross—Christ's own cross—and following him, brings salvation and joy, because through the cross is discovered his transforming presence and beatifying love. Here the emphasis is on the beatitude, not on the suffering; other passages have been concerned with the means, and emphasized the exacting side of Christianity, here we are concerned with spirit and value, and it is the joy that comes first—the joy of the soul's marriage with its Christ.

Eschatology

This is one of the esssential themes of the Gospel and one of the most important with regard to the structure of the Christian experience. Its difficulties are well known: it has been given a whole host of interpretations.[8] A few firmly established facts, arising immediately out of the various texts, will be sufficient for the purposes of our discussion here.

It may be worth while, to begin with, to reflect for a moment upon the mysterious time-continuum in which the world unfolds and we Christians live, frequently described in the Gospel as the *aiōn* (xiii, 39-40, 49; xxiii, 20). This continuum is made up of realities that pass away and of other realities that do not pass away. "Till heaven and earth pass, one jot or one tittle shall not pass of the law, till all be fulfilled" (v, 18). "Heaven and earth shall pass, but my

[8] See as representative of the general tendency of non-Catholic interpretations the article by F. M. Braun: *Où en est l'eschatologie du Nouveau Testament,* in *Revue biblique,* 1940, pp. 33 *et seq.* For a new interpretation of this central fact, cf. the articles by A. Feuillet, esp. *Revue biblique,* 1948, pp. 481-502, and 1949, pp. 61-92, and *Nouvelle Revue théologique,* 1949, pp. 701-722, 806-828. Cf. also O. Cullmann, *Christ et le Temps* (Paris, 1947), pp. 160 *et seq.*

words shall not pass" (xxiv, 35). The world passes away each day; it will pass away completely when the history of salvation is accomplished and the era of consummation opens. It is thus the scene —the material and spiritual centre—of a testing time, a growth; its continuity involves an unfolding process which is proceeding towards a climax; its entire cosmic aspect is merely provisional and will disappear beyond recall. But within this evanescent world there is a reality that time cannot erode—the Word of God, the Law of Christ, which defines the New World of God and makes it present within the old one. Here, then, we have a force that is supra-cosmic, supra-biological, truly divine, inserted into history and at work within it. The time in which we Christians live is made up of these two things —a visible reality, essentially evanescent, which will one day vanish before an ultimate reality, and within this an eternal reality at work —the saving Word, which lays within the old world the foundations of a New World that is imperishable.

But the Christian is a person who adheres to the Word of God and in whom the Word bears fruit: "Not in bread alone doth man live, but in every word that proceedeth from the mouth of God" (iv, 4). He is therefore both in the cosmic world and in the eternal world. In so far as values are concerned, he lives primarily above the order of cosmic time, in eternity. And if he declines to cosmic and biological values, if he gives them first place, if he immerses himself in their perishable waves, then he begins to suffer ontological dispersion—"he that gathereth not with me, scattereth" (xii, 30)—which is simply another name for death; he can gain the whole world, but he loses his soul, because he has changed his existence in the Word—his existence in God—into an existence in the world—in nothingness. Hence, again, he seeks the eternal beyond the transitory, and his search establishes him there. He must lay up unto himself (vi, 19-21) not "treasures on earth: where the rust and moth consume, and where thieves break through, and steal," but "treasures in heaven: where neither the rust nor moth doth consume, and where thieves do not break through, nor steal." And because "where thy treasure is, there is thy heart also," beyond the world of time in which all things pass away, he is already in the world of eternity, where everything abides. His soul is therefore always beyond the passing day, because it is above it (vi, 24-34). The grass that lives for one day is clothed by God, but he is above the days. The Father knows what he needs, and the Christian attaches himself to this loving, unchanging, endlessly present love, to calm his fears. He does not worry today about what the morrow may bring forth, because he is already above tomorrow, in God, who sees and loves and watches over him. In a region far above the difficulties of the days in which one whole side of his being is enmeshed, his soul is fixed by faith, longing and hope on the Eternal Kingdom—on God.

If we widen our point of view to take in not only a single life but the whole of human history, we come to the parables of the Kingdom, for example the one about the cockle (xiii, 37-43). The field is the world, in which men—the good seed and the cockle—live and grow through trial and hardship. The harvest will bring the solemn separation of the good and the wicked that is to inaugurate the consummation of the world. Time here appears as the true measure of this ordered growth, the intermediary between seed-time and harvest-time, the dimension within which humanity is pulled between the rival attractions of Christ and the Devil. And men are both within this movement and beyond it, in eternity. The just are in it by their fullness, as the seed of good grain that will be harvested for ever, the seed of glory that will make them "shine as the sun"; the wicked are in it by their emptiness, as the seed of cockle that can never be harvested, so that they will be cast into the fire. In the world of sin and the world of life, in time and out of time, such is the Kingdom and such the Christian. Consequently, the Christian is only partly out of time. He is in eternity in a partial, hidden, uncertain way; he is not in it entirely, or for ever, or in clear consciousness or full light. He is a swelling seed and a growing hope. He is by definition a being tending towards the fulfilment of hope, of growth, of life. All Christian existence is henceforth marked by this essential feature.

It is an aspiration towards reigning with Christ, a search for the Kingdom. The entire movement of faith is an effort at discovery, an impulse towards an infinite beyond, a crossing of appearances to enter into the hoped-for mystery, an aspiration towards the plenitude, the eternity, and the glory, that are all one. All petitionary prayer is of this nature. Since we are not given the plenitude of the Kingdom, we have to go on asking for the divine goods, tending towards them through a determined supplication renewed each day. "Ask and it shall be given you: seek and you shall find: knock, and it shall be opened to you" (vii, 7-12). The giving, the discovering, the entering within, are all always partial and provisional, giving rise to the same repeated demand, the same search, the same knocking on the door, and all consequently carried forward by the longing for the complete giving, the total discovery, the entry for ever into the Father's house. When the "outside" man becomes the "inner" man, then only will he have found all and received all. The whole prayer for the Kingdom is eschatological. The first three petitions of the Our Father[9] express the soul's movement towards that ultimate hour when the Name will be completely hallowed, the Kingdom fully come, and the Will of the Father done on earth as it is in heaven, because the children who suffer on earth will have become children in heaven—in the Promised Land of the Beatitudes. Thus at the very heart of the prayer which is obligatory for all Christians, there is an aspiration towards the Kingdom; and what is in the beginning no more than a spark hidden beneath the ashes becomes, with the soul's entry into God, a fire that sets it all aglow.

Christian joy is entirely eschatological. The poor, the meek, the pure, are blessed, because the Kingdom "already exists for them," but only in embryo: they possess it only as a promise, it flowers only in heaven. All the Beatitudes, therefore, are a beatitude of hope, which only achieves possession on condition that it tends continuously towards its fulfilment and is continuously elevated by desire. The cardinal beatitude from this point of view is the fourth, "Blessed are they that hunger and thirst after justice"—the beatitude of desire, seeking, aspiration, the beatitude that is at the heart of all the others, since justice denotes the divine goods, and poverty, meekness, and purity always mean for us an effort at denudation, de-hardening, purification, and tears and persecution make us call for trial and hardship to end in joy and peace. Full reward, full possession, are not given but are implied in embryonic form, and are active in the desire that is felt for them. The Beatitudes are thus a typical case of eschatology: an inchoate, partial, fragile possession, tending wholly towards the ultimate event—entry into the Kingdom, into the place where in everlasting plenitude we are in heaven.

Christian suffering too is eschatological. From the first, the beatitude of tears and the beatitude of persecution bring it within this perspective. For these beatitudes do not come through the joy they

[9] Lagrange, *Évangile selon saint Matthieu*, p. 129.

reveal and promise, but through the hazard they involve—we must "persevere unto the end" (x, 22)—through the strength they demand, through the imitation of Christ's persecution, death, and resurrection which they tend to realize. There is thus a "beyond" that is always present in Christian suffering and helps to transform it. We are told not to fear those who can kill the body, even when they are in the act of doing so, because we must fear him who can kill both soul and body in hell (x, 28)—in the beyond. We must, if necessary, be ready to pluck out our eyes, because "it is better for thee having one eye to enter into life"—into the beyond—"than having two eyes to be cast into hell fire." This beyond flows back upon the present and transforms it, enabling us to pass from temporal fear to eternal fear. Thus suffering in time is enveloped and taken up into the eternal.

If we widen our point of view still further to include the human situation as such, we find the parables of the Kingdom yet again. The mingling of the good and the wicked is found to be the established order until the end of time, and Christians must be surrounded by "cockle"—by evil in all its forms—until the ultimate separation. The aspiration towards the Kingdom thus becomes an aspiration towards deliverance; the suffering of the present time has at work within it a call to everlasting Beatitude; this anguished order of time is taken out of itself by the movement that carries it towards its "end"; it is raised up in a mysterious assumption that will end in a mysterious transfiguration.

And that is why the appropriate form taken by the Christian life is waiting and hoping. It is a waiting for the coming of the Lord, which will in the first place be a judgment (xxiv, 36-50). The time of this coming is an utter mystery, hidden from the eyes of men and angels and even from the Son; locked in the bosom of the Father. Consequently we must not only adore God's hidden will, we must also watch; not abandon our post, but wait in readiness for the coming, which will be like that of a thief. The meaning of this coming is likewise a mystery: the Lord alone knows what the judgment is to be; but the Christian must do his best to make sure that for him it will be a recompense by remaining faithful to his inner choice, to the service he has adopted, to his Master's will. The life that is a surrender to concupiscence is no more than a seeming reality, a dream, violent perhaps but evanescent, wrapped in sleep; faithfulness to God is the only real and awakened life (42) in which the soul can be clear and active, can breathe because given to God. Thus it "is ready" (44), and being ready means precisely to have fulfilled one's duty by waiting for the sound of footsteps, the opening door, and the appearance of the Lord.

Thus, within faithfulness, as within joy and suffering, there is this relationship of the soul to the mysterious coming, this waiting for the unknown hour, this hope of a judgment that will be the dawn of beatitude (46). A double uncertainty, but with very different characteristics in the two cases—an absolute uncertainty concerning the time of the Parousia, i.e. death and judgment, but an uncertainty with positive purpose and hope as regards the meaning of the coming and the judgment. The good servant is happy because he is faithful and thus ready for the marvellous, fearful Appearance.

The parable of the ten virgins (xxv, 1-13) brings out a feature that has already been touched upon (xxiv, 25). The waiting for the Lord is not a matter of any kind of illumination, avoiding its duties and devoid of reason and life under the pretext of faith. It is characteristic of the servant who is "faithful and wise." The parable accentuates this again by contrasting the "foolish" virgins with the "wise" ones (xxv, 2) who consider and look ahead—who are wise beforehand, in their refusal when first called; thus they are "ready" (10) and can go in to the marriage. Reason therefore has its use within faith: it is not destroyed, but transfigured; it concentrates on the coming as the ultimate fulfilment of all values; it uses every means it can to remain faithful and ready; and this is no more than what is required by a love, an obedience, and a desire that are all equally absolute. The miracle is that this vigilance is made up indissolubly of the intensity of the desire and the clarity of the vision.

The parable of the talents (xxv, 14-30) emphasizes the other aspect —the concrete fidelity, the proper use of the riches given, the need for inner growth, all with a view to the time that will come for the settling of accounts. Here the contrast is between the man who is "good and faithful" and the one who is "wicked and slothful." The entry into the marriage has become the entry into the joy of the Lord—of our Lord who owns us, who has filled us to overflowing and will reward us with his own joy. This is the eschatological aspect of the Christian labour. Finally, the judgment (xxv, 31-46) brings out the eschatological aspect of Christian charity. Mercy towards the "least brethren," who are Christ, makes Christians merciful as their heavenly Father is merciful and "blessed of my Father"—or rather, as a result of mercy there is realized within them an eternal benediction, "the kingdom prepared . . . from the foundation of the world" (34). Mercy shown here on earth contains its own judgment, and, as it is a love of Christ hidden in those who are his, it leads on to the judgment of love in glory. One thinks inevitably of St. Paul (Eph. i, 3-4) and the God of all blessings who has blessed his own with an immense spiritual blessing in heaven, in Christ.

If one makes a list of the words used in the Gospel to denote this convulsing, intoxicating end of all things, it appears as "the end" (xxiv, 14), identical with the ultimate limits of the spread of the Gospel, hence an aim and object; the "consummation of the world," hence the end of all becoming, in the fullness of growth; the "regeneration"[10] (xix, 28), thus an end which is also a beginning, the birth of a new world; lastly, as the Parousia of the Lord. A world made up of persons can only culminate in a personal act—the return of Christ in glory. Christ the Bridegroom, Christ the Lord, Christ the King: demanding faithfulness, foresight, labour, mercy; all turned towards the awful and blessed mystery of his coming in glory, rewarding perseverance in the faith and thus bringing fulfilment to an eternal choice and an eternal gift of self. The whole Christian life is enveloped in this eternal call; it realizes it in hope, while awaiting the time fixed by the Father when Christ will bring it to completion in truth, for ever.

Christ the Saviour

This is the point of convergence and living centre of all the other themes. The Christian experience is a series of relationships to Christ the Saviour. These relationships are all posited by faith; they each of them embody one particular aspect of faith in Christ by realizing an aspect of union with Christ, an existing before God and his Word that is typical of the Christian experience.

There is the relationship to Christ the Revealer. Christ reveals by his words, which make manifest the secrets of God; by his miracles, which manifest the glory of God; by his forgiveness, which is the

[10] For the meaning of this word, cf. A. Feuillet, *Nouvelle Revue théologique*, 1949, pp. 715-716 & n. 47. Cf. also the note by Fr. Benoit in *L'Évangile selon saint Matthieu* (*Bible de Jérusalem*), p. 116. n. 6.

actual accomplishment of the Word, the Good News of salvation. Faith is the adherence of spirit and heart and action to this Word of God, Christ, who is the bearer—and the object—of the message of salvation.

There is the relationship to Christ as God's Religious. Christ pays absolute homage to the Father who is in heaven. He prays to him, serves him, reveals his holiness and love. He teaches the prayer that gives him glory. He magnifies his mysterious, self-sufficient, absolute omnipotence. He insists on his sensitive, universal, indefatigable tenderness. He enables us to begin to see his consuming holiness and his fearful judgments. He dies to pay him the final homage of obedience, service, supplication, and love. Faith means adherence to this homage and the continuation of this homage, in prayer, adoration, supplication, "graceful" action, in sacrifice even unto death.

There is the relationship to Christ the Servant. Christ came to serve his brothers. He does not spare himself for them, he allows himself to be devoured by them. He encourages them, consoles them, feeds them, cures them. He takes up his cross daily for them, in poverty and fatigue, bearing their incomprehension, their hostility, their persecution, and death at their hands. Faith is adherence to this service and the continuation of this service. It is an imitation of Christ in his brotherly love, through joy and sorrow, and, if necessary, death.

There is the relationship to Christ the Lord. He has all the rights, and can make all the claims, of God. He claims to be loved above all things, he demands to be followed, believed in, served, confessed, even at the cost of life itself. To him belongs our whole existence, and to sacrifice this to him is to pay him the homage that is strictly his due and to save ourselves at the same time. He possesses all the power of God. He is Master over angels and devils as well as over men, the Master of the Sabbath and the Law, the Master of history and of everything that happens; he controls all things; and one day he will come back in the glory of the Father as the sovereign judge of the mankind he has called and redeemed. He possesses God's own joy. He promises the joy of the Kingdom to all who will become his disciples; he delivers from sin and terror; he helps us to bear heavy burdens; he transforms suffering; he makes us exult in God and leads us into the bliss of heaven. He possesses all the glory of God. He revealed it in his miracles, before which the crowds trembled in holy awe. He revealed it to the privileged few at his Transfiguration, with all the marvellous beauty of his being streaming forth from his divinity. He revealed it at his Resurrection, that mystery of the man passing into the other world, entering into the full glory of the Father, appearing then in this world of time and death as the very mystery of eternity and life in God. And he re-ascended to his Father, and this was the fulfilment of his mission. He is henceforth on the right hand of the Father; he holds the whole world—heaven and earth—in his hand, has sovereign power over it, animates it, transforms it. His existence is from now on, and more than ever, an existence with his own (xxviii, 20). He asks his apostles to teach and baptize and rule, but he is the soul of all they do, the invisible power behind all apostolic action. He is that presence, both present and to come, which is at work in the work of evangelization, but which will only reveal itself in all its fullness at the consummation of this present world—the presence that is at work within mankind on the march, so that one day it will be able to find its fulfilment in the joy of the Kingdom. A widening of faith and hope into which love may pour its measure of generosity, until the time comes for the reward without measure in the glory of the Father.

The Christian experience thus appears as a network of relationships all centred on Christ—as the Revealer, to whose "heart" and acts we must adhere; as the Religious, like whom we must do homage to the Father; as the Servant, like whom we must serve our fellow men; as Lord, King, Son, to whom there must be absolute obedience, self-giving, self-sacrifice; in clearness of mind, faithfulness, suffering, joy; in trembling aspiration towards the fulfilment, which is at once Parousia, Judgment, Beatitude, and the Kingdom of Heaven.

Concluding Remarks

There is a place for the Christian experience, and that place is to be found in the depths of the soul—in the heart, or the spirit—where God calls, forgives, and gives life, and where each man replies in secret, and is converted each day by choosing God. This means that the Christian experience is one of absolute inwardness. It takes place in man's most hidden depths; it involves his entire spiritual freedom; it only exists in this freedom; everything that can—and must—produce it outside, only has value as a reflection and an expression, a relationship to this spiritual source in the spirit. Since the Christian is a man who is being converted all his life, what goes on inside him determines the value of what goes on outside him entirely.

There are lines of force that govern this experience. It is not to be defined primarily as a matter of feeling. No doubt the deepest feelings—fear, trust, tenderness, joy—are all present in it; but they are integrated into a greater whole, and taken up in a movement of the whole person. The experience is to be defined in the first place in terms of spiritual acts, involving self-commitment and generosity of soul. There is the inward act of homage to the Father in the dual movement of adoration and love, detachment and attachment, supplication and exultation. There is the mysterious dialogue between the soul and God—an ascending line of Christian experience. There are the acts that make faithfulness real—the inner impulse is not in itself sufficient, and it would not be a true one if it did not bear fruit in obedience, purity of life and perseverance, in the clear-sightedness of an awakened and reflective soul. In particular, there is the love of the neighbour—serving, forgiving, bearing witness, and suffering for Christ. All these simply make up one immense act of homage to the Father, springing from the heart and inspiring to action, manifesting and nourishing true love. Inner and outer, act and action, are here both implied in each other: no true homage that does not bear fruit in service, no true service that is not rooted in inner homage. This is the "totalitarian" aspect of the experience, whose lines of force build up the whole field of human activity.

There is an atmosphere in which this experience is at home. First, joy, since Christianity is the good news of salvation and beatitude in God, and Christ is the Comforter, through whom comes the joy of the sons of God. But also, waiting and hope. For the salvation and beatitude are only in embryo, and only approaching their fulfilment. The joy and the suffering are eschatological; and the Christian is raised up by an immense aspiration towards Plenitude, Fulfilment, the Parousia. The gift is also a promise, the trust is shot through with fear, vigilance is fed by hope: this is the paradoxical mystery at the heart of the Christian experience.

There is a centre to this experience, and this centre is Christ. Through Christ come the call and all the gifts of God, and in him all the movements of the soul come together. He is the paradox in whom the paradox of ourselves is founded and explained. He is ultimately the place, the source, the light, and the fullness of all Christian experience. Although it is not exactly said, the Christian experience is an experience in Christ. It is a network of spiritual relationships that derive their existence, their density, their meaning, and their dynamism from Christ.

There is a root to this experience, and the root is faith, in the full sense in which it means that movement of the soul whereby one adheres to the Word and the Promise, and to Him who brings them. It is through faith that the call is received and interiorized, and fructifies; through faith that the Father reveals himself in Christ; through faith that the experience itself is embarked upon, develops, and finds fulfilment in an infinite aspiration. The Christian takes his existence from the mystery in which God who calls, and man who responds, meet; and it is from the mystery of this existence in God that the Christian experience springs. Thus the experience and the mystery are mutually involved within each other: herein lies the whole paradox of Christianity.

CHAPTER FIVE

The Experience of the Spirit in St. Paul

A Christian is someone to whom Christ has communicated his Spirit, and he is thus, rightly considered, spiritual (Gal. vi, 1). His life is a life in the Spirit, and the gift that he has received is personal and at the same time of the Church.

"In the beginning, in Jerusalem, the experience of the Spirit was communal (Pentecost, etc.), and this 'social' experience lies behind all individual Christian experience. The spirit which is given to all Christians is something that came down once and for all upon the community of the Messias and thereby introduced the new epoch."[1] This was continued in St. Paul. For at his conversion (Acts ix, 1-9 & xxvi, 12-18), under the influence of Christ, St. Paul underwent an experience that was at once intensely personal and at the same time involved the Church in three ways—because it revealed to him that Christ was present in its members, because it took him into the Christian community, there to be instructed and baptized, and because his own personal mission proved to be that of bringing pagans into the Church.

The experience of the Spirit by the rest of the faithful was also to be an experience of the Church. This was so, firstly, because the Spirit is given by the Church and received in the Church at the time of our initiation into Christianity: "For in one Spirit were we all baptized into one body . . . and in one Spirit we have all been made to drink" (I Cor. xii, 13); "Now he . . . that hath anointed us, is God: who also hath sealed us, and given the pledge of the Spirit

[1] L. Cerfaux, *La Théologie de l'Église suivant St. Paul*, 2nd ed. (Paris, 1948), p. 173.

in our hearts" (II Cor. i, 22); "in Christ . . . in whom also believing, you were signed with the holy spirit of promise. Who is the pledge of our inheritance" (Eph. i, 14); "God our Saviour . . . saved us, by the laver of regeneration, and renovation of the Holy Ghost, whom he hath poured forth upon us abundantly through Jesus Christ our Saviour" (Titus iii, 5). The gift of the Spirit is in Christian eyes sacramental.

It is of the Church in another sense too, for we receive it to the extent that we are incorporated into the Church, so that we may be united with all other Christians and built with them into the one Temple of God. This is the meaning of the famous passages in I Corinthians: "Know you not that you are the temple of God, and that the Spirit of God dwelleth in you? But if any man violate the temple of God, him shall God destroy. For the temple of God is holy: which you are" (I Cor. iii, 16-17). The temple of God is the "Christian community";[2] it is the Christian community that the Spirit first comes to sanctify; it is from the Christian community that Christians take their existence, and in it they are anointed and consecrated like living stones. And though the Spirit dwells in the depths of each individual soul—"Know you not that your members are the temple of the Holy Ghost, who is in you, whom you have from God?" (I Cor. vi, 19)—this is so that they may be "not their own" (*ibid.*) but belong to God in Christ and the Church, drawn completely into the single life of the one body by the spirit of unity. This is repeated in different words in the Epistle to the Ephesians: "Jesus Christ . . . in whom you also are built together into an habitation of God in the spirit." And the consequences of this are portentous, for it means that the Spirit is given to the Church, in the Church, and by the Church. There is no separate experience of the Spirit within the confines of any particular individuality: however deeply personal the experience may be, it is always something that relates to the Church. This conviction was to determine St. Paul's doctrine and attitude in the matter of the astonishing and magnificent, but highly dangerous, experience involved in the charisma of the Holy Spirit.

On the other hand, the effect of the Spirit on the regenerated person is more deeply personal than can ever be described. What

[2] J. Huby, *Première Épître aux Corinthiens*, Coll. "*Verbum Salutis*" (Paris, 1946), p. 113, with the passage from Cerfaux, n. 2.

takes place is literally a transformation. Before he is given the gift of the Spirit, man is a soul without any real strength, defeated by sin and the flesh and tyrannized over by evil and the Evil Spirit. After he has been invaded by the *Pneuma,* he is a different creature altogether: his *nous* has become a *pneuma* in the strongest sense of the word, because now he shares in the divine *Pneuma.* Henceforward his human *pneuma* is a spirit visited, purified, and vitalized in its depths by the Spirit of God, "the *nous* raised by faith and baptism to a supernatural order of being and acting"[3] and therefore deified by the power of the Spirit in its powers of knowing and acting, and with the ability, in Christ, to "approach the Father" and glorify him. Because there is rightly no opposition between the person and the community; because the person only draws life from becoming attached to the community in which alone he can find fulfilment; because he must serve the community if the community is to enable him to fulfil himself; because both person and community rediscover each other, exalted and consummated to the same degree, in the unity of Christ, the perfect man, person and community in one—therefore the gift of the Spirit is made to both at once, and endless prospects of development open up before the person within the body of Christ and the temple of God.

1. *The Spiritual Man*

The man regenerated by the Spirit has himself become spiritual, but only rudimentarily, and he is not yet able to have any experience of the Spirit. He is a child who has to become a man, an adult, one who is "perfect" in St. Paul's sense of the word. This theme is of the utmost importance in St. Paul; its central statement is to be found at the beginning of I Corinthians (ii, 4-16 to iii, 1-4).

About the meaning of this "perfection" recent opinion is in agreement:[4] the perfect person is the truly spiritual person. He is not the beginning Christian, whose virtue is not established, whose inner unity has not been achieved, whose soul has not grown habitually responsive to the Holy Spirit, and whose vision is therefore not suf-

[3] J. Coppens, *Confirmation,* in *Suppl. au Dict. de la Bible,* Vol. II, col. 139.

[4] F. Prat, *La Théologie de saint Paul,* Vol. II (Paris, 1929), pp. 49-51; E. B. Allo, *Première Épître aux Corinthiens* (Paris, 1934), pp. 39 *et seq.,* 52-54; Huby, *op. cit.,* pp. 85, 93, 97, 105 *et seq.;* J. Bonsirven, *L'Évangile de Paul* (Paris, 1948), p. 282.

ficiently purified, not sufficiently sharp, not sufficiently acclimatized to the divine mystery to enter into the revealed secret, the "wisdom of God." Nor is he necessarily a mystic, one who has had graces of prayer in the strict sense of the word, who has had God's presence in the depths of the soul revealed in full consciousness; nor necessarily, strictly speaking, a charismatic either, one who vibrates under the touch of the Spirit to produce the extraordinary phenomena described at length later on in the Epistle. He is the ardent Christian who has reached maturity after much effort and constant faithfulness, who through docility to the action of the Spirit has been purified, and learnt detachment and generosity of heart. The perfect are thus all whom the Spirit has helped to grow in virtue, who are "daily increasing their experimental knowledge of God and their power to read more deeply into doctrine";[5] all those to whom the scheme of redemption, summed up in the mystery of Christ crucified and resurrected, appears "lit up in bright light and assimilated more and more deeply by their experience and meditation"[6]—in short, all who in this Spirit have gained a personal knowledge, had "experience," of the mystery of God. The mature person, unlike the child, has the experience of life behind him; the perfect person, unlike the little child, has the experience of the things of God behind him. Let us look into this a little more closely.

"Howbeit we speak wisdom among the perfect . . . we speak the wisdom of God in a mystery, a wisdom which is hidden, which God ordained before the world, unto our glory" (ii, 6-7). That is the real field of experience known to the perfect:[7] a wisdom that is the mystery of God in the eternally secret scheme of Redemption, hidden in the "depths of God," in the will of God, "by whom you are called unto the fellowship of his Son, Jesus Christ our Lord" (i, 9); ultimately, in the actual mystery of Christ, who reveals and realizes the eternal mystery and is thus himself the mystery of God: *Christōs theou soirian* (i, 24). Always it is one Christian mystery with which we are concerned, but here this is not something that can be accepted immediately in the earliest stages of faith and affirmed as the Word of God; it is something that has to be experienced personally

[5] Allo, p. 54.

[6] Huby, p. 65.

[7] Cf. L. Cerfaux, *Le Christ dans la théologie de saint Paul* (Paris, 1951), pp. 203 *et seq.*

and assimilated into one's own life, and so savoured and understood much more deeply. The wisdom is defined objectively by its content: a new world opens before one, known truths are understood from within;[8] but this presupposes the influence of the Spirit, meditation, experience, and therefore a deep personal knowledge penetrating into the depths of the mystery of Christ, in whom are "all the treasures of the wisdom of God."[9]

Now this wisdom is transmitted by the Spirit: all the gifts of God that form this mysterious wisdom, "to us God hath revealed them, by his Spirit" (ii, 10-12). Since it is God's own secrets that are involved, we must be in God to understand them: now the Spirit is in God (as the spirit of man is in man), and this inwardness enables it to penetrate into "the deep things of God." God communicates his Spirit to us, so that the Spirit may reveal to us what it knows: "Now we have received not the spirit of this world, but the Spirit that is of God: that we may know the things that are given us from God" (ii, 12)—i.e., the participation in his mystery, his wisdom, his Christ, which constitutes the essence of the Christian life. Since those with whom we are concerned are "perfect," this knowledge is the result of the Spirit's teaching from within, it presupposes a whole labour of illumination and penetration and comprehension, and that is why it ends in "a doctrine of the Spirit" (ii, 13), for a doctrine, or discourse, is thought finding expression in words. An awareness of the mystery of Redemption and Beatitude in Christ, expressing itself in inspired words and producing the same sort of awareness in the perfect—that is what is meant by "speaking wisdom among the perfect."

Beginning from this, St. Paul—with his great fondness for widening horizons, and establishing general types—draws two distinctions, one explicit, between psychic and spiritual persons, the other implicit, between those who are perfectly spiritual and those who are only imperfectly so. The psychic person is (ii, 14) the "unspiritual" man, who is without the divine *pneuma* and "quite content to be so."[10] He

[8] HUBY, pp. 87-88.

[9] ALLO, p. 40. Cf. L. CERFAUX, *L'Église des Corinthiens* (Paris, 1946), pp. 42-44. The above pages had been written before I came across this excellent little book, chs. iii & vii of which should be read in this connection.

[10] HUBY, p. 98. This interpretation has been contested by J. DUPONT in *Gnosis* (Louvain, 1949), pp. 151 *et seq.*, who sees this passage as describing two kinds of Christians, who have either had, or not had, revelations about the after-life.

is shut in on himself, and can see nothing outside himself; and this is a frightful condition to be in. For the Word of God is exclusively concerned with the realities of the Spirit, and is only to be judged by the power of the Spirit. Because the unspiritual person lacks this power, the Christian mystery seems utterly absurd to him, and he is bound to reject it. The spiritual person is, by comparison, a man from another world (ii, 15-16). Possessing the Spirit of God, he is raised far above the psychic level, he escapes all its categories and cannot possibly be judged according to any of them—whilst at the same time he himself can judge all things, can judge the whole of reality, the whole Christian mystery and even those who reject it—all in profound humility, without any attempt to "teach the Lord his business," but as someone who has received the power of understanding whereby Christ penetrated into the mystery of God and expressed it in human thoughts and words. Because the Spirit of God has taken control of his own spirit, and transformed it, the spiritual person knows, possesses and can express the wisdom of God.

Besides these truly spiritual people, there are rickety spirituals like the Corinthians themselves (iii, 1-4). These are not "psychic," for they are Christians who have received the Spirit and so are embryonically spiritual; but they have not delivered themselves up to the Spirit: they are hindered and paralyzed by powers still carnal, egoistic, vain, worldly. They are like babes in that they do not understand what they have been given, and like children again they waste their time in silly quarrels. A prey to their passions, unamenable to the Spirit, deaf to its appeals, thinking and acting "like men," they are quite incapable of seeing and grasping the wisdom of God. Lacking unity, paralyzed by an inner discord, they are theoretically spiritual but behave in fact like "psychic" people, the men of the flesh. As they do not live according to the Spirit of God, they are unable to understand the gifts that God has given them, or experience any of the things of God; they stagnate in the puerile state to which their feebleness condemns them. The same features are mentioned again in Hebrews v, 1-11—Christians who have had time to become adults, "masters," but instead of developing have remained children; who are therefore unable to accept solid food (the doctrine of the priesthood of Christ), unable to "discern good and evil," and who thus need to learn the rudiments of the doctrine all over again.

Thus, then, St. Paul divides men into three spiritual categories.

First there are the "psychics," who are without the *pneuma* and know nothing about the things of God and therefore reject them as absurd. These people are usually in the power of carnal forces (cf. Romans vii, and viii, 4-14); they exist in the flesh, walk according to the flesh, live according to the flesh, and become "carnal."[11] The passage from psychic to carnal is inevitable, once the call of the Spirit has been rejected. Then there are the imperfect Christians—not beginning Christians, but Christians who have remained beginners—infantile, as distinct from infant, Christians. These are definitely not "psychics"; they have the Spirit—they have not cast it out—but they paralyze it so that it cannot act. The only way of following the promptings of the Spirit is by fighting against the powers of the flesh that remain active in every Christian; but these people have let themselves be defeated. It was normal for them to be children at first; it is abnormal for them to have remained children. And so they have become rickety creatures, for whom stagnation means regression. Henceforward they too are carnal, in the sense that they do not allow the spirit to act because they give way to the fleshly impulses that paralyze it. They are recalcitrant to the Spirit, opaque to its light, deaf to its appeals, no longer malleable like children but hardened by their lack of generosity. And the result is that they are unable to take the solid food of the complete doctrine, unable to distinguish properly between good and evil, to understand the hidden wisdom. In a word, they are unable to experience the things of God, unable to experience the Spirit. Of course, there are various degrees: the state referred to in Hebrews v, 11-14, seems vastly more serious than that envisaged in I Cor. iii, 1-4. But though the spirit has not been extinguished, it has been paralyzed in its vital spot—and the result is spiritual infantilism.

Finally, there is the perfect Christian. This is not "someone who has all the virtues,"[12] who has reached a stage when the flesh is no longer at war with the spirit. It is someone who does not usually give way to the powers of the flesh, and is usually responsive to the demands made upon him by the Spirit. Through conflict he has developed his spiritual organism, has disciplined himself, has grown up and become an adult. Because he has remained faithful, he has learned to

[11] The word does not occur in Rom. viii, 4-14. St. Paul uses circumlocutions—being, living, walking, according to the flesh.

[12] J. Bonsirven, *Épître aux Hébreux*, Coll. "*Verbum Salutis,*" p. 287.

understand the mystery of God, to distinguish between good and evil, to feel and follow the attraction of the spirit, to grow towards the infinite. He is able to experience the things of God, to experience the Spirit: he is spiritual. This, it seems to me, is the Christian St. Paul means when he speaks of the Christian as such. In Romans viii, when he is describing the Christian who has been liberated by the Spirit, he undoubtedly means the perfect Christian, for only the perfect Christian follows the promptings of the Spirit and walks in the Spirit and lives in the Spirit. This helps to explain St. Paul's repeated affirmations: it is the normal thing for the Christian to experience the Spirit, but to do so he must be a real Christian, adult, perfect, spiritual. We can now try to describe the experience of the Spirit that St. Paul attributes to the Christian as thus defined—i.e., the person who is in St. Paul's view the Christian as such.

2. *The Structured Experience*

The first thing to be noted is that this experience is not by any means a simple relationship between the soul and the Spirit, a sort of absolute, autonomous, self-sufficient contact between the soul and God. It is a structured experience that comes into existence and develops out of a network of extremely complex spiritual relationships.

In the first place, it is an experience within the Church. We have already seen that it is to the Church that the Spirit is given, so that it may become the Temple of God: it is only by being built into this great Temple—the only Temple—that each individual Christian can become his own personal temple in holiness of soul and body.[13] In another metaphor, the Church is the Body of Christ, and it is the Spirit (I Cor. xii, 4, 7, 11), "one and the same Spirit, [who] worketh, dividing to every one according as he will." There is thus great individual diversity within the truly divine unity of the one single efficient cause, the one single organizing will, the one single Person who imparts an infinite diversity to the ways of sharing in his own unique riches. All the various experiences will therefore be different and irreducible, but all will be equally unified in their source, which is the Spirit, in the point at which they all meet, which is the Body, and in their end, "the unity of the Spirit in the bond

[13] L. Cerfaux, *La Théologie de l'Église suivant saint Paul*, pp. 113 *et seq.* & n. 3. Cf. p. 27 & n. 22.

of peace, [for there is] one Body and one Spirit" (Eph. iv, 3-4). Built together (Eph. ii, 22), supporting one another (Eph. iv, 3), growing together, becoming conscious of their sonship together (Rom. viii, 16)[14] in the infinite diversity and mysterious profundity of their personal experiences—these are the things that characterize the true Christians. Finally, the Church is the people of God, the new people who are also a spiritual people—a people no longer under the influence of the flesh but under the influence of the Spirit *tois kata pneuma*[15] (Rom. viii, 5)—a people of the truly circumcized, "and the circumcision is that of the heart, in the spirit, not in the letter" (Rom. ii, 28); "for we are the circumcision, who in spirit serve God" (Phil. iii, 3); the people of the new testament—the testament of the Spirit (II Cor. iii, 6)—amongst whom everyone, great and small, has his own personal knowledge—the law written in his heart (Heb. viii, 10, & cf. II Cor. iii, 3), his own intimate acquaintanceship with God. One God, one people—because there is one Spirit who communicates himself to all and so transforms all by uniting them.[16] When it is remembered that the Spirit represents the first-fruits of the divine goods (Rom. viii, 23) and the pledge of the inheritance (Eph. i, 14), it will be understood that he raises the whole Church on earth towards its fulfilment in heaven, makes the temple ascend, the body grow, the people increase in one irresistible movement of longing, supplication, and love, whose impulse is felt in the deepest depths of each individual person's heart. But by this very fact, this personal experience will always be an experience within the Church, within a greater whole. It may be said that "Pauline theology is always concerned with the Christian's *esse christianum* and therefore his existence within the group,"[17] and that in the Pauline conception the individual and the Church "are inseparable. There is no atomistic, disintegrating individualism, and no all-absorbing totalitarian collectivism."[18] Instead, there are persons made for society and a society made for persons, since both persons and society are to be completed together, in the unity of the Spirit, in "one Man," Christ.

But the Church of the Spirit is also the Church of the Word of

[14] J. Huby, *Épître aux Romains*, Coll. "*Verbum Salutis*" (Paris, 1940), p. 290.
[15] L. Cerfaux, pp. 53 & 123.
[16] *Ibid.*, p. 183: "In the Pauline churches it is above all on the occasion of liturgical assemblies that the Holy Spirit is communicated. In this respect too, the whole of the Christian experience emphasizes the social life, the Church."
[17] *Ibid.*, p. 176.
[18] H. Koehnlein, quoted *ibid.*, p. 140.

God. It is by receiving the Word, and obeying the faith, that we enter—and remain within—the Church. The experience of the Spirit will therefore necessarily be linked with this absolute norm—the Word of God as preached first by the Apostle and after him by the Church. Let us take a few relevant passages.

"For our gospel hath not been unto you in word only, but in power also, and in the Holy Ghost and in much fulness . . . And you became followers of us and of the Lord; receiving the word in much tribulation, with joy of the Holy Ghost" (I Thess. i, 5-6). Two experiences are suggested in this passage—the Apostle's in preaching the Word, which manifests the power of affirmation[19] and the fullness of conviction that come from the Holy Spirit and give such solid confirmation of the testimony of Christ (I Cor. i, 6); and the experience of the faithful who receive the Word and live it in tribulation, with joy in the Spirit, and in this way follow Paul and Christ in their lives. The most important thing here is the Word: the Spirit comes and seals it in the Apostle and confirms it in the faithful.

In Gal. iii, 1-6, St. Paul appeals to the experience the Galatians had when they were converted. They received the Spirit, and "they were conscious of this, not only by miraculous outward signs . . . but still more by the change that took place within them, their sense of inner conviction, the enlightenment they received, the good desires they felt."[20] Now, they received the Spirit, not "by the works of the law," but "by the hearing of the faith."[21] Thus they "began in the Spirit," with the help of God himself, who "gave generously" (cf. Phil. i, 19). Here again it is by receiving the Word that one is filled with the Spirit and brought under its influence: faith in the Word gives entry into life in the Spirit.

"You know that when you were heathens, you went to dumb idols, according as you were led. Wherefore I give you to understand, that no man speaking by the Spirit of God saith Anathema to Jesus. And no man can say the Lord Jesus, but by the Holy Ghost" (I Cor. xii, 2-3). Here we find two radically opposite kinds of religious behaviour. The pagan is a man subject to obscure irrational forces; he lives under the sign of feeling, carnal feeling, and his passionate

[19] Rather, doubtless, than of miracles. This agrees with D. Buzy, *Épîtres aux Thessaloniciens*, in the *Sainte Bible* by L. Pirot, Vol. XII (Paris, 1938), in n. 1. For the opposite point of view, see Cerfaux, *op. cit.*, p. 140.

[20] M. J. Lagrange, *Épître aux Galates* (Paris, 1926), p. 58.

[21] "The opening (of the ear and the soul) that is faith."

impulses are given free rein and allowed to run riot. The Christian lives under the sign of belief, by a spiritual impulse informed and characterized from within by a word of God, whose utterances are strict and compelling. If some demoniac force takes possession of the Christian,[22] this is immediately made known and condemned by its hostility to the rule of faith. Conversely a clear affirmation of the formula of the faith—"Jesus is the Lord"—is the usual sign of the presence of the Spirit. It is only by obeying the Word that we can live in the Spirit.

One final section of Pauline theology remains to be explored—chapters xii-xiv of I Corinthians, where, during a discussion of the charisma, three essential facts concerning the structure of the Christian experience are brought out—its connections with the theological virtues (especially charity), with service to the community, and with reason. The main lines of St. Paul's teaching seem to reduce themselves to the following.

There are two kinds of charisma: charity—and all the rest. Charity is the actual heart of Christianity and the "only way." It is the fundamental gift of the Holy Spirit—"poured forth in our hearts by the Holy Ghost who is given to us" (Rom. v, 5). It confers Christian being to such a degree that without it we are nothing and the other charismata have neither use nor value. It is the only permanent reality, literally eternal, the living power of the Kingdom of Heaven introduced into the changing and growing body. It is at once love of God and love of the neighbour, and if in this passage St. Paul spends most of his time on its latter aspect, this is because he is discussing a problem of spiritual evaluation and practical behaviour within a community. Now this love which is man's primary power and which decides the value of his personal being (xiii, 1-3) is also the primary power in the community—it is literally charity that builds up the Church: *ē de agapē oikodomei* (I Cor. viii, 1). Cf. Eph. iv, 16: the body realizes its growth *eis oikodomen eautou en agapē*. This Agape of the Father, of Christ, of Christians, is thus a single current of power that completes the Redemption by creating the Body of Christ, the place in which the Redemption is properly achieved, the proper form of redeemed existence, the "fulness of Christ." Thus everything else has to take its place around this constructive force,

[22] On this obscure phenomenon, see ALLO, *Première Épître aux Corinthiens*, pp. 321 *et seq*.

and the charismata are to be judged according to the assistance they give charity in building up the Church. There are thus two incommensurable orders of spiritual reality involved here. And St. Paul wants two things to be realized—on the one hand, the primacy of what is invisible, charity being nothing preternatural, or miraculous, or solidly tangible, but an invisible force inserted into the heart and involved in life, all the visible miraculous side of the charisma being secondary and subordinate; and on the other hand the primacy of active over passive, for charity is the gift of self to the will of God, unstinting service of the whole body, while the whole passive, felt, experienced order of the charisma is, once again, inferior to charity and presupposes it as the basis of its value and effectiveness. Life in the Spirit is thus characterized by the absolute primacy of generous-hearted love; so that the first desire, the first prayer, the first endeavour, should be for the acquisition of charity: "Follow after charity" (xiv, 1). The essential Christian experience will thus be the experience of charity.

It goes without saying, of course, that charity is linked with faith and hope, its inseparable companions. St. Paul indicates this himself by putting the theological virtues in a group by themselves (xiii, 13). And other passages explain the connection; for example, "You are made void of Christ, you who are justified in the law: you are fallen from grace. For we in spirit by faith wait for the hope of justice. For in Christ Jesus . . . availeth . . . faith that worketh by charity" (Gal. v, 4-6). The spirit as "impulsive energy," and faith as the basic conviction, are "two operative principles distinct from each other" (Lagrange) but inseparable, because faith is an intrinsic part of the movement of the spirit. It rejects, in fact, justification by the law, and puts all its hope in Christ, but in this faith that works by love the spirit is active, drawing the soul towards hope—towards the divine goods that justification enables us to hope for. This passage is remarkable for thus associating the spirit with the three theological virtues and making it the basis of hope (cf. Rom. xv, 13).

It must be added that this force that is both a trinity and a unity governs the whole Christian endeavour, and introduces us into the full drama of the flesh and the spirit (Gal. v, 3, 26). The experience of the spirit is in marked contrast to the experience of the flesh; they are two opposed conflicting principles, each doing its best to hinder the other; but whereas one leads to slavery and sin, the other works for freedom and charity. Each manifests itself in its effects, the works of the flesh contaminating the spirit and the body and disintegrating the human being, the fruits of the Spirit transforming being and action and unifying man within and without in the image of Christ, as a power of freedom and benediction. The whole spiritual life—and particularly active charity, with its endless variety—is thus the direct result and the necessary sign of the presence of the Spirit; the whole life of virtue is to be found within the experience of the Spirit. This being so, it is not surprising to find that life in the spirit should be likewise a participation in the Kingdom of God: "For the kingdom of God is not meat and drink; but justice, and peace, and joy in the Holy Ghost. For he that in this serveth Christ, pleaseth God, and is approved of men" (Rom. xiv, 17-18). No doubt it is possible to isolate, as Fr. Lagrange does, the phrase, "joy in the Holy Ghost," and say that spiritual joy burns forth when the soul enters into justice, into peace with God, and that in this way the Kingdom of God is established within it; but one can go a good deal further and believe that "the Kingdom of God as it is in heaven . . . is transported into the soul . . . and produces the fruits of the Spirit there." The Spirit is then the power that "establishes the bond between heaven and earth,"[23] because it introduces the soul into the riches of the kingdom of glory. Here again the fruits of the Spirit comprise the whole Christian life—justice, peace and joy—but it is a kind of resurrected life, by which we find ourselves already living in heaven.

After this widening of the horizon, let us return to the charismata, and especially to the problem of their exact value. When they are properly subordinated to charity, their value is, on its own level, very real. The charismata are given by the Spirit for the advantage of everybody (I Cor. xii, 7), for the building up of the Church (xiv, 4, 5, 12, 17, 26). So far as they are concerned, the Body is the primary value:[24] "For in one Spirit were we all baptized into one body . . . and in one Spirit we have all been made to drink" (I Cor. xii, 13): at baptism and confirmation the Spirit is given for the sake of the unity of the Body. And the first end of Christ's activity (xii, 12) is the Body, for Christ "has many members and brings all

[23] L. Cerfaux, quoted and followed by Huby, *Épître aux Romains*, p. 462.
[24] L. Cerfaux, *La Théologie de l'Église* . . . pp. 182 *et seq.*

Christians into the unity of the Body."[25] The primary value is therefore to be found at the heart of all the diversity, in the unity of the body, expressing and incarnating the unity of the Spirit, the unity of Christ, the unity of God the Trinity (I Cor. xii, 4-6). Seen in this light, the charismata are entirely subordinate to the growth of the Church in Unity; and as they represent above all else the sudden control of individuals by the Spirit in the actual liturgical Assembly, the problem that arises for St. Paul concerns the vital tension between those who are thus inspired and the community in general. Hence the first rule: the charisma must "edify the Church" in the strict sense of the word, i.e. bind it together and not dislocate it; and therefore the principle upon which their relative value is to be ascertained will be their usefulness as constructive forces.

The requirements called for by the particular structure of the Body are here once again primary, and St. Paul gives their order very clearly, in xii, 27-30 at least. First come the charismata that serve the Word of God—those that appertain to apostles, prophets, doctors; next, miracles and healings; finally, very far behind the rest, speaking in tongues and interpretation. It is easy to see that it is the speaking in tongues, the "spectacular" charism,[26] that St. Paul is particularly concerned about. As it is a gift of God, there can be no question of rejecting it; but he is determined to keep it within well-defined limits. In the first place, it is inferior to the rest: chapter xiv is devoted to an exaltation of prophecy at the expense of it. Prophecy edifies and comforts the whole Church, whereas speaking in tongues only half-edifies the speaker, since it is confined to his *pneuma* and leaves his *nous* "without fruit" (xiv, 2, 4, 14); it does not, in itself, edify the Church, because the understanding of the faithful can find nothing in it for their own benefit or the praise of God. Or rather, it must indeed edify the Church, otherwise it would not be one of God's gifts, but it does so by appearing as something extraordinary and miraculous, and this supplies its second limit—it is dangerous. In the person speaking in tongues, the "spiritual emotion" (in Bergson's sense) that has overtaken the high point of his spirit arouses bodily emotion. He is gradually invaded by "prophetic fury," he vibrates under an invisible bow, he becomes

[25] L. Cerfaux, *ibid.*, pp. 217 *et seq.*, and Huby, *Première Épître aux Corinthiens*, pp. 286-288.

[26] Huby, p. 298.

oblivious of himself, he is at the mercy of passive feeling, he expresses himself in a language grown incomprehensible, a "barbarian" amongst "barbarians." Because a Christian does not lose his carnality, he runs the risk of being caught up again in the old pagan forces slumbering within him; because he may have once been a pagan himself, he runs a double risk of reviving old habits whose power has not been properly extinguished;[27] because his fellow Christians are men like himself, he runs the risk of arousing them, not to any spiritual communion, but merely to some vague kind of mental contagion, and thus—in the eyes of an outsider—transforming "the whole church come together in one place" into madmen (xiv, 23). One commentator has even referred to the "orgy of charismata that liturgical meetings were being turned into."[28] There was thus a danger of the "pathetic" stifling the spiritual, of Greek paganism stifling the young Christian faith. If God granted such charisma it was no doubt so that he might take hold of new converts in their whole being and manifest his power on the very level at which the power of demoniac forces had been active previously—a further example of that divine method of teaching[29] whereby the human being is spiritualized gradually. But such condescension is merely provisional, such miracles are meant to disappear, these inferior signs are destined to vanish in a purer light. Hence St. Paul's prudence: he exalts prophecy and merely gives speaking in tongues a "general pass"—"And I would have you all to speak with tongues. . . . Wherefore, brethren, be zealous to prophesy; and forbid not to speak with tongues" (xiv, 5, 39). Thus we have to record once again his severe criticism of all matters relating to feeling and the extraordinary, any succumbing to emotion; the primacy of the spiritual is never forgotten.

When he comes to the use of the charisma (xiv, 26-40), St. Paul insists very strongly on the requirements of reason—reason enlightened by faith, of course, since it pertains to those who are "in sense . . . perfect" (xiv, 20), who do not allow themselves to be carried away by their impulses but keep their self-control (xiv, 32), who are not believers in a God of disorder but in a God of peace

[27] A. J. Festugière, *L'Idéal religieux des Grecs et l'Évangile* (Paris, 1932), pp. 139 *et seq.*, and *Le monde gréco-romain au temps de Notre Seigneur*, Vol. II (Paris, 1935), p. 183.

[28] Cerfaux, *op. cit.*, p. 164.

[29] There are some excellent remarks on this in Huby, *op. cit.*, p. 349.

(32-33). Order (cf. Col. ii, 5), decency, respect for the Church, personal and general usefulness, the traditions of the Churches of the saints, obedience to the Apostle—these are the highly reasonable criteria which St. Paul adduces. But he does not primarily recommend them because they are reasonable, but because, being reasonable, they are also signs of a kind of respect that has a religious value—a respect for God, who is a God of peace (33), to whom prayer should give witness; a respect for other believers (xvi, 19, 26-31) and non-believers (22-25), who are to be edified; and a respect for oneself as an inspired person who must remain worthy of his God (32) and a member of a community which must be served (xiv, 2-6, 12-13, 19). Decency and order are a law of the Church because they are a way of paying homage to God—to such a point that, if a man is inspired to speak in tongues and has no interpreter handy, he must contain the movement of the Spirit within himself and keep its secret within his own heart: "But if there be no interpreter, let him hold his peace in the Church, and speak to himself and to God" (28). *Silentium tibi laus . . .*

This criticism of inspiration is of the utmost value for our present discussion, for it provides us with a threefold table of values—the primacy of the theological virtues, especially charity, over all other charismata; the primacy of the charisma of service over the extraordinary charismata; and the primacy of spiritual judgment over feeling and passive submission. The inspired person is only truly spiritual—and his experience only authentic—when he is included within the whole life of the Church and his experience is put at the service of charity and of that purity of spirit that is a homage to God. Since the supremely free manifestation of the Spirit is thus to be judged by its usefulness to the Church, this experience will include an extreme relativity in its visible forms and at the same time a permanent unity in its deeper content: the job of deciding upon it belongs to theology, and to the magisterium of the Church reacting to the spiritual mood of the moment. But throughout all this it is the absolute mastery of the Spirit that is manifest in this great experience, at once personal and of the Church, which has its roots in Christian initiation, is realized in the individual "manifestation" of the Spirit, and is ordained to the service of the Church.

3. *Personal Experience*

The Spirit as a Liberating Power. The main passage that we may take as our starting-point is chapter viii of the Epistle to the Romans, with its three great themes of deliverance, aspiration, and triumphant certainty. To get the first theme in its right perspective, we must go back for a moment to the very vigorous and highly schematized first draft in chapter vii.[30] Here the subject is man fallen and unregenerated by grace, faced by the obligations of the moral law as formulated by Moses, or as they appear in the natural law when the conscience is sufficiently strong and enlightened.[31] We may say in fact that the subject is the predicament of the religious man without the grace of God. He is torn inwardly, the centre of a conflict that ends in defeat, which in its turn ends in a kind of slavery. This lived contradiction is literally a deep mystery at the centre of his consciousness, and the man has in a way a direct experience of a mystery. "For that which I work, I understand not" (15, cf. 19). A lived experience of the violence to which action can subject the will, an acute awareness of the consequent slavery, a bitter experience of defeat, distress, and a longing for help—such are the essential elements of this complex of the flesh. The worst thing of all is that in this torn conscience the apex of the spirit, though tyrannized over by the flesh, remains perfectly clear, and is condemned at each new effort to the anguish of watching its own defeat. When the experience of the Spirit comes along, it inserts itself within all this misery, and for this reason it appears in the first place as a liberating force.

The facts of this experience are as follows. The Spirit dwells within the Christian (9, 10, 11): Christians possess the Spirit (9) as a deep, permanent presence of divine activity in that secret region of the spirit or heart which is the divine part of man, the holy of holies. But the Spirit is not an inert guest, and man is not a dead temple. The Spirit is the very power of God, it comes and transforms the *nous* and turns it into a *pneuma,* and the spirit, thus deified, becomes a redoubtable combative force that can henceforth face up to the flesh and beat it on its own ground. Spirit and spirit are

[30] Cf. P. Benoît, *La Loi et la croix d'après saint Paul,* in *Revue biblique,* 1938, pp. 481-509.
[31] Huby, *Épître aux Romains,* p. 256 & n. 2.

thus two realities that together make up a single complex, because the only purpose behind the Spirit's presence is to act as a spiritualizing force, and the *nous* only becomes a *pneuma* as a result of the endlessly vivifying action of the divine *Pneuma*. The Spirit asserts its life as a law, as a powerful, dominating force within the two other laws—the law of sin (and the flesh), which it destroys at the root, and the law of the *nous* (and of God himself), which it transfigures by bringing it into contact with Christ in baptism—which means dying and being resurrected in Christ. Henceforward "the law of the spirit of life, in Christ Jesus, hath delivered me from the law of sin and death." The new fact, as regards the experience, is not the Spirit of God himself, it is the spirit of man transfigured,[32] changed from carnal to spiritual, from impotent to effective, from slavery to freedom. This is the existential "conversion" by which the new man is made manifest, the new creation called into being by Christ at baptism; the beginning of that experience of the Spirit that characterizes all Christian life.

This experience is inchoate, of course, and the freedom is an effort to achieve liberation. Man is liberated completely but imperfectly—first, because though he is liberated in spirit he is not liberated in body except in hope (which does not mean, not really!), and secondly because even his spirit is only liberated as something to which victory has been promised, not given, so that it has to be fought for. Deliverance, for the Christian, lies precisely in this fact, that on the one hand there is no longer any cause for condemnation in him (viii, 1)—which means to say, no slavery to sin and death—while on the other hand he has within him the strength to triumph over the flesh. But he has to fight, to resist his appetites and tendencies—all the dead weight—of the flesh, to mortify the activities of the body by means of the spirit (13). The experience of the spirit is thus an experience of appetites and tendencies, and desires opposed to other appetites, tendencies, and desires (viii, 5), of a power that masters and annihilates other powers (viii, 13). It is a hard, pitiless struggle, from its humble beginnings, when the

[32] On 4, 6, 9, 10, 13, M. J. Lagrange (*Épître aux Romains* [Paris, 1916], pp. 196, 198, 201) takes grace to mean the life of grace. Huby (*op. cit.*, pp. 284, n. 3, 285 & n. 2, 286) explains it as "the supernatural principle of our actions, or—what comes to the same thing—the spirit of man renewed and possessed by the Spirit of God." In my opinion, as regards the beginning of this chapter, the latter expression gives a truer representation of St. Paul's meaning.

crucifying demands of the Spirit are felt to be a contradiction and man wavers between the flesh and the spirit (Gal. v, 17) so that slavery to the flesh has merely been exchanged for slavery to the spirit (Rom. vi, 12-23), through the slow, gradual ascent towards the light and service "in newness of spirit"[33] (Rom. vii, 6), until the time comes for that true liberty known to those who have interiorized the law, for whom it is no longer a constraining force but a direct appeal (Gal. v, 18-23), those who love whole-heartedly, who have been truly liberated by love and "walk in the spirit"—"in the way that produces love and is only hemmed in by love."[34] There is an immense distance to be covered, and St. Paul is always reminding us of the demands and joys to be met with on the way in all his "pareneses,"[35] which are simply one long description of this struggle waged by the spiritual in their efforts to increase their spirituality.

The Spirit as a Power of Knowledge. We mentioned this theme in our discussion of the wisdom of those who are "perfect"; here we need only return to the conclusions we came to then. The Spirit's function is to communicate this wisdom, which in God is the secret of salvation—a secret that is more in fact than a truth transmitted by the Word of God, for that would be faith, and wisdom is more than faith; a secret that is the very mystery enclosed within the Word of God, the movement of the life of the Trinity communicating itself, the beating of eternal love that comes and wakens our hearts so that they respond with love; a personal secret, Christ himself, the mystery, the light, the power of God—the living Wisdom of the Father. To possess wisdom means to enter into communion with Jesus Christ in a new way. And that is why this possessed wisdom comes from a deeper knowledge and love that are communicated by the Spirit, penetrating in an utterly new way into God's own inner life and seeing the mystery of eternal love in a new light. This wisdom is in us, therefore, as the revelation of love: a *revelation* (I Cor. ii, 10), because a truth thus grasped from within is a new truth so far as the intellect is concerned and throws light

[33] Cf. A. J. Festugière, *La Sainteté* (Paris, 1942), quoting Boussuet, "As on a spring morning" (p. 87).

[34] Chrysostom, in cap. 5, Gal., n. 5; P. G., 61, 671.

[35] These "pareneses" should be studied in detail for their description of the Christian endeavour. It is a subject we cannot go into here. Some of the most significant passages are: I Thess. v, 1-11; II Cor. vi, 14-vii, 1; Eph. iv, 25-v, 1-16; Col. 3.

upon the whole field of knowledge—"but the spiritual man judgeth all things" (*ibid.*, ii, 16)—and a revelation *of love*, because it comes from love and is addressed only to those who love—"for those that love him" (*ibid.*, 9)—and relates to the mystery of love; a revelation accomplished by the Spirit, who reveals and makes comprehensible the mystery of the good things promised by Love to those who love, because it is the Spirit that pours love into the human heart. Thus this wisdom is a great light arising in the soul led by love, and this light which is inseparable from love is a mysterious communication of the Spirit, a mysterious communion with Christ, a mysterious entry into the actual life of the Father.[36]

The Epistles of the Captivity return to this theme frequently and repeat it in detail—it is clearly a dominating idea, one that was continually recurring to St. Paul's mind. There is this highly concentrated passage in Ephesians, for instance: ". . . that the God of our Lord Jesus Christ, the father of glory, may give unto you the spirit of wisdom and of revelation, in the knowledge of him, the eyes of your heart enlightened, that you may know what the hope is of his calling, and what are the riches of the glory of his inheritance in the saints" (i, 17-18). He who gives is the God of Jesus Christ, for in the earthly Church the Father realizes the mystery of the Church in heaven. He gives a spirit of wisdom which is also a spirit of revelation, the power of understanding that springs from faith animated by love and penetrates into the mysteries of God. He gives enlightenment to the eyes of the heart—eyes received at baptism, by which the vision of the *nous* is transformed into that of the *pneuma*, and which in the perfect, under the influence of the Spirit, become more piercing still. Because the mystery of man redeemed is one with the mystery of Christ who saves man, the thing that the Father causes to be known in the light of the Spirit is hope—the marvellous inheritance, the riches of glory, to which we are destined by our personal vocation. The Spirit is from this point of view the power that reveals the mystery of the God of glory and the redeemed soul.

[36] L. Cerfaux has very well said (*L'Église des Corinthiens*, pp. 48 *et seq.*): "Knowledge of God and of the divine scheme of salvation does not simply mean knowing that men will be saved and the means whereby they will be saved; it means penetrating into the secrets of God, into the wisdom that is his essence, into the mysterious depths where knowledge and charity meet. . . . True intelligence flowers in love, just as love demands to be continued into a possession of knowledge. Knowing and loving are two aspects of a single act."

Other passages—which do not always mention the Spirit, but develop the same line of thought—sometimes emphasize the intellectual aspect of this immersion in God, in which wisdom and spiritual understanding are linked together (Col. i, 8), and sometimes the love that lies behind this light: "And this I pray, that your charity may more and more abound in knowledge and in all understanding; that you may approve the better things" (Phil. i, 9). Be "instructed in charity and unto all riches of fulness of understanding, unto the knowledge of the mystery of God the Father and of Christ Jesus: in whom are hid all the treasures of wisdom and knowledge" (Col. ii, 2-3). Here St. Paul explains in greater detail the idea that was to be found in I Cor. ii & iii. In wisdom, the apex of the spirit, which is both knowledge and love, finds itself once again deified by the Spirit. It enters into God in a single movement in which knowledge and love envelop—and develop—each other; it descends to the depths of the secret of Christ, the centre, the inexhaustible source of knowledge and love, whose effect is to transform and open the way to spiritual intelligence, i.e., contemplation of the divine mystery. And the power of the Spirit that gives this wisdom is so rich, so compelling, so strong, that it is always tending to overflow, to go further, to be carried further and further into the "inexhaustible concrete," the mystery of God.

The Spirit as a Power of Aspiration. Life in the Spirit does not only mean an effort towards liberation, and enlightenment through love; it also means aspiration. The Spirit is in us as a kind of pledge, an earnest, a first-fruits. It raises the whole Church in an immense movement of ascent, growth, and love towards full communion with God. The Christian soul is raised up personally by this irresistible call, which manifests itself in the finest spiritual feelings—as appears particularly in St. Paul's inexhaustible eighth chapter of the Epistle to the Romans.

The first of these is a cry of tenderness (Rom. viii, 14-17). The Christian, by definition, possesses the Spirit. The true Christian—the perfect one—allows himself to be impelled forward and governed and led by the guest who dwells within, whose one purpose is his sanctification. Now there is a meaning to this movement of the Spirit, because there is a meaning in its presence: it does not come to make slaves who fall down in terror before a God of fear; it comes to produce sons who in loving respect and tender reverence address themselves to a God who is their Father in Jesus Christ; it comes to enable that unbelievable sonship that is more real than anything else in the world to be heard in the cry that reveals its deepest impulse and its living power. This spirit of sonship, moreover, is also the spirit of love, because it is in love that we are chosen and called and justified, and therefore adopted; because this love is a permanent communication of the Spirit within us;[37] because it is so much the result of the Spirit within us that it must be attributed as much to the Holy Spirit which is its first principle as to our deified spirit which is its immediate principle. To say that the filial cry springs from love means that it springs from our spirit under the influence of the Spirit.[38] Everything comes from the Spirit, and everything comes from our spirit: both are present as two ontological principles concretely unified in one single act—the cry itself, which is thus the sign of the presence, and the action of the Spirit, its witness within us.[39] St. Paul sometimes says that it is we who cry in the Spirit (Rom. viii, 5) and sometimes that the Spirit cries in us (Gal. iv, 6). In either case, "the Spirit himself giveth testimony to our spirit, that we are the sons of God" (Rom. viii, 16). As a power of loving, regenerated by a love full of light (it is born in faith) and full of strength (it is born of agape), the spirit manifests the Spirit, and through the upsurge of tenderness our spirit experiences the Spirit.

The second manifestation of the Spirit takes place in the context of hope, and it has two sides to it. The first includes pain and sorrow, because hope always implies absence, trials, danger, painful growth: the world of hope is a world that the sons of God are brought into in the labour of growth and life. The second side is triumphant, because the world of hope is posited both in its being and in its becoming by the divine agape, the supreme power of creation, redemption, and beatitude, all in the sovereign power of Christ crucified and resurrected. The Christian Body is immersed in this mystery of painful and glorious parturition: it is the very mystery

[37] Rom. v, 5: *ekkekhutai*, poured continuously; *pn. dothentos* poured once, at baptism.

[38] Because this implies an opposition between two different economies (slavery-adoption), it is better to regard the action of the Holy Spirit not as a special gift but as the actual gift that makes us into adopted sons. Cf. Huby, *Épître aux Romains*, p. 288 & n. 3.

[39] The Spirit witnesses within us "by the effect of filial love which he creates in us" (St. Thomas); "by that very cry which he rouses in our spirit, that we are the sons of God" (Estius).

of the Church, which is at once a pilgrim in the shades here on earth and at the same time saved and in the glory of Christ in Paradise. "Saved in hope": that is the paradox, whose two terms supply the double rhythm for the whole development of the experience of the Spirit.

One beat of this rhythm comes from pain, and this has two sources. First there is the pain of the being in whom is accomplished the slow travail that produces a son of God, in a world in which there is being produced the body and house of the sons of God. It is clear that St. Paul's central thought concerns man and his destiny. But man is in fact rooted in a world which in its own way shares in his destiny. They suffer together, as they wait together for the day of their liberation: the world waits for man to be revealed in all his splendour as one of the sons of God, so that it can share in the brilliant triumph of his glory. But the way to this triumph is a way of pain. The "sufferings of the present time" are terrible: they make man cry out in his distress, they weigh upon him as a kind of slavery, they are the fangs of "corruption" pressing into a being who wants to live. They end in the great rending of death. St. Paul does not say this here, but he says it elsewhere, in the context of a number of expressions and ideas that are strangely similar (II Cor. v., 2-5). This suffering which culminates in death is only endurable because for the Christian it is a participation in Christ's suffering (Rom. viii, 17), because it is the proper means to his redemption, because regarded in this way it can become the pain of birth—the birth of a single being and at the same time of a whole new world. It is a paradoxical birth, accomplished not only through pain but through destruction. The Spirit of Christ makes us realize our slavery and distress; fills us with an ardent desire for the fulfilment of our being—i.e., the full adoption of the soul and the resurrection of the body; makes us "groan" within ourselves, as creatures who know that all they at present possess is a kind of first-fruits, a kind of seed that has to endure the trial of freedom, and that they must suffer and die before they can be finally born. But this very groaning is the groaning of hope, which continues through all the pain and through death itself, and opens out into resurrection and life. And the reason why the Spirit is a power of pleading and supplication and anguished hope within us is because at a still deeper level it is a power of deliverance, new birth, and freedom in the glory of God.

The prayer of supplication which St. Paul discusses next (Rom. viii, 26-27) is simply one particular example of this immense aspiration. It springs from the Christian's "weakness." This word is meant to describe the humiliated, wretched, impotent aspect of the human being at all levels; to all intents and purposes it is the human being himself considered as flesh, and there is an implicit antithesis between the "flesh," with the "world" which it implies, and the Spirit with its accompanying newness of life. When St. Paul wishes to "glory of the things that concern" his "infirmity" (II Cor. xi, 30, and xii, 5, 9) he mentions the way he was persecuted in Damascus, and his escape over the wall, through a window, in a basket; he mentions that mysterious humiliation, the sting of his flesh, the Angel of Satan, and, in the same list, "reproaches . . . necessities . . . persecutions . . . distresses for Christ." A humiliating impotence in the face of ourselves and others, in face of the war on two fronts that we are obliged to wage because of the temptations that come from within and the trials that come from outside, in the face of our lack of certainty, our ignorance of our own true good and what is to our own real spiritual advantage, God's concrete, particularized will for us—that more or less is what St. Paul means by our weakness: our wretchedness. Here he adds another source of wretchedness—the Christian's inability to control his prayers. The first reason for this is that "we know not what we should pray for as we ought." The Christian knows quite well that he must pray for his full adoption and resurrection, for these things are part of the very substance of his aspiration. But what he is actually asking for by praying for these things is a mystery which he knows only in the darkness of faith, whose meaning he cannot make out clearly, whose full realization he must leave to the next life, and whose immediate, personal means of realization remain unknown to him. He lives within a mystery whose ultimate meaning is hidden in God. How then can he pray properly? Even in what seem to be quite clear cases he makes mistakes. If he is buffeted by the Angel of Satan and prays to be delivered, he runs the risk of being mistaken, and in fact is mistaken. As for praying properly—he does not, weak, wretched creature that he is, know how to, he cannot see how to, he is utterly unable to. All that he can do is to abandon himself to that which is bigger than himself. Surrounded on all sides by his own mystery, which is suffused by the further mystery of God, he can do no other than abandon himself in the consciousness of his own powerlessness to the movement of the spirit which envelops him and raises him up to God in the midst of "indescribable groanings."[40] Because the object of desire is too remote and too profoundly hidden in God; because the source of prayer is too deep within us—not in any rational region, but in the deified *pneuma*, the image of God sealed within us; because this power of the Spirit, which takes hold of our weakness, this intercession, which takes such sovereign control of our own, is so unforeseeable, so profound, so powerful and sensitive, so divine, that it is simply one more darkness within us; because our consciousness of our wretchedness is so acute, in the midst of the mystery in which we are immersed as in the most intimate and secret parts of our being, and which nevertheless draws us towards the infinite as the frighteningly distant end of our pilgrimage—for all these reasons our prayer is full of groanings, and these groanings are indescribable. But they are understood by God, who sends his spirit into our hearts so that it may dwell there as the first and blessed source of all our aspirations, all our pain and all our hope.

But though darkness may envelop our deepest movements, there is at least one thing we know (*oidamen de*), and that is that our life is a mystery posited by love, and that if we love God in return we are sure to be saved. At the root of all this painful aspiration and groaning supplication is the love of God, the longing for union with the Father in the Son through the Holy Ghost. And from now on this aspect becomes clearer, the divine agape takes its place in the foreground, and, seen not from the side of human weakness but from the side of the all-powerful agape of God, our hope appears transformed, no longer groaning but joyful, not fearful but triumphant (viii, 28-39). When he speaks of those who love God—the saints (27)—St. Paul means the Christians as a group, the whole community. These love God because God has first loved them and his agape is active within them: from their election to their glorification, the divine will, as a manifestation of pure agape, remains unbroken by them, and they have no need of repentance. The Father loves those who are his, in Christ: he has taken sides with them,

[40] "It would be taking too narrow a view of St. Paul's thought to see in this no more than an allusion to speaking with tongues, or extraordinary states of prayer. The Spirit is present in those deep waves which lift up the Christian soul and transport it in an irresistible desire for the supernatural goods, the full possession of God" (Huby, *op. cit.*, p. 304).

delivered up his Son for them, he will give them in him all the graces they need. Christ loves those who are his: for them he died and was resurrected and sits at the right hand of the Father as an all-powerful intercessor—and all the hostile forces, all the things that formerly made us groan, are annulled, overcome, exterminated "because of him that hath loved us" (38).[41]

That is the other movement of hope. The whole Christian condition is the result of agape. The whole Christian aspiration arises out of agape. All this world of struggle, danger, and pain is in the embrace of agape and borne along by agape. We may feel secure, confident, joyful, and certain of victory, not because of what we are, but because of him who has loved us and given us our existence as Christians. We are pilgrims, but pilgrims who are citizens of heaven (Phil. iii, 20), pilgrims already in heaven with Christ even while we are still under trial and on the cross with him. The Christian is only saved in hope, but in hope he is already saved. Two facts, two movements, two different elements, compose the Christian attitude; as two beats in a single rhythm, which brings together into a living unity pain and joy, fear and certainty, anguish and triumph.

Now the Holy Spirit is at the heart of this attitude. We must remember to begin with that the Spirit appears elsewhere in St. Paul as a power of glory. There is II Cor. iii, 7-12, for example. Here St. Paul is speaking about the apostolic labour that leads to an ever more shining transformation in Christ, and he calls this labour the minister of glory: "For if that which is done away was glorious, much more that which remaineth [i.e., the Gospel] is in glory" (11). Now the power of glory is the Spirit, because the New Testament is the Testament of the Spirit (6), its ministration the ministration of the Spirit (8), and the Spirit writes the inner law on the hearts of believers (3). If the Spirit is really this power of glory at work in the New Testament, it is clear that it can lead the depths of the soul into the light, and enable it at certain times to experience the majestic presence of this glory. This is the meaning of the end of Rom. viii. St. Paul does not mention the Holy Spirit here—there is no need to. On the one hand, he is describing a movement entirely rooted in the Spirit; on the other, he is emphasizing the triumphant power of agape within us. But this agape "is poured forth"—and

[41] And that is why St. Paul can say in another place (I Cor. iii, 22-23) that these enemies belong to us and become our servants.

continues to be poured forth—"in our hearts by the Holy Ghost who is given to us" (Rom. v, 5), and hence its proper name is the agape "of the Holy Ghost" (Rom. xv, 30). St. Paul is thinking of "those who love God," but it is in the Spirit that we love, because the Father himself loves us in Christ and in the Spirit. The true images of Christ that God wills to realize (viii, 29) are also sons of God led by the Spirit (viii, 14), because it is the Spirit that accomplishes and perfects the likeness in which the sonship essentially consists. And that is why, what Christ does in heaven—i.e., intercede for us (viii, 34)—the Spirit does on earth, in our souls, in interceding for the saints (viii, 27). The same reality and the same experience are involved in both cases, but here earth is brought into harmony with heaven, and the light, the certainty, the glory of Paradise come down to enfold and transfigure the tragic condition of our pilgrimage. The agape of triumph surrounds the agape that is inserted within—and embraced by—faith and hope, and tears the human being from the clutches of the world of condemnation (viii, 1 & 34) and death; and the Spirit, through whom the new man and the new world are brought into existence, suffuses this time of pain and suffering with the bursting hope of eternal joy.[42]

4. *Formal Features of the Christian Experience*

An experience so mysterious inevitably raises a number of difficult problems. I should like to end by mentioning three of these. First, the problem of passivity. Passivity seems to have three stages, according to the three ways in which the Holy Spirit seizes upon the soul.

The first way occurs at conversion. Passages like I Thess. i, 5-6; Gal. iii, 1-6; Rom. vi, 16-20, describe the main features of this first stage. It is the response to an appeal, the acceptance of new insights

[42] The Epistles of the Captivity, though they do not give such a detailed account, have a number of features pointing in the same direction. We have already noted that the Spirit is a power of knowledge. In the Epistles of the Captivity it will be found to be above all a power of religion, inspiring prayer, homage, service (Eph. ii, 18; vi, 18; Phil. iii, 3); and a power of growth, building the temple and the body (Eph. ii, 21-22; iv, 3-4), developing a deep and sensitive charity (Eph. iv, 30; Phil. ii, 1), recreating the new man (Eph. iii, 16; iv, 23-24), strengthening hope in the midst of trials (Phil. i, 19; i, 27-28; cf. II Tim. i, 7, 14), making the soul sing and exult (Eph. v, 18-19). All familiar themes of the Christian experience, which no doubt became the common heritage of the Pauline Churches.

and attractions, a new obligation and beatitude; it clears the way for the action of the Holy Spirit that the Father and the Son institute within us to create the new man; it means obedience to the law that the Spirit plants within us and which makes us slaves to justice, obedience to the faith that defines and governs all our actions. The Spirit is not at this stage grasped consciously as a thing in itself, but its influence is conscious, and this manifests itself as a call, an illumination, an obligation and a promise. There is within us someone who speaks and acts first, a sovereign initiative demanding our response; the response is a magnificent act of freedom, but the freedom is grafted upon this sovereign initiative. This is the first form of the passivity. Every Christian experience thus begins, so to speak, as a matter of *laisser faire*, in an original *pati divina*, an original act of consent to the activity of the Spirit. And in this passive acceptance is accomplished the mysterious fecundation of the human spirit—its creation as a *pneuma*—by the power of the Spirit.

The second way appears in the actual growth of the Christian life. The Spirit is a compelling power, and the passivity of the soul will always mean docility to its impulses. But at this second stage the influence of the Spirit appears in the demands that are made by faith. The soul has believed and obeyed and given itself. It has done all this in the Holy Spirit, because the Spirit is the moving principle of the truths transmitted and also of the inner impulse to adhere to these truths. In this very full sense, "No one can say the Lord Jesus except in the Holy Spirit." The continuous action of the Spirit upon the Christian life takes place by way of this dual (inner and outer) influence of faith. It leads to a clearer and more heartfelt insight into the truths, and a stronger and more loving determination to practise them; to an ever clearer awareness that to obey in this way is to obey the Holy Spirit. The action of the Holy Spirit is thus indistinguishable from the actual movement of faith at the centre of the recreated life, and the appropriate form taken by docility at this stage is faithfulness—a minimum of passivity and a maximum of generous-hearted activity. Thus, "walking in the spirit" means rejecting the works of the flesh and realizing the fruits of the Spirit (Gal. v, 16-23); it means being detached, gentle, charitable (Gal. v, 25, 3). "Serving in newness of Spirit" means rejecting the slavery of the law, the flesh, sin (Rom. vii, 4-6 and viii, 4-8). "Not extinguishing the Spirit" means respecting its charismatic action, distinguishing clearly between good and evil, refraining from evil and holding fast to that which is good. "Not grieving the Holy Spirit of God" means respecting the first gift of the Spirit—charity, which edifies—and not sinning against it (Eph. iv, 30). Thus docility to the Holy Spirit turns out to mean faithfulness to the detailed concrete requirements of the faith. This faithfulness presupposes the clarity of mind, the courage, and the love that lie behind any living faith. But the progress of this unbelievably rich activity consists in seeing more and more unerringly, in the demands made by faith, the personal appeals of the Holy Spirit, who is the spirit of life in our hearts—*spiritu ex fide* (Gal. v, 5).

When the Christian gives himself in this way to the Spirit in obedience and love, he becomes one of the perfect, one of the spiritual, and he is now ripe for a further kind of influence from the Spirit, a more sensitive sort of response to its appeal; he is ready to be carried along in the full flow of its sovereign power. The immanent reward of his generous-hearted activity is precisely this "pneumatization," which renders the soul increasingly like Christ and surrenders it to the Spirit of sonship in the Church in which all are sons. In addressing himself to Christians as such, St. Paul is addressing himself to the community as such. And the highly personal experience which he describes is inserted with all its unforeseeable individuality into the experience of the Church as a whole. The Church is an assembly of sons, wherein the mysterious wisdom is revealed and the worship of the Father celebrated; it is an assembly of pilgrims, and from its midst arise the groans and aspirations of hope; it is an assembly of the citizens of heaven, the Jerusalem come down from on high—from Christ in glory, who enables it to live in the power of the Spirit—and from it rises the hymn of triumph of the redeemed. All the individual experiences of its sons and members are blended into the concrete universal experience of the Church, and the sovereign Spirit harmonizes the individual rhythms with the general rhythm set up by the immense body of the sons of God.

Consequently, at the summit of all this generous-hearted activity there opens before the soul the prospect of a supreme passivity through which the Spirit of sonship completes the soul's resemblance to Christ. Through prayer and painful aspiration, through supplication and triumph, the Spirit seizes the soul and raises it up to God, and all that the soul has to do now is to abandon itself, and let itself be carried towards what is greater than itself. This, once again, is a kind of passive acceptance, but it presupposes the substructure of faith, life in the Church, and a courageous faithfulness to the Spirit; it is a passivity which has no meaning except as the manifestation of the highest form of a given freedom, a passivity in which consequently, in a deeper way than ever before, the Spirit of God is united with our spirit, becomes the soul of our spirit.

What St. Paul's statements assert, in fact, is a mystery of union within unity. The Spirit and the spirit are two separate things, even when they are most closely united; in the Spirit we cry to the Father (Rom. viii, 15), and groan while awaiting our sonship (16, 23); to us the Spirit gives his testimony (16) and help (26). But this union is realized within a unity of life: the Spirit becomes the direct principle of the movements that spring from our souls, to such an extent that it is he who cries to God (Gal. iv, 6) and intercedes and groans within us (Rom. viii, 26). At the heart of the personal dualism that is always bound to exist between the Spirit and the Christian, there is an ontological unity between the Spirit which is given and the spirit which receives, and consequently a spiritual unity between them in the act itself, which springs, as from a single source and principle, from the divine Spirit and the transfigured, adhering, consenting weakness of our own spirit.[43] This problem needs to be taken over by theological thought and thoroughly investigated, but at least we can say that it establishes the fact of a supreme passivity, realized in the purity of a freedom that has been liberated, spiritualized and actualized by the sovereign Spirit; an extreme form of passivity, but one which is situated, integrated, and judged through being inserted within two things—a strictly structured personal experience, and a primary, normative, and nourishing experience within the Church.

The second problem concerns the immediate character of this experience. St. Paul knows of no pure and absolutely unveiled experience of the Spirit here on earth.[44] The actual hierarchy of the Christian life

[43] In conformity with the principle affirmed elsewhere, "He who is joined to the Lord is one spirit" (I Cor. vi, 18), which refers directly to the glorified Christ who has become the life-giving Spirit (Huby, p. 151). But it is by giving his spirit that Christ is a life-giving Spirit, and this statement therefore joins up with that made in Rom. viii.

[44] I have made no attempt to deal with the difficult apocalyptic passage, II Cor. xii, 1-10. Here St. Paul is in ecstasy, and speaks only for himself. This experience therefore lies outside the main lines of the Christian experience, and it is a problem how to connect it up with the normal experience of Christians.

is against any such thing, for we walk by faith, not by sight (II Cor. v, 6-7), we do not know face to face but darkly, as in a mirror (I Cor. xiii, 12). Thus, however luminous it may be in other ways, an essential obscurity envelops the whole experience of the Spirit—the obscurity of faith. Our experience is an experience through a medium, the medium of the testimony that the Spirit gives to itself in the development of our lives. We cannot grasp the Spirit except through the mediation of its own signs.

The first of these signs is provided by the truths themselves, which are the means used by God to reveal the mystery of his own person to us. If we go back to our major example of the perfect ones to whom God communicates his wisdom, we find that this wisdom is revealed to us as a mystery—the mystery of Christ in which all other mysteries are included. It was formerly a secret hidden in God; henceforth the secret is communicated—but (in accordance with the whole economy of the Gospel) it is communicated in the Word of God, in the message given by Jesus Christ, in Jesus Christ himself as the Word of God. The secret was "kept secret" (Rom. xvi, 25), it has now been spoken; but it cannot be seen; and it is on condition that we believe it to exist in the Word that we may hope one day to see it. Then it will not be a mystery or a secret or a spoken word that we shall grasp; we shall see the mysterious Being, the hidden God, the eternal Word, literally face to face. The experience of wisdom lies in penetrating into the mystery of faith in the direction of this face to face, without ever reaching it, but discovering God's personal presence more and more in his mystery and in the graces he grants us. It is for this reason that it is given us, not to see God, but to discern and penetrate into (and translate into act, when necessary) "the graces that God has granted us," the objective veil of the testimony between God and us; for this reason too we receive God's personal Spirit and God gives us Christ's actual intelligence. This personal power of thought gradually enables us to discover within the mystery the personal love of God, who seeks out "those who love him" so that one day he may satisfy them. But the mystery is never emptied of content, and the experience of the Spirit means plunging towards the divine depths, which are known fully only to the Spirit, but whose magnificent fruits are known to those who are spiritual, as present graces and promises for the future. Through signs more and more revealing and a spirit more and more transparent, we make a progressive discovery of the Spirit who travails within us, of Christ in whom our thought is rooted, and of the Father who is gradually leading us towards glory—until the time of the face to face when the long pilgrimage is over.

The experience of the Spirit is also realized in another, more particularized, more individualized form, in those spiritual movements described, for example, in Romans viii. Here we are no longer concerned directly with divine truth but with the reactions which it awakens within us, or rather which the Spirit rouses within us through our contact with it as we progressively live it. As a divine force at the root of our spirit, the Spirit enables us to combat and overcome the flesh, to realize our sonship, to aspire towards deliverance and to adhere to the divine agape in the joy of triumph. The soul has an experience of conflict and filial affection, distress and desire, victory in God—and through all these it experiences the Spirit. Spiritual acts and feelings are signs that reveal the Spirit. The experience takes place within faith, and excludes any vision or direct grasp; it has to be related to the norms of faith; it is only safe in communion with the Church, the Spirit's first dwelling-place; it involves a dual inward movement of effort and abandonment, possession and aspiration, sorrow and joy, fear and confidence, through which is revealed this virile, maternal, exulting power, a power of conflict, of spiritual generation, of triumph, which is the Spirit of God itself. This raises a second problem which needs to be investigated by theology—the problem of the direct experience of the Spirit that comes through the testimony which it gives of itself in the soul of the believer, the problem of the awareness of the Spirit that comes through the mediation of this great sign, the spiritual life itself.

What certainty does St. Paul accord this experience of the Spirit? This is not by any means a simple question, and one's answer needs to vary according to the various aspects of the experience.

Firstly, it is an experience in faith. Now faith is an obscure knowledge, because it is achieved by means of testimony given in human form but relating to realities entirely divine. St. Paul sometimes emphasizes the human form of this testimony, and therefore its imperfections, its deficiencies, its obscurity—"we know as in a glass, darkly"[45]—and sometimes the divine power expressed through it,

[45] This passage is taken to refer not to faith but to charismatic knowledge by L. Cerfaux, *L'Église des Corinthiens*, p. 94, n. 22, and by J. Dupont in a chapter of *Gnosis*, pp. 106-150.

and therefore its splendour and brilliance—"the light of the gospel of the glory of Christ" and "the glory of the Lord" (II Cor. iii, 18-iv, 4). Furthermore, it is the power of the Spirit that enables us to adhere to this testimony and to enter into the mystery which it reveals. From this point of view, the part played by our experience of the Spirit is to throw light upon the mystery enclosed within the testimony, to "reveal" (I Cor. ii, 10) more intimately what the soul already knows—in St. John's words, to enable the soul to learn what it has already been taught—not by getting rid of the testimony but by interiorizing it and illuminating it more and more.

To do this the Spirit devotes its activity to the inward side of the life of faith. It introduces a new kind of testimony within the first; it throws light upon the signs and gives a deeper meaning to the revealed truths; at the same time it strengthens the soul's power of adherence and love, arouses within the soul spiritual movements of a mysterious and utterly new kind, and leads it forward by ways that are surprising but sure. By this dual labour it educates the soul, makes it more and more like Christ, and enables it to see with ever greater clarity. But, of course, this experience is not a matter of separate phenomena and discontinuous sections, but a highly complex spiritual movement, proceeding according to a rhythm that can be felt but not foreseen, and bringing in its wake a whole world of new spiritual facts. The usual sort of certainty in a case of this kind is a direct certainty springing from the spiritual movement itself and adhering closely to it, embracing not an object but a sense of spiritual growth, linked not with the grasp of an abstract truth but with the discovery of a presence perceptible through its action, based partly on the unshakeable rock of faith and partly on the sovereign, unpredictable action of the Spirit, and therefore including within itself an element of abandonment, expectation, fearful trust, wonderment—an element of self-dispossession, since its origin is not within us and does not depend on us. It is also a lived certainty, expressing an attitude from which it is inseparable—dark like the mystery it transmits and feeds upon, luminous like the presence revealed through itself, firm like the God upon which it is based, uncertain and fearful like the weak creature in whom it grows; in short, a paradoxical certainty—the certainty of hope, in fact: "But you are not in the flesh, but in the spirit, if the Spirit of God dwells in you" (Rom. viii, 9). Let me try to explain these words, "You are . . . in the spirit." This statement has a twofold objective basis. The first is in the will of God, in the agape that is a gift from the Father and Christ in the Spirit, and which comes and takes man out of the toils of sin and brings into being the new creature. This in itself supplies a basis of absolute security. Secondly, there is the holiness of the Church, which is assured for all time because the Church is the Body of Christ vivified by the Spirit, the Temple of God, the Church of the saints and the elect. The fact that we are embraced by agape and included within the Church—both these things coming to us at the time of our baptism into Christianity—gives our certainty a twofold dogmatic basis. It remains a certainty within faith, for we cannot see the agape and the Spirit that sanctify us and make us members of the Church; we believe in them. "If it is true that the Spirit of God dwells within you . . ." We believe this, we are confident of it, but we have no evidence for it. Nor has anyone else. This is where a subjective element comes in (the inner state of each individual soul) and envelops the twofold objective basis in mystery. Between the objective and the subjective there is no bond of necessity; there is the dehiscence that always enters into any subjectivity, and the abyss that always opens in front of freedom. The passage from the community to the individual is not automatic. Whatever is revealed to be true of the group is only true for the individual on the condition, *si tamen* . . . The mystery—I do not say of predestination or election, but of personal adoption—is never taken by St. Paul out of the darkness of faith and presented as a reality known clearly in consciousness.

This reservation arises in the first place from the fact that our soul always remains a mystery to our consciousness. In St. Paul's view, our soul is a *nous* which the Spirit turns into a *pneuma* by transforming its latent capacities into an effective force. Or else it is something with mysterious depths—the "heart"—in which the eyes of the spirit have to open. But this strictly divine region exists at too profound a level ever to be reached by human vision. God, by definition, is "he that searcheth the hearts" (Rom. viii, 27), and he alone can comprehend the labour of the spirit in these depths. St. Paul, surveying his life as a "minister of Christ," writes, "For I am not conscious to myself of any thing, yet am I not hereby justified; but he that judgeth me is the Lord" (I Cor. iv, 4). These words mean that he recognizes that the Christian has such a partial awareness of his actions that his seeing himself as justified does not by any means mean that he is justified, and that the final judgment on the value of his acts can only be made by God; it means that the "heart's intentions" are absolutely "dark secrets," to oneself as well as to others,[46] and that Christ alone at his second coming will bring them "to light" and make them "manifest" (I Cor. iv, 5) to ourselves and to others. Thus our activity escapes us, as regards both its deepest source and its eternal value—and hence, all the more certainly, the source itself escapes us. The heart of man, as a thing acted upon by God and inhabited by God, is a mystery so divine that only God can bring it out into the full light; and it will need God's own appearance before this can take place. The unveiling of our being is reserved for the next world.

There is also another reason for St. Paul's reservation, and this is that there is no genuine experience of the Spirit except in fidelity to the faith. Now there is no infallible sign of this fidelity: no external sign can guarantee it fully: neither apostolic generosity, as St. Paul has just said; nor participation in the mystery of the Eucharist, when the faithful are gathered together in worship—for it is necessary for each to examine himself and prove himself and be fearful of receiving the bread of the Lord unworthily (I Cor. xi, 27-30)—nor the charismata since the most miraculous of them can co-exist with an absence of charity, and that means an absence of fidelity. Moreover, fidelity is never given once and for all; it is always accompanied by an essential risk. It has to be realized in a soul that is a mixture, in which flesh and spirit are at war; a soul that is "weak," in which its miseries weigh heavily upon it; a soul that is tempted, in which Satan can appear as an angel of light and his ministers as ministers of justice (II Cor. xi, 13-15) and so mislead it. Fidelity, therefore, cannot be regarded as something gained once and for all; it has to be re-won each day in the humble but magnificent endeavour of a redeemed freedom. Finally, fidelity is to be identified essentially with charity or the faith that works by charity, so that "love . . . is the fulfilling of the law" (Rom. xiii, 10). But in us charity is the mystery of God himself and the power of the Spirit, the mystery of an eternal (and everlasting) force within the soul, whose movements alone we can perceive—its desires, its suffering, its aspirations—and within the faith and hope by which it is surrounded, and which in their apprehensible aspect are also things of time and becoming, part of the pilgrimage.

[46] Huby, *Première aux Corinthiens*, pp. 119 *et seq.*

Charity as it is in itself is too purely divine for us to grasp; it is only recognizable by its fruits or signs; and that is why the certainty of being in the Spirit and living in the Spirit must always be surrounded by mystery. It is a certainty of faith, not of sight; of hope, not possession; stronger than all doubt and fear, but founded paradoxically upon a God who is invisible; held fast not from below but from above; thrown up like an anchor into the mystery of God.

This problem leads finally to another: does the certainty of being in the Spirit necessarily mean the certainty of being saved? Does the certainty of possessing the first-fruits and the pledge of the Spirit necessarily mean the certainty of possessing the Spirit one day in all its fullness? Is the spiritual person certain of salvation? St. Paul's reply is here again a continuation of his earlier reply, ". . . we are saved by hope" (Rom. viii, 24). In the matter of salvation the only certainty is hope.

The first reason for this is the fact that personal salvation remains a mystery hidden in God. Predestination, justification, glorification, are not realities about which there can be any kind of personal revelation. Election itself is not a fact of personal experience; it is actualized when that which did not exist comes into existence—"from my mother's womb" (Gal. i, 15)—and St. Paul has no knowledge of his own except through a strictly miraculous vocation (*ibid.*, 16), which makes it an exception to the general rule. Here on earth everything must be a matter of hope. God's redemptive will for me as a person remains an endless mystery. Furthermore, life in the Spirit is a seed growing towards its fulfilment, and between the seed and its full flowering comes the business of human collaboration—not only participation in the call to redemption through faith, but collaboration with the redemptive will through the charity that should animate the whole of our life and bear its fruit in the Spirit. Only, human freedom is a fragile thing; it is in a trial state; it is never fixed once and for all; it comes up unavoidably against scandal, suffering, the cross. We cannot be resurrected with Christ unless we suffer and die with him. And though our suffering on earth is as nothing compared with the glory that is to come, St. Paul knows very well that in itself it is a terrible thing that shakes the human being to his foundations—"yet so if we suffer with him, that we may be also glorified with him" (Rom. viii, 17). Thus a new mystery is inserted within the first: past and present are never infallible guarantees for the future. And indeed this mystery connects up with the first; for though it is man who labours, it is grace that enables him to labour —"not I, but the grace of God with me" (I Cor. xv, 10); though man works out his own salvation, God works in him "to will and to accomplish" (Phil. ii, 21); and consequently, since it is God who began the work, God will proceed with it until its culmination on "the day of Christ Jesus" (Phil. i, 6). Thus the mystery of what we today call final perseverance remains hidden in God. And so perhaps it should be said that for St. Paul the mystery of our justification and the mystery of our salvation are a single mystery, if it is true that here on earth our life is "hidden with Christ in God," and will only be truly made manifest "when Christ shall appear, who is your life, then you also shall appear with him in glory" (Col. iii, 4).

More than ever, then, in the matter of salvation, the only certainty is hope. Hope, in fact, forms the bridge between the security that comes from God and the insecurity that comes from us. Hope posits both sides of this irresolvable complex, and both have to be equally insisted on. Hope realizes the mystery and miracle of a confidence that springs from infinite poverty and rests on the infinite secret of omnipotent Love. Finally, hope, by anticipating the future and bridging the abyss, grasps the reality now, in its promise—not in peaceful possession, but in the boldness of an aspiration in which supplication and certainty meet.[47]

Hence we can understand the need for both St. Paul's lines of thought, the one reflecting man's fear and insecurity before his own weakness and the inscrutability of the divine judgments, the other the confidence and certainty of the Christian, "prevented," animated and enveloped by eternal, omnipotent love. "I chastise my body and bring it into subjection; lest perhaps, when I have preached to others, I myself should become a castaway" (I Cor. ix, 27). I wish "to know him, and the power of his resurrection, and the fellowship of his suffering, being made conformable to his death, if by any means I may attain to the resurrection which is from the dead. Not as though I had already attained, or were already perfect: but I follow after, if I may by any means apprehend, wherein I am also apprehended by Christ Jesus" (Phil. iii, 10-12). And contrariwise, "For I know that

[47] Cf. Huby, quoting Goguel (*Rom.* pp. 202): St. Paul's religious experience "is eschatological, since it can never be fully realized except in the next world; and it is mystical, since it is a reality and experience known here and now."

this shall fall out to me unto salvation, through your prayer and the supply of the Spirit of Jesus Christ, according to my expectation and hope that in nothing I shall be confounded, but with all confidence, as always, so now also, shall Christ be magnified in my body, whether it be by life, or by death" (Phil. i, 19-21; to which may be added 22-26). This is a tone we have heard before: St. Paul is applying to himself what in Rom. viii he applied to all Christians—their anxiety and their certainty, their pitiableness and their triumph—so that individual experience and collective experience coincide—inevitably, because in the Apostle's individual experience is revealed the experience of the whole Church.

The problem of the certainty of faith is thus the culmination of the previous problem concerning the certainty of the Spirit within us, and it resolves itself in the same paradoxical fashion, into the actual experience of hope. We are thus very far from the sharp opposition between the two which some have seen fit to discover in St. Paul's thought on these matters,[48] between a mutually contradictory distrust and confidence. In reality there is a concurrent, reciprocal opposition between two aspects of a lived mystery, two beats of a single spiritual rhythm. In this single mystery of hope, man, as a pilgrim far from his Lord, a creature on the way to a new birth, and God, as an all-merciful, all-powerful, concretely effective will to salvation, meet. Fear springs up whenever man's eyes turn towards his own tragic weakness, and joyful assurance takes its place when they turn towards agape, which saves even its enemies—how much more, then, those who are justified in the blood of Christ (Rom. v, 6-10)! In this single spiritual rhythm the two beats answer each other, and hope arises from the interaction between them: lamentation leads to hope, joyful assurance leads back to humble fear—this is the unchanging movement that leads to God, joins with God, holds God, in so far as the first-fruits of the Spirit allow here on earth, in a hope that is both fully confident and at the same time goes in fear and trembling—". . . we are saved by hope."

[48] M. Goguel, *Les fondements de l'assurance du salut chez l'apôtre saint Paul*, in *Revue d'Histoire et de Philosophie religieuses*, 1937, pp. 105-144. This work is full of interesting observations. But Goguel's categories lead him to misrepresent St. Paul. He believes that the essence of religion is irrational, and exists in contradiction to the rational; we believe that the essence of religion is supra-rational, integrating the rational and only rejecting its rationalistic deformations. And this seems to me to be the only way of doing justice to the whole of St. Paul's thought.

CHAPTER SIX

The Christian Experience in the First Epistle of St. John

THE problem of the *Prima Joannis* can be said to be the problem of the Christian experience. The theme underlying the whole of the epistle is in fact the communion of Christians with God and their fellow men in Jesus Christ. Communion, indwelling, possession—all these words convey the same mystery, the mystery of eternal life, which is God himself; which God communicates; and by which we live, as Christians, in the deepest and most mysterious region of our being.

What St. John aims to convey is that this communion is something which, so far as is possible in this life, we must try to live in the full light of, something we must experience, and must therefore grasp by means of that mysterious knowledge which comes from faith and love, and which, more deeply still, is the fruit of the Spirit who is Truth. There is therefore a Johannine "gnosis";[1] and for St. John,

[1] The word is of course simply a literal copy of the Greek: it is used here merely to emphasize the paradoxical character of this knowledge-communion spoken of by St. John. Let me add that though St. John was a Jew, and not a Greek, the attempt to wash him clean of "all suspicion of Hellenism" has perhaps been carried too far. Cf. the remark by J. STARCKY on the *Logos*: "Why should St. John, who had spent a long time in Ephesus where Apollos amongst others had spread the ideas of Plato, and where Heraclitus, five centuries earlier, had introduced Greek speculations on the *Logos*—why should St. John have remained deaf to all intellectual activity except that which faithfully followed the Bible and the Apocrypha? There is nothing to show that he had the ghetto mentality, surrounded as he was by Christians who had come from Hellenism as well as Judaism" (*Logos*, in *Supplément au Dictionnaire de la Bible*, Vol. V, col. 491). Even though J. DUPONT's weighty book has now appeared (*Gnosis*, 1949) the problem of early Christian gnosis still remains to be studied. For the case—still *sub judice*—of Clement of Alexandria, for example, see the important article by J. MOINGT, *La Gnose de Clément d'Alexandrie dans ses rapports avec la foi et la philosophie*, in *Rech. de Sc. relig.*, April 1950-Jan. 1951.

as for St. Paul, the perfect Christian is no longer in darkness but in light. He knows. He knows that he has passed from death to life. He knows God, and he knows love. He knows that he is of God and in God, and that God is in him; that he is in the truth and possesses eternal life. And if he turns his thoughts to himself, he knows that he knows God.

But the stakes that are involved in such a "knowledge" are so serious, this "gnosis" is so far from sight, illusions about it are so easily come by and so much to be feared, that St. John increases the number of tests that may be used to prove its genuineness and to enable one to live in safety by it. He is thus led on to describe the essential elements of the structure of the Christian experience; and it is this profound intuition, and the means of access to it, this mysterious possession, and its normative signs, that we must now do our best to grasp. One can have no illusions about the difficulty of such an undertaking: the obscurities that face the exegetist in the ramifications of St. John's thought are well known. Nevertheless I believe that much enlightenment is to be found there; and with the help of the good books that already exist on the subject, I shall simply try in the following pages to give a brief sketch of the complex structure of this experience. I shall make no attempt to follow the plan of the epistle itself—and advisedly so, for it might perhaps be a mistake to attempt to find in St. John's closely-packed and sometimes enigmatic writing any other order than Pascal's "order of the heart"—"which consists mainly of long digressions on every point that has any relationship to the end and yet goes on illustrating it all the time."

1. *The Main Features of the Christian Experience*

"That which was from the beginning, which we have heard, which we have seen with our eyes, which we have looked upon, and our hands have handled, of the word of life: for the life was manifested: and we have seen, and do bear witness, and declare unto you the life eternal, which was with the Father, and hath appeared to us: that which we have seen and have heard, we declare unto you, that you also may have fellowship with us, and our fellowship may be with the Father, and with his son Jesus Christ" (i, 1-5). The Christians to whom St. John was writing had never known Jesus. They had no normal way of knowing him other than the testimony of those who had lived with him. Hence the solemn proclamation with which the Apostle opens his epistle: he gives his own testimony so as to help them to share in his personal experience of Christ, of the Son and the Father, and through it in the full joy of the mystery of eternal life.

His experience is human in type: it is his soul and body, his intellect by way of his senses, that have seized Christ, the Word of life. The Word has "appeared" (i, 2) precisely because it has taken a human form, and St. John has been able to hear it, see it, handle it, and contemplate it at length. A spiritual perception arising from a sense perception: such is the starting-point of St. John's experience. What he has thus experienced is the Word of Life, which is also life eternal (v, 20): he who is turned towards the Father, is one with him, is God himself, the life-giving Everlasting Being. St. John does not say, "We have seen the Word," but "That which we have seen . . . concerning the Word." For "no man hath seen God at any time," and therefore John has not seen the Word. The Word has appeared, but through a body. His pure divinity remains inaccessible, it disappears in his transcendence: God is always something "greater." There has not been any pure grasp of the Word, of eternal life, but communion through what has appeared, through what could be seen, heard, and handled of the incarnate Word, and corporal and spiritual participation through the grasp of eternal life—in short, union with God through the greatest of all signs, the Man Jesus.

How can Christians share this experience? The answer is, through the testimony given by the Apostle, and communion with him. He gives testimony by bringing Christ's message, so that Christians may share in his spiritual life. It is by way of the truth, preached objectively by the Apostle, and subjectively accepted (by faith) and practised (by following the commandments), that they too can enter into communion with the Word of Life: it is through the witness and his testimony that they can have communion with God. St. John has known God through the mediation of Christ; Christians will know Christ through the mediation of St. John—in other words, through the mediation of the Church. The Apostle, the hierarchy, the Church, thus form one of the essential components of the Christian experience.

The centre of this experience is divine communion, and this means in the first place life in God. Now God is absolutely pure Light (i, 5), and he is in the light (i, 7), as in his own Kingdom. This light is pure and utterly beyond the reach of evil, a splendour of "glory," a transforming force: through the Blood of Christ it purifies us of all iniquity, dissipates the darkness in which we live, corrects our spiritual attitude and enables the whole man to live in truthfulness of life. Hence, just as God is in the light and is the Light, so we too must "walk in the light," learn to be more and more faithful to the Word, and, by dint of spiritual effort, approach towards the source of this infinite light; and this movement towards purity, towards uprightness of life and concrete truth, brings us into communion with God (i, 6) and our brothers (i, 7).

But God is also Charity (iv, 7-16). He is absolute generosity, which is pure through and through—because it conditions everything else, and has no other law than its own infinite superabundance; because it comes and takes hold of sinners; and because it gives itself in giving the Son as our Saviour, our living Expiation and Source of life. And this charity which is God is also from God (7). It is the power of God in us (cf. iii, 24); it tends to grow towards its own perfection, to become a pure return of love to its divine source: "Let us therefore love God: because God first hath loved us" (19). Hence, when we love God and our fellow men, when we abide in love, we are in God, and God is in us. Communion with God is therefore the life of bliss—through Christ (9)—lived in a purity and generosity that are both equally infinite; a participation in the Purity and Generosity of God.

This communion means a reciprocal immanence. God is in us and we possess him. "He that confesseth the Son hath the Father also" (ii, 23). "And this [eternal] life is in his Son. He that hath the Son hath life" (v, 12). "If we love one another God abideth in us" (iv, 12). Conversely, we are in God (ii, 6), and we must abide in Christ (ii, 28). "And he that keepeth his commandment abideth in him" (iii, 24). "And he that abideth in charity abideth in God and God in him" (iv, 16). ". . . that we may know the true God and may be in his true Son" (v, 20).

To understand this immanence we must go back to its source. Now this is a continuous divine action, a generative action by which at every moment God communicates to us our being as his sons. The proper name for the Christian in this epistle is "one who is engendered by God."[2] But this "kind of continuous divine generation" does not mean that we are outside God; on the contrary, it takes us towards him with all the force of the deified powers of our being. By faith and charity we embrace God, hold him, possess him. But in doing this we are simply returning to the original eternal Love that saved us and purified us and now engenders and deifies us. God gave himself by an act of absolute generosity, and by participating in this generosity we in our turn give ourselves: we are in God more than God is in us, because God is greater than our heart (iii, 20): he is the whole Light and Love in which in our own small way we only share.[3]

All this, moreover, is centred upon the Son. Objectively, it is by his blood and expiation that we are redeemed (i, 7; ii, 2; iv, 10-14). Subjectively, it is he who gives us life (iv, 9); by confessing him, we possess the Father (ii, 24); by possessing him, we possess life (v, 12); and though it is the Father who engenders us into eternal life, this takes place through Jesus Christ. Finally, for the Christian, being in God means being "in his true Son. This is the true God and life eternal" (v, 20). Christian communion is thus a personal relationship with Christ, in whom we are united with the Father. Our Christian being is a being-in Christ, because it is a being-of Jesus Christ, whose whole tendency is to make us belong-to Jesus Christ through faith and love.

It is not surprising that such an experience should be difficult to describe—all the more so as it is a "go-between," an intermediary ex-

[2] Cf. J. Bonsirven, *Épîtres de saint Jean,* Coll. "*Verbum Salutis*" (Paris, 1936), pp. 154, 157, 273, n. 2: "*o gegennēmenos,* perfect passive participle, denoting a lasting condition: the Christian, being a son of God, never ceasing to be the object of a kind of continuous divine generation."

[3] This for St. John is really "knowing God." In a remarkable article (*La Connaissance de Dieu dans l'Alliance nouvelle, d'après la première Lettre de saint Jean,* in *Revue biblique,* 1949, pp. 365 *et seq.*), Fr. Boismard has shown how St. John is continually returning to the Biblical theme of the "knowledge of God" (pp. 366-371, 385 *et seq.*). If I must record my disagreement with two connected points in the work (the fact that the starting-point of the "knowledge" should be conceived as "a genuinely mystical experience" (p. 390), and "faith" conceived as a purely external confession of the name of Jesus), let me emphasize that Fr. Boismard's general scheme—the presence of God and the transfiguration of man; the awareness of this presence; the witness to it in the profession of faith—seems to me to be absolutely right; and it is this that I too am concerned to explain here.

perience. Its place is between the two manifestations of Christ—the redemptive Incarnation and the Parousia. "And now, little children, abide in him, that when he shall appear we may have confidence and not be confounded by him at his coming. . . . Behold what manner of charity the Father hath bestowed upon us, that we should be called, and should be, the sons of God . . . Dearly beloved, we are now the sons of God; and it hath not yet appeared what we shall be. We know that when he shall appear, we shall be like to him: because we shall see him as he is. And every one that hath this hope in him, sanctifieth himself, as he also is holy" (ii, 28-iii, 3). The aim of Christ's first appearance is to deliver us from the Devil and sin (iii, 5-8), to purify us, to give us a new being—the being of sons—and thus to prepare us for the perfect communion of Paradise. The second manifestation will take place at the time of the solemn Judgment and our ultimate transformation in God. The Christian being is therefore a reality situated entirely between the Incarnation and the Parousia; based on the first, which gives it its ontological reality and efficacy, and tending towards the second, which gives it its meaning and governs it as its end. Consequently one dimension of the Christian experience is necessarily dynamic: the active connection between seed-time and harvest.

Abiding in God (ii, 28)—the divine communion that is achieved through faith and the practice of justice (ii, 29)—is a pledge that Christ will not cast us off but acknowledge us to be his own, and it therefore justifies a bold, joyful assurance at the terrifying prospect of the separation of the good and the evil. The communion is therefore directed entirely towards that future; it is an anticipation of our situation as we shall appear before the Judge in his final manifestation, an assurance at the prospect of Judgment. This communion is based upon the doubly mysterious reality of our divine sonship (iii, 1-3): it is mysterious to the carnal man, to the world, which has not accepted the love of God, has not allowed itself to be transformed by it, does not "know" God and consequently has no power of knowledge enabling it to understand the transformed beings who are the sons of God; and it is mysterious to the Christian himself, for he knows God but he cannot see him, since he is not fully transformed into his likeness. His knowledge is not complete because his being is not complete, because the Son of God, the direct source of being and knowledge, has not revealed himself to him. St. John himself has only known the Son through the testimony of his humanity; the Christian will only know him through the testimony of the apostle, and the testimony that God gives of himself through him. But when Christ manifests himself in the splendour of his divinity, and makes us perfectly like him, "what we shall be" then "shall appear," and in the light that comes from this revelation of Christ to us, and of us in Christ, our eyes will be opened, and "we shall see him as he is"—not through anything created, but in himself. The first—imperfect—revelation of the Lord leads, in faith, to the beginnings of the Christian being; the second—perfect—revelation leads, in sight, to the perfection of the son of God.

Thus in the experience that we may have of our sonship here on earth there is a double darkness—the darkness of what we are, which we know only by faith, and the darkness of what we shall be, which also we know only by faith, and which therefore intensifies the first darkness. Our actual reality as sons of God thus tends towards the hope of perfect likeness and perfect vision. As described in verse 2—"we are now the sons of God; and it hath not yet appeared what we shall be"—our Christian condition can be defined as a hope at the very heart of sonship. And therefore the sonship tends towards its fulfilment, as communion tends towards judgment—both tending towards that Parousia which will be at once an Appearance, a Judgment and a Transformation. Consequently—to repeat—the practice of justice (ii, 29) and the effort towards purification (iii, 3), in the image of Christ, govern the Christian's spiritual life, because they signify an increasing approximation, which on the last day will enable the sudden passage to perfect likeness to be accomplished. That Christ's appearance shall be followed by transformation into him, and a direct vision of his being—such is the Christian hope. It includes a discontinuity, known and understood by faith, between present and future, and it is inserted into the heart of the Christian experience so as to raise it under the influence of its powerful aspiration from faith to sight. In a word, for the Christian here on earth, ontological incompleteness leads to noetic incompleteness, and this twofold incompleteness is stretched to its full extent towards an ultimate completeness that is both ontological and noetic. Thus the hope of holiness and the effort towards it exist at the very heart of the Christian experience.

2. *Criteria of the Experience*

St. John's aim thus appears more paradoxical than ever—that of transmitting a certain knowledge of a reality that is by definition utterly mysterious. To avoid giving any opening to the kind of illuminism that has always been the bugbear of the "spiritually minded," he goes on to make a special effort to increase the number of criteria that can be used to ensure a reliable judgment; and these we must now study.

The essential idea is one of St. John's greatest themes. God is "the Truth," the one true God, and in him we do the truth: that is the real fulfilment of our vocation. Thus there is a *veritas vitae* originating in God and involving us wholly: our words, actions, and spiritual attitudes must conform to this truth, if they are to be real, true, and Christian, and are to bring us (or maintain us in) communion with God. This truth is therefore a total knowledge, which takes concrete form in faithfulness to the commandments—in faith and love. St. John sees this concrete totality as a thing to be understood, so to speak, in a series of waves, which advance upon each other and return upon themselves, endeavouring to reflect in their separate and intermingled repeated movements the inexhaustible wealth of one total ineffable experience. The beginning of all this is to be found in i, 5-7. To participate in God who is the Light, we must walk in light, not in darkness. If we say that we have fellowship in God when in fact we are walking in darkness, we are lying in word and in deed, we are not doing the truth. Walking in the light by imitating God who is the Light, means living with a generosity of heart and a moral uprightness that derive from our personal adherence to God's truth and to Revelation, purify us of our sins in the Blood of Christ, enable us to share in the light—the glory—which is the light of God in Christ, and consequently unite us with our fellow men. By what signs can we recognize that we are in the light, that we are doing the truth, that we are living in God?

First of all, by recognizing our sins. Here St. John is speaking of the "value judgment" we make upon our own spiritual condition: I say that I am a sinner, or I do not say this—in both cases, at the root of the judgment there is a spiritual attitude leading either to error and sin or to truth and salvation. In point of fact, "If we say that we have no sin" (i, 8-10), our judgment is partly sinful, an illusion coming from pride—"we deceive ourselves" (i, 8)—partly spiritual error, a lived lie—"the truth is not in us" (i, 8)—and an insult to God, whose Word is no longer a principle of truth for us, so that "we make him a liar" and "his word is not in us." Behind this assertion of our innocence, therefore, there is a pride that is both sinful and illusory, which leads us into lies and the deprivation of God. Conversely, "if we confess our sins" (i, 9), this is humility accepting its condition and judging itself in truth; it is also, and above all, an appeal to God: the humble look of the believer does not end in itself but immediately refers itself to God—who is faithful to his promise, is just and justifying, forgiving and purifying—and to Jesus Christ, who like his Father is just, and has become a propitiation for our sins and our advocate with God. This acute awareness of our souls as sinful, and of God as our Redeemer, implies an attitude of moral uprightness, living truth, homage and trust in God, that re-establishes us or maintains us in communion with God. The Christian, of course, should not sin[4]—"My little children, these things I write to you that you may not sin" (ii, 1)—as the ensuing criteria insist, since they all aim to exclude a particular form of sin, and the epistle returns to them later (iii, 4-18); but the Christian is too imperfect here on earth to be able to avoid sin, hence this duty of sincerity to oneself and to God.

Moreover, these sins that we commit in spite of ourselves are not continuous: there are days when our conscience does not reproach us, and rightly so. The question then becomes a broader one, and we are thrown back upon the problem of spiritual security and anxiety (iii, 19-24): how are we to know that we are in the truth and can thus have peace of mind at the thought of God? This truth and peace will depend on our "heart"—our spiritual intuition of ourselves before God. If our conscience reproaches us (which brings us back to the first case), we must not shut ourselves up within ourselves but take refuge in God—in him who is "greater than our heart,"[5] who transcends us by his knowledge, power, and love. He knows "all things" (as Peter says to Jesus—John xi, 17)—our sins and our repentances—and he will forgive us. This act of absolute abandonment to the God of mystery, in humility, adoration, and hope, is the

[4] On the impeccable Christian see the sound article by P. Galtier, *Mélanges de Science religieuse*, 1947, pp. 137 *et seq.*

[5] Cf. iv, 4 & v, 9: This very simple word emphasizes God's transcendence.

principle of our peace, and the sign that we are in the truth. If our heart does not reproach us, we can feel a bold assurance before God, we can pray to him who is "greater," and who cannot be reached in any other way except through prayer, knowing that our prayers will be heard. And our awareness is sure because it does not end in mere self-contemplation, but gives us a clear sense of our faithfulness: our practice of the commandments and of that which is "pleasing in his sight"—i.e., in concrete terms, faith in Christ and brotherly love. The awareness appears here as something wholly involved in the dynamism of our free acts, the reflective function of our spiritual activity, throwing us more and more upon God, either through our bold confidence and assured prayers or through repentance and humble adoration.

The second criterion is to be found, quite simply, in keeping the commandments and not breaking them. "We know that we have known him, if we keep his commandments" (ii, 3). This "practice" is not a sign external to the experience, which has to be applied to it from outside; it presupposes a voluntary obedience, a generous love, a real commitment at its root. "For this is the charity of God, that we keep his commandments" (v, 3). Here as in the Gospel[6] the commandments are in the first place faith and love (iii, 23): how can we practise them then except by first believing and loving? This practice therefore springs from the deepest impulse of the soul, and is an outward expression of the soul; consequently it brings its own light with it—it enables us to know that we know God (ii, 3), that we are in the truth (ii, 4), that our love is real and perfect (ii, 5). Thus, the lived connection with our free acts, the sanction and light that come from our activity, are one of the elements of our certainty, and hence an essential part of the Christian experience. The epistle comes back to this again and again (iii, 22-24; iv, 20-21; v, 2-3): conscious, voluntary faithfulness to the commandments is the sign, pledge and result of truth, love, and communion; it is the very light of the Christian experience.

More particularly, it is necessary to love one's fellow men in imitation of Christ, and not to hate them (ii, 6-12). This is simply a re-

[6] Cf. M. J. Lagrange, *Évangile selon saint Jean* (Paris, 1925), on John xiv, 21, pp. 386 *et seq.*, and cf. p. 381. Cf. *Theol. Wört. Z.N.T.*, by G. Kittel, Vol. II, art. *entolē* (Schrenk), pp. 549-563.

finement of the second criterion, but St. John is fond of insisting on it (cf. iii, 11-17; iv, 11, 20 *et seq.*; v, 1 *et seq.*)—no doubt because he sees it as the supreme sign of the descent of the new world into the old, the true light into the darkness. It is an "old" commandment (ii, 7), because for every Christian it is one of the first to be learned in the early days of faith; it is "new" (8), because it is as fresh as Christ and as fresh as the young Christian faith. Its importance is brought out immediately by a vivid contrast. The man who loves his brother is in the light, and he does not stumble (ii, 10). He who does not love is in darkness, he wanders about in the dark like a blind man (ii, 9, 11); he is not in the truth; he is a liar (iv, 20); he is "of the evil one"; he turns furiously against those who love; he is virtually a murderer, as Cain was in fact; he has death abiding in him (iii, 10-18). He who loves is in the light and does not stumble (ii, 10); he has passed from death to life and been born of God (iii, 10-15); he abides in God and God in him. Hatred and love of one's fellow men, selfishness and generosity, appear here as the two major forces struggling for the control of the human heart, and St. John does not suggest that there is any middle way between them. Here again, therefore, a fundamental human and Christian attitude is involved. This criterion will be understood all the better when it is remembered what this epistle regards as the three characteristics of brotherly love. It is the fulfilment of an essential commandment, of *the* commandment (iii, 11-23; iv, 21); and this duty is all the more strict, all the more necessary, and all the more significant, the more conscious it is, and the more it forms part of an experience that is direct and graspable and has no deception in it. "He that loveth not his brother whom he seeth, how can he love God whom he seeth not?"[7] (iv, 20). This love is more than a commandment; it is an imitation of God's love for us, for he has loved us by giving us his Son for our redemption. "If God hath so loved us, we also ought to love one another" (iv, 11). It is also an imitation of Christ's love for us: he gave his life for us, and we ought to give our lives for our fellow men, or at least help them as much as we can (iii, 16 *et seq.*). Lastly, this imitation is not done from outside, it springs from the very movement that leads us to love God, and brotherly love is simply

[7] I cannot think that this means that the neighbour is substituted for—i.e., identified with—God. The opening words of the verse emphasize the fact that it is a lie to say that one loves God when one has no love for one's fellow men.

an extension of our love of God; for, "every one that loveth him who begot, loveth him also who is born of him" (v, 1). The commandment and the imitation are interiorized and become identical in this single source, as the communication of the same life, springing up from the heart of God into the hearts of all his sons. Literally, loving one's neighbour means loving God, for it means loving the end of the creative love by the actual power of this love. It will be realized that this is the greatest sign of all, because it combines the deepest inwardness with the most distinct visibility: our neighbour is someone we can see (iv, 20), and we love him with a love that manifests itself outwardly, not only in words but in visible acts that prove our love to be true (iii, 18).

The antithesis becomes broader still with the addition of a new criterion: we must love God, not the world (ii, 15-18). There are not only "children of God" in the world, but "children of the devil" too (iii, 10); not only faith and love, but refusal, hatred, and the dreadful power of human lusts—in a word, "the world." This fact is an essential part of the Christian message,[8] and in this sense the world is the whole collection of forces that are opposed to God and make war on his Kingdom—the domain of evil, darkness, and the Evil One. But in this particular context the fact that the world is mentioned is especially important because it emphasizes an aspect of the struggle that is not very often brought out. Usually the world is presented in the Gospel as the whole collection of forces and beings that are governed by Satan and refuse to believe, and so persecute Christ and Christians.[9] Here it is presented as a temptation, the centre and source of all desire: "For all that is in the world is the concupiscence of the flesh, and the concupiscence of the eyes, and the pride of life, which is not of the Father but is of the world" (ii, 16)—the concupiscences of "the body, in so far as it impels towards sin,"[10] the ardent sensuality of sight (cf. Matt. v, 28), stupid flaunting pride—in short, the lusts of the senses and the lusts of pride, the forms in which evil appears at its most attractive.

These lusts have to be resisted. We must not "love" them, but

[8] J. Chaîne, *Les Épîtres catholiques* (Paris, 1939), p. 163.

[9] Thus John vii, 7; v, 23; ii, 31; xiv, 17-30; xv, 19; xvi, 8, 11, 33; xvii, 6; ix, 11, 25; and in the Epistle, iii, 13 & v, 4 *et seq.*

[10] Chaîne, *op. cit.*, p. 164.

resist their appeal; prevent them from enveloping us, since we are immersed in the world; avoid being seduced by them, since there is that within us which attempts to connive with them and we can so easily succumb to them. We must plunge our souls in God and "do his will." Then—once again—we shall attain to divine communion; we shall avoid the dissipation, illusion, and mendacity that are the world's true being—"the world passeth away and the concupiscence thereof" (ii, 17)—and enter into the communion of faith and love with the God who is and ever shall be, and in him our being will find its eternal destiny and reality and truth: "He that doth the will of God abideth for ever" (ii, 17).

Between the world and the Christian the opposition is therefore absolute; it can only manifest itself in a struggle to the death, in which one party is the victor and the other is vanquished. The Christian's answer to the world's hatred is faith, which represents his victory over the world (v, 4-5). The Christian believes that Jesus is the Son of God. All the lusts and appearances of the world league together to affirm the opposite. But when the Christian accepts the redemptive love of God in the Saviour Jesus Christ, he passes from death to life, from the world to God; he escapes from mendacity and is estabished in the light and in love. This is the first aspect of his victory. Furthermore, the world is always judging Christ, and Christ is always judging the world by his Spirit (John xvi, 8-11). But the world is already condemned, and the Spirit "gives the world the lie." The Christian, by affirming the divinity of Jesus Christ, unites himself with the judgment of the Spirit and condemns the world triumphantly—and this is the second aspect of his victory. Lastly, though the world may hate the Christian and persecute and kill him, the Christian still triumphs; for this too has been predicted. The Christian knows it, he "wonders not" (iii, 13), for he is being treated as his Master was treated, and he too dies only to be resurrected—and, in his being as a son, even here below he "lives for ever." This is the third aspect of his victory. Here we see the absolute opposition between two different kinds of being and life—"the whole world is seated in wickedness" (v, 19), it is already condemned and dead with the evil one; the Christian is in "the true God" (v, 20) and "in his true Son"; he is already saved and living with him. The very existence of the Christian, whose essential act is faith, is a condemnation of the world and a victory over it. And thus, "Whatsoever is born of God overcometh the world: and this is the victory which overcometh the world: our faith" (v, 4).

The last criterion concerns the same theme in another form, and keeps us still entirely within the domain of faith: we must reject all Antichrists, and continue to affirm the true Christ (ii, 18-23). With Christ the world has entered into its last phase,[11] the period of Messianic fulfilment and the time of the great battles by which the victory of Christ will be ensured. The adversary is here: he is Antichrist, who is against Christ, whose one desire is to take Christ's place. He appears as a variety of different antichrists, all denying that Jesus is the Christ, the Son of God, hence denying the Father, and all, therefore, having forsaken the Church. This painful state of affairs has led St. John to write one of the profoundest passages in the epistle, bringing out at one stroke the three elements—churchly, dogmatic, and mystical—necessary to communion with God. Before becoming heretics who left the Church, these antichrists had been in the Church. But they had belonged to the community, and hence to God himself, in appearance only; in reality they had never been of the Church, and their forsaking it proved this. By breaking their connection with the community (ii, 19), they broke their bond with God (ii, 23). This break was the result of an inner break with the truth—it was a lie, a denial that Jesus was the Christ and the Son of God, consequently a denial of the Father; leading to the spiritual loss of both (ii, 22 *et seq.*). And this break presupposed as a condition of its existence another lack, of a deeper nature still: the absence of "the unction from the Holy One" (ii, 20) which alone can teach from within. Having lost their union with the Church, failing to affirm the Truth, having no unction from the Holy One, these men are cut off from communion with God.

Conversely, Christians are in communion with God because they possess these three realities. They "have the unction from the Holy One and know all things" (ii, 20). We shall have to return later to the part thus played by the Spirit. For the moment, let us note that the text suggests that there is an inner action of enlightenment ending in knowledge of the truth, and that this is common to all the members of the community. Consequently, they know the truth, they

[11] On this whole subject cf. Bonsirven, *op. cit.*, pp. 134-136; for a very different treatment, Chaîne, *op. cit.*, pp. 167 *et seq.*

confess the Son and the Father, they possess them; the Father and the Son abide in them. Lastly, they have the unction and the truth, because they have remained faithful to the teaching of the Church as they have known it "from the beginning" of their Christian profession (ii, 24). This conformity to the received teaching—which causes the Father and the Son to abide in them—does not require any new teaching, because it is altogether a matter of faithfulness to the tradition and the unction (ii, 27). Thus, teaching and unction, the Church's magisterium and the Holy Spirit, are all bound up with each other and form a single spiritual structure; any one of them can be considered sufficient, as all imply each other. These three components—mystical, dogmatic, and churchly—describe the authentic structure of the Christian experience, in which the Church appears as the condition, the dogma as the object, and the Spirit as the inner source; and from the vital union of these three—and from it alone—springs divine communion, possession of the Father and the Son.

Affirmation of the dogma of the Church plays such an important part in the communion, it is such a necessary object of faith and at the same time such a clear criterion of "the being of God," that we find it again at the heart of the short passage devoted to the discernment of spirits (iv, 1-6). The word "spirit" oscillates here between two different meanings—one being the principle of inspiration or affirmation (of either error or truth), which has its origin in God or Antichrist, and the other being more concrete and meaning the person thus inspired. "Trying the spirits" thus means testing those who are inspired and the principle by which they are inspired.[12] The object of the discernment is a purely dogmatic affirmation—"Jesus Christ is come in the flesh"—and the criterion, as before, is conformity to the official teaching (iv, 6). Christians have simply to "apply" this criterion of orthodoxy, thanks to the spirit of God;[13] and their faith is a victory over the spirit of Antichrist—whom it unmasks and rejects—and over the world, both of which inspire the false prophets. Here again affirmation of the Church's dogma reveals the principle of inspiration.

[12] Must this be taken (as by Bonsirven and Chaîne) to refer to preternatural phenomena?

[13] The *nous* in verse 6 is ambiguous: in the first part it denotes the Apostle and those responsible for the teaching; in the second it refers to the Christians and ends the appeal made in verse 1.

Clearly, the criteria suggested by St. John are pretty comprehensive, and very closely linked together. Fundamentally they are a demand for—and a manifestation of—an "absolute moral integrity." This is achieved by means of a hard struggle, and in spite of their appearance of untroubled fervour these criteria reflect the Christian's tragic situation. Each in fact signifies an attitude that can only be achieved by the exclusion of a contrary attitude. The Christian is caught between temptation and inspiration, the world and God, Christ and Antichrist. It is only by an absolute concrete fidelity to the divine demands that he can remain in happy communion with the Father and the Son. One seems to glimpse through these opposing alternatives a whole attitude that was threatening the purity of the young Christian faith—the belief that people who had been delivered from sin were henceforth beyond its range; were above any mere obedience to the commandments; had no need to concern themselves with human beings, since they were entirely concerned with God; that concupiscence did not go down into the deep regions of the spirit where they loved the Father; that they could go beyond Christ and the Church, the visible and the human, and reach God, who is invisible. These seem to have been the fearful illusions that threatened the Christians of those days and which John was never tired of condemning. The true Christian only remains true if he denies himself, affirms himself, and conquers, again and again and again. He must therefore be humble, acknowledging his sins and his need for purification; faithful, practising the Lord's commandments; generous-hearted, not sparing himself in the service of his neighbour; detached, resisting his lusts; a man of pure faith, obedient and true, rejecting the lies and seductions of the false Christians—then he may be sure that he abides in God, and God in him. But before he can be assured of this communion, nothing less is needed than the daily giving of his life. It is because he insists so strongly on the necessary criteria of the Christian experience that St. John can insist with equal force on its depth, its certainty, and its inwardness.

3. *The Principles of the Experience*

We must now examine the actual principles of the Christian experience.

Its immediate principles are faith and love—though in fact to say two principles is to put it badly. If a spiritual force is known by its effects, St. John seems to say something like this: he who believes is of God, and born of God (iv, 2; v, 1-4); he who loves is born of God (iv, 7). He who believes has life (v, 13); he who loves has passed from death to life (iii, 13). He who believes abides in God and God in him (iv, 15), he who loves abides in God and God in him (iv, 12-16). The strongest words to denote the possession of God would seem to have to be applied to love, which is not only of God but God himself; yet they are applied to faith—it is the person who believes who possesses the Son and the Father and eternal life (ii, 22 *et seq.*; v, 12 *et seq.*). The strongest words to denote life in the light and the knowledge of God would seem to have to be applied to faith; yet they are applied to love—he who loves abides in the light and the truth (ii, 10 *et seq.*; iv, 20); only he who loves knows God (iv, 7, *et seq.*).

This is sufficient for us to be obliged to conclude that faith and charity are always mutually implied in each other, and that believing and loving represent for St. John two aspects of the same grace, the same spiritual movement, the same personal act, the same life in God. These two aspects are distinct: believing emphasizes the intellectual aspect, it always means confessing Jesus Christ to be the Son of God; loving emphasizes the generous aspect, it means giving oneself to God, to Christ, to one's fellow men, as the Father and the Son have given themselves to us. But these two aspects are inseparable: confessing Christ is the appropriate way for the intellectual being to give himself to God and live in the Truth; to love God and one's fellow men it is necessary to do the truth in one's heart and in one's life. And if we want to find the ultimate reason for this unity, we shall find it not in ourselves, but in God: for God is at once both Light and Love; Christ, in whom we find the Father, is at once both "the true God and life eternal"; consequently, the force that they communicate to us is a force of light and love that makes us beings "engendered of God"—living from God, by God, in God. According to whether St. John wishes to emphasize in man—imperfectly united and imperfectly like God as he is—the aspect of adherence or the aspect of self-giving, he refers either to believing or to loving; but as these two aspects are indissociable in the unity of a single life-movement, he attributes to them the same essential effect—communion with God, i.e. a knowledge entirely suffused by love, and a charity entirely enveloped in light. And that is why, again, he can join the two phrases together: "And this is his commandment, that we should believe in the name of his Son Jesus Christ: and love one another, as he hath given commandment unto us"; and, "He that keepeth his commandments, abideth in him" (iii, 23 *et seq.*).

Two highly significant features still need to be mentioned, however. "Every one that loveth is born of God, and knoweth God. He that loveth not, knoweth not God: for God is charity" (iv, 7 *et seq.*). To know, it is necessary to be. God is absolute generosity giving itself: anyone who does not reproduce within himself, with the help of the divine power, this movement of giving, has not acceded to the divine being, has not entered into his inner life, has not been assimilated to him, and consequently cannot know him from within. The kind of knowledge with which we are concerned here comes from assimilation, from similarity of being, and it exists, not on the level of affirmation or intellectual adherence, but of lived experience. It is a knowledge that is the culmination of faith; its dynamic principle is love, and it is identical with a lived and conscious communion with God.

The second point concerns the possession of the testimony of God through faith. "He that believeth . . . hath the testimony of God in himself" (v, 10)—the testimony given by God to his Son (v, 9 *et seq.*). This testimony is an act of God, on the one hand historical and dated (*Zōēn aiōnion edōken emin*—v, 11), on the other hand inward and permanent (*tēn marturian ēn memarturēken*—v, 10; cf. 9). The first phrase refers to the Christian revelation as historically manifested in Christ, and it includes, besides the Gospel, the words, the signs and the grace communicated by Christ; the second relates to the interiorization of this testimony by means of personal faith. There are thus two sides to this testimony—its proposition, so that one can believe in it, and following from this the words and signs, and the penetration by grace, that make up the actual call to faith. One may ignore this call, the testimony that God gives to his Son, and therefore refuse to believe either in the Son—the object of the testimony—or the Father, its author and guarantor; this means making God a liar (v, 10). Or one may respond to the call, believe in the Son by believing in the testimony given to him by the Father, and thus, in the words of the Gospel, "set to his seal that God is true" (John iii, 33). But then the testimony becomes interiorized:

by believing and becoming a true believer one possesses the Son, possesses the life that is in the Son (v, 10 *et seq.*), possesses therefore within oneself (v, 10) the testimony of God, which is the communication of eternal life, lived and experienced; thenceforward, too, one knows (v, 13) that one possesses eternal life. Faith has become a conscious possession of eternal life. This brings us back to the words of the Gospel: "Now this is eternal life: that they may know thee, the only true God, and Jesus Christ whom thou hast sent" (xvii, 3). This life is "the knowledge of faith that is a prelude to the vision of heaven," and "it is called eternal life because it is the fundamental act in the Christian's new life, which will know neither end nor interruption."[14] But the Epistle, in conformity with its aim, adds that the true believer has become aware of this life within him, and that he has "an intimate experience of this divine life in Jesus."[15] This is faith's highest privilege, which the Apostle experienced to the full, and which with his whole being he wants to enable his followers to discover: "These things I write to you that you may know that you have eternal life, you who believe in the name of the Son of God" (v, 13).

We have still not reached the heart of the problem. Faith and charity are indeed the immediate principles of the experience, but the deepest and ultimate principle is the Holy Spirit. St. John refers five times in the epistle to this part played by the Holy Spirit. In this he is taking up one of the main themes of the Gospel—the Spirit of Truth who teaches from within the truths enunciated by the Lord. If passages like John xiv, 26—"The Holy Ghost . . . will teach you all things, and brings all things to your mind, whatsoever I shall have said to you"—are taken to be direct references to the apostles and their successors,[16] it must be said that in the epistle St. John extends it to all the faithful. This Spirit, which he describes, in words that are stronger than any of the others, as "the Truth" (v, 6) is above all the Enlightener, he who teaches from within, who enables us to discern and embrace and comprehend the truth.

[14] F. M. Braun, *Évangile selon saint Jean*, in *La Sainte Bible*, by L. Pirot, Vol. X (Paris, 1935), p. 446.

[15] Bonsirven, *op. cit.*, p. 265.

[16] Braun, *op. cit.*, p. 431 (with A. Durand, *Évangile selon saint Jean*, Coll. "Verbum salutis" [Paris, 1930], in h. l.; J. Huby, *Le Discours de Jésus après la Cène* [Paris, 1942], in h. l.).

Let us take the first passage, ii, 20-27: "But you have the unction from the Holy One and know all things. I have not written to you as to them that know not the truth, but as to them that know it . . . Let that which you have heard from the beginning abide in you. If that abide in you, which you have heard from the beginning, you also shall abide in the Son and in the Father . . . And as for you, let the unction which you have received from him abide in you. And you have no need that any man teach you; but as his unction teacheth you of all things, and is truth (*halēthes*), and is no lie. And as it hath taught you, abide in him." Let us try to make a list of the things that characterize this unction. It is an inner communication of the Holy Spirit, made to all Christians. It abides in them: it is therefore a permanent principle of divine activity. It is in fact a permanent principle of knowledge: as a result of it all Christians know, and St. John writes to them as to people who know. This principle of knowledge refers to an object, which is the traditional teaching: "Let that which you have heard from the beginning abide in you"; and whereas a teacher teaches from without (ii, 27), this power of knowledge teaches from within, with an action that brings enlightenment. Its function is to enable people to adhere to the truth that is preached, to understand it and thus interiorize it within the Christian soul so that it may "abide in him." Though it would be a mistake to insist too much on St. John's "aorists" and "perfect ones," they must undoubtedly be given their full value when they are opposed to each other in two parallel phrases (ii, 27). Let us add, then, that the unction taught the Christians (*edidaxen*) when they acceded to the faith, and it teaches them continuously (*didaskei*) during their life of faith. This inner possession of the teaching may be lost; it only continues to be held through a free adherence and a free faithfulness (ii, 24); the unction remains in the soul on the same conditions. When as a result of the unction one remains faithful to the received teaching, one abides in the Son and the Father, in communion with God.

A permanent principle of divine life, communicated by the Holy Spirit, thus animates the life of the Christian. Its inner power and sweetness (it is an unction) enable the Christian mystery to be discerned, affirmed, and lived as it is taught in the Church (this is, essentially, Christ's divinity), and consequently lead to communion with God. If one is asked to give a name to this mysterious unction, it seems that one must recognize it to be the power of life that is known as faith and love, but seen from the point of view of its permanent living source in the Holy Spirit. It will have been noted, moreover, that St. John emphasizes the discerning function of the unction. The Christian world itself is saturated with errors. It has its false Christians, its false prophets, its antichrists (here should be added iv, 1-6), and all these deny Christ. One can only be a Christian by cutting oneself off from them and asserting against them the truth of Christ, who is both incarnate (iv, 2) and the Son of God (iii, 22 *et seq.*). This principle of discernment is in the first case called an unction and in the second, spirit, but it is the same thing in both cases—the principle of knowledge communicated by the Holy Spirit.

The same doctrine, I believe, could be found again in another form—the Spirit inserting the testimony of the Father within us.[17] This testimony is the action by which the Father communicates eternal life to us by giving us his Son; it implies Christ's whole mission, visible and invisible; it finally leads to that knowledge of the Father and the Son which is eternal life itself. We may believe, here again, that it is through the Holy Spirit that the Father gives us life—perhaps this is what St. John means in those mysterious verses, v, 6-8: Jesus Christ came by and in water and blood—the water of Jordan and the Passion? Baptism and the Eucharist? But the water and the blood would be nothing without the Spirit. And if all three give testimony, the water and the blood can only do so because they are vivified by the Spirit. Thus it is the Spirit, the invisible one, who gives the supreme testimony: he is "the Truth," as the Father and Son are the "True One"; and it is the Spirit who through blood and water, and ultimately through the faith and love which they nourish, communicates to us knowledge of the truth, eternal life, the testimony of the Father.

However that may be, the Holy Spirit plays a further part on another level: he enables us to become conscious of our communion with God. "And in this we know that he abideth in us, by the Spirit which he hath given us" (iii, 24). "In this we know that we abide in him and he in us: because he hath given us of his spirit" (iv, 13). The two things are slightly different: he has given us his Spirit, and he has given us of his Spirit. But the one is not complete

[17] Cf. Chaîne, *op. cit.*, pp. 213 *et seq.*, and Bonsirven, *op. cit.*, p. 146.

without the other: the Spirit cannot be possessed except by our possessing its unction—by sharing in it, i.e. the faith and love that come from it to enable us to know our communion with God from within. And this communion cannot be known unless its three aspects—mystical, dogmatic, and churchly—are closely linked together in the living act of faith, and are lived in unfailing faithfulness. Then there springs into being that sweet, luminous, blissful awareness that is the supreme flowering of eternal life here on earth. For St. John to insist so strongly on it, it must needs be real; for him to hedge it in with so many criteria, it must needs be mysterious. It is not something seen; it is a loving knowledge lived in faith. But this profound sort of intuition, this translucent experience, this concrete perception of our life in God, is so clear that we Christians do indeed know that we are in God and God in us.

When we try to take a bird's-eye view of the experience thus described, we are struck by the paradoxical nature of its unitive and active character. It is an experience of communion, and this communion is with a Trinity—in its source, for the charity of the Father gives us the Son and the Holy Spirit; in its object, which is (reciprocal) immanence in the Father and the Son, through the Holy Spirit; in its end, the transformation into God in sight. It is "Christly," for it is through Christ the Saviour that we become sons, and in the Son that we find the Father and eternal life. It is pneumatic, for it is the strength of the Spirit that teaches us faith and love and enables us to become aware of our life in the Father and the Son. This communion is therefore a life-relationship with the Trinity, a relationship becoming conscious of itself through faith and love. It is situated at the heart, or apex, of the spirit. It is a gift that can only be accepted; it is the highest passivity of the human being seized by God and hence holding God and held by God, in an embrace beyond all description.

But this communion is only possible as a result of the most purified, and generous, and continuous activity possible; and thus the experience of this communion is an experience of faithfulness, woven out of a living and active relationship with God—affirming Christ against the lies and persecutions of the world; acknowledging one's sins and purifying oneself in the Blood of Christ; rejecting the three kinds of desire and avoiding their strangling embrace; remaining faithful to the received teaching of the Church, to her commandments, to charity in action and in truth. Spiritual activity—an activity that is costing, incessant, and integral—is incorporated into the experience, and establishes its normative guiding lines of force.

Thus communion and faithfulness together make up a single experience: there is no spiritual activity without at least the suggestion of divine communion, and no real communion without generous activity. The spiritual activity is the result of the communion, since it draws its strength from it; it is its condition, since it alone maintains it; it is the sign of it, since it reveals the fact that it is effectively present. And the communion in its turn is the basic food of an activity that becomes more and more purified, vigorous, and joyful. If we add that the direct principle of the activity—faith and love—is also the direct principle of the communion, it will be realized that we are in the presence of an experience of an indestructible unity, in which outer and inner, action and suffering, integral faithfulness and full communion, spring from one and the same movement. It is therefore futile to attempt to separate these things and to stress any one particular aspect—the most visible (brotherly love) or the most invisible (the unction of the Holy Ghost); the most external (fidelity to the received teaching) or the most intimate (the testimony of God). This becomes more impossible still, when we remember that this entire experience is wholly a matter of life in Christ, a relationship to the True One, in whom we are given the one and only principle of life, faithfulness, and communion. The Christian experience, as presented by St. John, is an integral experience or it is nothing.

PART III
Structural Lines

CHAPTER SEVEN

The Christian Experience an Experience within the Church

EVERY Christian experience takes place within the Church: the Church relationship is a necessary and essential part of the experience. The Church is, in fact, "the field in which the divine life that flows through Christ comes to full power"[1]—Christ's "Plerome"—and no one outside her confines—for she is the organ of salvation, the spiritual and fleshly temple in which the Holy One is present—can be seized by the redemptive power of Christ and live with His life. Moreover, the Church comes before the Christian in point of time. Born of Christ's love, and blood, and glory, she is given by God antecedently to any kind of human activity. She is "the Church of God which he hath purchased with his own blood" (Acts xx, 28), the Ark which all must enter, the Kingdom in which all must be included, the Body in which all must be incorporated if they are to be removed from the world of sin and darkness and brought into the world of light and life—if they are to be "saved" (Acts ii, 47). Still further, the Church transmits to Christians her own spiritual being. She is the Mother; and she brings Christians into being by her intercession, by the Word of God, by the sacraments of her Faith. She is the mother's womb that no Christian can ever leave, because its life never stops being passed on to him—into the Church this life comes endlessly from its source, Jesus Christ. Lastly, as a result of this, the Church gives Christians all the vitality of her own spiritual life. By the Word that nourishes their faith, the sacraments that restore and increase their love, the rules that govern

[1] L. CERFAUX, *La Théologie de l'Église d'après saint Paul* (Paris, 1942), p. 260.

their concrete activity, the Church lies at the root of their religious attitude, at the heart of their decisions, at the source of their faith and their activity as Christians.

Thus, Christian beings are beings within the Church, the result of a whole network of church relationships that we shall soon have to describe. Consequently, the Christian experience takes place entirely within this network of relationships, which are its governing and determining conditions. Anyone who could fully understand this system of relationships—but it is impossible—would *ipso facto* understand the Christian experience in all its detail. In this chapter I shall simply try to describe some of the main aspects that characterize the Christian being in the Church, and consequently some of the main lines of the Christian experience. I am not—need I say?—attempting a complete theology of the Church; I begin by taking that for granted. Nor at this stage am I attempting to describe the Christian experience; I am merely trying to "place" it.

1. *The Mystery of the Church's Presence*

Living in the Church means living surrounded by mystery, and hence—because the Church is the Act of Redemption made permanent, lasting from the Ascension to the Parousia—it means living at the very centre of the movement that carries mankind forward. For Christianity, of course, there is only one mystery of salvation; it is a tremendous divine action that takes place, one may say, on three different levels.

There is in the first place the mystery of the God who desires our salvation. God, who is utterly remote, infinite, and holy, and yet at the same time endlessly present to all his creatures—even to those who are sinners—desires his creatures to be present to him too, and to return to communion with him. Consequently, he saves them by recalling them to himself, by forgiving them and sanctifying them—in a word, by introducing agape, which is eternal, into the heart of mankind, and into the heart of each individual man. Thus we have been—and are—sanctified by the will of the Father (Heb. x, 10). And God saves us in Christ. The love of God becomes effective through his gift to us of his Son: "God sent not his Son into the world to judge the world, but that the world may be saved by him" (John iii, 17). And he ordained that he should be called Jesus, "for he shall save his people from their sins" (Matt. i, 21).

In short, it is by the will of God that we are saved, but "by the oblation of the body of Jesus Christ once" (Heb. x, 10). Thus Christ saves us by one act of oblation, which began with his Incarnation and continued throughout all the actions of his life.

This Act of Redemption is a revelation: Christ is the image of the invisible God, without stain of sin, the living glory of the Father, the revelation of God's secrets; by his presence, his life, and his Word, God's existential Epiphany. It is also a reconciliation: it culminates in the Cross. God is "in Christ reconciling the world to himself" (II Cor. v, 19), and through the love that surrenders itself to be sacrificed Christ redeems us from sin and creates within himself the new man. And it is a transfiguration: its consummation is the resurrection. The Father can resurrect Christ because he is all-powerful; Christ resurrects himself, for he has "power to lay down his life" and "power to take it up again" (John x, 17). He thus becomes "the Spirit that giveth life," the principle of divinized existence, for the Father gives him "to have life in himself" (John v, 26) and to pass it on to others. Through this one act, in all the forms it takes in history, we are in Christ created for a new life. And always it is the same single mystery, of the God who desires our salvation—the mystery of the Father "who hath delivered us from the power of darkness, and hath translated us into the Kingdom of the Son of his love" (Col. i, 13).

These words bring us to the last stage of the divine intention—God saving us through Christ in the Church. The Church is the human, spiritual, and physical "medium" in which the Act of Redemption is expressed and operates. She is thus a theandric reality, constituted by the immanent power of Christ within her. Christ gives her her permanent foundation through the power that issues from his sacrifice; he gives her ever-present life and growth through the efficacy of the Act of Redemption which has been consummated once and for all; he creates her by his "influx" as her Head, that is to say, by the transcendent causality that implants the Church's being, and Christ's being, in every Christian—the "new creature." Her mediating functions are continued in three different ways—evangelically, through witness and the Word; liturgically, through worship and the sacraments; and apostolically, by fixing the standards of Christian activity. The Church is thus in a state of absolute existential dependence on Christ and God; she is the full, effective, permanent expression of the Act of Redemption; the mystery of God the Saviour, present and active amongst men.

This mystery of the Church has three essential features. In the first place, it is a mystery of unity. The Church is the holy people, created and gathered together by God from the beginning of the world to its consummation, in stages, in a variety of historic forms that must not be allowed to obscure its profound unity; a people heralded by signs and symbols, made actual in mystery, finding its fulfilment in glory; a people appearing fully at Pentecost; its direct principle the Spirit given by the Son and the Father, and its unity therefore profoundly personal since it reaches to the deepest roots of human existence; a means to perfect unity, because one single Spirit inspires all Christians, and entirely transcendent because its unity is always the unity of a new creation,[2] serving a divine purpose, the creation of the new man in Christ. Through faith and baptism the Christian is at once introduced into this tremendous, mysterious unity.

It is also a mystery of differentiation. The Church is the Body of Christ, and its unity is differentiated to a point beyond imagination. There is the differentiation of cultus as between clergy and faithful, and within this differences of vocation, of gifts, of function; at the root of all this is an ontological differentiation between all the various members, each of whom has his own way of imitating the one Christ. This infinite diversity is willed by the Spirit, so that something of Christ's inexhaustible riches may be revealed and made manifest; and the Christian is thus both enfolded within a unity, and given his own special place within it—given his own particular part to play, allotted his own personal position by the will of God and the call of the Spirit. And he is expected to accept his own unique vocation and increasingly do his best to fulfil it.

What is ultimately achieved through this unity and differentiation is a mystery of love. The Church is Christ's Bride. Christ "loved her and gave himself for her, so as to make her pure" and to be united with her in "a marriage that restores her virginity."[3] And in his own way every Christian is the Lord's bride and spouse—"prevented" and enfolded by his charity, made to respond to him in freedom and

[2] Cf. Cerfaux, *op. cit.*, pp. 48-50.
[3] St. John Chrysostom, P. G., 52, 400.

thus to enter into communion with him.[4] Because the Christian is not only a member, but a person, his bond with Christ is not only a means to his own particular incorporation in the whole but a means to a transfiguring personalization, and this comes from incorporation within the Church.

Finally, this mystery of the Church is presented, and expressed, and communicated, sacramentally; and this is its proper form of existence. For since man is a soul acting and expressing itself through a body, he is immersed in a world of symbols, and consequently the mystery of the Church is communicated to him by means of symbols. Just as Christ's humanity was once visible as the efficacious sign of the mystery of salvation, so the Church has its own humanity as the efficacious sign of the same saving mystery. Christian existence is essentially spiritual, being based on an *esse spirituale*,[5] grace; but, as communicated to human beings by the God-Man, it comes to us by way of the body, and is made effective in us by means of signs. The divine agape was first communicated through Christ's Humanity: it is now communicated through the Humanity of the Church.

Every level of reality is included. The divine truth is communicated in the Word of God, which first appears as human thought and speech, and ends in the Gospels, the *Credo* and the dogmatic teaching of the Church. The divine life is communicated by the sacraments —things, words, and actions that signify, contain, and transmit God's redeeming will and the life of the Holy Trinity. Both are communicated by men who have been consecrated, whose souls have been transformed and rendered suitable for the transmission of truth and grace by means of visible acts. Human words, human things, human persons, have all become efficacious signs of the Act of Redemption,[6] and been synthesized into one complex whole to continue Christ's own activity.

[4] Cf. the excellent passage from Father Damien, in H. De Lubac, *Catholicisme* (Paris, 1938), pp. 357-361.

[5] St. Thomas, *De Ver.*, 27, 2, c & 7^{m}.

[6] Y. Congar, *Esquisses du mystère de l'Église* (Paris, 1941): "The sacraments are not, properly speaking, new acts; in the spiritual mode of being of a symbolic-real celebration they are the mystery of the redemption accomplished by Jesus Christ actually present—substantially, in the Holy Eucharist, and at least in the aspect of sanctifying grace in Baptism and the other sacraments" (p. 33). Cf. C. V. Héris: "In some mysterious way the Act of Redemption, which is accomplished perfectly in the Holy Eucharist, must be perpetuated by and through the other sacraments." *La Maison-Dieu*, 14, p. 66.

But these signs communicate the mystery in their own way. They do so *really*, because they are willed and actualized by Christ who instituted them. As means of expression, they witness to the invisible Presence to which they give visible form. As means of action, they are a power, making the divine power active in the Church Militant. As means of communion, they actualize Christ's own mediation and make men one with God. But they do all this *under a veil*. The words and the things and the persons envelop and hide the mystery they transmit. They form an enormous fleshly and cosmic body round the mystery; they present it in the form of an image, which will symbolize it until the end of the world; they offer it in a history in which it will always be incarnate here on earth. Only the grace of God that forms the basis of the mystery thus signified can enable us to grasp it, to pierce the envelope and reach the actual substance.[7] In Moehler's words, the Church "is the permanent Incarnation of the Son of God."[8]

This aspect of the mystery of the Church governs one of the first lines of force of the Christian experience.

The Christian experience is the adherence to a mystery, the mystery of the Act of Redemption, hence the mystery of Christ the Saviour, in whom all other mysteries are included. It is by faith—which means participation in the mind of God and the beginning of eternal life—that we enter, live, and grow in the mystery of salvation, which is ultimately the mystery of the Holy Trinity. For the Spirit

[7] Cf. O. CASEL, *Le Mystère du culte dans le Christianisme* (Paris, 1946), pp. 54-58. On this point cf. Cahier 14 of *La Maison-Dieu*, particularly the article by Fr. I. H. DALMAIS, pp. 67 *et seq.*; also the summary by D. DEKKERS, p. 63, and the note by Fr. C. V. HÉRIS, pp. 65-66. If I had to give my own account of the problem, I should make a distinction between the Act of Redemption and the redemptive actions. The former is one and everlasting; it is made incarnate in the latter, which are many, 'historical,' and past. In this sense, it is not the historic actions that are present in the mystery of the Church—these are over and done with—but the Act of Redemption, which was the living soul of these actions—the one oblation, Jesus Christ. Cf. the important passage in *Mediator Dei:* "Hardly was the divine Word made flesh, when it manifested itself to the world in the richness of the priestly office, subjecting itself to the Eternal Father, as indeed throughout the course of its whole life it never ceased to do . . . and in a wonderful way found its consummation in the bloody sacrifice of the cross . . ." For the Beatific Vision, which lies at the root of this act, cf. *Mystici Corporis*.

[8] *Symbolique*, I, 5, § 36. For the meaning of this passage in Moehler, cf. in *L'Église est une, Hommage à Moehler* (Paris, 1939), the article by J. R. GEISELMANN, *Les aspects divers de l'unité et de l'amour*, pp. 174 *et seq.*

is the principle of the Church's existence; the principle of her unity, her differentiation, and her love. Christ himself is both her source, because he merited and gives the Holy Spirit, and the ultimate aim of her activity, because in her he forms "the one Man," the total Christ. And God the Father is her principle, because he gave Christ and the Holy Spirit, and her end, since the total Christ belongs to him and only lives to give him everlasting glory. Thus the Christian experience takes place entirely, and increasingly, within the translucent cloud of faith.

This mystery, it must be emphasized, is something that is given. Man is not called upon to make it or create it. It exists before him and calls him. His job, therefore, is to open himself to it, to accept it, and to insert himself within it. Through faith, again, he bows down in homage and submission before it as it unfolds itself to him: "The primary subjection of man to God is by faith."[9] By this absolute homage he embraces the mystery in all its three aspects: he enters into the redemptive action that saves the soul by making it divine, and, far from being absorbed by it, he finds himself as a result of this very insertion deepened and universalized, incorporated and personalized, to the maximum degree.

Lastly, it is a sacramental mystery, and the Christian enters into it according to the degree of his personal participation in it. He begins to understand the signs, and to realize their spiritual meaning, and to adhere to the efficacious presence of the Act of Redemption within them. He realizes these things by inserting himself within them: by means of the dogmatic statements of the faith he creates within himself a system of human thought that expresses God's thoughts; through the sacramental acts, by his intention, his faith, and his love, he grasps the divine life; through the hierarchy he meets the Lord, trusting the priesthood and submitting to them "as taking Christ's place."[10] Finally, through all the sacramental realities, he communicates with God—the God of Truth, the God of Love, the God who is the Lord. All the clarity and vigour of faith are needed if he is to accept this mediation and live his whole life according to it—for it is in the half-light of the world of signs and symbols that the Christian experience takes place.

This experience therefore involves a living relationship with a

[9] St. Thomas, *S. Th.*, II. II, 16, I c.
[10] *S. Th.*, III[a], 8, 6, c.

mystery. It originates in mystery, develops in mystery, and tends to re-create the mystery of redemption. As its source, as its structure, as its end, stands the mystery of infinite Love; and this it apprehends, lives, realizes, in a society that is a properly articulated whole—the visible Church, the earthly landmark and tangible medium of the eternal, efficacious, invisible Love concentrated in Jesus Christ, "whom having not seen, you love; in whom also now, though you see him not, you believe" (I Peter i, 8). It is a relationship with the mystery of the People, the Body, the Bride, whose dimensions and complexity, and whose very essence, transcend it on all sides, and so are continually throwing it into a state of existence beyond itself—into God. Christian being is a being-within the mystery of the Church; and the Christian experience is the condition, the consciousness, the realization of this mysterious "being-within." It is a relationship that can never be emptied of its content, because it is itself the determining factor in the experience—a psychological relationship, being made up of a continuous process of free acts, and a trans-psychological relationship, being God-centred, deriving its origin, its being, and its end from a God of mystery; a relationship which on the one hand is lived in the most secret recesses of the soul, in adoration, love, and praise—"Blessed be the God and Father of our Lord Jesus Christ, who hath blessed us with spiritual blessings in heavenly places, in Christ" (Eph. i, 3)—and on the other finds its due form and fulfilment in the mystery of the liturgy, in the "celebration of the mystery" that makes Christ present in the Act of Redemption, in that great Assembly in which all are united in Christ, and combine to form a single heart and soul which can be presented as an offering to the Father; in that "forest of symbols" in which the splendid ceremony, with its marvellous singing, unfolds to the glory of God; in the Church's great liturgy, the outline, the promise, the reflection and indeed the actual presence of the liturgy of Heaven,[11] because, at its living centre, is the homage of the Lord Jesus Christ himself.

2. *The Mystery of the Church's Mission*

The mystery of the Church is not merely a hidden reality of Redemption and Beatitude, to which we are united in love; it is

[11] Cf. Rev. Fr. Clérissac, *Le Mystère de l'Église* (Saint-Maximin, 1925), ch. iv, pp. 76 *et seq.*

also a mystery shared with man, a seed that has to be made to grow.

The Church on earth is the mystery of the unfolding of Christ between Pentecost and the Parousia. For the Church this means a time of development and growth, a time entirely devoted to the mission conferred upon her by him who was resurrected: "All power is given to me in heaven and in earth. Going therefore teach ye all nations . . ." (Matt. xxviii, 18-19). This mission describes the being of the Church as a source of activity.[12] Having received the mystery, she has to realize it in her life. After all that Christ performed by himself, there comes all that he wills to do through us. As her Lord and Head, he defines the Church's mission: it is the continuation of his own. He gives her the power to do this—his own power as our Redeemer; he gives the order (from outside) and the impulse (from within) to guide her, and to ensure that her mission will be fulfilled; and he addresses himself in the first place to those he has chosen for the purpose, those whom he sends, as he was sent by his Father.[13] The "power of an indissoluble life" (Heb. vii, 16) within him is henceforth entrusted to the apostles and their successors, who in his name are to "rule the church of God"—build the Temple, construct the Body, gather together the People. And all this means, in fact, making the original Act of Redemption explicit, and spreading it abroad amongst mankind by the grace of Christ and human endeavour. Henceforth, time and the human race and the universe itself have only one purpose, the fulfilment of this mission; and, when it is complete, time will reach its consummation, the universe will pass away, and the New Jerusalem will appear before God in all its glory. Meanwhile, however, there is work to be done, and all the faith that Christians can muster, all their love, all their industry, all their pleasures and pains, all their hope, are to be thrown into this task, which is always there to be continued, and pushed forward, and begun again from the beginning. This active mission

[12] On this mission, which is the Church's Aspotolicity, cf. Mgr. C. Journet, *L'Église du Verbe Incarné* (Paris, 1941), ch. x, pp. 642-647, and L. M. Dewailly, *Mission de l'Église et Apostolicité,* in *Rev. des Sc. phil. et théol.,* 1948, I, pp. 2 *et seq.*

[13] Cf. D. Gréa, *De l'Église et de sa divine constitution* (Paris, 1947), I, vi, p. 19: "The essence of the power conferred upon the hierarchy, the vital operation that is performed and transmitted in her, is a power unique and indivisible, enclosed within the unique and indivisible mission of Jesus Christ, and transmitted by him individually."

introduced like leaven into the dough of history is the Church herself, the mystery of the Act of Redemption, in labour.

But, as I have said, there are some who are specially responsible for this mission. In the beginning there were those who saw Christ and touched him; who for years were able to listen to his words and know themselves loved by him; who ate and drank with him after his Resurrection; and whom he nominated as his witnesses and as the pastors of his Church. Next comes the apostolic body, the Pope and the bishops, the hierarchy. This last is a great mystery,[14] its function being to utilize human freedom so as to make the Act of Redemption actual and efficacious. As such it is the efficient instrumental cause of the Church, subject to the causality of Christ its Head, who is himself subject to the utterly divine, exclusively creative causality of the Holy Trinity. Thus the hierarchy becomes the power that confers Christian existence: its magisterium prepares the human soul for the reception of truth and the gift of faith; its sacramental activity communicates the life and grace that are in Christ; by its juridical power it guides the spiritual activity of the faithful towards the fulfilment of Christ's will for them, which is the fulfilment of its mission. It is thus always a mystery, actualizing the redemptive power of Christ.

For its action, human, visible, and incarnate though it is, is impregnated through and through by the Act of Redemption: it is founded upon the invisible action of Christ, who inspires the hierarchy and prepares the souls of men to respond to its labours; it actualizes Christ's mediating activity; it leads to new and ever deeper activity by Christ in the soul. Consequently its function is vital and vitalizing—a maternal function of bringing to spiritual birth.[15] It is Christ who creates Christians, but it is the Church who—in and through Christ—bears them in her womb. Her maternity is purely spiritual. The priesthood is constituted as such by the ontological capacity for action which is its special characteristic and, normally, by grace; it becomes a priesthood in act when it unites itself to Jesus Christ in an intention—normally experienced through faith and charity—to do whatsoever Christ wills to do: through the junction of these two wills, and through the spiritual union that follows, the

[14] Cf. Mgr. C. Journet, *op. cit.*, pp. 29-30 & 645 *et seq.*

[15] Cf. M. J. Scheeben, *Le mystère de l'Église et de ses sacrements* (trans. by Kerkvoode in the Collection "*Unam Sanctam*"), Paris, 1948, pp. 86-90.

vital communication is established.[16] Thus, by a wonderful act of condescension, our Lord has made himself dependent on the hierarchy. Before he can be communicated in the mystery of the Church, the hierarchy has to provide him with the actual possibility of contact, through the free act that is comprised in the intention of fulfilling the mission. But his causality is always transcendent: through this simple act, which may be very poor from the religious point of view—the simplest intention to do what he wills—but which, psychologically, has to be performed, the redemptive activity, and grace and charity, are transmitted. The life passes through the hierarchy without ever coming *from* it—more precisely, without being *in* any particular member of the hierarchy, though it is in the whole Body and passes through it. And it is on this level—a vital, not a juridical level—that connection is established between the hierarchy and all the faithful—on a level at which life is communicated in its three stages: preparation, realization, fructification.

But this communication takes a standard form: it is imposed under certain conditions laid down by Christ. Since the starting-point, and the means, and the end of the hierarchy's action, are all determined by Christ, who is all-powerful, they are fixed irrevocably, and the hierarchy is similarly fixed with them. Its power, its control, its authority, are simply a continuation and application of Christ's own might and kingship and sovereignty. All power has been given to Christ; this power is passed on to the Church; and the first obligation laid upon any Christian is obedience in the faith. But nothing in the Church is purely external. There is only one Spirit in the hierarchy and in the faithful, the Spirit who "hath placed you bishops, to rule the church of God" (Acts xx, 28), and placed "the whole flock" (*ibid.*) round them to receive and fulfil the Lord's commandments. Consequently, the strength of the Spirit moulds, calls upon, impels the Christian to be obedient to the faith. He is made in such a way that he finds fulfilment in the Church according to the law of life given by the Lord, and finds his own particular place, his own personal vocation, in the body of spiritual members in accordance with the Body's law of life. In the Christian there is an ontological call towards

[16] In a sacrament, the rite itself (the canonists' matter and form) is simply the "matter"; the "form" is the human will in submission to the will of Christ.

hierarchization, because Christ in the Spirit has established his own Body hierarchically.

Take for example the matter of faith. It assumes that there exists within the believer the instinct of the Holy Spirit and the *determinatio credendorum*. The hierarchy's function is to teach, to clarify, to define the content of faith; its infallible magisterium gives it the power to express and clarify and construct the whole body of belief—to maintain the *Puritas ipsa Evangelii in Ecclesia*.[17] Faith is therefore a totality of truths presented authoritatively from outside and received by the believer in a spirit of obedience. But though the intellectual formulation may come to the believer from "outside," the same truths exist within him through the inner promptings of the Holy Ghost. The truth is proposed infallibly in the Holy Spirit, and accepted in the Holy Spirit by the believer: the instinct of the Holy Spirit inclines him towards acceptance of truths formulated in the presence of the Holy Spirit; and ultimately, because authority and obedience are both rooted in the same Spirit, the "outwardness," real though it is, derives from and culminates in a deeper inwardness, which is the actual mystery of the Church. And by immersing himself in the teaching imparted by the hierarchy, the believer immerses himself in the Holy Spirit and thus realizes his liberation and his personalization.

But we must not blur the necessary distinctions. The "determination" of the truths to be believed, of sacramental practice and spiritual behaviour, appears in the first instance as a law—because it either teaches what was previously unknown, or demands something not previously performed, or imposes something that goes against the grain. In the upbringing of children, in the new world of choice and decision opening before the eyes of adolescents, in the ordinary problems of everyday life, there is an external element, a moment of heteronomy, that may pass but will return again and again until the soul is perfectly conformed to the will of God. Because the call sounded in the depths by the Holy Spirit inevitably comes up against resistances in us, conflicts arise, the obstacles raised by carnal man set themselves up against the demands of the spirit, and the need for sacrifice appears: at every moment we have to deny ourselves to follow Christ, and lose our souls in order to save them.

Nevertheless, the Church's authoritative assertions take on in-

[17] *Concil. Trident.*, sess. iv, *Decret de Canonicis Scripturis.*

creasingly the appearance of a call. As faith and love increase, and the creature becomes more spiritual, obedience becomes a more inward matter, the product and manifestation of love: "he who loves me keeps my commandments." Spirit recognizes Spirit, love recognizes love, the soul becomes "connaturalized" with the propositions made by the hierarchy, and from then on obedience is experienced as a freedom embraced with ever greater willingness, abandonment, and joy. Christ gave us the ultimate example of this "coinherence" of obedience and love, obedience and freedom, and the Christian, after Christ and through him, has gradually to enter into the same experience. Thenceforward, an immense willingness, an immense desire, an immense devotion rise up from the soul animated by love, and in the very act of sacrifice a strength greater than all others leads to the utterance of that great affirmative that is the glory of God and the salvation of man—"Not as I will, but as thou wilt"—the affirmative that establishes the Church in the hearts of all who believe, and means the secret accomplishment of her mysterious mission.

We must go further. The visible Church, as we have shown, is indissolubly both "pneumatic" and "juridical". The "juridical" element is entirely at the service of the "pneumatic," the organism entirely at the service of the Spirit. Through the hierarchy, Christ communicates his Spirit; through the hierarchy, the faithful are brought into immediate contact with the Spirit; through the hierarchy, they are delivered, consecrated, animated, by "the law of the spirit of life in Jesus Christ"; through the hierarchy, they carry in their minds and hearts "the interior inspiration and impulse of the Holy Spirit";[18] through the hierarchy, they become "spiritual," lively, free, efficacious.[19] As a result of this, the faithful react upon the hierarchy itself.[20] Their welcome and acceptance, their desires and needs, their appeal, explicit or divined, weigh with the weight of love on the hierarchy, and govern the directions in which it acts. Through

[18] Encycl. *Mystici Corporis Christi* (*Selected Letters and Addresses of Pius XII*, Catholic Truth Society, 1949, p. 87).

[19] Cf. St. Leo, Sermon 75, 5: ". . . the Holy Spirit, by whom the whole Catholic Church is sanctified and the whole rational soul imbued" (P. L., 54, 403).

[20] Moehler has a profound sense of this, though he may not have expressed it as accurately as one might wish. See the most felicitous account (the basis of my own remarks) by Mgr. C. Journet, *op. cit.*, Exc. IV, pp. 630-640.

the Holy Spirit active within them, they ask for, and thus lead it to make, its decisions. Their aspirations, their efforts, their intuitions, their inchoate achievements, bring out new problems, and vaguely suggest the answers to them, and thus cause the hierarchy to take stock of new requirements, to separate the wheat from the chaff, to clarify and consecrate new lines of life. One has only to think of the problems raised for the Apostle Paul by the various Churches, the questions raised by the Corinthians—"the things whereof you wrote to me" (I Cor. vii, 1) . . . This is one of the Church's laws of life, and it is before our eyes today in the new forms of religious life that are arising, the questions concerning the liturgy, devotion to Mary, the mystical meaning of the Church, the insertion of the spiritual into the temporal, the creation of a Christian world. As a result of initiatives taken by the faithful there is a living interaction between the experiences submitted to the hierarchy and the new lines of development called forth by these experiences. Herein again appear the riches to be found in Christ, and thus again the Church's inner mission is realized in the unity of the Spirit.

Finally, there remains the faithful's essential function, which is to work for the growth of the Kingdom of God in the world. That is what the faithful are made for, because, with the hierarchy, they make up the Church. "Not only the sacred ministers, not only those who have dedicated themselves to God in the religious life, but in their measure also the other members of the mystical Body of Jesus Christ, are under an obligation to work zealously and energetically for the building and increase of that body."[21] The Church is given, and yet she is to be created, and the way she will be created is through "the collaboration of pastors and faithful"; for though everything is given in the Act of Redemption, Christ has entrusted the actualization of the infinite riches of this single Act to his sons' free disposition—which the Encyclical *Mystici Corporis* is not afraid to describe as "something truly astonishing" and "a redoubtable mystery."[22] Christians cannot perform this task unless they collaborate with Christ, unless they make the Church's mission their own, unless they become, in and through Christ, as Clement of Alexandria so magnificently said, "both saving and being saved."[23]

[21] *Myst. Corp.* (*Selected Letters and Addresses* . . . p. 102).
[22] *Ibid.*
[23] Quoted in *Myst. Corp.* (*Selected Letters and Addresses* . . . p. 81).

By their participation in the liturgy, by their personal prayers, by their service and sacrifice, they help the Church to grow, and see the sanctification of human beings "grow, so to speak, out of their labours."[24] It is all summed up by St. Paul: "From whom the whole body, being compacted and fitly joined together, by what every joint supplieth, according to the operation in the measure of every part, maketh increase of the body unto the edifying of itself in charity" (Eph. iv, 16).

The Christian experience derives one of its major features from this aspect of the Church: it may be characterized as a prodigious expansion of spiritual freedom. This freedom appears as a kind of obedience, which does not mean in the first place submission to a moral law but is a manifestation of faith and love, an actualization of the homage included in the theological virtues, a concrete form of adoration in Spirit and in Truth and a pure response to God. By means of this freedom Christians become in act what they are in being—"children of obedience," whose lives are fashioned not according to the former desires of their ignorance, but according to the will of the Holy One who calls them to holiness (I Peter i, 14). It is, further, a means to increasing liberation. If individualization (as something egocentric) can be contrasted with personalization (as something spiritual, leading to communion), then this obedience demands a more and more radical deindividualization for the sake of an ever deeper personalization, in Christ and as the image of Christ, with all that this must involve in the way of difficulty, obscurity, renunciation—and also in the way of conviction, fruitfulness, joy.

Nursed by obedience, the Christian experience manifests itself in the initiatives of a freedom that has been spiritualized, delivered from bondage, and consecrated. Far from preventing this expansion, obedience ensures its integrity and fruitfulness. Because the faithful are prompted personally by the Spirit; because they are thinking beings, who have to reflect upon their problems and solve them by themselves and for themselves, in obedience to the faith; because they are free beings, carrying their own inalienable responsibility, whose results have eternal significance; because they are animated by a charity whose initiatives originate in the one and only Spirit, and so help to produce the good of the whole Body, yet whose upsurge, as a created force, is strictly personal, suited to each separate soul

[24] *Myst. Corp.*

and adopted to its special vocation[25]—for all these reasons it is a result of the Christian's aspirations, and the unforeseeable choices made by his freedom, that his fruitfulness is made manifest in the Church, and that, in part, the mission entrusted by Christ to the Church is fulfilled.

Finally, obedience and initiative are directed towards the service of the Church.[26] Caught up in the immense task of the mission, the Christian must work for it as hard as he possibly can, with all that he is and has, in the situation in which he is placed by his vocation, taking his part in all the various forms of service: joining in the Church's liturgy, praying in supplication, sharing in her apostolic labour and redemptive suffering. He is a servant both by nature and by function. He has been ransomed and redeemed by Christ, he belongs to him, and in spending himself on the task he is only doing his duty as a little servant. But this duty is a consecrated act—it is an act of religious homage, because it springs from faith; it is a sacrifice, because it perpetuates our Lord's own dolorous offering; it is to the glory of God, because it reveals the power of Redemption in human activity; it is infinite in hope, because it performs a hidden service that will remain hidden until the day of Judgment. In short, this work is the fulfilment of the "reasonable service" (Rom. xii, 1) by means of which the Christian perpetuates the redemptive sacrifice, and fulfils himself by fulfilling the Church's mission.

3. *The Mystery of the Church's Mediation*

We have still not reached the heart of this mystery of the Church. The Church is the place where the mystery of Christ is enacted, and it is the instrument of Christ's mission; but it is also something more. It is Christ himself, because Christ as the Saviour identifies himself with his mediation, and the Church is the mediator of this mediation.

The Church is a reality, first amongst all realities—"the beginning of all things," in St. Epiphanius's famous phrase. But she is not a

[25] "Their freedom" (i.e., of souls), "and the supernatural action of the Holy Ghost in them, are a thing sacrosanct, which no man may under any pretext hamper or violate." *Mediator Dei* (*Selected Letters and Addresses* . . . p. 240).

[26] Cf. the excellent pages by Fr. H. Rahner in *Saint Ignace de Loyola et la Genèse des Exercices* (Toulouse, 1948), pp. 76 *et seq.*

thing that can be defined in herself or by herself. Nor is she an intermediary who joins things together from the outside and then loses her existence once the join has been made—she is no more this than Christ is an intermediary who brings us into contact with God from outside and then disappears. Like the Christ whose mediation she perpetuates, the Church is a mediator. Now, Christ unites us with God by his Act of Redemption, but also by introducing us into this Act; he unites us to God by means of himself, but at the same time by incorporating us into himself. The mediation is this dialectic between "by" and "in": when Christ touches a man and saves him, it is always "by a personal act of grace,"[27] but this act introduces the man into him who is perfect Man and perfect God, in whom Man finds God.

The same thing is true, proportionately speaking, of the Church.[28] Christ reaches us by way of the Church, but so as to include us within the Church: that is his way of taking hold of us and including us within himself. He communicates her existence to the Church, and this communication is absolute, permanent, and ever-present; but he only does this by communicating some participation in his own existence, therefore by inserting her into his own life. This influx of Christ is the full and perfect causality whereby he contains the Church more immediately and more fully than the soul contains the body[29]—more immediately, because the soul is not the efficient cause of the body, whereas Christ is the efficient cause of his Church; more fully, because the soul communicates itself to the body—as an act is connected with its own power—to make one thing, whereas Christ communicates his existence to the Church to make it both a body, that lives only by its participation in him and is one with him, and a Bride, who lives with his very life, as a person, free, loving, responsible, distinct from him. It is indeed the property of a transcendent

[27] *S. Th.*, III^{a}, 8, 3, 1^{m}.

[28] "Christ is a mediator, not as a third party acting as a go-between, but as being, in the unity of his one divine Person, God living amongst men. The same is true of the Church: she is not a mechanism acting as a go-between between Christ and the faithful, she is Christ himself to the extent that he comes and mystically lives amongst the faithful." E. Mersch, *La Théologie du Corps mystique* (Paris-Bruxelles, 1944), II, p. 227.

[29] Fr. E. Mersch is not afraid to write that the soul of the Church "is Christ's humanity, in so far as this is the universal principle of divinization," *op. cit.*, II, p. 213 (cf. pp. 157-158 & 200). As he himself recognizes, this statement is to be handled with care.

causality to realize such a mystery of unity and plurality, of incorporating unity and personalizing plurality. Consequently it is always through the Church his Bride that Christ engenders his children;[30] but it is always by immersing them in the Church as in his body that he causes them to exist. And when a Christian is born, he is born as a result of the activity of the Church vivified by Christ; the only thing is that he does not come out of the Church but enters into her and stays in her womb as his life's permanent setting.[31] Thus the Christian is born, and goes on living, in and through the Church, but for that very reason he is born and goes on living in and through Christ. The Church thus appears as a permanent mediation, constantly being actualized by the efficacious power of the Act of Redemption, and to be seen entirely as a relationship to that act. The Act of Redemption is one single act, beginning at the Incarnation, reaching its climax at the Crucifixion, finding its consummation at the Resurrection, and then being "applied" to mankind as a whole. The Church is the appropriate form taken by the Act of Redemption to reach mankind and bring mankind within itself.

This relationship has a dual movement, like Christ's mediation. It is a communication—"And of his fulness we have all received, and grace for grace" (John i, 16)—and it is an attraction—"And I, if I be lifted up from the earth, will draw all things to myself" (John xii, 32); yet one and the same relationship exists in the dual movement thus created—like the relationship in creation itself, which gives creatures their own being and at the same time leads them back to God.

Christ comes and takes hold of us by way of the Church, so as to immerse us within her and by doing so immerse us within himself. This can be demonstrated by the very theme that seems to draw the sharpest distinction between the Church and Christ—the theme of the Church as God's People. This means, in the first place, that the Church is made up of people who have been baptized. Now, at baptism man submits to the effects of Christ's death and resurrection and at the same time is introduced by the Holy Spirit into the unity of the Body. The new creation that was achieved by Christ at the

[30] "They were bound to imitate (Paul) as a father, in so far as he imitated Christ, who is the principal father of all." St. Thomas, *in I Cor.*, c. 4, lect. 3, 2, 2.

[31] Cf. G. de Broglie, *L'Église, nouvelle Ève . . .*, in *N.R.T.*, I, 1946, p. 10 & pp. 19-20.

Crucifixion and the Resurrection ends in this birth in water and the Spirit:[32] this is a personal application of the Act of Redemption, leading to annexation by Christ (the character) and vitalization by Christ (grace), by means of which he incorporates a particular member into his Body and creates his people. If the Church is the *congregatio fidelium,* it is through baptism that Christ brings it into existence; and from this point of view the Church can be described as a communicative relationship between Christ and man for the purpose of incorporating man within Christ.

Futhermore, this people that is composed of the baptized is divided into the faithful and their leaders; it is built up according to a hierarchy; and the hierarchy communicates Christ's own life to the faithful. But we know that it does this as Christ's "instrument" and "means." Let us be careful to retain the purified meaning that theology gives to these words. The hierarchy is Christ's unchanging instrument because of the unchanging nature of the Act of Redemption upon which its existence, its unity, and its efficacy are all based. But this instrument needs to be actualized by Christ whenever it is called upon to act, because it cannot act except in Christ's name and with the help of his power. Through the hierarchy, existence is communicated to the faithful, and thus through the hierarchy Christ personally makes his Church live and grow.[33] The hierarchy does not divide, it unites; it is a mediator; and with regard, for instance, to the faith that it communicates by way of its teaching, it must be said in all strictness: "Those who are in the Church are taught neither by the apostles nor by the prophets but by God himself; and according to St. Augustine the actual teaching that comes from a man comes from God who teaches within him."[34] From this point of view too, the Church, because of its transparency as a mediator, is a communicative relationship between Christ and his

[32] Rev. Fr. P. Benoît, *Revue biblique,* 1949, II, p. 317, n. 2: in the act that took place upon the Cross "all Christians were created in the person of the new Adam, before being born again through their own individual baptism."

[33] Rev. Fr. L. M. Dewailly, *art. cit.,* p. 21: "The duties and offices are performed as the result of an endless series of personal appeals addressed to a succession of new holders. And all these various successions become a single, multiple, everlasting succession that, strictly speaking, is the result of an abstraction—*or rather, if one considers the abiding Church, there is no succession at all.* There is the one Church, always the same, like its Head, Christ, yesterday, today and for ever."

[34] St. Thomas, *in Joa.,* 6, lect. 5 (Marietti, 195^{6}).

pastors, and between Christ and the faithful by way of the pastors, for the building up of the whole people.

Finally, the people of God are fed by the Bread of God coming down from heaven. The Eucharist is a reality, but it is neither a thing nor an intermediary. It is a sacrament which is also a sacrifice, presenting the mystery of the redemptive Passion, actualizing the Act of Redemption in the world of signs and thus communicating the Christ of glory, so that he may feed the People of God with himself, unify them within himself and consummate them within himself. The Church, once again, can be described as a communicative relationship between Christ and those who belong to him, so that the total Christ may be accomplished. She is thus the communication of Christ to men, in and through the society that he creates; she is the means and organ of contact between God and man, born out of his sacrifice, the divine medium through which and in which the Act of Redemption is expressed visibly and operates efficaciously. In short, she is the mediation of Christ by way of a mediating humanity which he will create for himself to the end of time.

It now becomes necessary to bring out into sharp relief one aspect that has been implied in what has just been said. Christ only communicates himself so as to draw us towards his life of glory; the Church only communicates Christ so as to draw us towards his existence in heaven. The Church herself, in fact, is not only an earthly reality here below; she is also a heavenly reality above.[35]

The Church, in the first place, comes down from on high. Christ has "departed," "ascended into heaven," is "seated on the right hand of God," i.e. has passed body and soul into the mystery of the Father. And it is from on high that he creates his Church, for "having received of the Father the promise of the Holy Ghost, he

[35] Descriptions of Christ as being "above," "in heaven," "on the right hand of the Father," are of course metaphors (cf. III^{a}, 58). What they all mean is that Christ has entered, body and soul, into God's own world, into the heart of the mystery, into the beyond that is all transcendence and divine glory. Christ's attractive power is to be understood as a spiritual action bursting forth from his soul and his spiritual body and bringing us into himself and hence into the reality of God. But images help us to imagine this, and for that reason we make use of them, just as the New Testament makes use of them (cf. on their noetic value, BERGSON, *La Pensée et le mouvant*, Paris, 1934, p. 52). Moreover, "above" and "below" describe man's condition theologically: cf. II^{a} II^{ae}, 7, 2, & I^{a} II^{ae}, 108, 4, c.

hath poured forth this which you see and hear" (Acts ii, 33). Our Mother the Church is consequently "that Jerusalem which is above" (Gal. iv, 25), which comes down from the agape of God into Christ, from the Resurrected One, who has now become the life-giving Spirit, spreading abroad the Spirit, "all the closer by reason of his divinity, as he had been distant by reason of his humanity."[36] She creates a people of those who are "resurrected from the dead," whose entire life-impulse aspires towards the things on high, towards where Christ sits enthroned in his own glory: "therefore, if you be risen with Christ, seek the things that are above, where Christ is sitting at the right hand of God" (Col. iii, 1). The downward movement only takes place for the sake of the upward one, the communication only exists for the sake of the attraction. And if the Church, which has come down from on high, finds expression and lives in the society below, in her members wandering far from their Lord, this is so that she may rejoin Christ in his glory at the right hand of the Father.

But the Church on earth herself exists on high, in the glorified Christ. She has been taken into his heavenly existence, and because of that she exists within him—in heaven. For the Father "hath quickened us together in Christ . . . and hath raised us up together, and hath made us sit together in the heavenly places through Christ Jesus" (Eph. ii, 5-6; cf. Col. ii, 11-13). Those words, it is true, are an eschatological anticipation, but such is precisely the Christian existence in its relationship to Christ.[37] Christian existence is at this moment a participation in the resurrected life of the glorified Christ, and in this sense "Christians too . . . in the reality of their supernatural life are present in heaven"[38] and are "rightfully, in invisible reality, what they shall be in the visible reality to come."[39] The whole mystery of the Resurrection is implicit here. If, before Christ was resurrected, the Spirit could not be given (John iv, 39); if, through

[36] St. Leo, *Serm.* 74, 4, P. L., 54, 398.

[37] *Paul Claudel interroge le Cantique des cantiques:* "This immortal creature, the Church, called into existence to breathe endless renewal, to fill herself with all the powers of her inmost depths at the source, she too looks with eager expectancy toward the rising sun. Tomorrow and tomorrow and tomorrow make up her endless present" (p. 380).

[38] L. Cerfaux, *op. cit.*, p. 256: We should not choose to add, as he does, "by a fiction, a mystic transference"—if these words are meant to imply that there is no reality.

[39] *Ibid.*, p. 254.

the resurrection of his body, Christ becomes the quickening Spirit (I Cor. xv, 45), "this means that after his glorification in the Resurrection and the Return to the Father he was to possess in his actual body the fullness of the Spirit, which he could then dispense through the sacraments."[40] It also means that the bodies of Christ's followers "are already united to his in the mystical union of baptism and the Eucharist; with him they have died and been resurrected. What is in his case an ultimate physical state is for them a mystical state awaiting completion but nevertheless real . . . If the bodies of Christians are even now, in St. Paul's words, "temples of the Holy Spirit," if they are sanctified and purified in their physical passions, it is because they are connected by means of the sacraments with the glorified body of their Master. They are members, they are preparing themselves to join him in heaven after their own resurrection, which is to take place at his Parousia."[41] But what is true of the bodies of the faithful is pre-eminently true of the Body of the Church, for it is the Church that is pre-eminently the "temple of the Spirit"; and what is true of their bodies is still more so of their souls, which are already resurrected to the spiritual life of Christ and the Church, which is this resurrected life henceforth present within mankind—for it is "by the faith of the operation of God, who hath raised him up from the dead" (Col. ii, 12) that the Christian is resurrected in baptism with Christ.[42]

Nevertheless, the Church is still on earth and belongs there. This resurrected life that she leads, leads to a paradoxical condition—it is hidden, because it is received and lived under the outward manifestations of the faith and cannot be grasped directly; it is a beginning, because it is only nourished by the "pledges" of the Spirit, and though it has taken control of the whole man it has not transformed him completely; and it is therefore threatened, because the soul, not being "saturated" by the life of God, is still subject to temptation and liable to succumb. Thus there is a threefold limitation—of the sign, the seed, and the "flesh"—that keeps our true glory hidden from us—"your life is hidden with Christ in God"—separates us

[40] Rev. Fr. P. Benoît, *L'Ascension*, in *Revue biblique*, II, 1949, p. 184.

[41] *Ibid.*, p. 182.

[42] On this point, Dom A. Vonier, *L'Esprit et l'Épouse* (Paris, 1947), VI, *L'Église de la Résurrection* ("The Church is intrinsically, by the very law of her being, the Church of the Resurrection," p. 72. She is "a function of the resurrected life of Christ," p. 75).

from our true essence—"now already we are the sons of God, but what we shall be hath not yet appeared"—and gives us the condition of "pilgrims and strangers on the earth" (Heb. xi, 13).[43]

This is a new aspect of the mystery of the Church. In her there is a duality of earthly and heavenly, humility and glory, the seed of incorruptibility in the creature still subject to corruption; and this gives rise to an infinite aspiration. Christ in glory draws his Church towards him, and that means that the life of the Church is to pass from imperfect existence to perfect existence—not in the first place "physically," from earth to heaven, but spiritually, from "justification" to "sanctification." That indeed is the way in which Christ's attractive power is realized, and the life of the Church means that she is to grow, gradually detach herself from this world of sin in which she dwells and return to the image of herself that is hidden with Christ in God; endlessly purifying herself of her blemishes, her blotches, her wrinkles, in order to pass from this world to the Father, and present herself to the Bridegroom radiant in her beauty. Here we touch upon the Church's eschatological dimension.[44] Her life is an everlasting journey, a perpetual Easter, by reason of the "virtue" of the Paschal Christ present within her. And this inner expansion is her permanent characteristic here below: between the time of symbols and the time when all is made perfectly plain, she is the time, the place, and the age of realities in symbols—of realities using symbols, and using them for their power of growth, until they burst and disappear in the pure and glorious reality.

The Church is thus the Paschal mystery perpetuated,[45] the passage from earth to heaven, from time to eternity, because heaven and eternity are present within her for the purpose of immersing her utterly within them. And this is precisely her mediation, her state of becoming being endlessly actualized by the Act of Redemption. The "communication-attraction" connection describes the mediation of Christ through the mediation of the Church, through which and in which the mystery of salvation is achieved. This is clearly to be seen in the case of the Eucharist: in the Mass, Christ becomes pres-

[43] For the meaning of this pilgrimage and exile, cf. the splendid passage by St. Gregory the Great, *Moral. in Job*, P. L., 76, col. 63, No. 48.

[44] For the "time" of the Church, H. I. Dalmais, *art. cit.*, in *La Maison-Dieu*, 14, pp. 77 *et seq.*

[45] Cf. the study, at once novel and traditional, by Fr. H. M. Féret in *La Messe et sa catéchèse*, pp. 212 *et seq.*

ent as the Saviour of his Body in an act of sacrifice; he comes down amongst us, so as to bear us aloft with him to the Father; by the Act of Redemption, made actual in the sacramental sacrifice, he gathers a dispersed people into his unity, an imperfect people into his sanctity, a pilgrim people into his eternity. He thus brings his people into heaven, because he brings them into himself—in a sacramental sacrifice which is his as a sacrifice, and the Church's as a sacrament, and which is one single sacrifice, because the mediation of the Church and the mediation of Christ are ultimately one and the same.

The Christian experience is included within this mediation in all its aspects: it is an everlasting journey into Christ.

It is realized in and through the Church, because it is through the Church as God's organ and the place of contact with him that it becomes joined to the Act of Redemption; and this act takes hold of the soul by way of the Church so as to make it live by God in the Church. It means an acceptance of Christ's communication and a response to Christ's attraction, because the Church in which it is immersed is essentially this dual movement itself: it thus comes from the intermingling of a passivity and an activity both equally necessary and equally lasting, though infinitely different from each other.

It is a movement to Christ and God within the Church—a movement that begins with the experience itself: the man who is converted passes from this world to Christ by way of an inner transformation—a movement endlessly repeated and growing ever deeper: the Christian, already within Christ, must penetrate deeper every day —a movement spiritual and hidden, because it takes place always through the medium of faith, the sacraments, and Christian endeavour—a movement that defines the Christian experience because it defines Christian existence itself as received in the mystery of baptism. Baptism immerses the recipient in the mystery of Christ, because it initiates a threefold relationship with Christ—with his Passion, his glory, and his ever-present efficacy. Baptismal life is thus a life which is "at the present moment" in Christ, but it extends from the Passion, of which it is the fruit, to glory, of which it is the seed. It is immersed in the everlasting Act of Redemption, actualized in time—in the rite of baptism—but it transcends and includes time. Consequently, the Christian who lives in the present by Christ is thrown back by the inner dialectic of his faith into the past, to the

Passion from which he derives his life, into which he was baptized, and which he himself is called upon to re-enact, and forward into the future, to the glory in which lives the Christ who calls him to himself.

This movement, within faith, is the movement of hope, based on the power of the Passion and directed towards the promised glory; animating a spiritual endeavour that unfolds in time, but in order to return to a reality that in Christ transcends and integrates time. By his movement the Christian ensures his permanence, his unity, his being, in Christ, but he can only do this because, by the lasting power of baptism, by the lasting mediation of the Church, he is enfolded within the mystery of Christ, which is the mystery of God assuming human form, of eternity assuming time, of glory assuming wretchedness, and which manifests itself in man in the mystery of an endlessly repeated acceptance, and a search, a possession, and a desire for the Lord Jesus.

At this depth, the Christian experience is a personal history, inserted within the great history of the Church; a spiritual development made incarnate and lived within the development of the Church; an endeavour to develop what is given, to discover what is hidden; to discover oneself in one's own mystery, by discovering, in and through the Church, the mystery of Christ the Saviour.

4. *The Mystery of the Church's Pilgrimage*

The Church is in a state of pilgrimage, not indeed by her essence, but as a result of her condition. She is the mediation of a mediation. This mediation which she herself is, is really the mediation of Christ, but her mediation does not coincide with Christ's absolutely. She is its organ and living centre, but not in a finished condition, because she is a mediation performed by way of signs, and reaches men *in statu viae*. She will be completed in Paradise, when faith will be consummated in sight, participation by way of the sacraments become fullness of life, obedience to the commandments change to spontaneous love. All the signs that were used for the mediation will disappear before the pure reality, and then the Church's mediation will coincide so absolutely with Christ's that it will become one with it. The whole spiritual distance that separates it from perfection will be annihilated, and the Church will reach the highest point of her perfection as a complete spiritual relationship with Christ in both her aspects; a perfect unity of spirit—*Quid adhaeret Deo, unus spiritus est*—making her the spiritual body of Jesus Christ, and a pure otherness of person making her his glorious Bride. Then Christ will be fully articulated in his Church, who will become "the fulness of him who is filled all in all" (Eph. i, 23), "that God may be all in all" (I Cor. xv, 28).

But here below, veil and distance remain, and, as a result, life in Christ remains imperfect. For the mystery of Christ's humiliation and suffering continues. God in his mercy willed that Christ should suffer and die for us, so that in him and through him mankind might redeem itself; and what Christ performed for mankind, mankind performs in the Church in completion of his work. The entire mediation is willed for a freedom that has to choose and take sides: the veil is a call to choose for faith, the distance a call to the desire for love, and both are conditions of the personal merit by which in Jesus Christ each man saves himself. But both also leave room for the freedom to refuse itself and grow hard. Like the mediation of Christ when he appeared on earth, the Church's mediation allows a choice between a positive—adherence to God, union with God—and a negative—indifference, evasion, refusal. We have the root of the matter in our own hands. And we promise the actualization of the negative possibility when we say that the Church is "in the world," and that "the world" is also in her children.

"The world," as it appears in the Gospels, is an essential, concrete category of thought with many meanings. It can mean all who are not included within the visible Church; or all the spiritual forces that motivate and govern these people; or all the achievements and institutions they create within human society and the material world; or more or less all these things at once. The Church is in the world in the sense that she is not coextensive with humanity but a particular grouping in human society, and her existence and progress are introduced within a different kind of existence and progress that condition her and which she tries to influence. The two realities are bound together in a series of tensions and meetings whose extent and complexity defy analysis.

From God's point of view all this makes up a single history, because mankind is intended for the Church and Christ; because through the Church grace works upon mankind to save it; because erring mankind itself plays a part in the supernatural growth of the world. But this unity is beyond us; it is God's secret, and only he can see into it; it is the mystery introduced into history and yet transcending history which will only be completed at the end of history, at a time which "it is not for us to know." From man's point of view, however, there are two histories, differing from each other in their ends and objects; the first aiming to humanize mankind and build the city of man, the second to divinize man and build the city of God. Sociologically they end in two different groupings—the people of men, and the people of God in the midst of the people of men. In the Christian view, the two peoples are designed to coincide, and partially and temporarily they sometimes manage to do this; but they can also draw apart and oppose each other, and this is a permanent fact of history. Within the single history written by God amongst men they provide two specific histories written by the powers of man. The man with no faith takes part in this double history without knowing it, the Christian is aware of it through faith. His job is to reconcile the two, by introducing human history within the history that is divine—and from this point of view all the tragedy comes from the world's ambivalence.

On the one hand this world is a world in travail, trying to grow, trying to understand and possess its own being, shot through with an obscure but ineradicable aspiration towards something better—mastery of the universe, freedom, justice, friendship, happiness. Mankind is thus labouring for its own increase, by reorganizing itself "in the unity of its immediate end and its mission in the world";[46] and in doing so it helps to provide Christ with richer material for transfiguration. And this is inevitable, for the nature that God has created is good, nothing can corrupt its essential principles, and God's grace transfuses it, healing it and helping it to succeed. On the other hand this world is also a world of sin. The human condition, in fact, is one of sin. All men come into the world deprived of the grace of God; outside of Christ all are subject to sin. And this great and terrible power is seen in its fruits: rejection of God, slavery to desire, hatred of one's fellow men, imprisonment within the merely human. The world thus becomes all the forces that refuse to give themselves to God, that set themselves up against him and try to destroy his existence within the hearts of men; aiming to give men a purely

[46] Encycl. *Summi Pontificatus.*

human freedom, a purely human existence, a purely human perfection, by means of purely human forces.[47] To the extent that the world is all this, it aims at a purely human history opposed to the history that God wills to write by means of the Church; it becomes an incessant obstacle to the Church; it creates a condition of things that resists the divine condition with the utmost harshness; it becomes for the Christian entirely a matter of temptation, a permanent threat of corruption, an incessant effort at his destruction. The road that it takes then is "a way without God, and in fact against God, without Christ and in fact against Christ."[48] To get to the root of the matter, it is the kingdom of Satan. It has an invisible head who has been essentially defeated by Christ but has been granted a "reprieve" and takes advantage of it to roam around loose—as far as God allows. The struggle between Christ the victor and the Devil, who is in a frenzy of desperation, fills the time of the Church. Seen in all its complexity, the world is in the locked embrace of hope and perversion, of —ultimately—the forces of sin controlled by Satan and the forces of grace that come from Christ through the Church.

Thus the part played by the Church in this world is truly tragic. By all the lawful aspirations and genuine hopes it bears, the world is the dough in which the Church is the yeast. It is the Church's duty to harvest the good and help it to increase, to take it into itself rationally, charitably, and with endless patience. By all the intentional revolt and actual perversity it bears, the world is the cockle that strangles the Church's good wheat. It is the Church's duty to fight against it and reject its rejection, to cast out its perversity, to give witness with the weapons of light, to suffer and sacrifice itself by and for it until the end of time. This dual, simultaneous task of acceptance and refusal; this discrimination between affirmation and negation; this concern for the human, and hatred for the sin that corrupts it; this love of all that is good, and even for the enemy who is wicked; this need for the endless, painful, hazardous search for new methods; this continual return to the job in hand, hoping in the midst of disillusionment and persecution—all this is indeed a fearful task. But for this the Church is made and, like Christ himself, she is

[47] When fully aware of itself, this attitude defines itself as follows: "The criticism of religion ends in the doctrine that for Man, Man is the only supreme being, and in the categorical imperative to destroy all social relationships by which Man is degraded, enslaved, forsaken and despicable. . . ." K. Marx, *Morceaux Choisis* (N.R.F., Paris), 1934, p. 232.

[48] Pius XII, *Christmas Message*, 1943.

sent "not to call the just, but sinners," and "to save that which was lost." The things that are impossible with men are possible with God —and possible with the Church, which has the light and strength of Christ.

And this brings us to another difficulty as urgent as the first. The Church is holy, but she is not simply a Church of holy people. She bears within herself sinners—and in one way or another all Christians are sinners. The Church is predestined from all eternity and always holy, but unequally so: on our level she is this only to the extent that Christians live by Christ. The dividing line in this case is within: every Christian is at once a Christian and a non-Christian, living by Christ and living by himself, with some of the deep regions of his being inhabited by the Lord and others still untouched by the Gospel. The Church finds herself at the foot of the Cross less from the activity of her enemies who stand without than from this human wretchedness in which the grace of God must work. The people of God are a mixture of saints and sinners: a changing people, in which the saint of today may become the sinner of tomorrow, and vice versa; an imperfect people, including far too many who remain puerile and undernourished "babes"; a people from which the "all too human" element is never eliminated, but "endlessly and endlessly renewing itself, develops like cockle amongst the wheat of the Kingdom of God."[49] The tragedy of this condition is that the transforming power of the Church is weakened by the sins of Christians, and this density of the flesh threatens to turn her from being a mediator into being an intermediary, who has to be crossed and transcended before the true Church and the true God can be found.

All her mediating functions are liable to be affected by this human denseness. They cannot be affected in their living substance, or in their essential rootedness within the Church, or in their universal efficacy, thanks to the assistance of the Holy Spirit and the presence of Christ; but they can be affected in the men or groups of men who exercise them, as a result of the admixture or interference of the "human, all too human" element.[50] The word of God, being hard to maintain in all its purity, is liable to become involved with all manner of im-

[49] Encycl. *Mit brennender Sorge.*

[50] "The giving of scandal can certainly be explained, and it touches the very essence of Christianity—its unity is the unity of a Redemption that takes place little by little; sin remains active in the world and the Church, and sin means rupture and schism . . . Thus the work of unity is performed amongst a process of splits and separations," etc.—E. Mersch, *op. cit.*, II, pp. 219-223.

perfections, misunderstandings, and errors; always coming up against new problems, it is liable to dodge some and compromise on others; being refracted through particular individual mentalities, it is liable to be subject to dangerous amalgamating and hardening-up processes. The administration of the sacraments, being a matter of human actions, is liable to lose its sap and its soul, to fall into mere routine and pharisaism. The hierarchy, being made up of human beings who remain human beings, occasionally bears besides fidelity and holiness "clear traces of our human condition of weakness," even "in the highest members of the Mystical Body";[51] it is liable to insensitivity, greed, failures of understanding, immorality even, liable to come to decisions—not in the order of infallibility but "prudential" or "biological" decisions[52]—that may be inappropriate, erroneous, or harmful. There is an opaqueness that affects the transparency of the Church's mediation.[53]

And though the Christian attitude should lead essentially to sanctity—"Be perfect as your Father in heaven is perfect"—on all sides there is evidence of Christian insufficiency in the fulfilling of this first of all laws. Christians capitulate to the attractions of money, the flesh, and the world; amongst Christians we find personal enmities, social enmities, ideological enmities; enmity between the faithful and the hierarchy, because of individualism or illuminism, between the "spiritually minded" and the "realists"; and engrossment and degradation in temporal affairs, in "business" and "politics." All these things are to be found already in germ, and in fact, in the letters of St. Paul, and they will always exist. There is thus an opaqueness in the Christian witness, a black mark running through the Church's earthly record; and this is a tragedy that makes it obligatory for every new generation of Christians to examine their consciences, beat their breasts, and endeavour to become fully converted.[54]

The drama of the pilgrim Church lies in the fact that it has to

[51] Encycl. *Myst. Corp.*

[52] Mgr. C. JOURNET's words. See his remarks, *op. cit.*, pp. 398 *et seq.* With regard to "the prudential decisions whose aim is to determine empirically the contingent relationships between the Church and the world, the divine assistance that we have described as a biological assistance will be of a particular kind. It will not spare her from difficulties or doubts or inconveniences, or even from actual errors," pp. 450, 451.

[53] Think of the terrible chapters written by St. CATHERINE OF SIENA against bad priests—"more devilish than devils"—*Dial.* CXXIII, 5.

[54] Cf. *Mit brennender Sorge.*

face the world, with all its hopes and sins, with the pure strength of Christ in the hands of unpurified Christians. For it to succeed, the first requirement is, not for it to turn a bold face towards the world, but to achieve a lasting inner purification that will enable the proper "purchase" to be obtained, by adapting the instrument to the pure strength of Christ, by purifying the sight, the will, the deed. It is by humility that the Christian gets "into the right position." With his sense of sin and holiness he can distinguish between hope and error; with detachment from self he can respond to the call of the world, and at the same time resist its attraction; with faith he can grasp or discover the particular job that is waiting to be done; with charity he can inject the power of God into the heart of mankind; with hope he can walk with unhesitating steps through the difficulties of his times, his work, his failures, his darkness. His effectiveness can always be nourished by one thing only—inner purification; his penetration, by interiorization; his constructive communion with men, by communion with Christ. Finally, the most transforming apostolate is rooted in the purest contemplation; because only then does the Act of Redemption express itself and operate through man with the maximum of purity and effectiveness.

This fact inevitably leads to a further element in the Christian experience.

Faced with the world present within himself, the Christian is called upon to make a continuous effort towards self-purification: to purify his will of the self-regard that cuts him off from Christ and his fellow men; to purify his heart of the involvement with desire that besmirches it and gives it over to the enemy; to purify his mind of the prejudices, the preconceived ideas, the false judgments that become engrained in it and prevent it from seeing properly; to repent, to do penance, to learn humility—all in love. Then his vision will be purified; for within his faith—which performs the first purification—will act the gift of understanding, which enables him to penetrate into the truths of God, and the gift of knowledge, which fathoms the truths about man. Then too, knowing Christ and himself, he will be able to understand the Church and the world.

Faced with the world which is in Christians and therefore in the Church, the Christian's first reaction cannot but be one of sorrow. Being bound to Christ and the Church by the deepest fibres of his being, and seeing Christ's face and the face of the Church marked by sin;[55] being bound to all his fellow men, knowing himself a sinner like them, knowing that their sins are in part his own, he feels all this wretchedness in a "heart broken and humiliated." He begs for forgiveness for himself and all men, he does penance, and, suffering under sin, he consents to suffer for sin. But his suffering is not fruitless, for it springs from love, and love desires the good of all men. With his will made up, then, and summoning all his strength, the Christian embarks on the struggle against sin and human misery—by example, for the conflict begins within himself; by word of mouth, testifying to his faith and spreading it abroad; by the "brotherly admonition" which at times becomes a duty for all men—so long as it is performed with all the tact and respectfulness—and daring—of true love; by every kind of action that may help to prevent, or extricate from, or repair the damages of sin. He does all this with reason and charity: if it is not rational, charity is insecurely based and liable to prove ineffective; and if rationality is not charitable it leads to sterile criticism and destruction. Great sorrow lies behind this effort at purification: it too springs from the Act of Redemption upon which the Church is founded, and it accomplishes this act within each separate member: "I . . . fill up those things that are wanting of the sufferings of Christ, in my flesh, for his body." Here too the Christian labours with a fundamental humility, with an unshakeable conviction that Christ is present within the Church, with absolute trust in Christ himself and a burning desire to give glory to God. Without all this he is no better than a Pharisee.[56] Pope Pius XI has said this in the strongest terms: "Every true and lasting reform has had its origin, fundamentally, in sanctity . . . On the other hand,

[55] "The human countenance (of the Church), like its Master's, is often bathed in sweat and blood. Like the Holy Face, it too is covered with blemishes": Cardinal E. Suhard, *Essor ou déclin de l'Église* (Paris, 1947), p. 19.

[56] St. Gregory's great words are well-known: "He who bears another, is borne by another" (St. Gregory the Great, *in Ezech.*, II, i, P. L., 76, 939, 5); but not so well-known, perhaps, is the energetic way in which these words are applied to the—interconnected—sins of pastors and faithful: "It is to be considered to what extent the sins of pastors and flock are interconnected. For when one of the flock sins mortally through his own fault, then he who is set above, because he kept silent, is responsible. Weigh well, therefore, my dearest brethren, that in so far as we are not worthy pastors, the fault is yours, through whom we are such prelates. If at times you fall into sin, the blame is ours, for in your evil desires you did not find us resisting you and summoning you back. Therefore you save both yourselves and us if you cease from wicked ways. We save you and ourselves, when we speak out about that which is displeasing" (*ibid.*, I. ii. col. 909, 9).

whenever reforming zeal has not sprung from personal purity, but has been an expression and explosion of passion, it has troubled instead of clarifying, destroyed instead of constructing."[57]

If we now turn to this world that calls to the Christian, tempting him and threatening him, the experience takes the form of witnessing—of being strong in faith. The first purpose of faith is to judge. The world judges the Christian, and the Christian—in the Spirit—judges the world. The world sets up its court of judgment on all sides, and on all sides the world must be replied to by the rational judgment of faith. This is no easy task, for there is no such thing as perfect error, because "all truths, by whomsoever said, come from the Holy Spirit,"[58] and because even when the Christian condemns anything, he must always be able to disentangle the element of truth that is involved in it. Faced with all the current theories that condemn Christianity and the Church he must be undismayed, and devote himself to the task of refuting them—in close contact with the hierarchy, and prompted by the instinct of the Holy Spirit and a sense of Christian values. This is primarily a task for the intellectuals, as Cardinal Suhard has pointed out so trenchantly;[59] but on a more humble level it is a task for all Christians, for all may find in their lived faith in the Church enlightenment enough to discover what is to be accepted and rejected.

The second task that faith is called upon to perform is resistance: "Love not the world" (I John ii, 15). The hatred that comes from the sinful world is a datum of faith and a constant in Christian history. Christians have to face up to this hatred, and, with all the violence of their love, reject its errors and faults, and fight against its attempts to seduce and destroy them. They know that in their fight against the Evil One who governs the world they have on their side the strength of the Spirit who can cast out devils. They know that Another than themselves is their support and inspiration and that he will bring them victory; they have faith in the victorious Christ.

Faith's third task is deliverance: "God so loved the world as to give his only-begotten Son . . . that the world may be saved by him" (John iii, 16-17). There are enemies present, a war on hand, and captives are taken: redemption means the announcement and achievement of

[57] *Mit brennender Sorge.*

[58] A passage which St. Thomas loved to quote, attributed to St. Ambrose; cf. *in I Cor.* 12, lect. 1; *in Joa.*, c, 8, lect. 6.

[59] *Essor.*, pp. 42, 58 *et seq.*

deliverance. It delivers man from the toils of sin, as we have already made sufficiently clear; but it also frees the human being himself, who longs to find himself, to achieve his fulfilment. The Christian has to help all the goodness that exists so supplicatingly all around him, to deliver itself from the evil that has fastened upon it, so that it may grow along its own true lines; and this he can only do by taking thought, and by playing his part realistically: following the thread of history, he must enter upon the gigantic task of constructing a world fit to be breathed in and lived in by Christians, a humanized world for men of good will—in short, a world animated by the charity of Christ.

These three tasks—judgment, resistance, and deliverance—are of course three different aspects of a single task. They integrate Christian action in the world—which is always all three together: judgment, resistance, and fulfilment. They involve the pain and suffering of sacrifice, because they are realized through the death-grapple of grace and sin; they are engaged upon with the certainty of hope, because they are the actualization of the Act of Redemption. Judgment is a function of Revelation; resistance, with the Cross it implies, a means of reconciliation; and deliverance, a first glimpse of transfiguration. Because human history is ambiguous and mixed, like the human heart itself; because evil is grounded in goodness, and lives upon it parasitically; because goodness can spring up so surprisingly and unforeseeably in the midst of evil—therefore the Christian experience is a process of becoming that always remains mysterious even to itself. It means a determined effort, made in communion with others and nourished by the realism, the patience, and the hope of all; a desire for true vision and real achievement, which, though it may be hesitant and shaky, is ultimately always effective. The Christian has simply one duty: to take his place alongside all men of good will and pledge himself utterly in their service. What God wants is his labour and sacrifice, the sweat of his brow and his heart's blood—and sometimes his neighbour requires this too. After which, God himself completes the work: "I have planted, Apollo watered, but God gave the increase" (I Cor. iii, 6). The Christian experience is thus an experience of sacrifice and joy, because it takes place within a Church that is both a pilgrim on earth and already in heaven—like its Master, who was both a traveller here below and supremely blessed in heaven.

CHAPTER EIGHT

The Christian Experience as an Experience in Christ

EXPERIENCE within the Church is an experience in Christ, because the Church's mediation actualizes Christ's own mediation in the world of time. The Church is thus the proper place for direct contact with Christ. At this point, therefore, the whole complex of direct relationships with Christ must be studied.

1. *Christ as the Way to God*

Christ is "the Way," and "by him we have access both in one Spirit to the Father" (Eph. ii, 18). The whole scheme of salvation, and consequently the whole structure of the redeemed material creation, are involved here. God the Trinity, as we know, is absolutely inaccessible: no one has ever seen him, no one has entered heaven, no man can ever appear before God as someone who has crossed the abyss by his own unaided efforts. Before man can be united to the Holy Trinity, God himself must reveal and give himself. Now if we take the word "direct" in a narrow sense as meaning "excluding any means to union," then God does not reveal himself to man directly. He does not give himself directly, at close quarters; he does not communicate himself directly to the finite mind by an act springing from his inmost depths and pierce it directly—one minute unknown, the next minute known. God does not reveal himself or give himself except in Christ: "And no one knoweth the Son, but the Father: neither doth anyone know the Father, but the Son and he to whom it shall please the Son to reveal him" (Matt. xi, 27). The abyss cannot be crossed, and has not been crossed, except in

Christ: it is through the mediation of the Man-God that we attain to God. The mediation is therefore not purely intellectual, by way of an idea or value; nor is it purely dynamic through some spiritual force that raises us upwards; nor is it an indirect mediation by way of an intermediary either. It is the mediation of a personal Being who is both Man and God—the eternal Word, with his two natures, divine and human. In the most precise sense of the words, we only attain to God by uniting ourselves with the Man who is God.

And here comes the paradox, and, apparently, the impossibility; for it would seem that if I cannot attain to God except through the Man Jesus Christ standing between God and myself, then there is a being not purely God blocking the way and acting as a sort of screen—and gone is the possibility of any immediacy in my relationship with God. But the truth is the exact opposite of this, because the Mediator is not an intermediary. Any man who acts as mediator between two different parties is always an intermediary: he exists in his own personal singularity and the density of his being inevitably interposes itself between the two. Moreover, when he acts in an endeavour to bring the two parties together, so that they will understand each other and come to an agreement in some sort of unity, his actions have a reality of their own and cannot avoid rousing similar thoughts or desires in the others, and the two parties will have to pass through them before they can be united as persons in a joint, free decision. For Christ not to be an intermediary, all this external element has to be destroyed in him, so that he can be a pure "instrument" of unity.

Now, in the first place, Christ is not an intermediary on the level of being, because he is not a being interposed between God and myself. He is not me, and the substance of my being will always remain untouched and untouchable, unimpaired even in the deepest union with him. But if he is not me, he is not any other being outside of God, because he is God himself, incarnate. His humanity is splendidly, perfectly real, as befits the humanity formed by the three Persons to become the humanity of the Word. But it does not exist except as posited *in* the Word; it does not exist in itself; it is posited *for* the Word, not for itself; in short, it only exists as assumed into the unity of a divine Person. So that the Word, who subsists eternally in the divine nature—with which he is identical—likewise subsists in the human nature—which he draws into his own subsistence

(S.Th., III[a], 2, 4). Thus, Christ's humanity exists, but it does not subsist; it does not end in itself, but in the Word; it is not a being, it has no being except in the Word—strictly speaking, it has no existence in itself, but only in the Word; no separate existence, but in-existence in the Word. In no way, therefore, can it interpose itself as a being between God and myself, or concentrate my attention upon itself, or fix my love upon itself, or restrict my communion to itself. Being the humanity of the Word, it rests upon a Principle that is both immanent within itself and infinitely beyond it. The consequence is that it always carries us beyond itself, and to touch it is to touch by means of it the Word that assumes it within itself; it is to be, not cut off from God, but oneself assumed into God. When Christ takes hold of me in his humanity, when I reach him in his humanity, it is the eternal Word that takes hold of me and the eternal Word I reach. In other words, Christ's humanity is the way to God, and when I touch Christ I touch God.

Again, being united with God means entering into the society of the divine Persons, and the incarnate Word is one of these, the Person in whom the mystery of the Trinity is made manifest and communicated. But the Divine Persons only exist in relation to each other—all three are simply one being; they do not lay claim to any being of their own, for as persons they are pure subsistent relationships and do not claim any being. They are real, infinitely real, but because they are really identical with the Divine Being. Being united by way of Christ's humanity to the eternal Word means being united to the Father and the Holy Spirit and, in them, to all the riches of the Divine Being. Once again—and this time from the point of view of the Holy Trinity—being united to Christ's humanity means being united to the Three Persons and the One God. And once again, to touch Christ means to touch God. Christ is not an intermediary, he is the Mediator.

What is true on the level of being is also true on the level of action. Man cannot be united to God unless God gives himself, and the movement towards union cannot come from man, it must come from God. In concrete fact, it comes from Christ sent by God, who takes hold of man and transfigures him. This "personal act of grace" is on Christ's side an act of his human freedom, his human love, his power as a human priest; it is the Act of Redemption itself, the very heart of the Mystery of Christ. The existence of the God-Man culminates in this supreme act, which is at once offering, expiation, and exaltation; which in the mystery of the Pasch embraces all mankind; which is eternally acceptable to the Father; and which becomes actualized in time in the reality of the Church, so that it may seize and save every individual human person.

By this act, access to the Father is ensured to man, definitively: ensured by its origin in the Incarnation, in which God and man are united for ever in the unity of the God-Man; ensured in right and in all fullness by Christ's death, which removed the obstacle of sin, destroyed the kingdom of the Enemy and reopened the gates of Paradise; ensured in its universal communication by the Resurrection, which made Christ the quickening Spirit, the Author of life, the living Fountain of the Spirit; ensured in its concrete communication and its individual application by the sacraments, which unite us with Christ's life-giving resurrected body, and by faith, which is our response to the Saviour's personal act.

Here again, this act does not put up a barrier between man and God, it makes man capable of being united to God. As a creature man is a stranger to God's inner life, as a sinner he is closed against God and condemned by God. The abyss has to be crossed, the obstacle has to be removed, and this is effected by Christ in the Act of Redemption: he redeems man and purifies him from his sin, takes him into himself and raises him up to himself—up to God—and thus makes him capable of grasping God by grasping himself, the God-Man, in the truth of his mediation. Because he comes to man in human form and behaves in a human way, he has to be accepted, he has to be believed and loved; he has to be submitted to and trusted, and his humanity adhered to as the sole way to God. Because he is God dwelling amongst us, in this man we grasp God's living thought, his efficacious Love, his very Reality.

It is thus by uniting ourselves to the divine incarnate Person that we accede to God. As regards the actual movement by which we accede to him—it is by way of Christ as the Way, the Messiah, the Manifestation of God, that this movement takes place. As regards the reality acceded to—it is in Christ as the Son of God, the Principle of life and communion, that contact with God is established and maintained. And since this access to God is nothing less than participation in the actual life of God; since this life is in the Son, and it is communicated to us in the incarnate Son and incorporates us with the Man Jesus Christ, therefore acceding to God means "that we may know the true God and may be in his true Son," because he "is the true God and life eternal" (I John v, 20) and unites us with the Father, with whom he is One.

Christ's mediation thus means infinite mercy, because God makes a man a way of going to him; it is an infinite paradox, because the inaccessible God is reached by way of a man; it contains a permanent possibility of scandal, because it seems to turn God into a man and put a man between us and God; but it is the source of all life, because it is the living link between man and God. All the humility and audacity of faith are involved here, and man is saved when he truly believes that Jesus Christ is the Son of God. Thus every true relationship with the true God is realized by way of Christ, established in Christ, and perfected by the Spirit in the Son, in whom we find the Father. And so it comes about that in all his various dimensions at once, man as a creature exists in Christ, for everything has been created in Him; he exists as redeemed in Christ, for in Christ everything has been saved; as a son he exists in Christ, for all sonship begins and ends in him; he exists as a brother in Christ, for in him all communion is founded and grows. All the Christian experience has to take place within the framework of these constituent relationships, and in this respect faith is the affirmation of our spiritual, ontological immanence in Christ, and the consciousness of our rooted foundation in the love of Christ.

2. *Christ and Christian Inwardness*

Inwardness is a relationship between spiritual presences; it requires a subject and an object;[1] it is established by an act of knowledge and love; and the specific dimension of inwardness is created by the spiritual—intelligible and affective—relationship between subject and object. By the inwardness of knowledge the subject becomes the other in an intellectual way—he can name him to himself in his mind, possess him within himself by means of this spiritual sign, and in the depths of his consciousness grasp the result of this intermingling of intellect and object in reflection. By the inwardness of love the

[1] In the normal theological sense, as the end of the act of knowledge or love. In the modern sense of the word, in true love the object is always a "subject."

subject possesses the one he loves, not only in his mind, but in the impression, the attraction, the affective charge aroused by the other in his will, which releases the movement of joy towards the loved one. By the inwardness of knowledge and love of self the subject names himself to himself in an act of thought more immanent than ever, and embraces himself in a movement of love deeper and more spontaneous than ever, because these two movements spring from the creature's own unity with itself. In all three cases can be discerned the "depth of intimacy" upon which inwardness is based.

Now, Christ creates the Christian inwardness because at the heart of the creature he forms the subject and the object in their relationship to each other.[2] He forms the subject of inwardness, because he forms the Christian within the man. Open to God by his nature, and capable of grace, the human person is called in Christ to supernatural communion, and thus directed positively towards the source of grace. Christ comes to perfect his capacity and fulfil his vocation. He gives the soul the Holy Spirit, who creates in man a deiform being with divine energies of knowledge and love. But this deiform being is the being of a son; this power of knowing and loving is a participation in the mind and love of Christ; and all this is realized by the Spirit, who is Christ's Spirit, "receives what is his" and communicates it to the Christian. In this sense Christ is the permanent principle of the Christian's communion with God, and he himself forms the subject of this communion within man.

Also, Christ forms the object of communion; and he does it by offering himself through his grace, his word, and his Church. He offers himself as the object of knowledge. He is the image of the Father: in him the invisible countenance shines in all its splendour, and he becomes God's existential epiphany: "Who sees me sees the Father." He is furthermore the perfect model of man as God wills him to be, his soul and body resplendent with God's own mind and love and glory. He is thus the One in whom is revealed the whole mystery of God and the whole mystery of man. He offers himself as an object of

[2] Cf. R. Guardini, *L'Essence du Christianisme* (Paris, 1950): "This inwardness is the place where man, having been saved by Christ, stands face to face with the 'God and Father of our Lord Jesus Christ,' and it is based entirely on him. Whenever Christ disappears, Christian inwardness at once disappears too" (pp. 11 *et seq.*). See also E. Mersch, *Théologie du Corps mystique* (Paris, 1944), Vol. I, pp. 91-109; F. Taymans, *Le Progrès du Dogme*, in *Nouvelle Revue théologique*, 1948, pp. 692 *et seq.*

love, because he is given by the Father for the salvation of men—the manifestation and the reality, in all ultimate finality, of the creative and redemptive agape. He offers himself as an object of service, because he is the model to be imitated, the leader to be followed, the Lord who must be adored. The inexhaustible riches of the wisdom and the knowledge and the love of God are wholly present in Christ; and the Trinity is wholly to be grasped in him.

Lastly, Christ establishes the bond between subject and object. Firstly, by the inner illumination that brings the truth of his Word before the eyes of the soul and enables it to be recognized, enables the truth of his Presence to be affirmed and the reality of his mystery as the God-Man to be adhered to. Next by that inner attraction which puts the person in harmony with him, makes the person truly tend towards him, and flowers in their affective union and conformity of wills. When through the grace of Christ there arises in the soul the faith that acts through love, Christian inwardness is realized in act, because there are realized the reciprocal immanence and otherness of the Christian in Christ and of Christ in the Christian: "I in him, and he in me." Moreover, this subject-object bond is given in the very formation of the subject and the object. For Christ forms them both in the believer by the same saving act, gradually preparing them in their reciprocal relationship and fulfilling them in the very act by which they are joined—the act of living faith, in which the object appears fully because the subject is fully formed. On the other hand, this inwardness, being realized in faith, remains mysterious. It is not a psychological phenomenon, but a reality in the order of grace; it is not seen, but believed; it is not perceived like an object, but posited as a structure of life. It is realized through the mediation of signs—the word of truth, the sacraments, the effects of grace—which both reveal and hide Christ's action, and demand the spirit's perfect homage, decentralization of the self, absolute response to the call of God.

It is in this relationship between presences that Christian consciousness begins to unfold. It is the consciousness of a member, because Christ is its Principle and End, its controlling Force and Standard of realization, its absolute Plenitude and Infinite Limit.

When the Christian fabricates the web of spiritual relationships that make up the Christian experience, he does it through Christ, for Christ gives him all the material of the experience by communicating his own being, his own energies and objects to him; he centres himself in Christ, because he participates actively in Christ's life and repeats in his own specific effort the actual movement of Christ's own knowledge and love; he expands in Christ, while preserving his own spiritual density, because the objects of his knowledge and love and service are the very objects of the consciousness of the God-Man. Thus he realizes a conscious, free, progressive assimilation to Christ.

But this consciousness as a member is a participation, and therefore subject to unavoidable limitations. The Christian cannot go beyond the subjective and objective world of Christ's own consciousness, for this constitutes the Christian consciousness itself, and for the consciousness thus constituted any going beyond it would mean self-annihilation. The Christian never reaches the infinity of Christ's own consciousness, because the consciousness of this Man who is God, which embraces the whole mystery of God and the whole mystery of man, and brings these two mysteries together, always remains transcendent to the Christian consciousness. All the Christian can do, therefore, is to imitate, in his own real but infinitely remote way, the infinite movement of Christ's own consciousness. He can add nothing to Christ; but he can go on drawing endlessly upon this inexhaustible mystery, and thus express in his own life the particular aspect of Christ that is meant to be his own personal vocation. When in the light of love he discovers the Father who is in heaven, the brothers whom the Father has given him in Christ, the Holy Trinity in whom the whole Christian reality is bathed, these discoveries are in each case a genuine, if infinitely inferior, participation in and expression of all that Christ has possessed and contemplated in all its fullness from the beginning.

And all the Christian consciousnesses together cannot do more than is done by Christ's consciousness alone, cannot embrace a richer or larger world than his; even taken all together they are no more than one single expression of his mystery, one single aspect of the realization of his world—the expression and realization fixed by the Father in his good pleasure and omnipotence as the perfect and eternal fulfilment of Christ in the fullness of his stature.[3] And Christ's consciousness bears all these separate consciousnesses, carries them to their full dimensions, and guides them with sovereign power to his

[3] "Christ having in himself, in an exemplary way, the splendour of all the saints" (St. Thomas, *in I Cor.* xi, lect. 1).

own personal unity.[4] Thus all Christian unity unfolds within Christ's own inwardness; the whole spiritual movement of Christian souls expands under his mediation; and the more any Christian consciousness is deepened inwardly, the more deeply it is immersed in Christ and in God.

A magnificent example of this expansion under the influence of increasing inwardness is given by St. Theresa of the Child Jesus in a passage describing how love, which is the very heart of the Christian experience, tries by its own movement to grow to the furthest limits of the redeemed world—to the limits of Christ himself. Theresa knows her vocation: it is to be Christ's bride and a mother of souls. But she feels within her other vocations—to be "soldier, priest, apostle, doctor, martyr." All these she longs to be—longs to have them all realized within her, each at its most heroic, most universal, most lasting. Once again, she longs for infinity, she wants everything. Finally she discovers the key to this mysterious vocation that embraces all others, and it is love—love being, so to speak, the heart that supplies all the rest of the body with its life-blood, the creative force behind all the various vocations, in other words the force that builds up the whole Church. "Love comprises every vocation, includes every time, every place, and exists for evermore." Theresa had found her place: "in the Church: within its heart I shall be love—and thus I shall be all" (*The Story of a Soul*, XI). To be the love in the heart means being at the point on which everything is centred and from which everything radiates outwards; but this centre of life and action has only one name, the Heart of Christ, and it was only by plunging into that Heart and hiding herself permanently there that St. Theresa was to embrace the universe.

3. *Christ and Christian Activity*

Activity is the expansion and completion of inwardness, and because it dilates the soul and makes it more open to Christ it prepares

[4] The Church's consciousness "is a synthesis of all the consciousnesses of all the members of the Mystical Body," . . . "realized by the divine life that contains them all and unifies them by joining them to Christ's consciousness through grace. Christ is always endlessly giving utterance to himself in each individual Christian who is attached to him in the unity of the Holy Spirit."—TAYMANS, *art. cit.*, p. 691.

the way for a deeper inwardness.[5] Now Christian activity—once again—is realized entirely in Christ.

Christ came to found the New Covenant and set up the New Law that was to be followed by all the sons of God. Now the New Law in its essence "consists chiefly in the grace of the Holy Ghost, which is shown forth by faith that worketh through love. Now men become receivers of this grace through God's Son made man, Whose humanity grace filled first, and then flowed forth to us" (I. II, 108, 1, c). As a product of living faith Christian activity expresses itself in two essential movements that are distinct from each other and yet at the same time intimately connected—a movement towards God, which is all homage and spiritual worship; and a movement towards man, a movement of brotherly love and service, extending if necessary to the point of sacrifice. But these two movements take place, and find their completion, entirely in relationship to Christ; and they can be said to have the three following aspects.

Christian activity is a conformation to Christ, and it is realized in his image. Every human act involves thinking and willing. Now the Christian's first duty is not to realize values or commandments as things conceived and formulated in the abstract, but to conform himself to a person, to model himself on the incarnate Son, who is an expression and affirmation of the spiritual values and fundamental standards that are involved in all thinking and willing.

Consequently, the only way of paying homage to God is by imitating Christ. Christ loved his Father; he obeyed him down to the smallest detail and up to the supreme sacrifice; he praised him and glorified him. And it is by imitating what Christ has revealed to us of his inner life that we shall do homage to God: he is the Son who has set us the example, and by acting like him we too shall become sons glorifying the Father of heaven. If our supernatural

[5] It is well known that Kierkegaard himself linked inwardness and outward behaviour very closely together; he has even been held to have been responsible for a "paradoxical revaluation of outward behaviour" (C. FABRO, *Foi et Raison dans l'oeuvre de Kierkegaard*, in *Rev. des Sc. phil. et théol.*, 3, 1948, p. 185, n. 22). Cf. *Postscriptum aux Miettes philosophiques* (French trans., Paul PETIT, Gallimard, s.d., p. 257): "The less outwardness, the more inwardness—*if there is any at all;* but at the same time, the less outwardness, the greater the possibility that the inwardness *remains purely and simply absent*. . . . The absence of outwardness may mean that inwardness is calling a man to enter into himself; unfortunately, *it may also mean that there is no inwardness at all*" (my italics. Cf. also, pp. 273-274).

being is a "resemblance by participation in the natural sonship of the Word," our worship of God cannot be anything other than a resemblance by participation in the worship paid by the Son. Furthermore, we can only love our brothers by imitating Christ: "Love one another, as I have loved you," i.e. with infinite respect for all, especially for the very humble, the very poor and insignificant; in day-to-day service; materially, bodily, and spiritually; by sacrifice, as he himself sacrificed himself for us.

This worship and service will be manifested in three different kinds of activity: in the living faith that enables us to adhere to Christ's vision, and to worship God in spirit and in truth in the way that he himself worshipped, loving our neighbours as brothers called in Christ to return to the Father; in our use of the sacraments, especially the Holy Eucharist, in which Christ takes us up into his own act of homage and delivers us to the Father, drawing us all together in the same desire for brotherly service; and lastly in our witness, through which in the strength of the Spirit we perpetuate Christ's own witness, confessing the Father before men and leading sinners to repentance and faith.

But Christ is not only our model, he is the Source; Christians are not only disciples, but members; and Christian activity is achieved in the strength of Christ. "All things come from God"—who loves us, gives us his Son, and inspires in him the love that is to redeem us. But all things come to us "through Christ," who merits, satisfies and redeems, who transfigures us and deifies us by the influx of his grace within us. And it is Christ's freedom, as a thing perfectly conscious of its ends and perfectly adapted to its purpose, that affects human beings and converts them and enables them to exist and act freely in him. At the root of all Christian activity is to be found the personal act of grace by which Christ enables us to act as sons: "Now grace is not vouchsafed to us by means of human nature but solely by the personal action of Christ Himself" (III, 8, 5, 1^m; cf. 2^m & 3, c). Christ's causality is therefore truly the first and universal principle in the order of grace—only it is not a force, but a being; not a cause, but a person. It is the knowledge, will and love of the Man Jesus Christ in act. And it is in this strictly personal union with Christ that Christian activity has its root.

Again, Christ does not give us the created grace that is in his soul, or the created gifts of light and love by which he is transfigured, for his soul is not our soul and the transfiguration of his soul can never become ours.[6] He gives us the actual principle of this grace and the actual source of these gifts, i.e. the Holy Spirit, who is his Spirit and becomes our Spirit, and who causes to spring up within us the very life he causes to spring up in Christ. St. Thomas's teaching is perfectly clear on this point: "Although the habitual gifts in Christ's soul are different from those in ours, nevertheless the same and only Spirit who is in Christ fills all who are to be sanctified. And from the unity of the Spirit comes the unity of the Church" (*In Joa.*, I, lect. 3; cf. 3, lect. 6). "There is in the Church a kind of continuity, deriving from the Holy Spirit, who, being unique and numerically one, fills the Church and makes it one. And therefore, with respect to his human nature, Christ is called the Head, because he spreads the Spirit within us" (*De Ver.*, 29, 4, c; cf. III^a, 8, 1, 1^m). Such is the mysterious action that makes Christ the Principle of our life and the direct Source of our behaviour, and ensures the unity and continuity between Christ and each of us and all who are Christians. But an unimaginable depth and transcendence are involved here; for if Christ "causes" the grace that is within us, he does not "cause" the Spirit—he gives it. And this pure communication is possible only because the Man Jesus Christ is in his Person the eternal Son, from whom, with the Father, proceeds the Holy Spirit; he who is the *Verbum spirans amorem*; he who, sitting beside the Father, communicates the Spirit into the soul in the world of time, because with the Father he is its Principle in the world of eternity. This Spirit his humanity received in all its fullness, because his humanity was that of the Son, and was to be the humanity of the Saviour; this Spirit it communicates in the holy and sovereign freedom of its love, because in it and through it the Word expresses himself, acts, gives life. Consequently it is in a mystery, which descends into the abyss of the Holy Trinity and takes us with it, that Christ communicates to us the One who prompted him, directed him and inspired him in his task of redemption; and the Spirit plays the same part in us. The Spirit inspires our activity, gives it his light, his enthusiasm, his efficaciousness. And through the Spirit Christ turns us into sons and enables us to act like himself—like sons: it is the power

[6] Cf. E. Vauthier, *La grâce du Christ et le Corps mystique*, in *Mélanges de Science religieuse*, 1949, pp. 63 *et seq.*

of the Spirit of Christ, communicated by Christ, that enables us to imitate Christ.

Lastly, Christian activity has one sole aim: to form Christ in the fullness of his stature. Now the constructive force is agape—which indeed is the only force at work in the new world and in the people of God, creating, recreating, giving life and growth. This force is truly divine, for in God it is the love uniting the Father, the Son and the Holy Spirit, and in us it is a participation in this love; and if it is revealed and given to us by Christ in the Spirit, this is so that Christ may be expressed and perpetuated in his members. Now Christ is not only the only-begotten Son joined to the Father in an ineffable constituent relationship; he is also the first-born, bound to all his brothers as the principle of salvation, divinization and unity in God. Seized by the Spirit of Christ and incorporated into his humanity, we participate in both these aspects of Christ: we become sons of God, participating in the love that unites Christ to God who is his Father, and brothers of Christ and of all the other sons in the saving Love that makes them one. Being rooted in the love of the Trinity, we are called upon to express this love in our lives and to extend it to all men—and this means, forming Christ. We shall find the three main features of this agape in the New Testament, in three different sets of passages.

St. Paul presents the Church as an enormous workroom: there is a great body, a great structure to be built—the temple of God, the Body of Christ, which grows through charity. There is a personal side to this growth. When Christ in his glory communicates himself to sinful man, he makes him a new man in the New Man which is himself. But the prospect before this creature born of grace is infinite, for he is a divinized spirit, called upon to grow, and to go on growing, until he has reached the fullness fixed for him by God in Christ. His growing-power is love, which takes him into the mystery of Christ and fills his soul with God, "unto all the fulness of God" (Eph. iii, 14-19), and this fullness of contemplation overflows as the lived fullness of brotherly love, which builds up not only the individual soul but the whole Church as well. For this growth has a churchly side to it. The Christian is baptized into the unity of the Holy Ghost and for the sake of the unity of the Body: the hierarchy and the charisma only exist to help build up the Church; the sole aim of all apostolic labour engaged upon in agape is the edification of the whole Body until the time of its full stature in Christ: the Lord gave "for the perfecting of the saints, for the work of the ministry, for the edifying of the Body of Christ"; he "maketh increase of the body unto the edifying of itself in charity," until it reaches "unto a perfect man, unto the measure of the age of the fulness of Christ" (Eph. iv, 11-16). Thus Christian activity is essentially motivated by agape, which builds up the glorious Body of Christ in secret until through agape Christ shall have satisfied all the creatures of grace to their utmost capacity, and thus filled "all things" (Eph. iv, 10).

St. John tends rather to emphasize the Epiphany of Christ and the Love of the Trinity in the Church. He sees the Love in its Principle, as between the divine Persons, and in its end, as between Christians, and in both cases this love is Unity—the living unity of persons who have given themselves to each other. Here again agape builds up the Church, and in two ways. On the one hand it binds the Christians themselves together and creates their communion and unity with Christ and the Father: this bond, this communion, this unity, is the Church itself. On the other hand, it draws the world to the faith. The unity which it reveals is truly a revelation of God, because it is set up in a world of hatred that rejects Christ and persecutes Christians (xv, 18-25). In this context it appears as a superhuman reality, charismatic, utterly divine. It is the testimony given before men, the sign of Christ's presence, the revelation of eternal Love. Through it, men recognize Christ as the Messias sent by the Father for the salvation of the world (xvii, 23); they recognize in Christians and in Christ the presence of the Father's unique love of Christ and his followers. Brotherly love is thus a continuation and manifestation of the love of the Trinity; and the faith of those who are converted is at once a discovery and an affirmation of this unique dual love: *credidimus Caritati, credidimus Trinitati.*

Now this brotherly love is properly speaking the "new commandment," the "commandment of Christ," because it is borne entirely by the charity of Christ. Christ's love is its model—we must love as he loved, and thus preserve his countenance before the eyes of men until the end of time; it is its principle—we must "remain within" it, as the shoot of the vine must remain within the sap of the stock; it is its end—Christians must be one as the Father and the Son are one (xvii, 11), because they must be one in the Son and in the

Father (xvii, 21), as the Father and the Son are one in each other. When the reciprocal love between the Father and the Son—communicated by Christ—is realized and expressed in the reciprocal love between Christians, the new commandment is realized, the new people is formed, and God is glorified. Seen in this light, brotherly love is not primarily a merely constructive force, it is the dazzling Epiphany of eternal love, revealed in Christ.

But to say that brotherly love builds up Christ, that it is a call to Christ and reveals the Trinity in Christ, means that it fulfils the Christian vocation and that it is by this love that we shall be judged (Matt. xxv, 31-46). Love is the standard of judgment, because during life it is the actual law of behaviour, the source, content, and form of the Christian's existence on earth. Now Christ came to save a race of men who are sinful, and hence in danger and misfortune. He assumed their condition, and in his love laid hold of the man of woe. He became that which he came to save, excepting sin. And loving him means henceforth loving all who are in misfortune—the poor, the captives, the blind and "them that are bruised," as Isaias says (Luke iv, 18-19); those who, as our Lord said, "are hungry and thirsty, strangers, naked, sick, or in prison" (Matt. xxv, 44). Helping or ignoring all these means doing good or evil, for it means helping or ignoring Christ. Once again—Christian behaviour ends with Christ; and human actions receive both their meaning and value here in this world, and their reward or punishment in the next, from Christ. The good and evil in our lives are defined by their relation to Christ; on the Last Day, Christ will simply acknowledge this, reveal it, and set his seal upon it.

Thus, all the relationships that go to make up the Christian experience are formed, and find their full development, in Christ. Faith and love are realized within an inwardness created by Christ; they manifest themselves in a kind of activity that derives entirely from Christ and fulfils Christ. In the matter of the Christian experience Christ is the Alpha and Omega, the Beginning and the End. But because he is the Mediator, everything that ends in him ends in the Trinity too. And that is why the centuries-old experience of the Church, single and manifold as it is, knows only one consummation: "That God may be all in all" (I Cor. xv, 28).

CHAPTER NINE

Affectivity and the Christian Experience

In the Encyclical *Humani Generis* occur these words: "Finally, they reproach the philosophy taught in our schools that, in explaining the process of cognition, it takes into account the intellect alone, neglecting the function of the will and the emotions. This is simply untrue. Never has Christian philosophy denied the usefulness and efficacy of good dispositions of the whole soul for fully understanding and embracing moral and religious truths. On the contrary, it has always taught that the lack of such dispositions can be the reason why the intellect, influenced by passions and bad will, may be obscured to the point of judging falsely. Indeed, St. Thomas thinks that the intellect can in some way perceive higher goods of the moral order, whether natural or supernatural, in so far as the soul experiences a certain affective 'connaturalness' to them, whether this 'connaturalness' be natural or the result of grace."

The following inquiry will follow the general lines laid down in this passage, but whereas the above observations are directly concerned with knowledge, I shall attempt to enlarge the perspective to include the Christian life itself. And I shall try to deduce from its most outstanding manifestations the general part played by affectivity in the living movement of the Christian life.

1. *General Remarks on Affectivity*

Affectivity and Suffering. The human person is self-subsistent, existing in his own inviolable secrecy and his own irrefragable uniqueness. But he is only given to himself as a kind of seed and hope; he is orientated towards various ends, and, through them, to the ultimate End in whom alone he can find fulfilment. He is called upon to build himself up, develop himself, complete himself, all quite freely and at all his different levels—organically, psychologically, socially, spiritually. Thus he is open to the world, to others and to God, and this threefold reality is necessary for him if he is to find his fulfilment. This presupposes a capacity for acceptance and reaction, an appropriate form of suffering and acting into which affectivity can be inserted.

Suffering signifies both the grandeur of a being made to receive everything, to become everything, to possess everything, and the misery of a being who has only a limited capacity—a capacity throughout his development permanently limited—for receiving the other, orientating himself towards it, and finding completion in it. Suffering is thus connected with the human being's radical potentiality and the ends by which this can be satisfied: it is the relation between the two. In a universe that is also a cosmos, in which finality is the deepest bond between beings, suffering can never be pure endurance or pure feeling: it must always be orientated towards something, specified by something, finalized by something, because it will always be the actualization of a potentiality by its object, the grasp of a reality at the heart of a being made to receive it: "For a thing is said to be passive from its being drawn to the agent" (*S. Th.*, I. II, 22, 1, c). And this arises from a general metaphysical law: "For every mover, in a fashion, either draws the patient to itself, or repels it from itself" (I. II, 23, 4, c; cf. 9, 1, c). When it strikes a being who is in a submerged state of desire, the object awakens him, makes him vibrate (in sympathy or antipathy) and gives rise to a movement of attraction or repulsion in him. Under this stimulus, the being suffers according to his particular potentiality, for his own good or evil. Suffering is thus, to be precise, a specified reception of the other within oneself, the actualization of a potentiality, either by attraction or repulsion. Suffering means being called, and responding to the call.

Suffering, however, can have three different meanings, each more restricted than the preceding one. The first concerns the whole human potentiality: suffering means receiving the other, and in this sense knowledge, both intellectual and sense knowledge, involves fundamentally a kind of suffering which is in fact a perfection—a *perfici* (I^{a} II^{ae}, 22, 1, c). The second meaning refers to the mode of reaction proper to the appetite as such, and this is the true sphere of suffering (I. II, 22, 2, c). The appetite, being ordinated to actual realities in their existential uniqueness, tends towards these by experiencing their attraction and allurement. It only perfects itself in a real union with beings, whereas the intelligence receives them and possesses them in itself; and if the appetite is more active than the intelligence, this is primarily because it is more passive before the actual things (I. II, 22, 2, 2^{m}), more dependent on the riches they can bring it, and hence limited by its actual susceptibility to them. Thirdly, suffering takes on all its full density, so to speak, when it brings the whole body into play and the reception of the other is accompanied by some organic modification: this is the case with "*passio*"—psycho-organic affectivity—and it can destroy the being as well as fulfil him. I shall use the word suffering in the second of these senses (which includes the third), and therefore regard affectivity as the appetite's capacity for reaction to its proper objects in matters concerning both sense and spirit.

But although I shall leave aside any discussion of intellectual suffering, which raises quite different problems, nevertheless, knowledge and affectivity clearly represent two fundamental human reactions and are therefore ultimately inseparable. Knowledge releases affectivity, and affectivity colours knowledge. So that affectivity is at once a reaction to knowledge and a reaction on it: it presupposes it and conditions it; it is bathed in it and modifies it. But it depends upon it in the first place for its actual appearance: before man can react to his objects, his ends, his true values, he must know what they are—and his affective reactions start from perceptions, or images, or ideas. This regulation by the known object is one of the major factors in our problem.

It is not the only one, however. For affectivity affects the subject in his entirety, in all three depths of his being: it affects the fundamental tendencies engrained in his nature—forces of instinct, and spiritual aspirations; it affects the modifications of these tendencies under the influence of the individual's own experience—psycho-organic and spiritual "habits"; and it affects the acts and operations that are produced according to his condition at any particular moment. Thus affective movements descend deep into the unconscious;[1] and from this they derive their frightful ambivalence, for the unconscious is both animal and spiritual; to it they owe in part too their suddenness, their unexpectedness, their violence, their beneficent or disastrous polymorphism. Affectivity thus appears as the meeting point of the inner world and the outer world, and these two worlds react on each other in a way that remains to be described.

The Affective Movement. Before we go any further, however, we need to indicate the three essential stages of the affective movement. Man is a being in a state of desire. He is orientated by a natural appetite towards the Good that will satisfy him completely—his last End. This appetite is his first, necessary, and unchanging movement. Until he reaches its end he is carried along by it irresistibly, in a great longing for infinity—he is open, desirous, hungry, needy. Now man never attains to his last end here on earth, but only to varying kinds of participation in it. He is immersed in a world whose ends are partial, provisional, conditional, running with or contrary to each other. As soon as he meets them and sees them for what they are, he is attracted by them, and then he either pursues them, takes hold of them and finds rest in them, or else he runs away from them, rejects them and is wounded by them—doing this again and again, unend-

[1] The first two layers, of course, raise the whole problem of the unconscious, and the differences between the various depth-psychologies on this point are well-known. In my opinion there are good grounds for admitting two kinds of unconscious—the *primitive unconscious*, the centre of biological forces (aggressiveness and sexuality, the Freudian instincts), psychic forces (Jung's "primordial images" or archetypes) and spiritual forces (the soul's aspiration towards values); and the *individual unconscious*, a resultant of the subject's own experiences, with all its components, "repressed" and, as Nédoncelle says, "renounced." To this would need to be added—above—a *third unconscious* of grace and the infused virtues, inserted into the centre of the spirit, coexistent with the other two and normally intended to polarize them towards its own ends. This is an unconscious by super-existence, unknown to the pure psychologist. No direct treatment of these problems will be found here. I have confined my investigation to the philosophical and theological level explored by St. Thomas: it seems to be the level at which inquiry is most urgently needed. When the part played by affectivity and freedom in the sphere of faith has been ascertained and explained, the problem of the connection between unconscious affectivity and free, conscious spiritual life will arise. It is a problem that awaits investigation on all sides. It is a necessary question, and it is a difficult one; but at the moment we have not got beyond the prospecting stage. Cf. the remarks by E. GILSON on memory and the unconscious in St. Augustine, *Introduction à l'étude de saint Augustin* (Paris, 1929), p. 131, n. 3 (2nd ed., 1943, p. 135, n. 2).

ingly. In man as a being proceeding towards his end, affectivity represents this fundamental, endlessly resurgent reaction towards the good, the "proper," the end—or towards their opposites. Man is thus always in a state of tension and desire. But this assumes and involves something further.

This desire, in fact, presupposes love, which is the basis of all affective movements. Now in love the will is always passive and active at once—the two different aspects are integrated in the identity of the same act. For the will is an infinite capacity of love for the good, but it is the good itself that transmits this capacity to the act.

To keep to the spiritual level for a moment—it may be said that the desirable reality—the end—moves the will; i.e., the reality enters into man by the mediation of knowledge, proportions the will to itself, makes it vibrate to its appeal, rouses its sympathy and attraction—in short, inclines it to love. This is its sympathetic aspect: the will is passive under the influence of the end and modified inwardly by it, and what it thus "receives" is a living impression, a vital impulse, a "*pondus*."[2] But this reception, which keeps the will open to the other, also makes it capable of movement, and induces it to make a reply. Thence there springs from the will an inclination towards the object, the living act which is the tendency towards the real end and the existing being—in other words, love itself. This is now no longer the sympathization and receptive aspect: it is the return and inclination aspect.

But these two movements are simultaneous, because they are two aspects of one single act. Thus love, as a modification caused by the object, is a passivity; as a modification orientated towards the object, it is an activity. Its activity is founded upon a kind of suffering, its vibration on a harmony, its impulse on an impression. And in each case these are two sides of the same psychological reality, two aspects of one single affective operation.[3] Love is thus a movement, but springing from a sympathization, an attraction, and based upon a communication. "The loved thing exists in the will, as inclining and in a way compelling the will to it" (IV C. C., 19). And again: "Lov-

[2] "Augustine compares love to weight, for by it one rises or falls" (*De Ver.*, 24, ii, 3^m).

[3] On this point, and for more technical details, H. D. Simonin, *Autour de la solution thomiste du problème de l'amour* (*Archives d'Histoire doctrinale et littéraire du Moyen-Âge*, 1931, pp. 199 *et seq.*).

ing is made perfect in the attraction of the one lover towards the being of the other" (*Compend. Theol.*, 46). And finally, in a passage already quoted: ". . . to tend to God by love, being as it were passively drawn by him" (I. II, 26, 3, 4^{m}). "To tend, passively drawn"; it is true of all love. And St. Thomas purposely emphasizes this aspect, which is so often ignored and yet so fraught with consequences. Love is in the first place a kind of suffering for the will whose expectation is fulfilled by the loved being; and as a spontaneous reaction to this suffering it is an activity—"a spontaneous movement of the lover towards the beloved" (II. II, 25, 2, c). Because it is the fundamental act of an appetite ordinated towards things as they are in themselves (I. II, 22, 2, 2^{m}), the passivity is at the basis of the activity—it is at the heart of a radical, permanent passivity that the activity unfolds; and the same movement appears from one point of view as the attraction of the object and from another as the inclination of the subject.

As the starting-point of the affective movement, love leads to desire, which in turn leads to an effort at real union with the end, and the possession of the end produces delectation. Delectation therefore presupposes possession of the object, and awareness of this possession: it is the affective manifestation of the flowering of this act of awareness, and consequently the appeasement of the love and desire by the possession of the end: "Repose in the end."[4] This gives some idea of its importance. For though man is in motion towards his last end, he needs occasional rests along the way. All real ends are stages in this journey, and inchoate manifestations of the final end; and in this endless dynamic process delectation is the time of rest, because it means a state of appeasement in joy. But as the possession is only partial, the flowering only temporary, and both ultimately insufficient, there is always a resurgence of movement, desire, effort, towards a new joy.

We must go further and say that of all the affective operations delectation is the first in importance. It is the end that is pursued, and therefore the principle of the affective movement. For, "Delectation and the good are desired for the same reason, for delectation is nothing but the appeasement of the appetite in the good . . . This is why, just as the good is desired for itself, so also delectation is desired

[4] I. II, 34, 2, 2^{m}; cf. 2, 6, 1^{m}; 34, 1, c; 2, c & 3^{m}; 4, c & 2^{m}. Also, "rest in the good obtained" (23, 4, c).

for itself and not for anything else, if the word 'for' signifies the final cause" (I. II, 2, 6, 1^{m}, & cf. 34, 2, 3^{m}). Love and desire come first in order of appearance, but they only exist for the purpose of that conjunction with the good which is fulfilled in delectation, so that delectation comes first in the order of ends (I. II, 34, 4, 1^{m}).

Delectation is thus the fulfilment of human activity. Something is lacking in any activity that is accomplished without it; it is strictly "the good which is added as a fulfilment"—*bonum completive superveniens* (I. II, 33, 4, c); consequently, no operation is perfectly good without it. And in this respect delectation may be compared with intellectual certainty. Intellectual certainty is the characteristic product of the possession of the true, in an intelligence that tends towards absolute Truth; delectation is the characteristic product of the possession of the good, in an appetite that tends towards the absolute End. "The appeasement of the mind in the truth, the appeasement of the appetite in the end": man only finds full satisfaction in certainty and joy; both are his life's necessary bread.

Such is the line followed by the development of activity. But we immediately have to complicate it. For the movement is one of love, desire, and joy; or, contrariwise, of hatred, repulsion, and misery; and these conflicting movements are mixed up with each other. On the one hand they stimulate each other: as any affirmation implies the negation of its opposite ("Affirmation of one thing always leads to denial of its opposite," I. II, 100, 7, 1^{m}), so any love implies opposition to anything that conflicts with it: love of anyone inevitably means opposing whatever hates or threatens or attacks the loved one. The affective process, which, for the sake of brevity, we have followed along a single line only, takes place in reality along two lines at once. Love and aggressiveness are bound up with each other from the most elementary reactions up to the highest forms of human activity: love of God inevitably means hatred of sin. On the other hand, it seems fairly certain that in the deeper regions of affectivity there is a paradoxical unity of opposite, associated tendencies, a unity that is "insulated against every kind of logic, inconceivable to the full consciousness," but affecting the whole psychic structure and bound up with the fundamental instincts.[5] "The path that runs along the top of the precipice by its mere presence arouses two opposite, inseparable tendencies within me—the tendency to go on, and the tendency to

[5] Cf. J. BOUTONNIER, *L'Angoisse* (Paris, 1945), pp. 39 *et seq.*, 266 *et seq.*

fall over the edge."[6] Children manifest this ambivalence in the games they choose to play, the frightening stories they ask to be told, in their attitude toward their parents, whom they alternately resent and caress;[7] they desire and fear, love and detest, both at the same time. Something of this remains in the adult, and love as an affective movement seems even in the case of its own object to be associated with aggressiveness—with the result that the very otherness of the beloved, with his limitations and deficiencies, and his excellences and superiorities, inevitably arouses the aggressive impulses; so that a great and genuine, pure and generous love cannot truly come into being except after a long struggle against aggressiveness. It will be readily understood what frightful dangers and complexities this introduces into the affective movement.

The Two Levels of Affectivity. Man is matter and spirit. Sharing in both, he brings them together in the unity of his being; open to both, he has need of both and is naturally attracted by them. In so far as the soul is the form of the body, all the material values are necessary and desirable to it: the soul goes in search of them and feeds upon them by way of its body. In so far as the soul is a spirit, and therefore, in a way, infinitely beyond the body,[8] it is open to spiritual values, desires them and feeds upon them by its spiritual operations. Man therefore knows two kinds of good, the one appertaining to the senses, the other to the spirit; and has two kinds of affectivity, the one of the senses, the other of the spirit.

The affectivity of the senses is psycho-organic, and it always involves both body and soul. It includes that "bodily change" which is implied in what is properly known as *passio* (I. II, 22, c, etc.). Whether it is an affective sensation that is involved—pleasure or pain—i.e., "an affective reaction, both psychic and organic, to a change in our own body, perceived as such"—or whether it is emotion, "an affective reaction, both psychic and organic, to an object either perceived as external to our own body, or imagined, or recalled to memory"[9]—in either case we are immediately transported into the world of the body,

[6] *Op. cit.*, p. 42.

[7] *Op. cit.*, pp. 154 *et seq.*

[8] "For since the rational soul excels the capacity of corporeal matter, that part of the soul which is independent of a corporeal organ, has a certain infinity in regard to the body" (I. II, 2, 6c).

[9] R. Dalbiez, *Psychoanalytical Method and the Doctrine of Freud*, trs., T. F. Lindsay (Longmans, Green & Co., 1941), Vol. II, p. 36.

obliged to "suffer" the world, moved by the most unmitigatedly organic impulses and governed by a polymorphous force of great power which we have within us—the power of images.

Spiritual affectivity is the reaction of the "rational appetite" to its proper objects. Whenever some good or evil is presented to the will, the spiritual movement of attraction or repulsion is set up. The will is an appetite and its act an inclination, and spiritual feeling is this pure upsurge of attraction or repulsion, in which no organic modification is essentially involved—"simple acts of the will having like effects, but without passion."[10] The will is thus to be understood here as the power of spiritual feelings, as well as—through its connection with the intelligence—the faculty of making free choices; and so it integrates the two functions of passivity and activity. And from the will spring great feelings like the love and desire for truth, goodness, and beauty; remorse and repentance;[11] admiration, reverence, gratitude, joy. These feelings mean something infinitely richer, more varied, more profound, more expansive, than the emotions, which are more violent and more weighty but more elementary and much poorer. And the more human activity becomes polarized upon the spiritual, the richer and stronger becomes this higher affectivity.

We have a first-class example of the difference between the two in St. Thomas's study of delectation. This is an essential part of human activity, as St. Thomas, quoting Aristotle, recognizes: "No man can be a long time in company with what is painful and unpleasant" (II. II, 35, 4, 2^{m}).

The delectation of the senses—pleasure—which immediately stimulates the body, is normal and necessary, because nature herself has joined it to the necessary activities of life (II. II, 142, 1, c), in particular to the preservation of the individual and the species (I. II, 31, 7, c). This is a normal dimension of our animality ("which we have in common with dumb animals," 31, 4, 3^{m}), by which we are connected with the movement of biological life. As these various kinds of delectation arise from the affective sensations and the emotions, and involve a modification of the bodily organs and the

[10] I. II, 22, 3, 3^{m}. Since there is no getting away from the necessity of using words, and philosophic usage is far from being cast-iron, I shall use the word "emotion" in connection with psycho-organic affectivity, and "feeling" in connection with spiritual affectivity. Cf. a brief but highly interesting account by J. MAISONNEUVE, *Les Sentiments* (Paris, 1948).

[11] So profoundly studied by SCHELER in *Le Sens de la Souffrance*.

"humours," they are tangible, "vehement," and at times irresistible (31, 5). As the good of the senses is the good of the composite as a whole, they affect both the soul and the body; they are able to monopolize the field of consciousness, polarize the forces of desire, and determine human conduct. And that is why so many people live by the senses.

Spiritual delectation—joy—springs from the spiritual operations, knowledge and love, "when delight follows reason" (31, 3, c). It is "in the mind" (31, 5, 3^m), and a pure spiritual act, "the mere movement of the will" (31, 4, c); it refers to spiritual goods or spiritual values—the contemplation of truth or acts of virtue (31, 7); it is man's normal fulfilment as a spiritual creature in the possession of his good, "which we have in common with angels" (31, 4, 3^m). In itself it is higher than the delectation of the senses (31, 5, c), because man is spirit rather than body; because spiritual goods are better than material goods; because the intelligence is nobler and more profound than the senses; because the union with the good, in the case of the spirit, is more intimate, more perfect, more lasting (cf. II. II, 141, 4, 4^m). Far from being a luxury, it is necessary for man's perfection. It strengthens the use of reason by attracting and fixing the attention, and by enabling joy to be found in intellectual and spiritual effort (I. II, 33, 3, c & 4, 1^m). It makes spiritual operations perfectly good, crowning the operation with a sense of fulfilment (34, 4, 3^m); it prepares the way for better operations by rousing attention, enthusiasm and diligence (34, 4, c); in fact, "no operation can be perfectly good without a sense of delectation in the good" (34, 4, 3^m). In particular, it ensures the vigour and wholeheartedness of virtuous actions by helping to root virtue in the soul, and no virtue can do without this joy: "It appertains to every virtue to delight in its own spiritual good, i.e. in its proper act" (II. II, 35, 2, c; cf. I. II, 59, 3, c & 4, 1^m)—to such an extent that in the virtuous person what is delectable has a certain moral value "for the sake of their inherent goodness which is delightful to the virtuous" (I. II, 70, 1, 2^m). Finally, delectation is the sign and rule of moral goodness: it means rest in the end, and the end confers upon the act moral goodness or badness (I. II, 20, 1); consequently, the moral value of a man is to be judged by his choice of delectations: "That man is good and virtuous, who delights in the works of virtue, and that man is bad, who delights in bad works." "He is good whose will finds rest in the true good" (I. II, 34, 4, c

& 2^m); and spiritual delectation is so "proper to virtuous men" (31, 5, 1^m) that it is practically a definition of them. As can be seen, it is difficult to imagine a profounder integration of affectivity and the action of the virtues, of joy and spiritual labour.

The Connection between the Two Levels. These considerations provide us with the preliminary matter of another problem—the relationship to be established between the two levels of affectivity. On the one hand, these two forces appertain to the same being, and they are destined to unite and collaborate. The ontological hierarchy between the two means that sense is meant to be obedient to reason; this ordination gives it its nobility (I. II, 50, 3, 1^m), and its obedience gives it a share in reason. Conversely, reason has the task of taking sense into itself and integrating it. And man's perfection is realized when the "two parts" are united in pursuit of the same ends.

Consequently, the good of man includes the right ordering of the passions (I. II, 24, 3, c). For man's good exists in the reason as in its root and principle; it is all the more perfect, the more it flows down into the other human powers. Therefore the passions are meant to be regulated by reason; they become morally good when they are subjected to reason, accepted or governed by it (24, 1, c); and man is perfect when he works towards his moral good with both his will and his sensibility, for any operation involving two distinct principles is only perfect when the two principles are both rectified (I. II, 58, 3, c). The function of moral virtue, therefore, is never to suppress the sensitive appetite and its acts (I. II, 59, 5, c), but on the contrary to help it to rectify its activity, so that it may contribute to the perfection of the activity of the virtues. Even bodily delectation is necessary for the proper use of reason (II. II, 142, 1, 2^m). Reason has need of sense-activity and the organs of the body, and man is therefore under an obligation to maintain his body in good order, so that the operations of the reason may be easy and delectable; and therefore "the good of the reason cannot exist if man abstains from all bodily delectation." Virtue is first cousin to the senses.

But the reason does not only govern, and the sensibility obey. To its governing function it adds another—that of awakening the sensitive appetite and drawing it along in its wake. When the movement of the spirit is intense, it communicates itself—*redundat*—to the sensibility (I. II, 24, 3, 1^m), with the result that the latter "in its own way tends to the spiritual good following the lead of the higher appetite" (30, 1, 1^{m}): emotion then becomes a sign of intensity of the will, a help to the work of the spirit (24, 3, 1^{m}); and spiritual joy brings the joy of the senses in its wake (59, 5, c). St. Thomas even recognizes that man "by the judgment of his reason chooses to be affected by a passion" (24, 3, 1^{m}): passion is awakened by the choice of the will—*ex electione*—and in this case the passion makes the virtuous action a better thing.

Though there should be a close union between these two kinds of affectivity, they may find themselves in opposition to each other, as a result of their comparative independence. The act of the sensibility depends in fact both on the sensitive appetite and on the disposition of the body (I. II, 17, 7, c) because it utilizes one or other of the organs of the body. It is true that the sensitive appetite depends on images, and that reason has authority over the imagination, as "the universal over the particular," and that therefore reason has power to control the acts of the sensibility; but this power is limited in two ways—by the weakness of the imagination, which often "cannot imagine what is being considered by the reason" (*ibid.*, 3^{m}), either because the thing is something incorporeal or because the imagination is weakened and hindered by bad bodily dispositions, and also by the power of the imagination (*ibid.*, c), which has an immediate effect upon the senses.[12] Again, the bodily dispositions are not subject to reason, and as they condition the sensibility directly the movements of the sensibility are not absolutely subject to reason. St. Thomas concludes, therefore, that "the appetitive faculty obeys the reason, not blindly, but with a certain power of opposition" (I. II, 58, 2, c), and that, in the celebrated phrase, the reason only has a political, not a despotic power over the sensitive appetite (17, 7, c & 58, 2, c)—a power of tutelage and persuasion, a slow, hard job of education. St. Thomas applies this, for example, to the sexual instinct. This instinct is more unamenable to reason than any other, and this is one of the penalties of sin (I. II, 17, 9, 3^{m}); but sin has "left nature to itself," and therefore there is a natural reason for this particular insubordination, which is that sexual thoughts and images arouse sexual emotion, which in its turn releases the movements of the "heart" and "sex"

[12] "The apprehension of the power of imagination is sudden and indeliberate: wherefore it can cause an act before the higher or lower reason has time to deliberate" (I. II, 74, 7, 4^{m}). Once again we touch upon the unconscious.

through an organic change that is outside the control of the reason. The image, the psycho-organic emotion, the bodily movement—here is a whole affective line, almost autonomous, that escapes the grasp of the reason: "I see another law in my members, fighting against the law of my mind" (Rom. vii, 15, quoted in I. II, 17, 7, 1^m).

We thus come upon oppositions of fact that make any cohabitation of sense and spirit very difficult. Each has its own particular weight, and tension between them is normal, but a slight shift of emphasis tears sensibility away from the spirit. Indeed, as man experiences himself in existence, he finds the weight of the affectivity of the senses very heavy, especially their delectation—whose function here we can only briefly indicate. These kinds of delectation conflict with the spirit by their suddenness—for they are connected with a multitude of objects and desires, and they are always coming across something that releases them, and then they spring up with the rapidity, the inevitability, and the audacity of animal instinct. They dominate the spirit by their violence (I. II, 31, 5, c): they are more powerful in fact than spiritual delectations, because they are realized in the world of the senses, which is known by material experience; because they have an organic component and thus affect the whole body; because the body itself is subject to appetites and pains and sadnesses that make man highly amenable to "the kind of deliverance and comfort" that can be provided by pleasure. Lastly, they make the exercise of reason and virtue difficult, sometimes terribly difficult (I. II, 33, 3, c; & cf. 74, 3, 2^m; & 77, 2, c). The human soul being single, if its strength is monopolized and its attention distracted by the senses, the reason becomes correspondingly weak; furthermore, violent and excessive delectations are against reason and they corrupt its practical judgment—in the last resort, bodily disturbance, by perturbing the senses and the imagination, can put an end to the right use of reason.

And here we come to one of the main, and highly dangerous, functions of affectivity. Being a reaction of the soul to objects that fulfil it—goods and ends—affectivity is dependent upon the knowledge that presents it with its ends: though the appetite is in a state of desire, at the root of every act of desire we find an act of knowledge—some affective sensation or perception, some image or thought—and this regulates the appetite objectively. But an end is not a thing. It is something that seems good to the subject—in St. Thomas's very expressive word, a *conveniens* (I. II, 9, 2, c). Now an object seems fitting to a subject according to what it offers and according to the person who perceives it: the *conveniens* is a relationship between these two terms, and depends on both—"fitness is spoken of by way of relation; hence it depends on both extremes" (*ibid.*). The subject to a considerable extent controls the appearance of the object: he determines whether it is good or bad for himself; he is psychologically the master of his own good and his own evil. In other words, though every real end is ontologically a genuine value by reason of the fullness which it derives from God, it does not appear as a value or get grasped as one except by a subject who recognizes it as such through an act of evaluation. This assertion can only have meaning for those who acknowledge a clear distinction between ontological reality of ends and values, and the knowledge that we may have of these; and who consequently grant man the power, not to create the reality of these ends and values, but to create their appearance. Such a doctrine is capable of assimilating all that is true in what recent investigations have discovered about the subjectivity of values, without, like them, taking upon itself a creative function beyond its range. It recognizes the credibility and importance of this appearance, which is a composite result of knowledge, affectivity, and freedom, and the fundamental condition of any grasp of values and ends. Man does not invent moral and religious realities, but he does invent his own relationship to them; he thus invents his own world of ends and values, by creating himself as he wants himself to be. The importance of affectivity, therefore, lies in the fact that it is a necessary element in the appearance that conditions our spiritual perceptions; and this importance is all the greater from the fact that it takes place before any conscious deliberation. *Talis unusquisque est, talis finis videtur ei:* as the being is, so appears the object to him (Rousselot). This is a universal principle, which St. Thomas applies regularly.[13] "In all matters, the person who has the right disposition will have the right opinion about singulars; but the person who suffers within from a lack of rectitude will also lack rightness in his opinions": whence arises the difference in this matter between the man who is awake and the man who is asleep, the healthy and the sick, the weak and the strong,

[13] I, 83, 1, 5^m^; I. II, 1, 7; 2, 1, 1^m^; 9, 2; II. II, 24, 2; 45, 2; *De Ver.*, 24, 10, c; *De Mal.*, 1, 5, 10^m^; 2, 3, 9^m^; *in Rom.*, 8, lect. 1; *in I Cor.*, 2, lect. 3; *in Joa.*, 14, lect. 4, etc.

the virtuous and the vicious, the spiritual and the "animal" (*in I Cor.*, 2, lect. 3).

Now the affectivity of the senses, with its psycho-organic reactions, is particularly virulent and redoubtable. It literally transforms the subject, and hence the appearance of the object. This is true of a simple affective sensation or a simple emotion. "It is clear that man is in a certain sense changed by suffering and the sensitive appetite; hence, according to the suffering by which he is affected an object seems to him fitting which would not appear so outside this particular suffering: to the angry man things seem good which do not seem so to the man who is at peace. And in this way, *ex parti objecti*, the sensitive appetite moves the will" (I. II, 9, 2, c). And again: "And such as a man is by virtue of a corporeal quality, such also does his end seem to him, because from such a disposition a man is inclined to choose or reject something" (I, 83, 1, 5^{m}). It is even truer when there come into play those deep and stable dispositions integrated in the being himself—the habits—which act like a nature, make a whole series of objects connatural with themselves, and, so to speak, determine the will's judgment and choice in advance (*De Ver.* 24, 10, c & 12, c): "He whose soul is informed by a *habitus*, good or bad, judges of the end by the exigences of that *habitus*" (*in Rom*, 8, lect. 1). And this is all the more so as the acts and choices refer to the singular (I. II, 9, 2, 2^{m}) and the appetite is orientated towards the singular as such. The property of any deviated affectivity is thus to transform man ("When a man falls from virtue into vice, he becomes in a sense another man"; Aristotle, quoted in *De Ver.* 24, 10, 1^{m}), to burst forth in violent unpremeditated movements, to corrupt the practical judgment and ultimately to destroy his chance of election (*De Ver.*, 24, 12, c). There is always the reason, of course, and it can pass judgment upon this released emotivity, fight against it, and overcome it; but when man has abandoned himself to it he is not always able to get the necessary grip upon himself. Sensitive affectivity thus appears as a formidable power to transmute man—to transmute his judgments, his desires, and his acts. The object regulates the desire, but the desire to a great extent fabricates the object. In human, moral, and spiritual matters, it is necessary to love to be able to know, and it is necessary to love well to be able to know well.

Affectivity and Freedom. As it has been necessary to "compose" the two levels of affectivity, so now it is necessary to "compose" affectivity and freedom, for to a great extent the drama of the spiritual life is made up of the continuous dialogue between them.[14]

But, in the first place, what does affectivity bring to freedom? It is freedom's purveyor, because it provides the objects between which freedom can choose. Every object grasped by the reason is available to freedom in so far as it possesses an affective coefficient: it offers itself as fitting, desirable, delectable—or the reverse. Freedom is thus spontaneously attracted or repelled by objects through the mediation of affectivity, which makes them appear good or bad. And the objects are very truly so many summonses to choice, for they put freedom in the position, or under the obligation, of having to accept or refuse. The perpetual upsurge of loves, desires, delectations—actual, or imaginary, or remembered—produces an immense mass of material at the disposal of freedom, and a perpetual invitation, or demand, for choice.

Affectivity goes further, for it supplies forces that orientate the choice. At any given moment the affective tendencies draw man towards specified ends and definite choices; when these ends and choices are absorbed by the vital organs, and become part of the nature, they find themselves, so to speak, pre-formed in them, and freedom is in danger of becoming the captive of its own determinants—unless it can manage to polarize itself more than ever upon the calls of the spirit. Obviously, in this situation unconscious forces play a most important part, and what pushes out into consciousness is simply the tip of a whole world of subterranean, animal and spiritual powers that are mysterious and rather frightening. Thus freedom is obliged to take its place and its bearings, and to be achieved, in relationship with an affectivity that feeds it and polarizes it: the act of freedom is to a great extent a reaction to affectivity.

But, of course, freedom can react with its own strength. It has the power to judge affectivity, to follow or refuse it, to weaken or

[14] I should not like this distinction to be misunderstood. I take the Thomist view to be that human powers can be divided into knowledge and affectivity (cf. the recent essay by Rev. Fr. Chenu in *Le Coeur, Études carmélitaines*, 1950, p. 126). Within affectivity, there is instinctivity and the will; within the will, spiritual feelings and free choices. But the choices are necessarily related to the intelligence, and the free act is always a "willed judgment" as well as a "judged will." Consequently, the concrete problem in any kind of spiritual life concerns the relations between emotions and feelings on the one hand and free choice on the other. It is in this sense that in the following pages I distinguish between freedom and affectivity—so as to unite them.

strengthen it. It is so made that it can mould it according to its own choices and give this great lump of brute material a fully human form. According as it chooses animality or spirituality it confers upon man his condition and value: man becomes carnal or spiritual according to the kind of affectivity he allows himself.

Not that freedom is a sort of absolute power enthroned over passive matter. I have already emphasized the appeal, the seduction, the weight, the hindrances that sensible affectivity can suggest against or impose upon freedom. Even spiritual affectivity is made up of contrary movements, loving or aggressive, selfish or generous, sad or happy; and a—partial—definition of freedom as a reaction to affectivity suggests that it has conditioning factors as well as power. Nevertheless, leaving aside any purely pathological factors, it is true that freedom can never be entirely suppressed; it retains its power of judging and choosing; it can always reconsider its inclinations, no matter how habitual, how deeply rooted, how strong these may have become, and resist them and be reconverted (*De Ver.*, 24, 10, c & 12, 4^m, 5^m, 12-19^m). This may not be easy; it may demand that long and concentrated attention whereby man acquires self-restraint—*nisi multa deliberatione seipsum cohibeat* (*De Ver.*, 24, 12, c)—it may be impossible without the grace of God; but it is the property of the spirit never to be absolutely satisfied, absolutely riveted, absolutely bound, here on earth. And the man who abdicates in the face of his affectivity still does so by an act of freedom.

Consequently, a man's value is to be judged by the value of the affectivity he has freely conferred upon himself, beginning with that which is given him by his nature and developed by his surroundings. It is his freedom that gives him his connaturality with the loves, desires, predilections, and delectations that make up his spiritual physiognomy and determine his human value. He is made from the mass of "matter" that he has refused or taken into himself, integrated or rejected, strengthened or weakened, and which in the end has become either external and foreign to him, or more inward and personal to him than his own flesh and blood. "For it is evident," says St. Thomas, "that a habit of moral virtue makes a man ready to choose the mean in deeds and passions" (i.e., activity and affectivity). "And when a man fails to make use of his virtuous habit in order to moderate his own passions or deeds, the necessary result is that many passions and deeds fail to observe the mode of virtue, by reason of the inclination of the sensitive appetite and of other external agencies. Wherefore virtue is destroyed or lessened through cessation from act. The same applies to the intellectual habits, which render man ready to judge aright of those things that are pictured by his imagination. Hence when man ceases to make use of his intellectual habits, strange fancies, sometimes in opposition to them, arise in his imagination; so that unless those fancies be, as it were, cut off or kept back by frequent use of his intellectual habits, man becomes less fit to judge aright, and sometimes is even wholly disposed to the contrary, and thus the intellectual habit is diminished or even wholly destroyed by cessation from act" (I. II, 53, 3, c).

The dialogue between affectivity and freedom is thus one of the main factors in man's moral, spiritual, and religious life. It is a constituent part of the human being; it develops as the individual himself develops; it goes on throughout his life, following the impulses of affectivity and the choices made by freedom, mutually enveloping and enveloped by each other, like the give and take of an endless dialogue. But freedom is rooted in affectivity only so that it may control it, interiorize it, humanize it; if it fails to fulfil its task, it is because the man himself has failed.

2. *Affectivity and the Christian Experience*

If affectivity plays such an enormous part in human life, it is only to be expected that it will play a similar part in the life of the Christian: *gratia non tollit, sed perficit naturam*. If the Christian life is a life freely given to God, this freedom too is permeated by affectivity. If the Christian life, as it exists in us, is in the first place the gift of God, the gift of a new existence in Christ, we shall expect to find that it includes a new kind of suffering and a new kind of affectivity.

The Two Kinds of Affectivity in the Christian. In the Christian the old man is destroyed at the root in baptism, in the sense that the fundamental orientation of his being is changed and his relationship with God is transformed into an entirely new one: having been seized by the Love of God, he has become capable of loving God above all things. But the renovation achieved by this transformation is not magical; it is merely a new beginning. Man is changed at the very centre of his spirit—"the new man is the spirit renewed inwardly" (St. Thomas, *in Col.*, 3, lect. 2)—but the rest of him is not changed in this way, and he still remains a battlefield. "The new creature is the grace that renews, but the old man still lives on in the flesh. If you follow the judgment of the new man, then you are clothed in the new man; if you lust with the desires of the flesh, you are clothed in the old man" (*ibid*). The old man is dead but he won't lie down; in somewhat the same way as the Devil has been vanquished by Christ and yet goes on attacking his Kingdom.

On the one hand, the old world of ends and values—human, separate, at enmity with Christ—still solicits his attention, his heart, his hands. His most animalistic instincts—aggressiveness and sexuality—are not subject to grace, or penetrated by it, in their specific activity. Man still feels pride and the lust for power, still has his old egoism, his cowardice, his hardness of heart. He remains "flesh," in fact, in St. Paul's sense, and a whole side of his psycho-organic and spiritual affectivity remains foreign or hostile to Christ. This is not sin any longer, but it is the result of sin and the promptings of sin—the old affectivity at the heart of the new man.

But the new man too has his own affectivity. He has entered upon the "new world" revealed to him by faith, the world of supernatural ends and values, of the Christian mystery, of Christ in all his different dimensions. He has been given a new principle of reaction to these values—grace and the infused virtues, the new nature with its principles of knowledge and appetency. The new affectivity is grafted upon everything right and excellent in his natural affectivity. It springs up under the influence of the Holy Spirit and a nature cured and transfigured. A whole world of forces, desires, and aversions, likings and repugnances, joys and sorrows, gradually invades the soul, to nourish and call and comfort its newborn freedom in its choice of the Christian mystery. A whole new kind of affectivity—primarily spiritual, but, when necessary, psycho-organic too—then begins to develop under the impetus of freedom and the increasing influence of charity. Spiritual writers and theologians have always seen signs of this in a large number of passages of Scripture, which they have meditated and expatiated upon lovingly, as we shall see later.

At the beginning of the spiritual life, and for a long time afterwards indeed, this new kind of affectivity is given as a starting-point: it begins at the highest point of the spirit, and only through the struggle with the old affectivity does it manage to spread down into the lower zones. St. Thomas has described the difficulty of this process in the following passage: "The continual corruption of the sensuality is to be understood as referring to the 'fomes,' which is never completely destroyed in this life. . . . However, this corruption of the 'fomes' does not hinder man from using his rational will to check individual inordinate movements, if he be presentient of them, for instance by turning his thoughts to other things. Yet while he is turning his thoughts to something else, an inordinate movement may arise about this also: thus when a man, in order to avoid the movements of concupiscence, turns his thoughts away from carnal pleasures to the considerations of science, sometimes an unpremeditated movement of vainglory will arise. Consequently a man cannot avoid all such movements, on account of the aforesaid corruption" (I. II, 74, 3, 2^{m}). The situation in which the beginning Christian finds himself can therefore be described as a coexistence of two different kinds of affectivity; a contamination of the new affectivity by the old; a gradual extrication of the new affectivity as the result of a continuous effort at purification—in short, as a dialogue between freedom and affectivity.

We can even study the change from the one kind to the other in the progress towards justification—either, in the case of conversion, from unbelief to faith, or in the change from a life of sin to a life of grace. It is God who instigates this process, maintains it and completes it: in other words, in the person who is called upon to be a Christian, but has not yet arrived at that condition, God will raise the affective movements that are necessary if there is to be a response from the person's freedom, and which are therefore necessary for justification. He calls to the sinner through all that he is, through all that can possibly respond—his reason, his heart, even, if necessary, his body. He arouses, excites, attracts the whole force of his longing. And the man suffers God's action—God who is all-powerful and all-merciful, and who wants him to respond. The call to *metanoia* cannot be made without the whole being being turned upside down, for the whole man has to be remade, a sinner has to become a child of God. And it is through new thoughts, new feelings, new emotions, that this transformation is prepared for and takes place.

The Council of Trent made a sort of blue-print of the movement from the state of injustice to that of justification,[15] indicating all the essential feelings. When the sinner realizes his condition as it appears in the eyes of a God who is all justice and mercy and who has redeemed us through Jesus Christ, the following spiritual movements take place—faith, by which he adheres to the truth of all that God has revealed and promised, especially the justification of the ungodly; fear at the thought of God's justice, which gradually changes under the influence of his hope for mercy and forgiveness; incipient love, which is a desire for purification, liberation, peace with God; and repentance, through which his soul returns to God, hating and detesting the sins it loved. These are all so many spiritual movements, communicated by grace and received by freedom; they signify the awakening of the new affectivity under the influence from on high. It is worth noting that in order to emphasize God's primacy and the human being's receptivity, the Council continually uses the passive mood: sinners are "awakened and helped" by grace, "freely moved towards God" by faith, "struck" by fear, "raised to hope" and "moved against their sins." "Believing," they "are turned" towards mercy, they "begin to love." Here, then, clearly indicated, we find that awakening of affectivity which is an appeal to freedom, leading to "the decision (*proponunt*) to be baptized and begin a new life and practise the commandments of God."

These feelings, of course, do not come one after the other; they are all awakened together; making their presence felt, and then disappearing; combining and separating; but always pulling in the same direction—roughly or gently—towards the affirmative—or the negative—to be finally uttered by freedom. They form part of a fundamental questioning of the whole of existence, a radical reorganization of being; and this highly complex and unique composite of feelings and free acts creates a single upsurge of the whole soul, called upon—and consenting—to pass from sin to grace, from death to life. What man feels at this time, without always clearly realizing it, is a *trahi ad Deum*, an unrecognized kind of suffering, a grasp that becomes tighter and tighter upon him the more he gives way under it. It is a lived experience and a conscious call. Man perceives it, not as something infused or supernatural of course, but as something real and absolutely new, drawing him towards God. It is the first experience of the new affectivity, conferring upon and revealing to

[15] Sess. vi, cap. 6. Cf. J. Rivière, *Justification*, in *Dictionnaire de Théologie catholique*, Vol. VIII, 2, col. 2180.

his soul a new dimension—and all the rest of his life will bear the mark of this experience.

If freedom responds affirmatively and surrenders the soul to God, justification leads through faith to perfect contrition and charity. These acts are conscious; but they are the result of an infused reality that is not conscious. Through sanctifying grace man is re-created, receives a new spiritual being, exists in Christ. By faith, his intellect is enlightened and reflects God, is remade and receives the impression of the light of God and the seal of the original truth. By charity the will is drawn and united to God, and is granted a share in the eternal Love. But this re-creation is no more a conscious thing than creation, no more conscious than the communication of natural being or the lasting creation of the intellect and the will. This suffering is so deep, has come so recently from God's own hands, that unless he experiences a special grace no man can feel it: all the experience that takes him forward to meet God stops at the threshold of communion; and it is in a dark light, in the homage of certainty and faith, that he surrenders himself to his Lord. Here already, knowing leads to unknowing, feeling to non-feeling, experience to that which lies beyond experience, the affectivity that has been consented to, to the mysterious union that lies beyond all affectivity, because man finds his fulfilment in a God who is present but unknown. After which, as his reward, he enters for a time into joy and peace.

Affectivity and the Infused Moral Virtues. Once he has passed from death to life, the Christian has to deliver his members not to sin but to holiness and bear the fruit of justice. He has not come to the end; but he is now able, and obliged, to tend towards his end. But he is not dragged irresistibly by the new spiritual movement; it is by his own efforts, "prevented" and maintained by grace, that he must gradually unify himself. The function of all virtuous activity is to assist the penetration of spirit into every human being (I. II, 55, 3, 3^{m}, & 74, 5, 2^{m}) and to assert the primacy of ordered love in every human act (55, 1, 4^{m} & 62, 2, 3^{m}). The function of these powers of grace, the infused moral virtues,[16] is to make the redeemed reason lord over the affectivity of the senses and human

[16] The explanation differs somewhat according to whether one admits the existence of infused moral virtues as special powers of grace with their root in charity, or rejects them as such and extends the power of charity itself to each of the moral virtues. But the process of transfiguration that has to be realized remains the same.

behaviour ("*circa passiones et operationes*"), and thus to purify, and bring order into, and Christianize, the Christian's affectivity. The governing rule of the infused moral virtues is not human reason only, but reason elevated by grace and governed by the Word of God, and their aim is not a merely human order but an order that is fitting for the sons of God and the city of the saints (I. II, 63, 4)—in short, "*propter similitudinem coelestem*" (*Virt. card.*, 4, 2^m^), so that man may resemble Christ. I shall now try to indicate the part played by these virtues with respect to the affectivity of the senses.

The affectivity of the old man is not affected directly when grace and the virtues are infused into man by God. It still retains all the complexity of its normal elements—bodily dispositions, helping or paralysing a particular kind of virtue (I. II, 63, 1, c, & 65, 1, c); primitive instincts, rooted in the psyche and manifesting themselves in the egoism of pride or sensuality; passionate impulses, rising up from the encounter of instincts and their objects; deep and powerful habits, forcing the inclinations to take a particular direction. All these forces tend towards their act and delectation instantaneously, before the spirit can intervene; independently, either agreeing with or opposing the desire of the spirit; inordinately, as a result of original sin, or of sins that have taken a social form, or of personal sins. Though natural and good in their essence, in actual fact they have broken loose from reason and oppose its ends, and are consequently a danger to, and a corrupting influence on, the Christian's human and divine good.

In particular, sin sets up a falsified reality, from which man has to free himself and substitute for it another reality more in conformity with supernatural truth. This means that the Christian's being needs to be re-created by grace, so that it may be given—or given back—its connaturality with true values and supernatural values, and thus learn to experience them as good. It means too that freedom must use the new affectivity to help it to fight against the continual resurgence of the old, so that the grasp of the true, natural and supernatural ends and values may become spontaneous and efficacious. The end of this effort, which is only attained by the saints, is the restoration of human existence in its full unity: on this level man is unified within himself in the movement that carries him towards his end, and unified with the world of true values and the values of faith, because these values and realities appear to him from now onward as they really are. What affectivity had unmade it has now remade; and man, restored in his being, realizing an appearance of values that corresponds to their being, is freed from error and moves about in "real life."

Hence the real function of the infused moral virtues is to polarize affectivity to the appeals of grace, to subordinate affectivity to the demands of charity. The forces that are in revolt against virtue have to be subjugated, i.e. their attractiveness has to be resisted and their violence curbed. A consent to a carnal delectation, for instance, means deliberately choosing that affectivity shall be inclined towards the act that causes it (I. II, 74, 8, c); it is a consent by freedom to an inner orientation; and the subjugation of this movement means in fact resisting the inclination by an act of free will and curbing its expression. Whenever these forces are not contrary to virtue, virtue must control them and make them serve spiritual ends. It is the spirit's proper function to direct these forces in this way—including the delectations of the senses themselves, which have their "*primum movens*" in the reason (74, 6) and which reason must make use of in so far as they are necessary to right activity (II. II, 141, 6, c & 142, 1, c). Ultimately it must transfigure the powers of the senses by making them amenable, docile, and friendly to the spirit and grace.

But as the infused moral virtue achieves this integration it develops correspondingly the affectivity of the new man. It gradually makes the activity of the virtues more rapid, more easy, more delectable, because it makes the appetite connatural with its own ends. It never gets beyond the need for struggle, and often has to work without feeling any pleasure "by reason of certain contrary dispositions remaining from previous acts" (I. II, 65, 3, 2^{m}): man then "feels no pleasure and complacence in the act, on account of some impediment supervening from without"; he only knows the "*delectabile propter finem*" (II. II, 123, 8, 2^{m}). But normally the spirit emerges triumphant, growing in strength and acclimatizing itself to the spiritual order and developing there in joy. Then alone can man be said to be truly virtuous—in God's eyes even more than in his own: "Every act of virtue has two aspects, one being the kind of act it is and the other the way in which it is performed by the agent. If the two aspects do not coincide in any act of virtue, it is not virtuous *simpliciter:* thus the virtue of justice is only truly fulfilled when the works of justice are performed with pleasure and joy. And although in the eyes of men, who see only the appearances of things, it is sufficient to perform an act of virtue according to its kind—e.g., an act of justice—nevertheless, in the eyes of God, who sees into the hearts, it is not sufficient merely to perform that particular kind of act, the act has to be performed in the required way, i.e. with pleasure and joy." And that is why God does not love anyone who merely gives, but "He loves the person who gives joyfully"—not someone who murmurs sadly: "Serve God joyfully" (*in II Cor.*, c. 9, lect. 1).

We find a particularly clear example of this inner development in the matter of chastity,[17] for this very reason that it can be realized on two different levels, according to the relationship that exists between the spirit and the sexual instinct. At the first level, spirit and instinct are at war: the reason knows that it is necessary to avoid sin, the appetite desires its fleshly satisfaction, and the will is pulled both ways, between feeling and obligation.[18] By chastity, the will chooses against instinct, which does not want to submit but is hostile and dangerous; the will controls the instinct from outside by resisting it and restraining it, so that it may adhere to God. Man thus experiences the heterogeneity of the two zones: his virtue is in the will, it is not yet in the appetite; and this sort of chaste person is no more than continent (II. II, 155, 3 & 4), because he is still obliged to use force to master an instinct that is incessantly in revolt. Thus the difference between the continent and the incontinent person is not to be found in the reason (whose judgment is right) or in the appetite (whose desire is bad) but in the will, because the first rejects and the second accepts the promptings of the instinct. This is an excellent example of an appetite in revolt being mastered by the spirit that has submitted to God.[19]

But this kind of chastity is only a beginning. With prayer and generosity of soul, the affectivity of the senses gradually yields to the calls and demands of the spirit; it becomes obedient, integrated into the movement of virtue, subject to right reason and right love. Man becomes unified, the battle calms down, chastity becomes the accepted master of the thoughts and images, the emotions and desires

[17] In the modern sense of the word. St. Thomas's analysis of the matter is highly complex, of course (cf. II. II, 163).

[18] I. II, 77, 2, 5^{m}.

[19] All the more significant in that the object of virtue involves matter so remote from reason (II. II, 141, 7, 1^{m}).

(II. II, 141, 3, c) that sprang from the instinct and made it so imperious, and the instinct submits because it has been conquered and purified. The person who was formerly chaste has now become temperate (155, 3-4); body, instinct, and all its impulses have been penetrated by true reason and love; the natural harmony has been established between the various parts of the soul (141, 1), the good of reason has reached even to concupiscence (155, 4, 3^m^), affectivity is integrated with the spirit, the assurance that comes from strength takes the place of fear (*verecundia*, 144, 4, c); lastly, peace—an "armed peace," of course—has followed upon war. In this sense, sexual activity has been sublimated,[20] and virtue has fulfilled its function of unifying man in his movement towards his last end. Thus in this case there is an absolute difference between the temperate man and the intemperate man (II. II, 156, 3^m^) because habitually reason, appetite, and will form a single unity in both, but on the level of instinct in the case of the latter and on the spiritual level in the case of the former.

The function of the infused moral virtues is therefore not to get rid of the affectivity of the senses but to reform it. A just man is not someone without any passions, but a man whose passions have been purified and integrated with the effort to be virtuous and so greatly increase his strength in the love and service of God. Our Lord was impassioned when he drove the buyers and sellers out of the Temple with a whip; so was St. Paul, when he gave the false Christians such a rough handling, and his followers such a shaking; so was St. John, when he hurled his condemnations against the world and the heretics and those who persecuted the name of Christian. Stoic *apatheia*, far from being accepted by the Christian tradition, has always been vigorously rejected as a form of self-mutilation, an impossibility—in

[20] The word has by no means a clearly defined single meaning in the literature of psychoanalysis. The following remarks seem to contain a good deal of truth; they are made by GUSTAVE THIBON in *Médecine et Sexualité* (Paris, 1949), p. 201: "The purely genital can never be superelevated or transfigured. . . . What can be sublimated and passed over into the service of the spirit, is everything in sexuality that is not specifically sexual—the halo of images, feelings and desires which are polarized round sex, elements not merely biological but psychological, which in themselves are neutral and indeterminate so far as sex is concerned, but which sex can always utilize to its own advantage. Let us take a particular example: an erection can never be sublimated, but the images and emotions that cause it or accompany it can be sublimated. And this means a great deal, considering the great part played by psychic life even in our most carnal motions."

proof of which, here from amongst a hundred others of a similar nature, is a passage from Julian Pomerius which is all the more significant from being so unoriginal: "We find (the passions) necessary to life because on earth we simply cannot live without them. And for this reason, if a man does not fear and dread the possibility of losing his own faith during his life on earth, or the possibility of someone whom he loves in Christ doing the same; if he does not have sorrow for his own sins or for those of his neighbour; if he does not feel joy or sorrow at the progress he makes; if he neither wants nor desires the good—then not only is he not living correctly; he is not even a man (*sensum ipsius humanitatis amittit*)."[21] St. Thomas's observations on virtue in general are equally valid here: a Christian is perfect, and his virtuous acts are perfect, only when the affectivity of the senses is itself polarized round the spirit, helping the play and increasing the power of faith and charity.

Affectivity and the Theological Virtues. The theological virtues introduce man into the world that is truly divine. They enable him to make direct contact with God, and orientate him directly towards God. They thus imply, and produce, a radically new kind of spiritual affectivity that fights against the old kind in an effort to subjugate, purify, and integrate it; and they can only develop properly in the atmosphere of an affectivity that is entirely in harmony with God. Let me try to show briefly how this is so in the matter of faith and charity.

The first thing required by faith is a purification of the affectivity of the senses, because this conditions intellectual vision. Man being situated between the world and God (II. II, 7, 2, c & I. II, 108, 4, c), purity of spirit means adhering to God, whereas impurity means "submission to the temporal by love." Now faith demands and achieves a radical purification of the spiritual creature, because it makes him rise above the world, tend towards God alone, and unite himself with God in an act of perfect homage: in this sense, only the pure in heart can see God. A double purification is thus demanded of the affectivity of the senses.

In the first place, faith demands the purification of the disordered affections (II. II, 8, 7, c); for if the spirit remains bound by love of the temporal and the carnal, its desire inclines it towards carnal delectations, its strength becomes focused on these, sometimes ex-

[21] *De Vita Contemplativa,* III, c. 32 (P.L., 59, 517).

hausting itself completely, and "in consequence man's operation in regard to intelligible things is weakened" (15, 3, c, & cf. 1, 3m). Gradually the spirit becomes blunted and blinded, and the man falls into *hebetudo* or *caecitas mentis*. He must be purified by faith from this carnal adherence and opaqueness, and brought to abstinence and chastity, so that his spirit may recover its purity, its freedom, its strength, its power of penetration. This "purification of the disordered affections"—*praeambula et dispositiva ad Deì visionem*—is performed by the virtues and gifts that control appetite (8, 7, c), and it is called for and demanded by faith throughout the whole course of its development. But the purification of the "carnal" is not enough; there must also be a purification of the "sensible." If reason has to abstract the intelligible from the sensible, the more it is free from the imagination, "the more thoroughly will it be able to consider things intelligible, and to set in order all things sensible" (II. II, 15, 3, c). Now a disordered affectivity produces images of a frightful density and highly resistant opaqueness, that have a fierce hold on the spirit and interfere with the ascent to God. As, in the matter of faith, it is always a question of recognizing "supernatural truth, to which the right will needs to tend" (II. II, 8, 4, c)—in other words, a truth that is utterly spiritual, and at the same time thoroughly charged with affective value—it is necessary for all this sense-material to be able to be drained off, and for the soul to loose itself from its adherence to it, so that faith may unfold freely in the widening and deepening air of divine truth. Only then can man obtain that "*munditia mentis depuratae a phantasmibus*" which prevents him from receiving what is revealed by God as though it were a matter of bodily images, and which thus completes (*completiva*) the knowledge of faith (8, 2, c). This purification is achieved by the gift of intelligence, which only exists in a soul rectified by charity, but which in such a soul plays a part in the whole movement of faith.

Faith's second function is to purify and develop spiritual affectivity. Faith, being the radical submission of the spirit to God, "the perfect homage of mind and will" to the Lord, meets on this level in fallen man a fearful adversary—pride, "inordinate desire of one's own excellence" (II. II, 162, 2, c), which distorts one's true estimation of oneself—"*de se majora existimat quam sint*" (162, 3, 2m). The proud man makes himself his own judge in his thinking and acting;

he raises himself above what has been determined for him by the divine ordinance—instead of bowing down before God in fear and reverence (7, 1, c), he equates himself with God, sits in judgment on the divine laws, refuses to obey the commandments (4, 7, 3ᵐ), and refuses to pay God the homage and submission that are his due (162, 5, c). Consequently, he corrupts the true supernatural knowledge of God (162, 3, 1ᵐ): "Knowledge of truth is twofold. One is purely speculative, and pride hinders this indirectly by removing its cause. For the proud man subjects not his intellect to God, that he may receive the knowledge of truth from him. . . . Nor does he deign to learn anything from man. . . . The other knowledge of truth is affective, and this is directly hindered by pride, because the proud, through delighting in their own excellence, disdain the excellence of truth; thus Gregory says (*Moral.* XXIII., *loc. cit.*) that the proud, although certain hidden truths be conveyed to their understanding, cannot realize their sweetness: and if they know of them they cannot relish them" (*ibid.*).

Now the spontaneous upsurge of pride is one of the Christian's endless temptations, and it attacks the specific motive of faith, which adheres to the truth *propter auctoritatem Dei revelantis*. It tends to weigh man down in the opposite direction from the movement of the Holy Spirit, trying to bring faith down to a merely human level; and it is endlessly arousing instinctive movements of opposition, resistance, and refusal. Discussing the two acts of the intelligence—simple intuition and deliberation—St. Thomas writes: "In respect of simple intuition it can have an inordinate movement about divine things, as when a man suffers a sudden movement of unbelief. . . . Now it is possible for one of the articles of faith to present itself to the reason suddenly under some other aspect, before the eternal law, i.e. the law of God, is consulted, or can be consulted; as for example when a man suddenly apprehends the resurrection of the dead as impossible naturally, and rejects it, as soon as he has thus apprehended it, before he has had time to deliberate and consider that this is proposed to our belief in accordance with the divine law" (I. II, 74, 10, c). Faith has therefore to fight against this essentially spiritual impurity, to develop humility and the feeling of homage, and to strengthen the fundamental impulse, made efficacious by grace, that leads the soul to subordinate itself joyfully to God because he is God—transcendent, entirely other, utterly mysterious:

Tibi se cor meum totum subjicit
Quia Te contemplans, totum deficit.

Then, bathed in this atmosphere of humility, reverence, adoration, man attains to the *voluntas prompta*, the lightheartedness, the devotion, the trust, that are the true signs of true faith (II. II, 5, 4, c).

He gains even more: he gains a greater certainty of his faith. This takes place, in fact, in the order of affectivity.[22] Supernatural love, with all that it implies in the way of connaturality, complacency, desire for unity in union, is the "entry" into living faith, it is its light and strength. When the spiritual affectivity is released, canalized, and fed by charity, it makes man's free response and free gift of self prompt, joyous, and invincible; it makes faith glow with greater ardour. Activity, with the freedom that produces it, is the oil that gives light to the lamps of the wise virgins in the night of absence and waiting.

As for charity, it is even richer in affective values. St. Thomas describes it as a kind of love which is both "a certain union of affections" and "good will" (II. II, 27, 2 c, & 2m), in other words, as a composite of affectivity and freedom, feeling and generosity. It is impossible to separate these two elements. On the one hand, charity is a *dilectio*; by its very nature it implies a free choice, an absolute preference for God: it is a love of God above all else. But on the other hand we cannot, as St. Thomas always insists, reduce it to an unconstrained movement of freedom—benevolence—on the pretext of spiritualizing it. The nature and function of this affectivity can therefore be studied in the total movement of charity.

To understand this affective union that constitutes charity, we must turn to the analysis of human love—or at least to that part of it known as the love of friendship—that is made by St. Thomas in the *Prima Secundae*. This union is fundamentally love itself: "love itself is this union or bond" (28, 1, c), "(this union) is essentially love itself" (*ibid.*, 2m). It is made up of a twofold relationship (28, 2, c & 1m): the person who loves bears the other within himself, with the complacency that is the impression of the loved one in his heart; and again, the person who loves enters into the other and with him makes up a mysterious unity: "desiring the same for his friend as for

[22] *III Sent.*, d. 23, q. 2, sol. 1. Cf. G. de Broglie, *La Certitude de la foi*, in *Recherches de Science religieuse*, 1950, p. 22.

himself." The essential thing is the spiritual identification that love realizes in a dual movement: first by decentralization, for the person who loves goes out of himself, establishes his centre in the other, and this supplies the ecstasy proper to all love; then by harmony of wills: the person who loves looks upon the other as himself, "inasmuch as he reckons what is good or evil to his friend, as being so to himself" (28, 2, c), until ultimately he looks upon himself as the other, "looking on his friend as identified with himself" (28, 2, c). He sees and lives the other's will as his own, sees and lives the other's good and evil as his own. By this affective identification, in every love of friendship, "I," if we may be allowed to use Rimbaud's words, "is Another" (cf. II. II, 27, 2, c).

Now this aspect is also to be found, analogically, in charity, as St. Thomas was keen to emphasize. "Charity realizes an infinite end when it unites the soul to God by justifying it" (II. II, 23, 3, 3^{m}). Faith and love attain to God as the source of all light and goodness, but "charity attains God himself that it may rest in him" (23, 6, c); and whereas faith and hope involve a certain separation from God, "charity implies union with that good" (*ibid.*, 3^{m}). "To love is indeed an act of the will tending to the good, but it adds a certain union with the beloved" (27, 2, 2^{m}). "The interior act of charity has the character of an end, since man's ultimate good consists in his soul cleaving to God, according to Psalm lxxii, 28: It is good for me to adhere to my God" (27, 6, 3^{m}). Lastly, "Hence charity, by loving God, unites the soul immediately to him with a chain of spiritual union" (27, 4, 3^{m}). "Union of affections" (27, 2, c), "spiritual union" (27, 4, 3^{m}), "union of the spirit" (82, 2, 1^{m}), "spiritual fellowship with God" (I. II, 109, 3, 1^{m})—all these expressions signify the union that constitutes charity itself. Because it alone unites the soul to God as its last End, charity adheres to God as the absolute end of all contact, desire, abandonment, union, joy. Because it alone unites the soul to God immediately—in the very act of love (*diligendo*) (27, 4, 3^{m})—by the mutual and perfect bond of friendship, it repeats analogically all the features of affective union described above: decentralization, because man's centre has become God, loved above all else and more than oneself; coincidence, because God's will, God's good, God's interests, all become man's; ultimately, spiritual identification, because though in their personal reality man and God remain utterly distinct and infinitely remote from each other, nevertheless charity effects the *unitas spiritus* between them. All the great mystics are agreed about this,[23] and they do no more than repeat St. Paul's words: *Qui adhaeret Deo, unus spiritus est.* But because in charity man refers himself entirely to God, with all that he has and is, this union is realized in reverence and holy fear and adoration and to the accompaniment of graces, and it is therefore enveloped in a metaphysical and spiritual distance that the Beatific Vision itself will only deepen.[24] This distance, moreover, intensifies the infinite movement of charity, "the inclination of grace" (26, 6, c), tending towards its first Cause and last End, and producing in its own movement the whole development of supernatural affectivity, with its three stages of love, desire and joy (28, 4, c).

In passing, it may be worth while to note that the modern distinction between affective and effective love does not seem to have been made by St. Thomas, for whom love was by its very nature an affective reality, being an inner act of will (a mixture of spiritual feeling and freedom). This act is the essence of charity, and it has its own intrinsic value, for it is an end. But precisely because it is an inclination of the will, it needs to be translated into other acts, both inner and outer, which are its necessary effects, its products and signs.[25] The affective-effective distinction is a proper one, and in practice very useful, but it lies on another level, criteriological rather than metaphysical, psychological rather than theological. To anyone who wants to know whether his charity is genuine, the answer is, Consult your visible actions, not your invisible ones—and therein lies true wisdom; always on condition that it is remembered that outward

[23] "Man and God, because they are not one in substance or in nature, cannot be called one; nevertheless in certain and absolute truth they are said to be one in spirit, if they adhere to each other by the glue of love. This oneness is not achieved by coherence of essences but by agreement of wills."—St. Bernard, *Serm. in Cant.*, 71, 10, P. L., 183, 1126. Cf. E. Gilson, *La Théologie mystique de Saint Bernard* (Paris, 1934), ch. v, *Unitas Spiritus.*

[24] I. II, 19, 10, 3^m: fear means submission to God, and also separation, "in that he does not presume to be equal to God but is subject to him; it is in charity that the separation is found, in as much as he loves God more than himself, more than all things; whence an increase of charity does not diminish reverential fear but increases it."

[25] Cf. 26, 6, 3^m: "The inner act of charity has the value of an end . . . external acts are a kind of means," 28, *Prol.*: ". . . the effects which result from the principal act of charity, which is love: (1) the interior effects (joy, peace, mercy); (2) the exterior effects (beneficence, alms deeds, fraternal correction) . . ." Cf. 31, *Prol.*

actions too can be deceptive: "And if I should deliver my body to be burned, and have not charity, it profiteth me nothing." But from the point of view of theological analysis, the distinction is not without its disadvantages: it may tend to focus the attention—and the sense of values—on outside things, and neglect those within—love, and its inner effects; it may tend to displace the centre of gravity and weaken the sense of the richness of the mystery of love.[26]

If we now turn to the growth of charity, we once again come across the freedom that is at the heart of supernatural love, purifying, developing, and unifying the affectivity.

Charity is meant to grow. It is not perfect from the beginning, but has to earn its perfection through effort and struggle. Following tradition, St. Thomas divides this growth into three stages—as experienced by beginners, Christians making progress, and the perfect (II. II, 24, 7, 6). These stages are marked according to the conscious, voluntary effort (*studia*) that the individual has to make, and at each stage this effort implies a specific condition of the affectivity. The chief thing that beginners have to do is to struggle against sin. Their affectivity is characterized by a very lively and very painful experience of the attacks and attractions of sin, a strong sense of their own vulnerability, and hence a sort of perpetual disquiet. This condition is therefore one of division, experienced at the centre of the struggle for victory. As we progress, we aim primarily to develop the virtues. Their affectivity becomes predominantly that of the man at war, less susceptible to the power of sin, cool in the midst of battle, struggling towards perfection with a general feeling of security. This signifies a progressive purification of the appetite and concupiscence, as the spirit progresses. The perfect seek union with God and the fruition of God. Their affectivity has been subjugated, purified, integrated with the aspiration of the spirit; they have been delivered and are intent on union and joy. Love has expanded to its fullest capacity. We thus witness the gradual re-creation of the old affectivity under the influence of generosity, through the gradual disentanglement and development of the new affectivity.

[26] St. Francis de Sales spoke more accurately of the two exercises—affective and effective—of our love for God: *Traité de l'Amour de Dieu*, VI, 1. Cf. J. de Guibert, *Études de Théologie mystique* (Toulouse, 1930), p. 271, and *Theologia Spiritualis* (Rome, 1937), nos. 61-62 (in which both expressions are used, but with a very clear explanation of the meaning of each).

This growth has another aspect—the unification of the subject, and therefore of his activity, under the influence of love. Charity, in fact, governs all the acts of the virtues and directs them towards its own end, integrating all the affective forces in the ascent to beatitude. It centres them upon God: "The love of God is unitive, in as much as it draws man's affections from the many to the one. . . . But self-love disunites man's affections among different things" (I, II, 73, 1, 3^{m}). Everything that can be properly ordered in human affections—natural friendship, for example—charity sets in order and integrates with the prime and all-important affection for God (II. II, 26, 7). In the man who is fragmented and weakened by sin it re-establishes unity and strength—it is able to do this because increasingly it injects its own strength into the soul. Charity grows, in fact, by becoming rooted in the subject (24, 5, c): it summons all his potentiality, transforms it into action, subordinates it to itself, and transfigures it spiritually (*ibid.*, 3^{m}). This unification by interiorization (25, 7, c) prevents any inner swelling of the soul, and helps it to love itself as it should. Loving God purely, we find man beginning to love himself properly, and able to live happily with himself; whereas the sinner does his best to escape from himself to avoid, as Pascal said, his "unbearable inner man." "The good love themselves, as to the inward man, because they wish the preservation thereof in its integrity, they desire good things for him, namely spiritual goods, indeed they do their best to obtain them, and they take pleasure in entering into their own hearts, because they find there good thoughts in the present, the memory of past good, and the hope of future good, all of which are sources of pleasure" (25, 7, c). Thus charity interiorizes our spiritual being and deepens our self-awareness and self-knowledge, thanks to the truth, the uprightness, the strength, the joy that it gives to the soul. The "evil" is driven out of the self, because it has chosen to be separate, the "good" is fully restored with all its riches of nature and grace, because it has established itself in God.

Lastly, the normal manifestation of charity is joy and peace (28 & 29): there is joy in the soul because God is infinitely happy and the soul possesses him through love, and peace because all the appetites are united in pursuit of the same good and in one fundamental movement of love. The joy and the peace are not perfect, any more than the possession and the unification are perfect: the joy has its sorrow and the peace its disturbances, because of all that still resists the possession of the divine good and the united harmony of the desires. And the joy and the peace are not felt when the flesh's repugnance to grace is too strong and the struggle too hard. Let us consider this matter of joy for a moment. St. Thomas's own doctrine raises the problem: virtuous behaviour should be voluntary and delectable, the teaching of the divine law itself being: "Serve the Lord in gladness" (I. II, 100, 9, 3^{m}). St. Thomas replies to this objection by making the following distinction: to act sorrowfully means without fundamentally wanting to, and this is a thing that charity never does; nevertheless charity does not always act joyfully. "That works of virtue should be done without sadness, falls under the precept of the Divine law; for whoever works with sadness works unwillingly. But to work with pleasure, i.e., joyfully or cheerfully, in one respect falls under the precept, viz., in so far as pleasure ensues from the love of God and one's neighbour (which love falls under the precept), and love causes pleasure: and in another respect does not fall under the precept, in so far as pleasure ensues from a habit: for *pleasure taken in a work proves the existence of a habit,* as stated in *Ethic.* ii. For an act may give pleasure either on account of its end, or through its proceeding from a becoming habit." There may therefore be a repugnance of the sensitive appetite which prevents the joy from being felt, and hides a deeper, utterly naked joy that is not perceived and yet is strengthening because it comes from being faithful to love—*delectabile propter finem*. St. Thomas explains this elsewhere (*De Car.*, 11, 8^{m}) when discussing St. Paul and the struggle between charity—the longing to die and be at one with Christ—and nature—the desire not to die: "The more perfect charity becomes, the more perceptible by the senses becomes the victory of charity over nature; and this is a result of the perfection of charity. On the other hand, in people in whom charity is imperfect, charity can do no more than win the battle, and the resistance that comes from nature makes the victory imperceptible to the senses. . . . But that, nevertheless, the soul, even without feeling it, prefers the fruition of God to union with the body, follows necessarily from the nature of charity" (cf. *De Car.*, 12, & *in II Cor.*, 5, lect. 1). We therefore find, as we should expect, the same growth in the joy of charity as in the activity of charity: joy is the reflection of activity and the sign of its success, and it appears, disappears, or grows according to the degree of perfection of the charitable impulse and the ensuing activity. Whenever a major difficulty hinders the charitable movement, the felt joy disappears—whether it be in the grosser resistances that have to be overcome by the imperfect, or in those deeper, more subtle impurities that the light of God endeavours to remove in the perfect. Yet even in the midst of this hard and painful suffering there remains the joy that is so purely spiritual that it seems utterly foreign to the soul, the joy that comes from faithfulness, submissiveness, and union with God—the *delectabile ex fine*. And perhaps it should be said that though the soul at these times may not experience joy, it still knows peace, because "the chief movement of the soul finds rest in God" (II. II, 29, 2, 4^{m}). But, as will be seen, the line of development is always the same. From the coexistence of the two kinds of affectivity, and the struggle between them, the way leads on the one hand to the weakening and attenuation of the sinful affectivity, and on the other to the freeing and full development of the new affectivity, in the struggle waged by freedom with the help of grace.

* * *

These reflections should really be extended, particularly as regards the problem of "spiritual feeling"; but despite their sketchiness they should at least enable us to raise a problem and hint at a solution.

The fact that affectivity plays such an enormous part in the Christian life arises mainly from man's "structure": the spiritual life is essentially a matter of self-giving and the consecration of one's freedom to God. But affectivity prepares the way for, then goes hand in hand with, then crowns, the movement of liberty; unless, conversely, it successively blocks it, paralyzes it and dries it up. Furthermore, the modern world is characterized by a great outburst of affectivity. Modern man is exploring and using the world of affectivity to a prodigious extent—one has only to think, for instance, of all the techniques developed by psychoanalysis and propaganda. Again, cultural developments have led to a formidable development of affectivity, for three reasons at least—because the frightful conditions—material and psychic, economic and political—under which we live, tear man from the life of the spirit and drive him back upon affectivity; because the absence of any moral and religious education means that his consciousness is dulled and his outlook restricted to merely hedonistic and utilitarian values, so that any sort of spiritual freedom has great difficulty in manifesting itself; and because the means of culture—the press, the radio, the cinema—sink human beings in the world of images and feeling. The result is that the masses cannot avoid materialism or their daily anxieties except by a pathetic escape into some compensating kind of affectivity. In the sphere of culture there is all too often a hiatus between the deeper investigations made by the technical and critical intelligence and the surrender to affectivity. The result is that there seems to be a complete disappearance of the middle region of reason, conscience, and morality, with the humble, vigilant, and ever-faithful freedom that goes along with it, and often of the region of pure spiritual aspiration too.[27]

Faced with this sort of collapse and mutilation, Catholic thought must first of all try to give affectivity its rightful place.

Catholicism recognizes a natural affectivity that is both of tremendous value, because of the fact that freedom depends upon it, and terribly dangerous, because in actual fact it is disordered, and freedom has to fight against it to subjugate it, purify it, and rectify it. Further, Christianity introduces and develops a new—supernatural—kind of affectivity; this begins as a seed given by the grace of God, and it has to grow bit by bit into its own characteristic purity. If affectivity is the appetite's reaction to its proper objects, Christianity offers man the world of faith, with its primary values—the Church, Christ, the Trinity, and, through them, salvation and beatitude—and its subordinate values, above all the Cross, the death of man to a whole aspect of himself and to the world: renunciation leading to fulfilment, detachment bringing communion—affectivity crucified in order to be beatified. Again, grace gives man a new appetite and new inclinations: through the theological virtues, grace inclines man to affirm, desire, and love God himself; through the infused moral virtues, the human movement tends to be integrated with the theological virtues; while the gifts of the Holy Spirit supply the proper principles of passivity to and acceptance of the inspiration of the Spirit. By these means Christ introduces into the regenerate man a radically new kind of affectivity that tends to extirpate the old

[27] Similarly, E. Bréhier has noted acutely, in contemporary French thought, "an immediate change-over from sensuality to spirituality" and the disappearance of the "moral virtues" in books in which all the credit goes to the "theological virtues."—*Transformation de la Philosophie française* (Paris, 1950), pp. 183 *et seq.*

sinful affectivity, to integrate the natural affectivity, and to develop, itself, into docility to the Spirit.

This will give some idea of the part played by supernatural affectivity in the Christian experience. For the sake of brevity I shall dwell only on its positive side. First, it supplies a sort of ground base for freedom to work upon. It prepares the way for the Christian life, sounding a continual summons through all the desires and antipathies, attractions and repulsions, liking and repugnances, that it brings into being from day to day. It accompanies the Christian soul as it travels forward towards God through all the vicissitudes aroused by the alternating presence and absence of the Beloved.

It is, moreover, a constituent element of the Christian life. The essential act of this life is the "faith that works through love," the freedom that chooses to adhere to God, to obey God, to sacrifice all to God when called upon to do so. Now affectivity is to be found within this movement; for adherence to God, and obedience, and sacrifice, can only be chosen if the truths of Revelation are grasped as objects of personal beatitude in God—the commandments being a means to personal union with God, and homage to the point of sacrifice being the ultimate assimilation to the person of the Saviour. But the appearance of the truths of Revelation, of the commandments, of sacrifice, is conditioned by the affectivity that is given by God and developed by the redeemed freedom. Knowing and choosing here go hand in hand with experiencing—I do not say feeling—and they mutually involve each other, because in matters of affective knowledge and affective union, being and appearance are the same thing. Cajetan once said this, with his usual vigour: "In matters of appetite there is no difference between being and appearance. And consequently delectation is caused by whatever one thinks one has, whatever one thinks one possesses, whatever one imagines will be enriching, etc.; and not only by actually having, possessing, being enriched by, etc."[28] There is thus some kind of image and thought at the heart of the affective movement; not only that, affectivity has an influence on the actual birth, and quality, and value, of the image and thought. This inevitable bond is found at the heart of a living faith: freedom and affectivity grow up together there, and ascend together towards Christ; and the more the soul really tries to be pleasing to God, the more it is pleasing to itself in God—unified in

[28] *Com. in* Iª IIªᵉ, 32, I, no. 5.

its journey towards God by the joint transfiguration of freedom and affectivity.

Lastly, affectivity crowns the generosity of love. The end of full communion with God here on earth is the joy of communion; as the end of the Beatific Vision is the joy of that vision. But before this end is reached there must be the rough sketches, the foretastes, the intermittent participations in communion that are experienced along the way, and consequently joy is mingled with sorrow, the longing is painful as well as pleasant, and the movement of adoration and supplication, of all the activity of the graces, may be sweet or it may be dry. Even the Cross is enveloped in the Father's blessing, the Son's love, the Spirit's strength: "Blessed are they that mourn, for they shall be comforted." The union is paradoxical during the earthly pilgrimage, until the time of joyous consummation in Paradise.

And herein alone is to be found the ultimate meaning of supernatural affectivity for the being who is on pilgrimage: it is a healing and transfiguration because it is a foretaste of eternal joy. The affectivity of the flesh tyrannizes over man, and so long as he is dominated by it he is both bad and unhappy. Supernatural affectivity delivers him from this tyranny and makes him good and happy. Spiritual freedom, in fact, is not man's last end, it is the person's essential power, and it only finds fulfilment when it finds God and takes pleasure in him; when, however humbly, it has entered into the joy of its Master. It is vain to hope to heal man, who longs for happiness, unless he is given true joy to take the place of false joy. And Christianity's strength, once again, lies in the fact that it offers man the bread he truly needs instead of his own poor nourishment—offers to him too the one intimate, urgent, shattering invitation that alone can raise him from his misery and carry him off to his Father's many mansions. *Gaudete in Domino semper.*

CHAPTER TEN

Spiritual Feeling

"The language of current ascetical psychology is very far removed in style from that of Augustine. Where the saint says that the grace of God gives pleasure, modern directors of souls are very careful to distinguish between the dry, naked will—the only thing that in their opinion is necessary for an action to be virtuous and meritorious—and pleasure, which they always seem to mistrust. Clearly, by pleasure they mean a delectation of the senses, and undoubtedly they are perfectly right to prevent any confusion between merit and enjoyment, grace and 'consolation.' But this kind of mistrust is a serious handicap to psychology, to truth, and to their followers, as the most clear-sighted of ascetics and mystics have always known quite well."[1]

These very penetrating remarks by Fr. Rousselot form a suitable introduction to this chapter. It is impossible to deny such an essential element in human life as feeling without running a great risk of producing some disastrous compensations; and though Catholicism may be to a great extent a doctrine that centres upon the purification of nature, it never encourages its negation. It thus becomes necessary to put the matter of feeling in its right theological setting. The problem has been tackled directly by the mystics—necessarily, from the nature of their experience—but it is a problem that is always cropping up in the ordinary devout life,[2] and that is the level on which I intend to discuss it here. I shall therefore describe some of the main

[1] *La Grâce d'après saint Jean et d'après saint Paul*, in *Recherches de Science religieuse*, 1926, p. 103.

[2] Cf. the classification of the "affections" by St. Francis de Sales, *Traité de l'Amour de Dieu*, I, 5 (natural, reasonable, Christian, supernatural); I, 10 (spiritual, reasonable, sensual); I, 11 & 12.

lines of the problem, and thus try to explain how Christianity calls not for the negation, but for the purification, the integration, the "assumption" of feeling.

1. *The Existence of Spiritual Feeling*

By "feeling" I mean the Christian's affective reaction to his objects and ends in the spiritual order—i.e., his emotions and feelings, in so far as these are directly experienced in consciousness, and to the extent that, rightly or wrongly, they seem to be aroused by the action of God, and to be directed towards the search for God, union with God and the service of God. This reaction is one of the normal elements of human passivity before God, in St. Thomas's sense of passive suffering—i.e., as an activation of sense and spirit by grace.

The Spiritual Senses. In this domain everything seems to suggest that the Christian has been endowed with a supernatural organism capable of experiencing the things of God, and is provided in his inner man with spiritual senses; as though the best analogy to describe his spiritual experience should be taken from his bodily senses. Seeing, hearing, breathing, tasting, touching—these words are all used in Scripture to describe man's commerce with God; and the means he uses to unite us with him are, similarly, light, words, scent, taste, touch. Christian thinkers were quick to collect all the passages in which these and similar phrases occur, and used them to develop a whole doctrine of the spiritual senses. As is well known, this doctrine was applied to the mystical experience, and thence developed into a special method of prayer.[3] But in the beginning it may have been something rather different. In his essay on the *Application des sens,* Fr. Maréchal has written: "Sometimes a number of passages are quoted from St. Thomas which only have a very indirect connection with the theory of spiritual senses, unless this is to be confused with a theory of spiritual experience in general."[4] It is precisely this latter point of view in which I am interested here.

In the first place, it seems quite clear that this doctrine was con-

[3] Cf. the two essays by K. RAHNER in *La Revue d'Ascétique et de Mystique: Le début d'une doctrine des cinq sens chez Origène* (April 1932) and *La doctrines des sens spirituels au Moyen-Âge, surtout chez saint Bonaventure* (July 1933). Also J. DANIÉLOU, *Platonisme et Théologie mystique* (Paris, 1944), esp. pp. 235 *et seq.*

[4] *Dictionnaire de Spiritualité,* Vol. III, col. 826.

cerned with the general conditions of the Christian life. The recently discovered *Dialogue with Heraclides*[5] by Origen[6] seems to be written from this point of view. There are two men in all of us, says Origen—"The Scriptures say that man is two men"—and there is a homonymy between the two. Therefore, Scherer comments, passages in Scripture that refer to the bodily senses must be given "a symbolic or mystical meaning—in other words, be related to the inner man." Origen takes a number of passages from the Bible and applies them to the Christian's spiritual reality and activity: the eyes represent thought; the ears, our openness to God; the nostrils, taste, touch, signify those spiritual organs by which we perceive the good odour of justice, the sweetness of God, God's presence. But although Origen uses the phrase "the mystical subject" to denote the inner man, this collection of images refers to the fundamental dimensions of the ordinary Christian life: we gain "a deeper insight" by "observing the commandments"; we are free either to "open" or to "stop" our ears; and the "touch of God" is known only "through faith." Clearly Origen is entirely concerned here with the Christian's normal equipment: we are in the world of faith, which alone leads into the new world in which we can meet God.

There is an example of the same kind of thing in Augustine. The whole of Sermon 169[7] is devoted to this problem. Man experiences delights of the bodily senses which are material and necessary to life. They become good or bad according to use—the meaning given them by freedom—and therefore according as whether, for instance, pleasure is taken in a psalm or a bawdy song, in the smell of a flower or the incense arising from idols, in one's wife or a harlot. But there are also spiritual delights, found in faith and justice, and these are greater and better, and should come first, for they refer to the world of invisible realities. Hence, "Justice is to be loved even more than any lawful pleasure or delight of the body. If thou hast senses within thee, all these senses within thee take delight in the delights of justice. If thou hast eyes within thee, use them to look upon the light of justice: '*For with Thee is the fountain of life; and in Thy*

[5] Edited by J. SCHERER: *Entretien d'Origène avec Héraclide et les évêques, ses collègues* (Cairo, 1949).

[6] Of whom K. RAHNER has written: "It thus seems as though in Origen's view the spiritual senses can be the organs of a mystical knowledge" (*Revue d'Ascétique et de Mystique*, 1932, p. 136).

[7] P.L., 38, 867 *et seq.*

light we shall see light.' Of this light the psalm saith: *'Enlighten my eyes that I never sleep in death.'* Likewise if thou hast ears within thee, listen to justice. He was looking for such ears who said *'He that hath ears to hear, let him hear.'* If thou hast sense of smell within thee, consider what the Apostle saith: 'We are the good odour of Christ unto God in every place.' If thou hast sense of taste within thee, consider: 'Taste and see that the Lord is sweet.' If thou hast sense of touch within thee, hear what the bride singeth of the Bridegroom: 'His left hand is under my head, and his right hand shall embrace me.' " But there is conflict between the two kinds of delectation, and man must struggle, and choose, so that the spiritual delectations may win: "Your flesh finds delight in forbidden delights; may your souls find delight in justice, which is invisible, beautiful, chaste, holy, harmonious and sweet, that you may not be straitened before her by fear."[8] Clearly, we are not on any mystical level here, but in the middle of the field of combat that is to be found in every Christian soul. The world suggested by analogy with the world of the senses, and made up of specified perceptions and delectations, is the world of faith. Here again the mysterious spiritual senses are part of the Christian's normal equipment.

Other passages with the same meaning may be found—for instance, in connection with the Eucharist. The old mysticism is known to have been highly sacramental in character, and from the writings of the early Fathers there may be garnered a whole store of passages that seem to regard eucharistic communion as the direct principle of a certain kind of mystical experience. But these need to be closely scrutinized; for many of these passages seem almost certainly not to possess the full mystical significance that we are tempted to give them. This has been made very clear by Fr. Daniélou in his essay on "*Les Repas dans la Bible et leur signification*."[9] After referring to the well-known passage by St. Cyprian on the "spiritual intoxication" produced by the Eucharist, he observes: "The Blood of Christ is a wine that intoxicates. This intoxication means, essentially, leaving the world of sin and entering into the world of grace. It means that the old man is forgotten. Again, wine brings joy; and the Blood of Christ is the principle of spiritual joy. There is a sacramental symbolism and at the same time a mystical symbolism, the transformation effected

[8] *Ibid.*, 870.

[9] *La Maison-Dieu*, no. 18, pp. 22 *et seq.*

by the sacrament producing an experience of the things of God in the soul." The same is true of St. Gregory of Nyssa: "Here intoxication describes the effect of the Eucharist, which is to take man out of his natural life and introduce him into the life that is divine. The meaning is dogmatic, not mystical."[10]

Finally—to cut the matter short—we shall refer to a very interesting passage from St. Thomas.[11] He is commenting on "Let this mind be in you which was in Christ Jesus"; and he writes "Let this mind be in you—i.e., hold by experience that which was in Christ Jesus": "See the light of Christ, in order that, being illuminated by it, you may be conformed to him; hearken unto his wisdom, that you may be beatified; breathe in the graces of his sweetness, that you may run to him; taste the sweetness of his piety, that you may be always in God; touch his virtue, that you may be saved." "Be of this mind, as touching him by the imitation of his actions." The imitation of Christ is the principle of contact, and hence of spiritual experience: we are here still within the pure activity of faith, and we can begin to glimpse the structure of an experience that is entirely related to Christ, bound up with definite acts and, so far as feeling in the ordinary sense of the word is concerned, very limited. At any rate, the "spiritual senses" are seen to refer in turn to the Christian's inner equipment, the joy of the Christian life, and contact with Christ through the sacrament or spiritual effort. There is a polyvalency of feeling.

Delectation. If the foregoing is true we must conclude that feeling has a normal part to play in all sections of the spiritual life. This is expressed by Augustine in what he considered to be a doctrine of the utmost importance: the doctrine of spiritual delight. As he expresses it, this idea is to be understood in a way that is both very deep and very purified. Very deep, because delight is a necessary part of the Christian life. Augustine will not admit that carnal man can have his joys and the just man not have his: "Who can live without affections? Do you think, then, brethren, that those who fear God, and honour God, and love God, have no affections?"[12] "Could the drunkard rejoice, and not the just man? . . . Unhappy is that man, even when he is drinking; happy this man, even when he

[10] *Art. cit.*, p. 24.
[11] *In II Phil.*, 5-6, lect. 2; Vivès, II, 371.
[12] *In Ps.* 76, 14; P. L., 36, 278.

is hungry and thirsty . . . Let him see the pains of that man, and his own joy, and think of God. He who even now gives us such joy of faith, hope, and charity, and the truth of the Scriptures, what is he not laying up for us at the end?"[13] God in fact is in every way better than his creation, and for that reason is the pure source of true delight: "There is a pleasure in the Lord, who is the true Sabbath and the true Repose . . . Who can give as much delight as the One who has made everything that gives us delight?"[14]

Moreover, Augustine had his own personal experience behind him to teach him—if that was necessary—that carnal delight can only be overcome by spiritual delight. For the soul really exists where it loves and rejoices in loving. "The soul's 'place' is the delight which it rejoices to have attained to through love—a harmful delight, when it follows upon cupidity, but fruitful when it follows upon charity."[15] This is why, when a man is converted, he finds new delights: "Every man who has been converted to God witnesses a change in his delights and pleasures, for these have not been taken from him but changed."[16] And it is charity that enables the soul to experience the "sweetness" it so needs. Commenting on the words in Psalm cxiii, "Teach me sweetness and discipline and knowledge," Augustine writes, "Why does the Psalmist say, Teach me sweetness, but that the grace of God may become known to him increasingly through the sweetness of its goodness? . . . Therefore, the man to whom God 'makes sweetness,' i.e. in whom he mercifully inspires a delight in goodness; or rather, to put it more clearly, the man to whom God gives the love of God, and of the neighbour for the sake of God, must demand instantly that such a great gift may increase in him; so that for its sake he may not only despise all other delights but bear all sufferings too. For instance, to the sweetness will be added salutary hardship. And so it is necessary to ask, and ardently desire, that this hardship may be added not merely to a tiny morsel of sweetness or goodness (I mean of holy charity) but to sweetness so great that the hardship fails to strangle it in its embrace."[17] And because Christian truth must be both known and enacted, "God teaches us, so that we may know what we must know, by opening

[13] *In Ps.* 57, 22; *ibid.*, 691.
[14] *In Ps.* 32, 2, 6; *ibid.*, 281.
[15] *In Ps.* 9, 15; *ibid.*, 124.
[16] *In Ps.* 74, 1; *ibid.*, 946.
[17] *In Ps.* 118 *enarr.*, 17; *ibid.*, 1547 *et seq.*

the truth to us; he teaches us to do what must be done by filling us with sweetness."[18]

But this delight needs to be understood in a highly spiritual sense. Discussing verse 65 of Psalm 118, *Suavitatem fecisti cum servo tuo, Domine,*[19] Augustine observes that *suavitas* is a rendering of the Greek word *krēstotēta,* which was also translated as *bonitas.* And as there is a sweetness in evil and in permissible carnal pleasures, *suavitas* must be understood as the Greeks understand their *chrestotes,* "as referring to spiritual goods"; so that the passage comes to mean, "Thou hast made me delight in the good." Now for Augustine this good is essentially the Truth—which is Christ. Of Mary Magdalen at the feet of Jesus he writes, "She delighted in the Truth, she listened to the Truth. She ate that which she heard. . . . The delight of the human heart is the light of truth, abundance of wisdom; this is the delight of the human heart, the faithful heart, the holy heart—there is no pleasure that can be compared with it, even remotely."[20] And there is of course the well-known passage in the treatise on St. John,[20a] in which Augustine describes the soul drawn by love and joy "towards Christ revealed by the Father," delighting in Wisdom, Justice, Truth and Eternity—"in everything that is Christ." *Da amantem; et sentit quod dico.*

Finally, when he is analyzing the connection between grace and freedom, Augustine concludes that "with the Holy Spirit, pleasure lies in not sinning—and that is freedom." He thus identifies delight with love and choice, which make up freedom: "Delight is simply love, which is simply the weight within the will, which in turn is simply free will itself."[21] Love, delight, choice; these are three aspects of one single and entirely spiritual act that is given to the soul at the same time as the soul performs it; a suffering, an acceptance, a consent. Fr. Rousselot has expressed this with his usual excellence: "Augustine saw that God's operation in the will, his grace that enables the willing to be done, really consists in changing the soul's love, in changing the ego's greatest and governing pleasure. . . . This indescribably sharp, sensitive, topmost point of my personality, which

[18] *Ibid.,* 1549.
[19] *Ibid.,* 1547.
[20] Sermo 169, 5-6; P.L., 38, 868 *et seq.*
[20a] 4-5; P.L., 35, 1608 *et seq.*
[21] E. Gilson, *Introduction à l'étude de saint Augustin* (Paris, 1929), p. 205, n. Cf. the very faithful account by Fénélon, *Instruction pastorale en forme de dialogues sur le système de Jansénius,* Vivès, XV, pp. 264 *et seq.*

inserts itself into the other . . . this spiritual flame, the highest expression of my self, is led by God wherever he pleases—and it pleases me. God works my own pleasure within me, he makes me prefer this to that, makes me love, makes me pleasing to myself. As St. Augustine says, *ut delectet.*"[22] Thus this doctrine integrates spiritual feeling with the essence of Christian activity: it is incomprehensible without the affectivity given from on high to heal and deliver sinful man: it develops by developing the tragic story of the struggle between the two kinds of affectivity, the two kinds of feeling, the two kinds of love, that rend and tear apart the pilgrim far from God.

The essence of this doctrine is to be found again in a different form in St. Thomas. In particular, the part played by delight in the free act appears here, in the teaching about *consensus* and *electio* (I. II, 15). When the spirit adheres to a reality, it "takes delight" in it: the experience of this delight is the consent (*cum-sentire,* 15, 1, c). Now the consent refers to the means, the adherence to the end being a *simplex voluntas.* Consequently, consent is connected with choice, and its function is as follows (15, 3, 3^{m}): "Choice includes something that consent has not, namely, a certain relation to something to which something else is preferred: and therefore after consent there still remains a choice. For it may happen that by aid of counsel several means have been found conducive to the end, and through each of these meeting with approval, consent has been given to each: but after approving of many, we have given our preference to one by choosing it. But if only one meets with approval, then consent and choice do not differ in reality, but only in our way of looking at them; so that we call it consent, according as we approve of doing that thing; but choice according as we prefer it to those that do not meet with our approval." Thus choice always takes place within some kind of delight, and St. Thomas's *quod placet ad agendum* takes its place beside St. Augustine's *quod delectat.* There is therefore no act of choice that does not arise from some kind of delight, and, through it, from some radical inclination.

On the supernatural level God gives both the gracious inclination (the infused virtue) and the spiritual delight (the *delectable ex fine,* at least); this is the context in which the act of Christian freedom is made; and man enters into true freedom when through generosity

[22] Fr. Rousselot, *art. cit.,* p. 101.

of spirit he has interiorized the demands of faith and performs them spontaneously from love. St. Thomas explains (e.g. in *C.G.*, III, 129, end) that man is inclined both from within and from without to observe the justice laid down by the laws of God: "From within, when he makes it his will to observe the commandments of the law of God, and does this from his love of God and the neighbour. For anyone who loves anyone gives him back what he owes him spontaneously and joyfully, and is even glad to add more; and for this reason the perfect fulfilment of the law comes from love. . . . Such people are therefore disposed to perform what the law ordains voluntarily and spontaneously. And therefore they are a law unto themselves, because they have the charity that inclines them towards the law and makes them act well gladly." St. Thomas's words are perhaps even more striking when he shows (*C.G.*, IV, 22, 4-5) that the Holy Spirit frees us from a dual bondage—moral, because it makes us want to perform the genuinely good, and psychological because it makes us want to do this spontaneously and from love: a twofold deliverance, for man acts henceforth, on the one hand, in accordance with the radical inclination of the will, which is in conformity with being and is obligatory (*ordinem voluntatis*), and on the other hand in accordance with the actual spontaneous movement of his own will (*motum suae voluntatis*). "The Holy Spirit so inclines us to act, that he causes us to act voluntarily, in that he makes us lovers of God." Inclination, love or delight, choice: three realities form a single whole for St. Thomas as for Augustine.[23]

"*Devotio*." The same facts will be discovered in connection with the problem of *devotio*. As explained by St. Thomas (II. II, 82), this is the act by which the will abandons itself light-heartedly to God in its zeal to do homage to him and serve him. St. Thomas notes particularly its affective fulfilment (82, 4, c): "The direct and principal effect of devotion is the spiritual joy of the mind." The will that abandons itself to God finds its fulfilment in seeing the divine goodness, and that leads inevitably, in the first place, to delight ("I remembered God and was delighted"), and accidentally to sadness, because of the imperfect nature of this enjoyment of God ("My soul has thirsted for the living fountain"). But to abandon himself entirely to God, man must escape from his wretchedness, and he

[23] For this, cf. the splendid chapters by St. Francis de Sales in *Traité de l'Amour de Dieu*, II, 12 & 13.

does this by way of devotion: hence his sadness at seeing his personal miseries, and his joy at the thought of God's goodness and in the hope of God's help (*ibid.*, 2^m). Joy and sadness before God thus spring from spiritual devotion. Elsewhere,[24] commenting on "*Clamans, Abba, Pater,*" St. Thomas explains that "he cries, not with the strength of his voice, but with the strength and fervour of love. We cry 'Abba, Father,' in fact, when through love we burn with desire for God in the strength of the Holy Spirit."

Later spiritual writers, in conformity with the general development of a "reflective age," were to show even more interest in this connection between *devotio* and joy. Take that very pious and very copious sort of *Summa*, Alvarez de Paz's *De Inquisitione Pacis*. Here we find three different kinds of devotion described.[25] First there is substantial devotion, the pure movement of the will that surrenders man to the service of God. This kind of movement can be separated from any sort of feeling and realized despite all the revolts of the flesh and the senses. Then there is accidental devotion—sweetness, or spiritual consolation. This is a true means to the creating of man: it strengthens him against the weakness of the flesh, restrains his sensuality, detaches him from temporalities and produces "all kinds of wonderful effects." It is not always felt as such, but it is always a deep delight of the will in the good, a kind of fervour and perfection of substantial devotion. It must be asked for as an excellent means to growth in virtue; it is a "great mistake" to despise or reject it; the desire for it is a sign not of effeminacy but of strength and wisdom, of the man who knows his own wretchedness, his impotence, and wants consolation so that he may love and serve God. And de Paz is not afraid to write, "Anyone who thinks otherwise does not know himself, does not really long for perfection, and knows nothing of the true and lasting riches to be found in this sweetness" (p. 488 *b*).

Lastly we have devotion, or sensible consolation. It is spiritual, because its object is spiritual and divine; and sensible, because it "is experienced not only in the will but in the fleshly heart, in the senses and the appetite, and is accompanied by a bodily reaction." Sometimes it is a backwash of spiritual devotion on to the senses and the body. Then it makes for peace and unity in love; it is more precious

[24] *In Gal.*, 4, lect. 3, Vivès, II, p. 181.

[25] Lib. II, part III, cap. 1 (Vivès, V, pp. 578 *et seq.*). The same doctrine is developed more subtly by SUAREZ in *De Oratione Mentali*, II, 6 (Vivès, XIV, pp. 139 *et seq.*).

than spiritual sweetness, for it includes this and overflows beyond it; it marks a sort of return to the innocence of original justice; and it would be stupid to despise it. Sometimes it is given by God suddenly—to tender souls, to new converts, to the weak. It is a great gift, but inchoate and dangerous, and it is not to be taken as an end in itself: "We are consoled not for the consolation's sake, but that we may gird ourselves to labour" (p. 492 *b*).

Furthermore, this is only one aspect of spiritual feeling: besides feelings of joy there are feelings of sorrow. Vicissitudes of this kind are the inevitable lot of the pilgrim while he is on earth.[26] Trials, temptations, sins—all these bring bitterness into the Christian life. Disgust follows devotion; aridity follows sweetness; desolation follows consolation. And all this is necessary to purify and fortify the Christian soul, and to conform it to the death and resurrection of Christ into which it was introduced by baptism: at certain times it is necessary to go to God "crawling on hands and knees" (p. 512 *a*). But this felt absence of feeling is one of the hardest trials in any generous life, capable of paralyzing even the best. This again shows the importance of feeling in the Christian experience, and supplies one more reason why we must attempt some sort of critical estimate of an element that is at once so important and so dangerous.

2. *A Critical Estimate of Feeling*

To help us in this somewhat difficult inquiry it may be worth while to distinguish between three things—feeling in itself, as a thing unqualified; sensible feeling; and spiritual feeling.

Feeling in Itself. By this I mean the passive side of spiritual emotions and feelings, as things at the disposal of freedom.

This kind of feeling is in the first place always something to be gone through. Sometimes it means a preparation for, a summons to, freedom. Emotions or feelings can tend to make us hate sin and cleave to God, serving him and trying to please him: they are a means, and they have fulfilled their function as affective movements preparing the way for freedom when they have led up to some kind of consent and decision. To stop at them would be to falsify their significance

[26] This theme of vicissitude is one of the main features of the tradition. It is expressed in a variety of ways by, for instance, St. Gregory the Great (e.g., on the instability proper to fallen man, in *Moralia in Job*, VIII, 10, 19; P. L., 75, 813).

and to refuse our actual response to God's call. Sometimes, again, feeling may be the fulfilment of freedom, joy in the end possessed. But here again the true end of activity is the Good to which the spirit desires to be united—i.e., God and the will of God; and though the same movement of freedom desires both the end and the delight, nevertheless the delight is only desirable because of its proper object, the good possessed (of which it represents the consciousness); because it only ensues upon this possession as "its proper accident" (I. II, 2, 6, c), and because in this sense "all seek delight because of the good and not conversely" (*ibid.*, 1^{m}). Being a satisfaction found in a (partial) possession of the divine good, delight is polarized entirely upon this good, and any feeling is simply a connatural concomitant: God himself, not the joy found in God, is the proper end of any true spiritual impulse, and to stop at the mere feeling, or to go after the mere feeling for its own sake, would inevitably mean missing the feeling and God too, the sole last end of all desire. There thus needs to be a detachment from feeling, a purification of feeling, even when it is most strongly felt.

Again, it would be highly dangerous to regard feeling as the necessary starting-point of all supernatural activity. Into this error, throughout the history of the Church, have fallen all those false mystics for whom the genuinely Christian life could only begin when God's action began to be felt. We may take Molinos, with his Quietism, as an example of this; for Molinos, in trying to escape from feeling, only fell back into it more irrevocably than ever, and all the errors formulated on this point by earlier heretics are found in him with surprising regularity.[27] Quietism is the virulent corruption of a

[27] As an indication of the immense amount of literature on this subject, besides dictionary articles, see on the Montanists: Oracles 5 & 14, in Fr. de Labriolle, *La Crise Montaniste* (Paris, 1913), pp. 45-47, 73 *et seq.*, 131 (on Tertullian, pp. 366-370). On the Messalians: M. Kmosko, *Patrologia syriaca*, Part I, Vol. III, pp. cxvi et seq. (texts, pp. cxxxiii *et seq.*; on the whole, pp. clxxii *et seq.*), and E. Des Places, *Introduction* to Diadoque de Photike ("Sources chrétiennes," Paris, 1943, pp. 9-19). Some essential texts in J. de Guibert, *Documenta ecclesiastica christianae perfectionis studium spectantia* (Rome, 1931), nn. 80-87; cf., for the Brothers of the Free Spirit, *Doc.*, 213 (78); for the Alumbrados, *Doc.*, 407 (11). For Molinos, Fr. Dudon, *Le Quiétiste espagnol, M. Molinos* (Paris, 1921); *Le Gnostique de saint Clément d'Alexandrie, de Fénélon* (Paris, 1930): also Fr. Pourrat, D.T.C., *Quiétisme*, and *La Spiritualité chrétienne*, Vol. IV. For a brief account of the condemned propositions, cf. the summary by N. Terzago in *Analecta juris Pontificii*, VI, pp. 1576 *et seq.* (cf. X, pp. 574 *et seq.*).

number of great truths; as formulated by the theologians and acknowledged by its author—and condemned by the Church—it seems to come down to this:

Behind it all, there is a kind of sin of angelism. Molinos is obsessed by a longing for pure spirituality, a sort of physical purity of spirit. In its depths, he seems to say, the soul as it issues from the hands of God is utterly pure, because it is literally divine. The Christian effort should therefore be to extract this spiritual kernel from all that is not itself, to restore it to its original purity, and to make it coincide with the divine essence that is its living principle and its origin by identifying itself with it, so that there are no longer two realties but one (Prop. 5). Consequently, this process of ontological purification cannot possibly be a matter of morality: neither mortification of the spirit nor abnegation of the will can lead to it. The process must be psychological, and in a way physical—the exclusion of every impure element, the annihilation of everything within us that is not purely spiritual, is not a reality that can be deified by identification.

Now God is pure Spirit, and man is spirit and sense; and this leads to an absolute rejection of all things appertaining to sense, because by the very fact of their so appertaining they are "abominable, defiled, impure."[28] This denigration is extended to the whole domain of feeling, to all objects and movements of devotion through the senses.[29] God is Absolute Rest, and man is activity; therefore any spiritual movement of any kind whatsoever is opposed to God, the very fact of its being activity excluding any possible identification with God. Hence the rejection of activity as such,[30] of all acts of knowledge and spiritual mediation,[31] all acts of virtue and will,[32] all resistance to temptation and self-love. At the end, man is dead, with the death that means the annihilation of all activity—"the soul annihilates itself in its operative being"[33]—and from this very fact comes absolute abandonment to God and transformation in God. For once the im-

[28] Undoubtedly the Quietists had the idea that everything experienced is a matter of sense, and that the will cannot be felt: cf. PETRUCCI, in DE GUIBERT, *Documenta*. . . . 483 (29).

[29] Props. 18, 27, 35, 36, 63.

[30] Props. 4, 5.

[31] Props. 6-8, 9-11, 58.

[32] Props. 2, 6, 21, 31, 35, 61.

[33] Prop. 5.

pure elements have been removed, man's spiritual essence is identical with God's essence, and the soul is found to be fixed on God,[34] in the everlasting, inamissible actuality of contemplation.

Two things follow. First, when the soul is dead to its own activity and identical with God, everything else becomes a matter of indifference. Since God has taken away the soul's will, and it has no will left,[35] it has become impeccable,[36] and nothing can affect its deified essence. Hence temptations, sins, acts of obscenity, become utterly unimportant; they are foreign to man and have no significance—or rather, they are means whereby the soul may be still further annihilated, made purer, more holy, more at one with God.[37] Secondly, since God alone is active in those who are perfect—"in us without us"[38]—and increasingly active in them,[39] the soul must surrender itself to his action entirely, must not try to rouse any devotional impulses itself,[40] and must repress any that spring up of their own accord,[41] unless they obviously come from a special impulse from God:[42] "the soul that has been truly annihilated cannot but operate under the impulse of God, and it is not she who acts, but God within her."[43] Thus we reach the point where it is necessary for a divine movement to be felt before there can be any activity.

And so this doctrine, which begins by denying all feeling, ends by surrendering to it on all levels—on the sense level, as being utterly unimportant, and on the spiritual level, as being a necessary sign. The fundamental mistake lies in the fact that any action by God is regarded as incompatible with any action by man, and divine grace is regarded as the destruction of, and perfect substitute for, human freedom. The result is that spiritual mortification by way of the destruction of evil is replaced by the physical annihilation of human powers, and for the living passivity of the soul welcoming its God and responding with love is substituted the lifeless passivity of a soul that has lost its will, its freedom, and its faculty for action.

[34] P. Dudon, *Molinos*, p. 276.
[35] Prop. 61.
[36] Props. 55-57, and Dudon, *op. cit.*, p. 286.
[37] Props. 46, 47, 52.
[38] Props. 4, 13.
[39] Prop. 20.
[40] Prop. 33.
[41] Prop. 32.
[42] Prop. 32.
[43] Dudon, *op. cit.*, p. 288.

This is an absolute corruption of the Christian life, at whose living root lies "faith working through charity"—the divinely infused power that makes us connatural with supernatural Beatitude, so that we tend towards it spontaneously, just as natural powers tend towards their natural ends (I. II, 72, 1 & 3), the inner law of life inscribed upon the heart by the Holy Spirit (*ibid.*, 106, 1, c), who both enlightens and leads us, as the natural law does with respect to human ends (*ibid.*, 2m). This "grace of the Holy Ghost, which is shown forth by faith that worketh through love" (*ibid.*, 108, 1, c) is a kind of infused *habitus*, "a sort of instinct of grace" (*ibid.*) that bears fruit in inner and outer acts. The rule of our activity is supplied by the Word of God in the Church, and faith means adherence to this Divine Truth. Under the light and impulse of inward grace, and faced with its precise objects and well-defined ends, human freedom thenceforward has the power to make decisions and to act. It has to practise the commandments, and make up its own mind about those aspects of the worship of God and service of the neighbour that are not laid down in the Law (*ibid.*, 108, 1, c & 2, c). But it is always the grace of the Holy Spirit that inclines us to act well, and enables us to do freely the things that are in accordance with grace, and to avoid the things that are against grace (*ibid.*, 108, 1, 2m).

The Christian has not by any means, therefore, to wait for any feeling of grace. He knows by faith that God will assist him; he relies through hope on this help; and by charity he freely chooses to obey God and serve him. Freedom, thus "prevented" and maintained, unconsciously but really, by grace, is primary and sufficient.[44] To wait for a feeling of grace is therefore both a fundamental mistake, because the action of grace is normally imperceptible in the continuous process of the spiritual life, and a frightful danger, because by restricting the soul to a deliberate vacuity[45] this attitude

[44] Cf. the excellent passage from Bossuet quoted by P. Pourrat, *op. cit.*, Vol. IV, p. 292: Letter to Mme. de Maisonfort, 21 March, 1696 (*Correspondance de Bossuet*, ed. Urbain-Lévesque, Vol. VII, Paris, 1913, pp. 350 *et seq.*).

[45] Cf. Gregory the Great, *Moralia in Job*, XXXI, 55 (P.L., 75, 709): "There are some who flee the actions of the world but make no effort to practise the virtues. Such are in a torpid sleep, their spirit is asleep and they are unable to see any spiritual realities . . . For most of the time, in fact, the more they are safe from external action, the greater grows the babble of the impure thoughts that they garner in their sloth." And devils come into it: "the result being that the more the soul is removed from external actions, and the more it imagines itself to be serving God, the more it is in reality under the sway of the devil by reason of its evil thoughts," etc.

leaves it a prey either to sloth and inertia or to the disastrous forces of an unpurified consciousness. The *Articles of Issy* express the true Catholic teaching on this point. "The Christian is not allowed to wait until God inspires his acts in a particular manner; all he needs, to be enabled to perform such acts, is faith, which acquaints him with the will of God, made manifest and declared aloud by his commandments and the examples given by the saints; always assuming the assistance of exciting and prevenient grace."[46]

Furthermore, though it is true that when God wants to make his action felt in the soul he can do so, the absence of any such feeling is as normal as its presence. The first reason for this is that the Christian, being on pilgrimage here on earth, is travelling along a way of vicissitude. Spiritual life cannot be arrested any more than psychic life can, and love's unchanging vision of God is reserved for Paradise. Immersed in the world, and at the same time tending towards God, divided within himself in all his innermost aspirations, the Christian is obliged daily to undergo endless alternations of ease and difficulty, longing and dryness, ardour and distaste. Also, so long as he has not attained to perfection, he remains in need of drastic purification. He is not ready for total union with God, or capable of experiencing and following all the subtle variations of the movement of the Spirit. Helped by grace, he has to purify himself through all the labour of virtuous effort, until God himself takes over the task of purification from its foundations and casts both sense and spirit into the crucible of passive purgation: then only is affectivity restored to the condition of purity willed by God, and really able to taste how sweet the Lord is. Lastly, here on earth the Christian must imitate Christ, and carry his cross as he did and in company with him. So long as he is inhabited by the "*reliquiae peccati,*" it must be in pain that he learns detachment and rises towards God. And when he is really purified, then Christ makes him share in his redemptive Passion and Agony. Then the saint enters into dereliction and crucifixion for the sake of the salvation of the world. Wrapped in the great peace of the friends of God, he experiences the "holiness of justice," the deprivation and annihilation of all feeling of joy. And

[46] *Documenta. . . .* 493, 11 (cf. 25-26). It should be noted that Fénélon in his counter-suggestions made no objection to the article: cf. Dudon, *Le Gnostique. . . .* p. 282. Cf. Bossuet, *Instruction sur les États d'oraison,* I, iii, 11: "Their presumption puts them on the level of men subject to the illusions of their hearts, prepared to call God whatever suits them best."

God rewards him, when he pleases, with a joy that transcends all feeling, and which the lower part of the soul can never experience even when the spirit is living by it.

Feeling is thus from every point of view an instrument, something never to be waited on, something that always needs to be transcended and sacrificed, whenever God wills. For this reason the Catholic spiritual tradition has always been highly suspicious of more or less permanent states of consolation.[47] "Because he is good," says St. Bernard, "Our Lord Jesus Christ makes it his custom to attract lesser souls by such touches. But let those who are in this state know that such graces are not given them but lent them, so that in time of joy they may remember sorrow, and in time of sorrow they forget not joy."

Sense-Feeling. The spiritual life is not a thing without emotions. The saints weep at the thought of their sins and the goodness of God; their hearts beat to bursting-point within them; they shout and dance for joy; they die to see God. In their own much lowlier way ordinary Christians experience similar perturbations, in which body and soul react in unison before God: "My heart and my flesh have rejoiced in the living God" (Ps. lxxxiii, 2). The question thus arises, how much significance and value is to be accorded to all this feeling?

When it is given by God, of course, it is an excellent grace. God has made man a composite of body and soul, and he calls him through both. St. Teresa, with her admirable realism, says, "When God grants spiritual sweetnesses to souls still far from detached, this is because in his infinite wisdom he sees that these will tend to make them leave all things for love of him."[48] This feeling generally seems to be found at the two extremes of the spiritual life. First, in the newly converted, whom God takes when and as they are, still suffused with all their past delights and still deeply involved in the life of the senses. He takes hold of them through these things, and for a time attracts them to himself by "sensible consolations" that divert them from their wicked joys and familiarize them with the spiritual world. When St. Augustine said that the convert sees "his delights change," and that these "are not taken away from him, but changed,"

[47] Some passages on this subject will be found in J. B. Scaramelli, *Le Discernement des Esprits* (trans. Brassevin, Paris, 1910), pp. 246-248 & 275-284. The passage from St. Bernard occurs on p. 278.

[48] *The Way of Perfection,* XIII.

we may take it that he was not only thinking of disembodied delights and highly refined pleasures, as a glance at his *Confessions* should show.[49] St. Gregory the Great, again, has described the three stages of this experience with his usual precision—first the struggle between flesh and spirit, old and new, aspiration and desire; then the victory of grace, with "a great joy that warms the heart" and "an experience of the great sweetness of consolation"; and finally, so that the individual will not imagine himself a saint and grow proud, the return to the journey through the desert. Consequently, "in the beginning they know only charm and sweetness; in the middle, the trials of the testing time; in the end, the perfection of all fullness."[50] These new emotions are normal, but they are not necessary, and in the case of souls already deeply religious the change-over may take place in darkness, God leaving the soul naked before its duty. A person who passes from Protestantism to Catholicism, for instance, knows and loves Christ personally already; in his faith there is a solid foundation that has been lived through in its sacrificial aspect: God may call to him through this painful faith, in absolute dryness, reserving the joy for later.[51]

And then again this sensible feeling reappears at the summit of the spiritual life in the great mystics. God has purified them to the bone, they have submitted to the "vigorous washing" with a crucified and unshakeable love. They are thus remade, newly created in their whole being, restored to a condition that brings to their minds the state of original innocence. Because they are truly prepared, detached from everything that is not God, divine joy can flow even into their bodies.[52] But the difference is clear: in the case of the convert, the sensible feelings come to him from outside, into a soul that is imperfect and which God wills to bring to freedom: they are not "at

[49] Before conversion there is a split in the will and the soul: hence shame, hatred, fear, self-disgust (VIII); after conversion, an experience in which emotion and feeling express and reinforce the spiritual aspiration—hence every sign of agitation, cries, shivers of fright, joyous hope, tremblings, complaints, divine sweetness, "tears of joy."

[50] *Moralia in Job*, 24, 11; P.L., 76, 300-302. Similar observations might be made about all beginnings in the spiritual life. The man who is converted to a life of fervent piety, and the man whom God introduces into the path of mysticism, generally experience the sweetness of God that detaches them from created things and draws them towards union with himself.

[51] Cf. the case of Mgr. Benson, in J. Huby, *La Conversion* (Paris, 1919), pp. 75 *et seq.*

[52] Cf. *infra*, the *Note on the Affectivity of the Senses in St. John of the Cross.*

home" in him; they are bait to encourage spiritual effort, and they will disappear. In the saint, the feelings are normal, because they arise from the spirit into a body and senses that have been purified; and they prepare the way for more searching purifications or a still more heroic service of God and human souls.

Lastly, when we come to the case of emotions that are linked up with an intense spiritual impulse, we find that they may have a very large part to play in certain phases of the spiritual life. There is, for instance, in particular, the mystery of tears. Mme. Lot-Borodine has reminded us of the part played by tears, and their significance, in Greek spirituality,[53] and she lays considerable stress on their mystical character. Fr. Hausherr, correcting Mme. Lot-Borodine's point of view, and adopting a wider view of the problem altogether, in his highly original book on that mysterious thing *Penthos*—a kind of mourning over lost salvation, a compunction of heart producing tears, consolation, happiness—makes it clear that this tearful compunction is fundamentally a matter of faith and asceticism—of faith,[54] because man must get to know the true good, must know that he has lost it, must meditate on his wretchedness and therefore "go into mourning" and "enter into the blessed way of penthos"; and of asceticism, because the ancients aimed to recover their lost unity no matter what it cost them. Until they reach the stage at which they can experience perfect peace, their instincts having been unified with their will, their imagination with their intelligence, and their will and intelligence with the will and mind of God, they go on chastising themselves, knowing themselves to be far from the absolute health that is their aim. When the unity is restored, the "emotions" are determined by the "intellections," and the "mourning" by the lost good. Hence, "forcing oneself to shed tears simply means endeavouring to restore the disturbed equilibrium between the lower senses and the higher";[55] it means performing one's duty, walking in the way of the commandments, and therefore striving towards a kind of compunction—sorrow and tears—that is "always within our power."[56] Of course there are some people "ill-advised enough" to beat or whip themselves into

[53] *La Vie Spirituelle*, Sept. 1936, pp. 65 *et seq.*

[54] I. Hausherr, *Penthos, La Doctrine de la componction dans l'Orient chrétien* (*Orientalia Christiana Analecta*, 132), Rome, 1944, pp. 178, 183 *et seq.*

[55] *Ibid.*, pp. 186 *et seq.*

[56] *Ibid.*, pp. 193 *et seq.*

tears,[57] but they are mistaken: the real way is through the heart's repentance, though prayer and longing—"Weep and shed your tears before God in intention," said St. Nilus, and in this way, "by dint of faith and prayer . . . the rock of your soul will be changed into a running spring."[58] All this takes us into a world remote from that of our usual spiritual habits; but the really remarkable thing is that these tears form part of a spiritual whole: they are desired and petitioned for, but in a context of faith, repentance and prayer, and thus the spiritual feeling is protected against itself by taking its place within one great spiritual effort.

Despite all this, Catholic spiritual tradition has always been severe on the part played by sensible feeling in Christian life, and has always regarded it as dangerous. For one reason, psycho-organic affectivity, being bound up with the body, inherits the ills of the body, and is therefore burdened with a heavy load of carnality, none of which is directly purified by grace; and it is thus to a great extent nourished and governed by the human being's animal instincts. It is easy to understand why spiritual writers should show such mistrust of emotions arising from forces unrefined by grace and always largely hostile to its influence. Again, this affectivity can breed the most fearful illusions. Man is naturally a religious animal. In the eyes of the psychologist he is a being endowed with a religious instinct manifesting itself as a synthesis of all his higher instincts—his love of truth, goodness, and beauty. In the eyes of the theologian he is a being naturally inclined to love God above all things, this inclination being the ontological root of his entire spiritual activity. When his being is transformed by grace and his spiritual inclinations are transformed by the theological virtues, the supernatural religious impulse comes from the very centre of the spirit and can "move" the whole of his psychic life. But the impulse remains spiritual; and though it may—indeed must—involve the powers of the senses, it does not in fact involve them directly. If the Christian lacks the courage to get down properly to the work of purification, he will find himself sidetracked by compensation: judging of things entirely by his emotional hunger for them, he will be tempted to look for emotion only, and to accept and foster all his emotions without making any attempt to criticize them. And there is always a danger that these may come

[57] *Ibid.*, pp. 97 *et seq.*
[58] *Ibid.*, p. 191.

from an imagination and an instinctive life that have remained unpurified. Then, they are food without nourishment, for they do not come from God; they deceive man by giving him the impression that he is feeling or tasting the action of God when he is actually swallowed up in self; and they fix him in egoism, by diverting him from any genuine effort to be purified and united with God. All of which tends to make him vulnerable to the wiles of the Devil. For it is in the region of the senses that the Devil, the Father of Lies, is most at home:[59] there, thanks to the readiness of the carnal instincts to co-operate with him, he can work at his ease. A man may easily imagine himself to be following God, when in fact the Devil is simply leading him "up the garden." Thus, here more than anywhere else we find man situated between inspiration and temptation, subject to the frightful polyvalency of the religious emotions—which may be daughters of God, or of the unconscious, or of the Devil. Clearly, any abandonment to these feelings, any deliberate encouragement or passive acceptance of what is unpurified or uncontrolled, can be one of the greatest dangers in the spiritual life.

Finally, the feelings connected with the senses exist in any case on a low level, at which there can be no union with God or service of God. The primary value for Christianity is always one thing only —the free homage of the mind and will to God, the whole man's free service of his Lord. At this height the senses do not exist. Absence of feeling cannot prevent the soul from ascending to God, nor can its presence ensure it, and when feeling is sought after and enjoyed for its own sake it prevents it. In this sense—which incidentally has nothing in common with the views of Molinos—feeling has always to be transcended, until the stage is reached at which it is an overflow of the spirit on to the senses; and again, since it is no more than an effect, a reflection, it must always be penetrated through and through by the pure light of a spiritual impulse centred on God alone.[60]

Spiritual Feelings. These are normal for two reasons. Firstly, they are necessary for freedom, which is animated and supported through-

[59] On this classic affirmation, cf. Mgr. Catherinet, *Les démoniaques de l'Évangile, Satan* (*Études carmélitaines*, 1948), pp. 324-37. (English translation, *Satan*, edited by Father Bruno de Jésus-Marie, O.C.D. [Sheed & Ward, London and New York, 1952].)

[60] For the part played by sense feelings, cf. the vigorous chapter in Fr. A. Massoulié's, *Traité de l'Amour de Dieu* (Brussels), II, V.

out its development by great spiritual feelings. An unembodied freedom existing in a pure state, unencumbered by instinct, impulse and emotion, is, as we have seen, a myth. But a freedom untouched by spiritual affectivity and deaf to its appeals is also a myth. Freedom is brought to life by "objects" loaded with affective value, which release the feeling that provokes and orientates the choice. The sinner's freedom is called to conversion by remorse and repentance, by the longing for forgiveness, by the—truly spiritual—thought of Christ on the Cross, or the gentle Mother of all succour. And the freedom of the just man is moved to generous effort by the gratitude he feels at the thought that he has been redeemed, and the loyalty he feels as one called upon to serve; by his longing to imitate his Saviour and help spread the Gospel—in short, by love. In the second place, spiritual feelings are the overflow and efflorescence of freedom. Joys and sorrows, increasing longings, outbursts of adoration, or exultation, or supplication, light-heartedness—these are the feelings that accompany our acts of decision; and at the same time, of course, they are excellent graces, enabling us to be pleasing to God and to ourselves in God—which is not forbidden us: far from it, as St. Thomas has explained in his defence of "tempting" God (II. II, 97, 2, 2m). "To tempt" someone, says St. Thomas, means to try to procure from him some direct experience of his knowledge or power, his goodness or his will; and Scripture seems to regard this as perfectly legitimate in the case of God's goodness—"Taste and see that the Lord is sweet" (Ps. xxxiii, 9)—and his will—"That you may prove what is the good . . . will of God," etc. (Rom. xii, 2). Therefore it is permissible to "tempt" God? Answer: "There is a twofold knowledge of God's goodness or will. One is speculative and as to this it is not lawful to doubt or to prove whether God's will be good, or whether God is sweet. The knowledge of God's will or goodness is effective or experimental, and thereby a man experiences in himself the taste of God's sweetness, and complacency in God's will, as Dionysius says of Hierotheos (*Div. Nom, ii.*) that he learnt divine things through experience of them. It is in this way that we are told to prove God's will, and to taste his sweetness."

But these spiritual feelings have nothing like the same density as the emotions. Being purely spiritual, they are difficult for the insufficiently purified to perceive or grasp. They are usually mixed with the senses, indeed enveloped by them, "obnubilated" by the inertia or interference of the senses, covered over with superficial agitation, occupation, dissipation. Often there is no clear consciousness of them at all; they disappear into aridity, in which all that can be perceived is the naked desire, or memory, or faithfulness. Often, again, they form part of the painful sharing of Christ's Cross—in dryness and weariness, in the tragic suffering for sins, in heartrending awareness of the indignities suffered by Christ. But this suffering is undergone in love, and the soul would not have it end; and when love reaches its fullness, suffering can at times become such joy that the soul complains at not being able to suffer more. Spiritual feelings thus share in the Spirit's infinity, and the endless wealth they bring is beyond all reckoning. But their function is always to help the soul to do God's will increasingly, to abandon itself to his action, to serve God and sing hymns to his glory.

Therefore—once again—it is the final end of spiritual feelings that gives them their value, and to take pleasure in them for their own sake means arresting the movement of charity. And for this reason spiritual writers recommend that we shall not become engrossed in them, but detach ourselves from them[61] and not think about them deliberately. "Avoid becoming attached to things of sense and to the pleasure of devotion and the things of God; for this is a very common failing, and dangerous," writes Fr. Rigoleuc. "Carefully avoid any reflection on the light God gives you or the things he causes to happen within you. Such thoughts are worthless. . . . They are all the more dangerous in that they expose us to the illusion created by our Enemy, occasion pride and self-esteem, are opposed to the nakedness of faith that is such a precious thing in the realm of the supernatural, destroy the emptiness that faith creates in us, and, by attracting the soul to the lower level of sense, debase and degrade it from its high estate as pure spirit."[62]

3. *The Integration of Feeling in the Spiritual Life*

A critical estimate of feeling should end with a discussion of its authenticity and value in some particular kind of spiritual life. It

[61] As regards St. Teresa, see the remarks by M. Lépée, *Sainte Thérèse d'Avila* (Paris, 1947), pp. 237-239.

[62] Quoted by Rev. Fr. H. Pinard de la Boullaye, *La Spiritualité ignatienne* (Paris, 1949), p. 347.

seems to me that the essential criterion in this case is to be found in its integration into the totality of the Christian experience. In accordance with my original distinction,[63] then, I suggest that—all due allowance being made for subordinate criteria—feeling is genuine when it is lived and reflected upon, not on the empirical or experimental, but on the experiential level.

The problem arises on the empirical level when emotions or feelings are valued for their own sake entirely. Taken in their given existentiality as the brute matter of the spiritual life, emotions and feelings cannot be explained in advance, they are polyvalent, and when any particular religious feeling or emotion arises it always raises the question as to whether it comes from God or the self or the Devil, and hence what its value is. Because God's supernatural actions are not usually registered in consciousness, and the real sources of any affective movement are usually unconscious and intermingled with each other, and because any action by the Devil is usually inserted into the activity of our own partial determinisms, therefore there is no infallible criterion for discovering whether any particular spiritual feeling, which seems to conform to the inner law of the spirit and the demands of faith, does or does not come from God. This explains why theologians, and spiritual writers generally, are so severe and sceptical about any such feelings, and about the Christian experience itself when this is regarded as an empirical matter concerning a number of affective states experienced directly. Taken by itself, as a material reality, feeling is not a revelation of God.

On the experimental level—i.e., the level at which feelings are provoked—the difficulties are even greater. In the first place, the movement of freedom refers directly to the end—i.e., God himself—with which man is meant to unite himself, not to any delight that may accompany this union. Secondly, the effort of freedom is concerned with acts to be performed—the worship and service of God—not with affective states that may be felt. Any attempt to provoke a particular feeling seems therefore to be condemned in advance, as tending to interfere with the free manifestation of spiritual freedom. Experimentation is bound to be dangerous, because it diverts freedom from essential to secondary matters; it is bound to be illusory, because states that have been psychologically provoked come to be regarded as communications from God; it is bound to be an insult

[63] *Supra*, ch. I, p. 15.

to God, because it appertains to God alone to give himself to be enjoyed when he wills, and man can only wait for this grace in humility, penitence, and purity of life. Experimentation, as something aiming to provoke mere feelings, has no place in the Christian experience.

Feeling only assumes its proper part when it is absorbed and integrated into the totality of the Christian experience, i.e. inserted in its proper place in the tissue of spiritual relationships that make up the experience—in short, on the experiential level. The first group of relationships is created by the inward acts of the theological virtues —particularly charity—which ensure a real communication with God through a right orientation of the mind, a fundamental rectification of the powers of sense and spirit in their ascent towards the ultimate End: by these, the new feeling is aroused, extricated, and polarized. The second group of relationships comprises acts of virtue—acts of the theological virtues, and of the moral virtues prompted by charity —as a result of which the spiritual feeling is preserved, kept within limits, and integrated with the redeemed freedom. The third group of relationships, intrinsic to both the others and particularly important for our present purpose, concerns the mortification, abnegation, and purification that are necessary in every Christian life; by these the new feeling is delivered from the old and becomes genuine and fruitful for the soul. And all this, of course, is lived within the Church, in obedience to the Word of God and one's lawful superiors. Inserted and integrated in this way, feeling recovers its normal function, which is a practical necessity; it takes its part in a living dialogue with freedom; it enriches the soul's dialogue with God; it helps towards a deeper experience of the mystery of the joys and sorrows of the Christian life—the mystery of Christ. Endless examples could be given: we shall restrict ourselves here to a mere handful.

To begin with an extreme case: even experimentation now becomes legitimate. We have already described the attitude of the old ascetics, who wanted, and laboured to attain, the blessed *penthos*. But it must be remembered that this attitude was simply one aspect of lives that were entirely controlled by faith, lives that were all prayer, purified by a severe asceticism and an obedient submission to the Ancients; and that—apart from a few known eccentrics—these simple, uncultured men aimed *per modum unius* at a spiritual sort of dolour —a mourning over "Paradise Lost"—and the tears that were at once the sign and the result of this mourning. Their "experimentation" was perfectly genuine because it was governed by the whole tenor of their spiritual life, austere, pure, fervent—and therefore itself absolutely safeguarded.

St. Ignatius provides another example of the same thing at a later period of time. He too knew about the charisma of tears,[64] and in a quite extraordinary way. For long periods of his life he was literally invaded by tears—before Mass, during Mass, in his prayers, in his meditations, in contemplation. He was finally obliged to try to stop this incessant flow, and prayed to God to take these tears away from him "if that was all the same to His divine Majesty" (50), but he continued to be invaded by them: his journal "for the last nine months is simply a detailed account of the daily manifestations of the gift of tears."[65] "A strange and typical fact,"[66] says our author—all the more so as Ignatius was so hard on graces of this kind and very guarded about this particular gift ("the gift of tears is absolutely a thing not to be asked for") and realized both the danger that lay in becoming attached to such tears and the fact that it was God's will that he should be the greatest example of them. They seem in fact to have been the organic repercussion of infinitely precious favours which he received, and any record of them was a recollection of a visit God had paid his soul. But they were always simply one element in a strongly structured total experience: "In the journal, as in the *Exercises*—along with the same primary concern to discover the will of God and then embrace it, to discover it first by inner experience, without in any way repudiating the use of reason enlightened by faith, and the same longing for divine confirmation of any decisions taken—we find the same devotion to the Most Holy Trinity, the same respect for the Divine Majesty, the same sense of the infinite distance between God and us even in the midst of the most vital outpourings of love; we find the same large place given to mediators. . . ; we find, again, the same subordinate but useful and beneficent part attributed to the imagination and the sensibility,

[64] I have made use of the information given by Fr. J. de Guibert in *Mystique ignatienne* in *Revue d'Ascétique et de Mystique*, 1938, pp. 113 *et seq.*, esp. pp. 125-129. I hope I will be forgiven for introducing an example from the mystical life.

[65] *Ibid.*, p. 125.

[66] *Ibid.*, p. 129.

which do not appear as our born enemies, to be got rid of at all costs, but as real helps, though secondary and needing a watchful eye."[67]

There is nothing surprising, therefore, in the fact that on some particular points Ignatius should suggest an actual spiritual experimentation as a means to learning the will of God—as for instance embarking on a series of tests to discover the right amount of food or penance that will be found personally appropriate in these matters,[68] "as a result of the experience of the knowledge, consolation, and inspiration" that will often accrue. But as Fr. de Guibert observes, this experimentation takes place amidst graces that have all the marks of contemplation; it is simply a correlative to the normal rules of supernatural prudence, and even so it does not always need to take place; and finally it signifies simply one moment of spiritual research that takes its place within the total dialectic of the *Exercises* and the whole extremely closely-knit effort that St. Ignatius expects his disciple to make. Here again, the isolated element finds its meaning and the guarantee of its authenticity in the structure as a whole.

The immense problem of the discernment of spirits is to be judged by the same criteria. If we confine our attention to the case of spiritual consolations as described by Scaramelli,[69] whose work is on the whole a summary or reorganization of the work of his predecessors, we find that the Devil can undoubtedly excite "tendernesses and sensible consolations"[70] in the soul in order to "catch" it within its clutches. The fixation of the soul in this sweetness, the pursuit of the delight to be found in it, the use of prayer as a means to pleasing self instead of God, the neglect of one's duties and a lack of charity for the sake of this consolation, the habitual falling into the same faults—in other words, a falsification of the spiritual impulse, and sloth in the "effort of virtue"—such are the signs of illusion. The judgment is different[71] "if besides the tender consolations of sense there also exists in the understanding a sober knowledge of the divine truths and in the will a profound affection for holy things and solid virtue; if after these sweet prayers the reli-

[67] *Ibid.*, p. 133.

[68] J. de Guibert, *Theologia spiritualis ascetica et mystica* (Rome, 1937), pp. 1280, No. 139. (English translation, *The Theology of the Spiritual Life* [Sheed and Ward, New York and London, 1953-4]; see p. 119.)

[69] *Le discernement des Esprits* (trans. Brassevin, Paris, 1910).

[70] *Ibid.*, no. 145, p. 215.

[71] *Ibid.*, no. 165, p. 245.

gious soul is more mistress of itself, more circumspect in the avoidance of faults and more diligent in the performance of acts of virtue. If this is so, it may be firmly believed that consolation is a true effect of grace and a real gift from God." In other words, enlightened faith, a right will, a growth of strength and generosity in act—these are the signs of genuine consolation. And as always, the structure judges the element.

Finally, to take an example not drawn from any special problem but from the essential piety of Christians in general, we may turn to the *Sacramentary of Leo*.[72] Whatever its actual origin may be—and historians are still arguing about this[73]—it appears as a genuine, indeed magnificent, document of the *Romana devotio*,[74] and supplies us with a wealth of passages for our purpose. Occasionally pure consolation seems to be asked for: "Fill us, Lord, with the grace of thy sacred gift, and what we feel with a sweet veneration with our bodily taste let us feel more sweetly still with our minds."[75] "Filled with the taste of thy grace and strengthened by the sweetness of thy heavenly table, we give thee thanks."[76] "May the sacraments we have received purify us from all error and pour into our hearts the sweetness of thy fragrance."[77] But generally petitions of this nature form part of a whole determined by the general structure of the Christian attitude. For instance, there is this passage, in which the spiritual joy that lies at the heart of the process of salvation is connected with the Eucharist (as a remedy), deliverance from the flesh, religious homage, and the hope of salvation for the entire man: "May the

[72] P.L., 55.

[73] Cf. M. ANDRIEU's discussion of A. STUIBER, *Libelli Sacramentorum Romani*, 1950, *Revue des Sciences religieuses*, April, 1951, pp. 201-202. It is considered to be a collection of masses "composed separately by various Popes," kept in the Lateran Archives and collected (end of 5th century?) into a *Liber Sacramentorum* for the use of Roman ecclesiastics. "The editor of the original copy has clearly taken his material from the collection of papal Masses in the Lateran. The use of the phrase 'Gelasian Sacramentary' is not necessarily an error." The result was an "official book for the use of priests . . . as well as for the Pope himself" (p. 202). Since these lines were written a corner of the veil seems to have been raised: see A. CHAVASSE, *Messes du Pape Vigile dans le Sacramentaire léonien* (*Ephemerides liturgicae*, LXIV, 1950, pp. 161 *et seq.*).

[74] P.L., 55, 134 A.

[75] *Ibid.*, 69 C.

[76] *Ibid.*, 96 A.

[77] *Ibid.*, 125 C.

participation in thy divine sacrament, O Lord, be a lasting defence for thy people, may they not be kept in slavery by the vices of the body, may they be delivered by spiritual delights, may they be subject to your Majesty in perfect devotion, may they always await, and receive abundantly, salvation of mind and body."[78] In another passage, joy is linked with detachment from temporal things and the things of the body, and the struggle against the Devil: "Deign to pour (thy grace) into our feelings (*sensibus*), lest, through cleaving to our earthly affections, we fail to raise our eyes towards heaven; lest, being occupied in base pleasures, we be unable to elevate our minds to where our Saviour has ascended; lest, following in the Devil's footsteps, we may lose our true inheritance, which is Christ—for no one can delight in the one true sovereign King, unless he has previously destroyed and trampled under foot the malignant claims of the tyrant."[79] Finally, there is a passage in praise of the free gift of consolation, linking it with God's honour and the desire for love: "O thou who alone accomplishest great and wonderful deeds, who not only dost not punish us for our sins as we deserve but even grantest unto us beyond our deserving the gifts of thy consolation, (deign) to prompt us to worship thy Name by the bounty of thy fatherly gifts, rather than by constraining us by just punishments; and be propitious to us in thy clemency, that slavish fear may be transformed into the affection of sons."[80] These splendid passages, which could easily be multiplied, far from despising feeling, place it in the context of the general movement of the spiritual life, and give it authenticity by inserting it into the fundamental structure of this life. Once again let me repeat that it is the organic whole of spiritual relationships that gives feeling its meaning and value: there is no real Christian experience outside the realm of the experiential.

Any attempt to clarify the role of feeling still further would be an immense task in which two series of facts at least would have to be studied in detail.

The first would be the general, never-ending evolution of sensibility. This is evident in the development of Revelation. Speaking of the Holy Spirit's appearances to the prophets, the Rev. Fr. Dumeste

[78] *Ibid.*, 124 B.
[79] *Ibid.*, 38 B.
[80] *Ibid.*, 128 D.

writes:[81] "To these prophetic messengers God communicated himself throughout the centuries, in a way that shows an evolution and progression which he himself directs, and for which, in his infinite Wisdom, he has not failed to make use of secondary causes. Religion did not have from the beginning that ultimate perfection which it acquired when the Son of God himself intervened in the New Testament. Each separate stage of prophetic development manifests the supremacy of God's action. . . . But whereas in 'primitives' like Balaam and perhaps Micah ben Jimla the divine impulse often seems to irrupt into the subconscious areas of the soul of the charismatic, prompting him to words and deeds whose significance he himself does not understand, later, with the development of consciousness and the feeling for personality, and a more reflective type of mind, prophecy gradually emancipates itself from these lower forms until with the great seers of the classical period it rises to a very high level of spirituality. It is difficult to exaggerate the marvellous nature of this divine teaching, which spoke to each succeeding epoch in the language it was able to understand." But the human soul is never at rest; it is always discovering new or neglected aspects of itself according to the culture that surrounds it. In a "reflective age," for example, the inner eye undoubtedly tends to concentrate on an inner spirituality, and it would be a mistake to regard this as an aberration or an impoverishment: in itself the exploration of the inner man is a gain, a growth, and an enrichment. Danger only comes from any one-sidedness in the developments that are thus instituted.

In the field of mysticism, for instance, St. John of the Cross and St. Teresa describe an experience that has led to a considerable enrichment of our knowledge of the world of grace. Moreover, they were simply continuing a venerable line, including Origen, Augustine, Gregory of Nyssa, Diadocus, Gregory the Great and St. Bernard. On a lower level, no doubt, but one that is of more immediate importance for the spiritual life of the ordinary Christian, the *Imitation of Christ* provides similar testimony. When one studies the argument of this work, it soon becomes clear that two distinct spiritual lines govern its development. The first line is the eternal one of the relationship between God and the soul. The whole field of external activity is abandoned, as befits the life of a

[81] *La Vie Spirituelle*, July 1938, p. 41.

monk, and likewise the whole field of inter-personal, social, neighbourly relationships. The drama centres entirely on the pure search for God, in complete inner solitude, by way of spiritual combat, humility, compunction, abnegation, desire, and love. In the truly gospel-like tones of this book, with their penetrating sweetness, every Christian soul can recognize itself immediately.

But a second line inserts itself very clearly into this first one; a second theme can be heard continuously through the first. This derives from the level at which the search takes place, which is not that of dogmatic principles but of spiritual experience. A very clear example of this is to be found in the famous (and unjustly criticized) chapters on nature and grace.[82] Here there is no attempt to study the ontological structure of these two separate principles: nature means corrupt nature, nature corrupted by sin, and grace is a supernatural force that is introduced into the soul and governs its activity. There are not two principles, but two complexes—almost St. Paul's "flesh" and "spirit." But the Pauline theme is brought down from the level of the "historic," universal experience of man fallen and redeemed, to that of concrete, particularized experience. The grace in question here is not grasped from above in its ontological and dogmatic aspect, but from below, in its psychological aspect, as something lived and clearly known. It remains faithful to St. Paul, but as a continuation and application to the order of the lived and felt, as involved in the fluid world of spiritual vicissitude. Grace, which heals and triumphs, here expresses its victory in terms of experience, consolation, security, devotion, and tears. And this is as much a sign of a particular age as of a particular soul.

One of the major features of this experience can be understood by studying the visible or concealed presence, the continual resurgence, of the theme of consolation. There is no hesitation about the judgment to be passed on this: it is desirable, though secondary; delicious and nourishing when given by God; often absent when desired, for that is part of our trial here on earth. But the really significant and revealing thing is the way the theme continually recurs—and whenever it occurs, it is as affectivity in action. Consolation attracts and polarizes: we know that we are unworthy and that the Lord must refuse us consolation during our earthly pilgrimage; nevertheless, it is something we hope to find at each

[82] Book III, chs. liv & lv.

turn of the road, rising up before us like some blessed presence. Fr. Chenu has described this exactly, in the following words: "All this compunction tends towards joy, jubilation, swooning at the heavenly visitation, for if the Friend wishes it so, it is still a consolation to be without consolation."[83] It is well known that this "little book" has been for generations of countless souls a guide, comforter, and friend on this way that is ever-old and ever-new.

There remains a second line of investigation to which some reference must be made. If it is true that feeling becomes authentic from being inserted into a total experience, it is only to be expected that these lived syntheses, which are very difficult to analyze—they are called "spiritualities"—will differ considerably in this respect. The great forms of spirituality answer some of the eternal needs of the human soul, but they bear the impress of the saint who first lived them in an experience that was at once individual and universal, and they still have the mark of the times in which they first appeared and of the problems to which they first gave an answer. Consequently, some of them tend to welcome feeling, while others tend to eye it rather suspiciously; some are glad to concern themselves with the problems raised by feeling, whereas others ignore them; some are indulgent towards it, others severe. These differences are inevitable and perfectly legitimate: so long as the whole structure in which feeling is integrated remains balanced and in conformity with the essential requirements of Christian truth—and when the Church approves, this is bound to be the case—no doctrinal problem can arise. On the other hand, it is very difficult to compare feeling, as it appears in these various forms of spirituality, because its position and function and significance depend on the structure as a whole: it is the whole syntheses that have to be compared if any worthwhile conclusion is to be reached. In this matter, diversity is lawful, even at the heart of unity: it is a manifestation of the spiritual catholicity of the Church—the soul comes to life and grows in its own way under the breath of the Holy Spirit, "dividing to each as He wills," and the theologian can only study and admire, once again, in its inexhaustible riches, the mystery of Christ in his saints.

[83] *Introduction à l'Imitation de Jésus-Christ* (Paris), p. 28.

A Note on The Affectivity of the Senses in St. John of the Cross[84]

The dialogue between affectivity and freedom is one of the major factors in every Christian life, and the victory of the healed freedom over unpurified affectivity is one of the essential prerequisites of spiritual progress. For the benefit of the souls he directed, St. John of the Cross analyzed this dramatic dialogue with unique insight.[85] He showed what an enormous part was played by affectivity at every stage of the "Ascent of Mount Carmel," and he explained how affectivity had to be purified before it could flower and die to be reborn. In this note I shall leave aside all discussion of the purification and transfiguration of knowledge and spiritual affectivity, and limit myself to the problem of the affectivity of the senses; and I shall try to describe the threefold purification that conditions a threefold flowering.[86] This is emphasized by St. John throughout his whole work, but especially in the *Ascent of Mount Carmel* and the *Dark Night*. As Fr. Lebreton has so truly said, the problem with which these books are concerned is the attractive power of God, "the most profound feature of mystical asceticism."[87]

1.

The *Ascent of Mount Carmel* opens with a radical condemnation of every creaturely appetite, and this extreme attitude has never

[84] All the quotations that follow are taken from the *Complete Works of St. John of the Cross,* translated by E. Allison Peers.

[85] It must be remembered that for the ancients the will was the faculty concerned with spiritual feelings and free choice: it included both affectivity and freedom. Hence an inevitable ambiguity of language. But in conformity with the scholastic tradition St. John distinguishes the two aspects quite clearly: cf. *Dark Night,* II, 13; II, 11; and the important passage in the first *Fragment* distinguishing between the feeling and the operation of the will.

[86] In Baruzi's view the end of the "Ascent" is "the regeneration of perception" (*Saint Jean de la Croix et le problème de l'expérience mystique, passim,* cf. pp. 584-585, and in the *Histoire générale des religions* (Quillet), Paris, 1st ed., 1924, IV, 185). It would be just as true to describe it as a regeneration of affectivity. But in any case this kind of regeneration is not the end, it is an effect and a means. Let me add that the searching analyses to be found in Baruzi's great work are always well worth reading, even if one cannot always entirely agree with them.

[87] *Tu Solus Sanctus* (Paris, 1948), p. 55.

ceased to startle people. It must be realized that St. John is getting a firm and comprehensive grasp of his subject from the start. He is like a man who has just come down from a long and difficult climb, and who turns round to take one last look at what he has left behind: he sees the great masses of rocks reaching up to their towering summits in a vague and indistinct outline, and he knows what vast abysses there are between the various levels that seem so continuous from below. So St. John of the Cross at the beginning of the *Ascent:* he leans towards his brothers to describe the way to them, and thinking of those summits hidden in glory, and the wretchedness of those who live below, he immediately announces the absolute demand—the divesting of all one's appetites if one is to advance towards God. Thus this radicalism is to be seen in the first place in the light of the end pursued—transforming union with God, fruitful possession of God: "that which God seeks to do is to make us gods by participation" (*Points of Love,* 28), and next in the light of man's concrete situation at the beginning of the ascent, i.e. as a creature who is fallen and sinful. St. John refers to this at the beginning and again at the end of the first book of the *Ascent:* "The soul sings of the happy fortune and chance which it experienced in going forth from all things that are without, and from the desires and imperfections that are in the sensual part of man because of the disordered state of his reason" (*Ascent,* I, 2, 1). "For the soul, on account of original sin, is truly as it were a captive in this mortal body, subject to the passions and desires of nature" (*Ascent,* I, 15, 1). The concrete nature of man is fallen, sinful, stained, captive; and it is the "sensible" likings and attachments of his nature that St. John means. Ontologically, man's nature is good, because it has been created by God; but "normally," as a result of the weight of its instinctive desires, each particular nature is disordered. And as the world appears to man in the light of what he is, both his appetites and the view of things that they lead to are equally impure. Hence the general attitude to be found in these opening chapters: every affection, every attachment, every liking of the soul for creatures, is opposed to the love of God, reduces the soul to the level of creatures—where all is base and vile—and makes it a place of utter darkness, compared to the pure light of God. So all must be sacrificed.

On this level, in fact, and seen from this angle, creatures appear as false values opposed to God, and this leads to the frightful litany in which, compared with God (the one true Value) the being of creatures is described as a nothingness, their beauty ugliness, their wisdom ignorance, their power slavery, their joy torment, their wealth poverty (*Ascent*, I, 4), and in this sense the affection for creatures and the affection for God are contraries and mutually exclusive (*Ascent*, I, 6). The only appetite that has the right to remain is the following: "to keep the law of God perfectly, and to bear upon oneself the Cross of Christ" (*Ascent*, I, 5, 8.). In these general remarks St. John seems to allow creatures no escape from their two kinds of misery—their ontological misery, since they are infinitely remote from God, and their spiritual misery in so far as they are the objects of a distorted perception and the source of an inordinate appetite. St. John describes in vigorous terms how inordinate appetite blinds the soul and falsifies the appearance of things: "It is well known by experience that, when the will of a man is affectioned to one thing, he prizes it more than any other; although some other thing may be much better, he takes less pleasure in it" (*Ascent*, I, 5, 5). And again: "For he that is blinded by desire has this property, that, when he is set in the midst of truth and of that which is good for him, he can no more see it than if he were in darkness" (*Ascent*, I, 8, 7). Thus we are not concerned here with the true and ultimate essence and meaning and value of creatures—for as they come from the hands of God they are miraculous and their beauty indescribable (*Canticle*, V & XXIX)—but with the appearance and meaning and value conferred upon them by carnal man when he separates them from God, takes them at their face value and "compares them with God." This is why sense has to be entirely recreated, and to this end emptied of all its appetites and all the "remnants" that these have left behind in the soul, all its old ways of desiring and feeling (*Ascent*, I, 5; cf. *Maxims*, 98). And the only thing that can do this is true love, because this means an effort by the soul "to labour to detach and strip itself for God's sake of all that is not God" (*Ascent*, II, 5, 7), and again, because it "consists in having great detachment in suffering for the Beloved" (*Points of Love*, 6). Clearly these remarks are directed against distorted perception and inordinate appetite—the "old man" and all his likes—and they are absolute because they are seen in their connection with the ultimate end: St. John will later be more precise and detailed about them in connection with the various stages reached by the soul in its journey towards God.

2.

The first and essential effort that "beginners" have to make, is to detach themselves vigorously from the "likings of sense." We may take "sense" to mean the affectivity of the senses, with its powers—the bodily senses and the sensitive appetite—and its acts—its loves, desires, and delights. But St. John immediately makes a distinction between the natural appetites—which we may take to be the spontaneous movements of appetite—and the voluntary appetites. At this stage the former are not really dangerous and do not interfere with the spiritual life (in any case they are unavoidable) and when the will fights against them they become a means to spiritual progress (*Ascent*, I, 11 & 12). The latter, however, are a major obstacle. When the will consents to their spontaneous movements it forms a solid block with them, and it is this sensible affectivity-plus-freedom complex that St. John is almost entirely concerned with. That is why he speaks sometimes of the sensitive part in which all the appetites are housed (*Ascent*, I, 15), and sometimes of the will that accepts and moves them, as in the words, "Withhold . . . thy will from the indulgence of the desire" (*Ascent*, I, 6, 6; cf. I, 4; I, 5; I, 9; I, 10; I, 11). He is thus concerned both with this region of being—the senses—and the source of its value and meaning, which is the will. This complex he calls appetite, affection, liking—"the sensible spirit," in contrast to "the spirit which is purely spiritual" (*Ascent*, I, 6, 2).

Now, in this sense, liking is the source of all evil as soon as it becomes disordered and inordinate, i.e. as soon as it becomes a voluntary appetite for mortal sin, or venial sin, or any imperfection (*Ascent*, I, 11). The least habit of the smallest imperfection is an obstacle to union with God: no matter whether it is a thick rope or a slender thread, it hinders the soul and threatens to make it lose everything (*ibid.*). St. John insists that though only the appetite for mortal sin can totally deprive the soul of God (*Ascent*, I, 12), every inordinate voluntary appetite in its own way does the five essential kinds of damage—fatigues the soul, torments it, darkens it, soils it, and weakens it (*Ascent*, I, 6). The reason for this is that any inordinate voluntary appetite is strictly opposed to God (*Ascent*, I, 4) and its existence an insult to God: "He that will love some other thing together with God of a certainty makes little account of God, for he weighs in the balance against God that which, as we have said, is far distant from God" (*Ascent*, I, 5, 4). It is therefore necessary to divest oneself, empty oneself, strip oneself, of every inordinate liking and appetite, to tear one's will from the consent it gives, and make a brave resolution to serve God and imitate Christ and deny oneself for his sake (*Ascent*, I, 13), not omitting the tiniest liking or the least appetite.

But man is bound to find this impossible unless God comes to his aid and gives him a liking that drives the other one away, and thus gives the spirit the strength of renunciation. "For, in order to conquer all the desires and to deny itself the pleasures which it has in everything, and for which its love and affection are wont to enkindle the will that it may enjoy them, it would be necessary to experience another and a greater enkindling by another and a better love, which is that of its spouse, to the end that, having its pleasure set upon Him and deriving from Him its strength, it should have courage and constancy to deny itself all other things with ease" (*Ascent*, I, 14, 2). The mechanics of this transformation are explained in connection with visions, in a passage that can be applied generally (*Ascent*, II, 17). Since the soul is still weak and fleshly, God adapts himself to it and gives it the food for which it hungers and which it is capable of receiving: he perfects it according to the inner and outer senses, "communicating spirituality to it first of all through outward and palpable things, adapted to sense, on account of the soul's feebleness and incapacity." He incites it "to make use of good things which are natural"; and it begins to find happiness in sermons, in the mass, in bodily penance, meditation, holy talk. Then he perfects it by means of supernatural favours—visions, scents, words . . . So sense "is greatly confirmed in virtue and is withdrawn from a desire for evil things"—in short, it is detached, purified and gradually disposed with "order and with sweetness" towards a more spiritual union. To join these two opposite extremes, the soul and God, there is usually no other way: however imperfect and inchoate these graces may be they are necessary at this stage (*Ascent*, II, 7), and the soul must welcome them, without growing attached to them: "And, when thou comest to possess it wholly, thou must possess it without desiring anything" (*Ascent*, I, 13, 12).

What he says of sense St. John also says of the will, and hence of the affectivity of the senses. He made a long study of the joy of the will from this point of view, and the nerve of his argument is this. Joy comes from the possession of a good. Possession of any other good but God means wretchedness and danger. It is therefore necessary to empty oneself of every inner possession achieved by love before one can enter into the true joy that comes from the true possession of the true good. Freedom thus finds itself obliged to sacrifice one joy before it can be given another—it must sacrifice an appearance for truth, an illusion for reality, creature for Creator (*Max.*, 67). But this appearance, this illusion, is dreadfully solid and has a formidable power over fleshly man. St. John puts the case for renunciation by showing the havoc wrought by the voluntary appetites and the corresponding advantages of the stripping he describes. He supports his argument by the fact that man is made for the joy of God; that he is spontaneously drawn to lower kinds of joy; that he must die to these to rise to the first; and that he can only rise by stopping to seek them out and by looking for God instead. "We must not set our rejoicing upon any other thing than that which tends to the service of God" (*Ascent*, III, 18, 6). To forsake the present joy and to seek out, not future joy, but ways in which to worship and serve God—these are the two sacrifices that can alone lead into true joy.

But here the problem of the affectivity of the senses arises again, for the will can take its joy from sense as well as from spirit. At the beginning of the *Ascent* St. John had criticized the likings of the senses that were voluntarily accepted; now he criticizes the likings of the will relating to the senses. But this does not mean merely a change of emphasis; a profounder demand is made. In the first case the likings were connected with sin or imperfection; now they are likings that are good in themselves, and given by God himself, but which for this very reason are dangerous to carnal man: the will, more than ever, must purify sense. St. John has explained his mind on this point in three extremely valuable chapters (*Ascent*, III, 24-26). Here he discusses the joy that can be procured by the bodily senses, inner and outer; and the particular point he concerns himself with is the essential baseness of sense. Sense cannot know or understand God as he is, because it is of the body, whereas God is spiritual (*Ascent*, III, 24); so that to stop at sense means inevitably failing to find God. The only value of any joy of the senses therefore is as a means to rejoicing in God (*ibid.*). If as soon as the soul feels any such joy it immediately refers it to God, it can and should make use of it, "for then such things of sense subserve the end for which God created and gave them, which is that He should be the better loved and known because of them" (*Ascent*, III, 24, 5). But this "liberty of spirit" can only be reached after a severe purification; as far as beginners are concerned, such joys are always likely to prove a snare, paralyzing the soul, turning it away from God and focusing it on themselves. And the soul then falls into all the "harms" which St. John goes on to enumerate so relentlessly—obsession with the created and distaste for God, inner dispersion and the tyranny of desire, softness and cowardice and hardheartedness towards others, the blunting and corruption of the spiritual judgment, with the reason "as useless as a broken vessel."

It is therefore necessary for the soul to seek God alone, and to renounce all joys and likings, until "the animal life being mortified, (the soul) must be journeying to God" (*Ascent*, III, 26, 6). Then man is delivered, recollected, purified, and, receiving back a hundredfold, finds in the things of sense "the delight of delectable knowledge and contemplation of God" (26, 5) and God in all things: "such a man, being pure in heart, finds in all things a knowledge of God which is joyful and pleasant, chaste, pure, spiritual, glad and loving" (26, 6). Will has purified sense; here, as always, renunciation has been found to be the way to the fullness of joy.

3.

The soul does all it can, but its all is not enough. The impurity of sense is too deep, too far-reaching, too subtle, for human nature to be able to get rid of it even with the help of grace. But what man is unable to do, because he cannot get close enough even to see what is to be done, God himself will do; and this is the passive side of the night of the senses.[88] This is not the first passivity, which is intro-

[88] On this, cf. the just remarks by J. Paliard in *Saint Jean de la Croix et la Pensée contemporaine* (Tarascon, 1942), pp. 16-17.

duced by grace into every Christian soul; it is a second and very special kind, deriving from a new and sovereign initiative from God, who "prevents" our human initiative and changes the direction of our efforts. For beginners there is danger in the fact that the pleasure found in God is experienced by a soul still far from perfect. As the soul begins to be "converted to the service of God," the grace of God—"its loving mother"—"makes it to find spiritual milk, sweet and delectable, in all the things of God, without any labour of its own, and also great pleasure in spiritual exercises" (*Dark Night*, I, 1, 2). These likings are excellent graces; but their function is to detach the soul from worldly sweetnesses, to strengthen it in God and deliver it to God (*Dark Night*, I, 8). If the still unpurified soul desires these likings, and grows attached to them, it is stopping on its way: and to prevent it from doing this, God deprives it of the favours with which he formerly overloaded it (*Dark Night*, I, 1). St. John bases his observations on the evidence supplied by mortal sins. Here we can confine ourselves to his example of spiritual gluttony (*Dark Night*, I, 6). Gluttonous souls find divine sweetness in their spiritual exercises, and become so enamoured of them that they end by being enslaved by them. The result is that they lose the essential thing: they weaken themselves with fasts, and do their best to kill themselves with penances—but fail in reason and temperance; they ignore advice, or argue with their director and refuse to give way—and so fail in obedience; they seek their own pleasure gluttonously, avidly, shamelessly, in communion and prayer—and so fail in the fear of God; and, being feeble and cowardly when faced with the need for real mortification, they fail in generosity of heart. Such is the wretchedness of these beginners, caught up in their own puerility, weakness, and impurity. "A low way of loving, a low style, reflecting very accurately their self-love and liking"—such are the things from which God wills to deliver them through the dark night.

He will dry up the source, plunge the soul in darkness, wean it "from the breasts of those sweetnesses and pleasures," give it "pure aridities and inward darkness" (*Dark Night*, I, 7, 5), make it eat crusts, and gradually change the powers of sense to spirit. In other words, if affectivity means love, desire, and delight, God is to suppress all feeling of love, take away all delight, and put emptiness in their place. As for the desire, that is bound to remain in any spirit that goes on loving God, but as it is weaned at its root (in love) and in its flowering (in delight), it becomes an unsatiable hunger and thirst, a frightful torment. If this void continues, the frustrated desire is liable to turn to disgust and plunge the soul back into the delights of sense. The whole question then becomes whether the spirit will hold out against the hungering senses. There is now no sweetness in sense or spirit (*Dark Night*, I, 9), and the spirit will only hold out if God gives it the strength and courage to operate (*Dark Night*, I, 9) and that dry, dark contemplation which is beginning to take place within it without its knowing it. So man enters upon "the first purgation . . . bitter and terrible to sense" (*Dark Night*, I, 8, 2). But if the soul yields and holds, if it knows the joy of being led and encouraged, it enters into a new world—sees its own wretchedness and vileness and the greatness and excellence of God, and slowly attains to the purity of love, acting "for God's sake alone" (*Dark Night*, I, 13, 1). Then God gives it its reward, and for a time "it goes about the things of God with much greater freedom and satisfaction of the soul, and with more abundant and inward delight than it did at the beginning" (*Dark Night*, II, 1, 1).

4.

It might seem that by now the sensibility had been re-created and purified and made transparent to the light of God; but such is not by any means the case. One hurdle has been surmounted, but man is still on his journey, still spiritually a child (*Dark Night*, II, 3), and the senses are still not really purified—because the spirit has not been purified. For man is one, sense and spirit are bound together in the unity of the person (*Dark Night*, II, 1), and as the soul controls the body, so the spirit confers its own value and purity on the senses. For every religious attitude is rooted in the spirit, and therefore "all the imperfections and disorders of the sensual part have their strength and root in the spirit, where all habits, both good and bad, are brought into subjection" (*Dark Night*, II, 3, 1).

Thus the situation is this: through the two nights of sense a certain purification of the spirit has already begun—it has been purified itself in its connection with the senses, but it has not been purified in itself, in its connection with God. Contrariwise, the senses are already purified in themselves, but they are not yet purified in their rootedness in the spirit. Consequently, so long as the spirit is not directly purified, the roots of the impurities and imperfections of the senses, far from being extirpated, have not even been touched, and so the purification of the senses remains extrinsic and superficial—coming from outside, its real inwardness has not been reached; coming from below, the appetite has only been mortified with regard to its objects and not with regard to its source. Thus all that has been effected so far is a certain adaptation of sense to spirit: the senses have been relieved of their grosser impurities, they find the spirit less repugnant, and have become "in a certain way united and brought into agreement" (*Dark Night*, II, 3, 1). But because all this remains extrinsic, the night of the senses "may and should be called a kind of correction and restraint of the desire rather than purgation" (*Dark Night*, II, 3, 1). In short, the senses have been tamed, not transfigured; so that what remains is for sense and spirit, "in a certain way united," to be purified together through the purification of the spirit—"the purgation which is effective for sense coming upon that of the spirit begins" (*Dark Night*, II, 3, 1)—and this heralds the "horrible" night.

Now the actual root of the impurity, as insisted on by St. John, seems to lie in the fact that the powers, appetites, acts, and likings are human realities. This means that in the first place they relate to man, and so are infinitely remote from God, too feeble to attain to God in truth, desiring and operating and tasting God in a low fashion; and secondly that they relate to the old man (*Dark Night*, II, 16) marked by original sin and all subsequent individual sins, ensnared by the traces and remnants of sin and so acting in an impure way. These two aspects are combined in every spiritual activity: St. John, it must be repeated, is concerned with this complex all the time[89]—and it is the violent contrast between this low

[89] On this delicate point, see the very just account by Rev. Fr. Lucien Marie, *À la recherche d'une structure* (*Études carmélitaines*, 1938, II, pp. 264 *et seq.*). "When (St. John) attacks the soul's 'natural' way of acting, he means the concrete nature, the fallen nature which the author of the *Imitation* criticised so harshly" (p. 264). Cf. the quotations on p. 276. The "old man" who appears in the *Dark Night*, II, 16, is perfectly explained in the *Living Flame*, II, 6, with reference to a classic passage from St. Paul. The Rev. Father refers to "two purifications, the one within the other" (p. 271); perhaps we should speak of two aspects of a single purification, because it is the spirit in its dynamic unity that is involved, and it is its impure baseness that has to be eliminated.

and impure reality, and the absolute—ontological and spiritual—transcendence of God, that makes all this purification necessary (*Max.*, 38-39).

Since it is necessary to leave behind the "ordinary and common" mode of feeling before one can rise to the "Divine sense, which is a stranger and an alien to all human ways," we have to be tragically "begotten anew" in suffering and emptiness and absolute strangeness (*Dark Night*, II, 9). Since the inclinations of the senses (*Dark Night*, II, 14) are "vile," their operations "base," and their abilities "short," and all their actions because of their "uncleanness" and "clumsiness" (*Dark Night*, II, 16) hinder the reception of spiritual goods, therefore all this has to cease and all these powers have to become purely receptive. Since we receive according to what we are, and our faculties and desires are "base, impure and wholly unnatural," and can only receive "things supernatural and divine . . . after a base and a natural manner," therefore they have to allow God to prevent their acts and operations, so as to lose "their own manner, which is human and base," and acquire "purity . . . strength . . . capacity to receive and taste things that are supernatural after the manner of those things, which manner is Divine," "receive, feel and taste that which is Divine and supernatural after a sublime and lofty manner" (*Dark Night, II*, 16, 4). "A sublime and lofty manner"—that is to say, not in their low human way, but in the marvellous divine way that alone is fitting. Height and depth have a metaphysical and spiritual value for St. John: they symbolize the dimensions in which the mystery of the Sacred exists. But this re-creation is a terrible thing, and the soul stands bewildered, confused, lost, like a traveller in a foreign land (*Dark Night*, II, 16).

And so man enters into the horrible night; and there is darkness and torment, and the purification seems like destruction and annihilation—enough to make anyone howl like Job and moan like David's dogs (*Dark Night*, II, 9)—and yet at the same time there is the longing for God, the fire of love, the wound of love. There is no need to describe this again here, but we do need to ask what happens to the affectivity of the senses when the night of the spirit is being thus endured. The *Night* says nothing about it: it is unfinished. But the *Spiritual Canticle* can tell us.[90] From the

[90] There is no need here to attempt to settle the question of the relative position of the *Spiritual Canticle* with regard to the *Ascent* and the *Dark Night:*

plethora of its images let us take three particularly significant ones. The first is the image of the old wine and the new (16). New lovers are like new wine, "for the fermentations of the wine of their love take place wholly without, in their senses," and they are governed by them; old lovers are like old wine: purified and "delivered from the fermentations" of the senses, they take the divine sweetness "in the substance and savour of the spirit and truth of action." The boiling of the senses is over: this is the first stage. Next there is the analogy of the flock—abandoned for the sake of a higher work, the work of love (18-20). The imperfect soul is inhabited by a flock of likings, appetites, imperfections, but, when it is purified, it "feels itself to be free from all these childish likes and dislikes and follies, which it pursued" (17, 14). And because its spirit goes wholly to God, its body, senses and powers go thither too: they are rectified to such a point that even in their first movements they usually tend to operate in God and for God; all their care and endeavour is devoted to the service of God, and the movements—whether active or passive—of the senses, as well as of the mind, always cause the soul "ever greater love and greater delight in God" (19, 8). The senses have recovered their divine spontaneity as given to them by God in the state of original innocence and again in baptism.

There remains the extraordinary stanza 39, the last stanza in the *Canticle*, in which St. John sings the praises of the transfiguration of the sensibility. Here the whole glorious movement ends with passages of the most exquisite feeling. Here, unfortunately, we must make some attempt to analyze these concluding pages. The sensibility, pacified and purified, subject to and united with the spirit, is "reformed and purified in conformity with the spiritual part." It has, so to speak, moved out of one world and into another. Detached from creatures, remote from them and a stranger to them, "they cannot move it by their sweetness to desire them, nor by their wretchedness and misery to dislike and be troubled by them." The sensibility is now no longer sensitive from below, but only from above—"the mouth of desire must be opened towards heaven" (*Letter* V). Consequently the appetites, conformed to the inner spirit and lost in recollection with God, have their own share of enjoyment in the

---

it is quite self-sufficient. (To the discussion should be added the remarks by J. Vilnet in *Bible et Mystique chez saint Jean de la Croix* (Paris, 1950), pp. 179-183). The point is that it supplies the conclusion we are looking for.

goods of the spirit: the sensibility "with its sensual faculties and natural forces is recollected and has participation and fruition, after its manner, of the spiritual grandeurs which God is communicating to the spirit." "After its manner": St. John never relaxes. The senses are not in themselves capable of spiritual goods, but when they are united to the spirit they receive a "backwash" that fills them with joy and attracts them towards interior recollection, "wherein the soul is drinking of spiritual blessings." In this way, the bodily powers and senses "taste . . . of the overflowing which is communicated from the soul to them."[91] It is at once the greatness and the limitation of the senses that they are not spirit but can share in things spiritual, so that the whole man is steeped in divine goods. It is worth noting, from our present point of view, that the last passage from the Bible quoted by St. John in the *Spiritual Canticle* is the verse from Psalm lxxxiii: "My spirit and my flesh have rejoiced in the living God."

A study as brief as the foregoing hardly allows of a conclusion. I shall therefore end by simply making three observations.

In the first place, we must not let ourselves be misled by the simplicity of St. John's language. His vocabulary does not contain any of the tormented, abysmal features that have been used by some speculative mystics in their attempt to convey their experience. But through the severity of his thought and the demands he makes for spiritual effort there shines an extraordinary sense of God's transcendence. Man is separated from God by the two abysses of finitude and sin. God is enthroned above in his utter strangeness and holiness; man exists below, short-lived, vile, sinful. So long as both remain as they are, there can be no union between them; hence everything that is impure—sin, and all that is left behind by sin—and all that is low—all human ways of thinking and loving and acting

[91] Cf. the *Living Flame*, II, 20: "And of this good which comes to the soul a part sometimes overflows into the body through the union of the spirit, and this is enjoyed by all the substance of sense and all the members of the body and the very marrow and bones, not as feebly as is usually the case, but with a feeling of great delight and glory, which is felt even in the remotest joints of the feet and hands. And the body feels such glory in the glory of the soul that it magnifies God after its own manner, perceiving that He is in its very bones, even as David said: All my bones shall say, 'God, who is like unto Thee?' And since all that can be said concerning this matter is less than the truth, it suffices to say of the bodily experience, as of the spiritual, that it savours of eternal life."

—has to be destroyed at its root, before the soul can be changed from "old" to "new," can be transformed and literally deified.

But the ontological lowness of the senses—their status as psycho-organic affectivity—cannot be gainsaid; and this means that they are doubly impotent—first, because of their inability to purify themselves, so that they need to be purified by the spirit, and secondly because of their inability to share as they are in themselves in any of God's goods, so that they need to derive their participation from the spirit. The great fact behind St. John's severity is that everything below the spirit is incapable of God. Below the level of spirit the ontological limits are absolute: only on the level of spirit can there be any consideration of the problem of the infinite "elevation" of any being whilst it retains its own ontological status. Despite its finitude, and because it is the image of God, the spirit possesses the kind of infinity and family-likeness with God that enables it to be truly deified and to enter into the conversation with God that is "addressed by pure spirit to pure spirit" (*Dark Night*, II, 17, 4). But however closely involved with spirit the affectivity of the senses may be in the unity of human nature, it exists below this level and can never get beyond it—the senses having no "proportionate capacity for this, either in this life or in the next" (*Spiritual Canticle*, 39). They are too "low" and God is too "high."

This doctrine does not lead to the destruction of man; on the contrary, it means the exaltation of man in God. There is great humanity in St. John of the Cross. In his eyes man is one, and the senses are an integral part of man's unity: man is a composite, and the senses are one of his component principles on the level of conscious appetency: there can be no transfiguration of man unless the senses have a part in it corresponding to the part they play in human nature and their openness to God. That is why St. John establishes such a close connection between the senses and spiritual freedom; why he integrates the purification of the one with the development of the other; and why he is able to describe so magnificently the growth of this spiritual freedom, which in its highest form is identical with love itself, and which as it rises takes the senses with it. Since the night is both active and passive, freedom must work as hard as it possibly can to purify the soul and deliver it up to the all-consuming flame of God; so that according to all the dimensions of its mystery, as a power that can both conquer and receive, it may give man to God. The senses are so immanent within the spirit that their impurity can only disappear when the centre of the spirit is absolutely pure.

Conversely, when the spirit has been transformed, the senses share in the transfiguration. For the senses too have been made by God and for God; and St. John has given incomparable expression to the joy of the senses united to the spirit and hence to God. We are here at the opposite pole from any sort of Quietism: the primary value is a constructive spiritual freedom—St. John has no contempt for the things of sense and does not condemn the senses for what they are in themselves. But because unpurified sense provides one of the major difficulties of the spiritual life, St. John subjects its impurities to a pitiless analysis, so that he can ultimately restore it to its proper place and position in the pure praise of God. St. John's humanity, indeed, is part and parcel of his tremendous catholicity: for him the whole man—which means his entire spirit, and all his senses, down to their most fundamental impulses—must be delivered over to Christ, so that ultimately all together may be changed into divine operations (*Living Flame*, II, 6).

Lastly, this tremendous adventure of the spirit is from beginning to end a drama of death and resurrection in Christ. St. John does not himself exploit "Pascal's theme," as we should call it today, but he lives at the heart of the same mystery. Again and again he says that the end of purification is "the uprightness and cleanness" that God gave the soul in "the estate of original righteousness"; but he also adds "or on the day of her baptism" (*Spiritual Canticle*, 37, 1). This is a highly intentional transposition of the mystical journey into a Christological journey. Our real original justice comes through baptism; mystical transformation only serves to reveal and rediscover all its marvellous fullness. Baptism inaugurates the mystery of Christ within us, and the whole mystical life is simply a development of this. That is why on earth every death is the way to a resurrection. The senses must die to their fleshly pleasures, but to be resurrected to spiritual pleasures; die to spiritual pleasures, but to be born to the pleasure that is to be found in God; die even to this, but to be resuscitated through a new upsurge of the spirit transformed by love. Dying to be reborn is the unchanging law of spiritual ascension: mortify yourselves, says St. John of the Cross, "if perchance there is still aught left in you that has yet to die and that impedes the interior resurrection of the spirit" (*Letter* V).

Finally, this whole drama of death and resurrection simply emulates and realizes within us the essential movement of the imitation of Christ, which governs the mystical life as it governs the Christian life; and we realize that in one single movement this process ends with the entry—objectively—into the "lofty caverns" of the mystery of Christ (*Spiritual Canticle*, 37, 3) and—subjectively—"into the centre of its spirit, which is perfect life in Christ" (*Living Flame*, III, 2).

CHAPTER ELEVEN

The Christian Experience an Experience within Faith

1. *Living Faith as the Starting-Point of the Experience*

THE living principle of the full Christian experience is the "faith that works by charity." Whether it is informed or uninformed, faith always keeps its essence and its ontological structure. Even when it is uninformed it is a gift from God; it cannot be a "bad habit," and its "uninformedness" is not part of its essence (II. II, 4, c, & 1^m, 2^m, 4^m; *De Ver.*, 14, 7). But if faith is envisaged in its actual state, one has to add to its essence the concrete position of the subject with regard to the Last End; and this leads to considerable differences between the two states of faith.

Uninformed faith, in so far as it is faith, is a magnificent grace, left to the sinner by a merciful God, and keeping him Christian.[1] But, in so far as it is uninformed, it means sin and the absence of charity, this being the true cause of its "uninformedness." In this case the act of faith cannot respond fully to all the demands of its being, because its root in the will is an imperfect love, and the will does not will as it should (I. II, 65, 4); it becomes "an imperfect act, which awaits its perfection by charity" (*De Ver.*, 14, 5, 7^m); it does not fulfil the demands made by its function as a means to salvation—the just man lives by faith—for it is the act of a dead faith, of no effect towards salvation, and in this state faith itself only exists "in a sort of inchoate state."[2] The act of informed faith is thus the

[1] "If anyone shall say . . . that he who has faith without charity is not a Christian, let him be anathema."—*Conc. Trid.*, sess. vi, can. 28.

[2] I. II, 65, 4, c: Cf. *Supplem.*, I, 3, c: The uninformed habit becomes an informed habit; the act of uninformed faith does not become an act of informed faith.

only perfect act of faith; in Bossuet's words, the act of faith is then in its "natural state," whereas previously it had been in a "violent state."[3] We must now try to discover what exactly faith and charity are, in an informed faith.

Faith provides charity with its object. This is a law: "the last end must of necessity be present to the intellect before it is present to the will" (II. II, 4, 7, c). A movement of faith is thus implied in every movement of the soul towards God (*De Ver.*, 28, 4, 9^m), and charity can only love the intelligible "divine good," which the supernaturalized intellect alone can apprehend and propose as the object of love. It therefore "loves what is affirmed by faith" through what is enunciated, and surrenders to it (II. II, 24, 1, c & 1^m); and, since faith heals and elevates the intellect, it must be said that charity cannot come into existence without this radical rectification of the intellect, for "the will cannot tend to God with perfect love, unless the intellect possesses right faith about him" (II. II, 4, 7, 5^m).

Furthermore, charity means friendship with God. And this is such an extraordinary, superhuman phenomenon, that before one can accept it as a fact, and consent to it, and give one's belief to it, one needs to be absolutely convinced that it is true, and to be able to hope that such friendship is possible to the wretched creature that one knows oneself to be. Thus at the root of charity there must exist faith, by which one can "believe in this fellowship and colloquy with God, and . . . hope to attain to this fellowship" (I. II, 65, 5, c). Lastly, faith imposes its own conditions upon charity. The First Truth is both the Object and the End of faith, and the end of faith—the divine Good—is the object of charity. But this object is grasped through the indestructible veil of faith—"under the aspect of something unseen" (II. II, 4, 1, c)—and though everything in faith centres upon Jesus Christ, it is the Jesus Christ whom "having not seen" we love (cf. I Peter i, 8). Charity is thus enveloped in the obscurity proper to love, and it is within a kind of luminous cloud that it develops and comes to merit eternal life. Faith is thus the permanent foundation,[4] the necessary condition, the appropriate environment, of the charity of the Christian pilgrim.

[3] *États d'Oraison, Second Traité*, ch. liv (ed. Lévesque, Paris, 1897), p. 143.

[4] At least partially, as a basic reality and in accordance with the perfection that it always involves (II. II, 4, 7, 4^m; cf. I. II; cf. also *De Spe*, 4, 14^m).

Charity, in return, links faith with God as the Last End. Having faith means believing in God as one who reveals himself, one who gives testimony of himself, one who offers himself as the End that brings beatitude—and it is in this last respect that charity completes faith (*De Ver.*, 28, 4, 6^{m}). As something by itself and apart from charity, uninformed faith implies a certain bond with the Last End, a bond formed by imperfect love—the bond of hope. It implies a certain orientation towards the Last End, arising from imperfect and ineffectual desire, indeed according to the actual imperfection of the love. Consequently, being enclosed in spite of itself within this circle, uninformed faith leaves us cut off from God our Last End and subject to the distance appropriate to the virtues of the Christian pilgrim, who believes in God without seeing him and desires him without possessing him.[5] By uninformed faith and hope man is orientated towards the Last End remotely, but not immediately, and hence not effectively. The grace of faith as it is in itself without charity is on the one hand received fully in the intellect, and "embryonically" (*De Ver.*, 14, 77, 6^{m}) in the will; but on the other hand it is blocked in the will because the will has not been "decentralized" from itself by any all-compelling love, and so refuses to give and receive fully. Thus there is no direct contact with the End, and no real possession of it, and hence no effective orientation towards it: "due ordination to the last end is lacking" (II. II, 23, 7, 1^{m}).

When charity enters into the soul it transforms the subject: it realizes "that spiritual union, whereby we are transformed with a view to the end"—in a word, "the assimilation to the end by love" (I. II, 3, c & 3^{m}; cf. II. II, 4, 4, 4^{m}). Consequently, though charity does not lead to seeing, and does not abolish the intellectual distance from the object (that would mean abolishing faith), it does lead to possession, and by a movement of grace that the intellect is unable to grasp it abolishes the affective distance from the end;[6] it makes the Last End immanent in the will by "decentralizing" man from self so that he may deliver himself up to God completely. By this decisive fulfilment of the will the gap is bridged, the proper ordina-

[5] Faith and hope "in their very nature, imply a certain distance from the object: since faith is of what is not seen, and hope is of what is not possessed" (I. II, 66, 6, c).

[6] "Faith . . . only shows the object . . . this appetitive movement towards its object surpasses human knowledge" (I. II, 66, 6, 1^{m}; cf. II. II, 23, 6, 3^{m}).

tion to the end is realized, and in accordance with the *Credere in Deum* the faith is vivified from within and becomes a means to justification, unification, and new life itself, through the charity by which it is informed.

Here then is faith, strengthened in its most inward movement. Since it gives its full assent to the Word of God, it is a magnificent act of homage; but when the will becomes perfectly obedient to God through charity, the assent itself becomes involved in this firmly-based, effective, infallible movement towards the Last End (II. II, 4, 5, c), and as the intellect has given its assent so that it may reach the Last End (*ibid.*), this assent of the intellect finds itself strengthened too.[7] In the order of action, indeed, in which we are involved by the movement towards the end, the perspective is reversed, and what was accidental with respect to the essence of faith becomes essential to its being as a theological virtue (*De Ver.*, 14, 6, 1^{m}): the whole element of knowledge now appears as "a kind of matter" (*De Ver.*, 14, 5, c) that charity is to inform; and as the object of faith does not carry the intellect along by its own force, but in accordance with the movement of the will, so that the end has primacy over the object (*De Ver.*, 14, 2, 12^{m}), therefore, when charity does in fact enter into it, "its own perfection overflows, so to speak, upon the intellect" and thence "not only upon the act of faith" but "upon faith itself" (*De Ver.*, 15, 5, 9^{m}), and thus charity completes the orientation of faith and realizes its finality (II. II, 4, 3, c). Faith has then become the real foundation of the spiritual life, because it has become its basis, and this basis is linked with all the other virtues by charity, *vinculum perfectionis* (II. II, 4, 7, 4^{m}).

Finally, charity makes faith active. It would be a mistake, of course, to imagine that faith is never active on its own account. By its own power it believes and adheres to and pays homage to God; it is stronger than sin; it can lead to confession and the defence of truth; it is a way of bearing witness—all because it is a divine power within man, and the sinner a fragmented being in whom partial health, and what are separately right orientations of mind and act, can exist alongside a fundamental orientation that is misdirected. Uninformed faith can even be so strong—in an unbaptized convert, for instance—that it can achieve the level of martyrdom, through which the mercy

[7] "Thus when anyone has been led by hope to charity, then he also hopes more perfectly, fears more purely, just as he believes more firmly" (*De Spe*, 3, 1^{m}).

of God transforms it into a living, justifying faith.[8] Nevertheless, faith only comes into full activity through charity. In the order of activity it is the will that lies behind all human acts, and love that produces all the movements of the soul. In the order of supernatural activity it is the inclination of grace towards the Last End—i.e., charity—that directs all the supernatural acts towards their one end. It carries them along in its royal progress—effectively, because it proceeds from a real union with the end; universally, because it loves God above all things, and carries all else towards its proper end; infinitely, because it is a participation in infinite charity (II. II, 14, 7, c) and its object infinitely lovable, and this invasion of the soul by charity enlarges its capacity for love. And the first thing that is thus carried along is faith.

In the first place, since charity is founded upon faith, and enlightened and governed by faith, and unfolds into faith, it is indissolubly linked with faith and cannot avoid carrying it along with it. But also, the same thing is called for by the greatness of faith itself. Being rooted in the intellect, and its primary function being contemplation, faith is not an immediate principle of action, but only a remote occasion of activity, and it is thrown into action by the mediation of love (*De Ver.*, 14, c); but faith calls and clamours joyfully to be thus driven, for it adheres to the First Truth, "which is the end of all our desires and actions" (Augustine, quoted in II. II, 4, 2, 3^m). Hence faith and charity advance together towards the conquest of the divine Good, towards communion with the Beloved, bringing along in their wake the whole company of virtues and all human activity. The theological virtues come first. As St. Thomas is never tired of repeating, man is situated between God and the world, and he has to choose, i.e. both opt for and at the same time exclude: he can only realize himself through these twin processes of adherence and refusal. Sin means "despising God and adhering to a changing good"; merit means "despising the created and adhering to God as one's end." But the end is a better thing than the means, and when man despises the world and adheres to God, it is the adherence that in the first place gives the act its value and makes it meritorious. "And so these, namely the theological, virtues whereby he adheres

[8] Cf. the general attitude adopted by theologians towards the baptism of blood, for which the requisite condition is not necessarily contrition but merely supernatural attrition.

to God in himself, are greater than the moral virtues, whereby he holds in contempt some earthly thing in order to adhere to God" (II. II, 104, 3, c). First in dignity, in value, in power, the theological virtues are life, self-giving, animating all its functions. And this is true in a special way of living faith, as St. Augustine, echoing St. Paul and St. John, says: "I came that they might have life—i.e., the faith that works through charity."[9]

Thus, taken in their concrete activity, faith and charity are intrinsic to each other, like intellect and will,[10] but to a quite extraordinary degree. Charity takes its object from faith, is based upon faith, is guided by the light of faith, unfolds in the luminous darkness which is faith's condition of existence here on earth. Faith in return receives from charity its effective movement towards the Last End, its real object, and is impelled forward by charity, the highest of all God's graces; and the divine sap, rising from its root in the will, enlivens and transfigures it from within.

They thus together form a single principle of action: "faith that worketh by charity" (Gal. v, 6). St. Leo the Great has described this inner reciprocity in a splendid passage: "Charity gives faith its vigour and faith gives charity its strength. Consequently the true reality and fruition of each are realized when they remain indissolubly connected. But when they are no longer together they find themselves lacking together, for they are a source of light and help to each other,[11] and ever shall be, until the longing felt by belief shall find its fulfilment in seeing, and that which now cannot be loved without faith or believed without love shall be seen and loved unchangingly. Since, as the Apostle says, in Christ Jesus what matters is the faith that works by charity, therefore let us strive to have both faith and charity, which are the two wings whereby purity of spirit may fly up magnificently to merit and see God, no longer weighed down by the burden of fleshly cares. For he who said, 'Without faith it is impossible to please God,' also said, 'And if I

[9] *Tractatus in Joannem*, 45, 15; P.L., 35, 1727.

[10] "The will . . . is in the reason: wherefore charity is not excluded from the reason through being in the will." It can therefore be said that "Charity is in the reason by a certain kinship of will to the reason" (II. II, 24, 1, 2^{m}).

[11] To this may be applied St. Thomas's discerning remarks on a similar saying of St. Gregory's: "Its reference is to faith, hope and charity as virtues" (*De Spe*, 3, 8^{m}).

should have all faith, so that I could remove mountains, and have not charity, I am nothing.' Therefore, that the divine mysteries of the paschal sacrament may be received with the submission that is due to them, may these two things, in which is gathered together all the teaching of the commandments, be desired with the utmost ardour, that through them each one of the faithful may become a living sacrifice and a temple of God. May faith endeavour to hope what it believes, and charity to make what it loves propitious to itself; for both are proper to him who loves and him who believes."[12]

To be precise, the connection between the two virtues is here twofold. There is an objective connection, because in the theological virtues object and end coincide (II. II, 4, 1, c): the First Truth, the object of faith, is also the Last End, the object of charity, and thus the object of faith is essentially (*per se*) the object of divine beatitude (II. II, 4, 3, c). Faith only knows and adheres to its object with a view to love and union (I. II, 62, 4, c), and the act of faith is ordained, as though to its end, to the object of charity too—the divine Good (II. II, 4, 3, c)—so that faith begins and ends in love (*De Ver.*, 14, 2, 10^{m}). There is also a subjective connection; for the motive behind the assent of faith is not the evident truth, but love of the end, and in a living faith the assent is the result of charity: because the Truth is my beatitude, and because I love and desire it, I adhere to it fully and absolutely. The greater the love, and the more it opens out to the grace that brings it into being, the more firm and decisive becomes the movement that fixes the intellect, and the more firm, solid and certain becomes the assent. Virtue, act and object form a joint harmony: the complex unity of the act reflects the nature and concrete conditions of the object proposed. From both the objective and the subjective points of view faith and charity unite to form in concrete fact one single living force. And that is why for St. Thomas the essential thing about the "New Law" inscribed on the heart of the Christian is the grace of the Holy Spirit, which consists in—and expresses itself in—faith working by charity (I. II, 108, 1, c). Here we are at the very heart of the Christian experience: we have reached its main root, which is neither faith nor charity but "faith working by charity."

[12] *Sermo* 45, P.L., 54, 289-290.

2. *The Object of the Experience in Faith*

The object of the Christian experience is God, and communion with God.

To the question, what is it that essentially appertains to faith, the seeing of which will bring us absolute bliss, St. Thomas replies that two mysteries are involved: "the hidden reality of the Godhead, the vision of which gives us bliss; and the mystery of Christ's humanity, by which we have access to the glory of sons of God" (II. II, 1, 8, c). I have already discussed the mystery of Mediation; now I must say something about the ultimate mystery—the actual secret of the Divinity. He whom sight will reveal to us, with whom we shall be enabled to communicate through faith, is the true living God, the one true God, the God who is holy, who is Spirit and Love, the One God in the Trinity of Persons.

This God is above all else a God hidden in mystery—a God who would not tell Moses his name, who lives in light inaccessible, whom no man hath seen and lived because his absolute holiness and the unbearable splendour of his glory separate him from all created sinful being. But at the same time he is a God who longs for human beings from their deepest impulses to their highest aspirations, a God who himself crossed the abyss and chose friends for himself from amongst men, the God of Abraham, Isaac, and Jacob, who spoke to Moses as with a friend, whose tenderness it was granted to Osee to know and sing, and with whom Jeremias had such shattering conversation. A God who is awful and yet invincibly attractive, remote and at the same time familiar: such is the first aspect of his mystery.

But the further Revelation develops and approaches towards its culmination, the more transcendent and at the same time the more immanent appears this God. More transcendent than ever, because this God who creates all things by his Word, who raises and transforms man through his Spirit, and inspires and nourishes him with his Wisdom, this one God is Father, Son, and Holy Ghost; and his unity and his plurality are both equally transcendent, his Unity beyond all solitude, his Trinity beyond number, and the reciprocal Inwardness of his Unity and Trinity utterly beyond us. There is only one way of approaching God, and that is to know that one does not know him; the more he is known as unknown, the higher becomes the knowledge that we have of him (cf. II. II, 8, 7, c, and *Contra Gent.*, 1, 5, etc.). At the same time, he becomes more immanent than ever. The Trinity adds to the mystery of unity the mystery of a society of Persons, and indeed these Persons love us, save us and bring us into communion with them. Enclosed within their own inviolable intimacy, the Three "come" and make us their Temple; they dwell within us, and we within them. We become their dwelling-place because they give themselves to us as the living principle and object of our knowledge and love; they become our dwelling-place because the whole movement of our knowledge and love causes us to adhere to them, relates us to them, plunges us into them as in an infinite ocean of Divinity. The intimacy of God the Trinity remains absolute and inviolable, because we are utterly unable to enter into the pure activity, beyond all movement, by which the Father engenders his Son, and Father and Son breathe forth the Spirit, and the Three are posited together and together given to each other, their inwardness to each other and their distinction from each other both being equally perfect. And yet by the mediation of Christ we are taken up into their life; and through the Son, in the Spirit, we have access to the Father—we enter into society and communion with God.

The relationship uniting us to God is therefore one of love and adoration—the adoration of love. God separates and is separate, because he is "elevated unspeakably" above man, and we have to see the mystery of his plenitude, his riches, his absolute self-sufficiency, against the other mystery of our nothingness, our poverty, our utter dependence—see ourselves as "dust and ashes" at the feet of the "living God." Furthermore, God condemns sin and forgives the sinner: he is the Holy One who consumes, and the Saviour who justifies and gives life; and man has to recognize his sin and damnation, and die to his sinful being, so that he may be reborn, reconciled and transfigured, in newness of life. Finally, God unites man to himself in a marriage beyond flesh and blood. And man's love is all the truer and deeper, as he is more conscious of and receptive to the infinite distance, both ontological and spiritual, that separates him from God; all the more pure, the more his worshipping in spirit and in truth becomes the inner law of his activity.

Faith tends through the Word of God to God himself; through the rising movement of grace that inclines it towards God, charity unites itself to God himself. This communion with God brings flashes of enlightenment and reveals new sources of attraction, develops and becomes enriched with all the new spiritual movements that are aroused by grace and tend towards God and unite with him. And as they form part of a living communion with God, there comes a knowledge of the gifts of God; and this is a further object of the Christian experience.

St. Thomas touches upon this problem frequently, and his remarks are extremely valuable. He starts from two points. First there is what is strictly speaking a fact of metaphysics, which theology cannot deny: "It is requisite for man's perfection that he should know himself" (II. II, 132, 1, 3^m); and then a passage from St. Paul (I Cor. ii, 12) that allows him to move from this metaphysical necessity to the life of faith: "We have received . . . the Spirit that is of God; that we may know the things that are given us from God." St. Thomas comments on this passage: "It may be taken to mean that the Spirit of God is given to the saints that they may know the spiritual gifts unknown to those who do not possess the Spirit," according to the words of the Apocalypse, "To him that overcometh I will give the hidden manna."[13] St. Thomas applies these words to the Pauline theme of the *gloriatio*, the good and bad ways of glorifying oneself. And he shows, first, that "it is not a sin to know and approve one's own good" (II. II, 132, 1, c); next, that "everyone should glory in the Lord in the goods that God has given him, and no others" (*in II Cor.*, 5, lect. 2, 6); and, finally, that "if anyone glories in any of God's gifts as in something received from God, this is 'good glory,' because by so doing he is glorying in God; whereas if a gift is gloried in as coming from oneself, this is a bad way of glorying" (*in II Cor.*, 12, lect. 2, 5). St. Thomas can come down to a more subtle, more human level: "It is requisite for man's perfection that he should know himself, but not that he should be known by others." Nevertheless, though this second knowledge may not be desirable in itself, it can become so if it is useful, either so that men may glorify God and thus make progress in the good, or "in order that man, knowing by the testimony of others' praise

[13] *In I Cor.*, 2, lect. 2, 2nd interpretation.

the good which is in him, may himself strive to persevere therein and to become better" (II. II, 132, 1, 3^m^). The same teaching applies to the affective knowledge—i.e., experience—of the sweetness of God: we are indeed told by Scripture to desire it and achieve it: "Taste and see that the Lord is sweet" (II. II, 97, 2, 2^m^); and one of the bad things about pride is precisely the fact that it centres us upon ourselves and prevents any experience of this sweetness of God (II. II, 162, 3, 1^m^).

Lastly, speaking of humility, St. Thomas distinguishes between the value of what there is in us that comes from God, and the worthlessness of what comes from ourselves. He reminds us that humility includes reverence for God, and goes on, "Humility does not require a man to subject what he has of God's to that which may seem to be of God's in another. For those who have a share of God's gifts know that they have them, according to I Cor., 12: that we may know the things that are given us from God. Wherefore without prejudice to humility they may set the gifts they have received from God above those that others appear to have received from him" (II. II, 161, 3, c). Thus man should know himself, and when God loads him with gifts—which in the Christian's eyes he is always doing—he should recognize that he is being thus favoured, and do this with a kind of recognition that is not merely notional and abstract, but affective, practical and concrete; this being the conscious presence of oneself to oneself, one's existing and acting utterly suffused by the grace of God. The object of the experience is therefore both the God whom the Christian knows through the truths of faith and loves through the impulse of charity, and the actual mystery and fullness and movement of this life of God within him, which he can perceive and rediscover each day in its own intrinsic activity.

Two of the main features of the Christian experience follow from the nature of its object. Firstly, it is an integrating experience. God is the one and only absolute Last End of all human aspiration. Consequently, experience in faith means that the human person is involved in his most hidden inwardness, his profoundest aspiration, his ontological and spiritual totality. The experience therefore brings all his powers into action—his intellect, because the experience is founded upon faith; his affectivity and freedom, because it rises entirely from love; his will to action, because it has to be built up, beginning with inward acts and proceeding to visible actions in which the whole person is involved; his body, because it purifies and takes up into itself the reactions of the senses, and the body too has to expend itself and offer itself in homage as a pleasing sacrifice to God; and his communion with others, because it springs from a being who is part of a community, made to love others and to build up the whole body with them. It goes further, for it involves the Church whence it derives and within which it unfolds; it involves, through the Church and in the Church, Christ himself, the everlasting living source of all Christian existence and activity; it involves the entire world, since it is expected to utilize it and penetrate it through and through, and so consecrate it to Christ; and it involves communion with God, the communion by which man fulfils himself on every level of his being, and so prepares himself for eternity.

It is an integrating experience in an even deeper sense, because it takes all these powers and elements and aspects of man and unifies them, interiorizes them, and personalizes them in an ever-increasing degree. The main distinction made in this respect by Christian thought is the fact that sin dissociates, whereas charity unifies.[14] By cutting man off from his Last End, sin deprives him of the only principle that can give his powers their proper hierarchy and unity; by encouraging him to pursue things temporal, it dissipates desire amongst an endless sequence of passing goods, and shatters the soul upon the rocks of multiplicity. Conversely, charity, by concentrating all the powers of the soul upon the search for and service of God, and detaching them from their anarchic desire for all partial goods, animating them and bearing them along in the uprush of its own impulse—charity leads the soul from multiplicity to unity—"the love of self, disintegrating; the love of God, integrating." Of course, only the saint has any acquaintance with this kind of peaceful unity; but the actual progress of the Christian experience gradually tends to realize it too. It is a unity shot through and weakened by daily sin, but restored by conversion and penance; a unity that is purified and strengthened as the soul passes from fear to faithfulness and pure love; a rich unity, rejecting nothing but evil and increasingly integrating all that it saves and snatches from

[14] I. II, 73, 1, c & 3^{m}; II. II, 25, 7; 29, 1, c.

sin; a unity that is the endlessly repeated and affirmed negation of inner and outer division, because charity tends with its whole might towards unity—*tendit in Unum;* a unity in which alone the person can find his true vocation, because in the deepest depths of his intellect, the most secret places of his heart, the most decisive moments of his freedom, the most powerful moments of his activity, it is a "communion with the Son, Jesus Christ."

Again, since the Last End is situated in infinity, and never completely possessed here on earth, the Christian experience is necessarily dynamic. It is essentially a movement, something that cannot be arrested because on earth there is no end to it. It is utterly dependent upon a call—a call making its own demands and producing its own reality, the call to an ultimate resemblance with Christ the Firstborn—and by our continuous response to this call we are continually being drawn onward. The essential thing about this response is that it involves an ever deeper openness, an ever more complete self-giving, to what is required of us by infinite love in its unique obligations towards a being uniquely loved. It is directed towards a perfection truly divine: "Be ye perfect, as your Father in heaven is perfect." Its starting-point—the grace of baptism—is a seed that we are expected to develop beyond any assignable limits. Even if we were entirely faithful in our response to this call for every moment of every day of our lives, this would not be too much to bring us to the stature fixed for us by the Father in Christ; for this, and this alone, is what life is given us for. But as our faithfulness is usually intermittent, shaky, half-hearted, we should despair of ever reaching the true stature if the "little hope" was not there to help us raise our eyes and our whole soul towards the God of Mercy.

Furthermore, this movement is always a death and resurrection in Christ. We can never finish dying to sin that we may live to God. We begin to think ourselves "full men," and we find that all we have acquired does us no good at all, and have to start stripping ourselves again. We imagine ourselves poor, and find ourselves encumbered with too many things—which we have to get rid of. We think we are on the road—the right road—and then there is suddenly no road at all, the top of the mountain is lost in darkness, and we know not where we are or which direction we should follow. And only by accepting all these facts of abnegation, penance, darkness, insecurity, clumsy-footedness, and yet at the same time throwing ourselves with all our might into the mystery of the unknown God, can we find light for our feet again, and the path of life. Thus the process is inevitably indescribable; it is not a way that can be marked out once and for all; we have to make a new beginning every day, forgetting what lies behind and concentrating entirely on what lies ahead, until we reach the final fulfilment of our eternal vocation, hidden in the heart of God.

If we now try to grasp this movement as it works at the centre of the human being, we find that it is a thing at once expansive and unifying. It impels us increasingly towards the service of God and our neighbour. It literally takes us out of ourselves. It fixes our mind and heart, our will and activity, upon the Kingdom of God, upon our fellow men who need our help, and upon the Church that is still to be built. It shatters our most legitimate expectations; it takes us farther than we ever imagined possible; it carries us both inwardly and outwardly "where we don't want to go." Is there any soul that has not sometimes found itself stretched beyond the limits of endurance, liable to crack up utterly under the impact of the Holy Spirit? But at the same time and in the same movement the soul becomes concentrated in a single impulse, unified in a single love, simplified through a proper hierarchization of its powers, and recollected in an ever-increasing determination to love God and act for God above all things and in all things. It is like a great tree that can push delicate fronds into the wind and the sun because everything inside it is animated and developed and maintained by its own strong sap. Charity leads to action and service and at the same time is fostered by them: it brings them into existence, and they make it grow. It is, in fact, self-giving, and the more it gives itself the more it is; the more it unfolds, the more deeply rooted it becomes; because the more it gives itself, the more it "passes into action" with ever-growing purity, depth, and power. "Extended in all things, I am made strong in Thee": these words of St. Augustine state the law. And the saint himself proved this up to the hilt: absolutely consumed and absolutely recollected, absolutely self-giving, absolutely unified, because absolutely present through love in all that he did.

3. *The Mediation of Signs*

But the main problem still remains. Experience means lived knowledge, and Christian experience means the Christian's awareness of his relationship with God in Christ. But faith does not mean that we see God: we grasp him through something—something other than himself—through the truths he reveals to us, the gifts he grants us, the spiritual movements that bring us into spiritual relationship with him. What is this awareness, this knowledge?

Preliminaries. In the first place, we have a direct knowledge of the acts and states of our Christian life: "The spirit of man knows what is in man": it sees its own acts and in these acts the principle behind them.[15] Now a Christian act is a free act, and therefore, like all acts of choice, a conscious act. Affective states—or rather, affective operations—have grace and the reaction of the appetite as their joint principle: the reaction is a conscious one, and since it is usually accepted or refused, which means grasped by freedom, it shares in the consciousness of freedom. Furthermore, the principle of the experience is faith working through charity. Now freedom lies at the very heart of the act of faith. The intellect is "determined to it by the will, which chooses to adhere consciously to one particular side" (*De Ver.*, 14, 1, c); it "assents to something . . . through an act of choice, whereby it turns voluntarily to one side rather than to the other" (II. II, 1, 4, c). In the same way, freedom lies at the heart of charity. For though charity does not exist in the will "in its aspect of free will" (II. II, 24, 1, 3^{m}) but in its aspect as an impulse of love towards the End, it signifies a choice and a preference for God. It is in fact a "dilection"; and it is not sufficient that it should be merely admitted in principle that God must be loved more than anything else, "it also requires the act of choice and will to tend towards this preference as a highly particularized object of choice" (*De Car.*, 6, 15^{m}). Thus the acts of the faith that works through charity take place in the full consciousness of freedom; and it naturally follows that they are perceived, and can be reflected upon.

Some remarks by Bossuet are relevant here. The Quietists, in the name of some essential purity of spirit, had denigrated the value of conscious acts in souls that had reached perfection: such conscious-

[15] "We actually perceive that we have habits from the acts of the habits of which we are aware in ourselves" (*De Ver.*, 10, 9, c).

ness, they said, being self-regarding, must be impure. Bossuet soon deals with this. He first reminds us that our ignorance of ourselves and our actions is one of the wounds and effects of sin; that even the "greatest souls" are sometimes aware of their "feelings" and sometimes not; that it is difficult to decide which is better, but that "normally speaking, as a sin is more evil the more deliberate it is, it would seem that in the same way a virtuous action has more goodness in it the more intentional and the more fully conscious it is." And he ends, "I will take it upon myself to say—and, as will be seen, not rashly—that actions that are clearly perceived are in themselves the more perfect."[16]

Nevertheless, the problem returns. These acts and states are supernatural: what then do we know by knowing them? To begin with, let us make it clear that for the moment we are leaving aside the acts by which we refuse the call of grace and ignore God's call—i.e., sins. Of these acts the one real cause from the moral point of view is human freedom. They are acts that are fully known, since their object is a created good, their principle a choice in favour of the created, their nature a free refusal of God (I. II, 112, 5, 3^{m}). They are objects of direct experience in their very being: "My sin is always before me" (Ps. li, 3). But we are here concerned with genuinely supernatural acts, whose principle is both God and man, grace and freedom. In practice, the question boils down to the problem of the central act of the Christian experience, the act that is the source of all Christian activity and the principle of all its value: the act of charity. What do we know of the act of charity? The answer can be given in two words—which immediately raise a whole host of problems: there is no "science" of charity, there is a knowledge of charity by way of signs.

Our Ignorance of Charity. If "science" is given its technical mediaeval meaning as a certain knowledge reached by way of causes, then the answer given by the theologians is quite clear: the Christian cannot know, in this sense, that he possesses charity.[17] Charity is a *habitus*, a stable supernatural determination of the will. Now we know a *habitus* through its acts; and we grasp our acts directly in their relationship with their objects: thus our knowledge of the act and the *habitus* is measured by our knowledge of the object, because

[16] *États d'Oraison, Traité* I, v, nos. 12-27 (Vivès, Vol. XVIII, pp. 465-476).
[17] *De Ver.*, 10, 10, c.

the object (like the end) governs them from within. To know whether we possess charity we need to know what charity is, and also that it exists within us. But we know neither of these things. Charity is the inclination of grace towards the supernatural Last End; its object and end are God the Sovereign Good, who brings man beatitude. But we do not know this God. Faith reveals him to us, but it does not allow us to see him (I, 12, 13, 1^m^). It tells us of the "effects" of God, "more in number and more excellent" than any known by the reason, and characteristics of his being to which reason cannot reach. But it only reveals God through those "created forms" that enable us to stammer out the Uncreated (I, 12, 2, c), those complex enunciables we create so that we may grasp his utterly simple Being (II. II, 1, 2, c), in an act in which the intellect is not actuated or the assent determined by the object alone. Thus whatever light we may be given by faith, what God is, what God is in himself, remains not only incomprehensible but unknown. "By the revelation of grace we do not know what God is in this life, and thus we are united with him as with something unknown"—*quasi ignoto conjungimur* (I, 12, 13, 1^{m}). Certain knowledge means a knowledge of principles, and the principle, the object, and the end of grace are all God himself, but "because of his excellence," "because of the immensity of his light," this God "is unknown to us"—*nobis ignotus* (II. II, 112, 5, c & 3^{m}).

Since we know neither the object nor the end of charity, we can never know what charity is or whether we possess it: "What charity is ordained to is incomprehensible, because its object and end are God, the sovereign Good, with whom charity unites us. Consequently a man cannot know, from the act of love which he sees within himself, whether he is managing to live for God in the way that is essentially required by charity" (*De Ver.*, 10, 10, c). The mystery of the object affects both the act that aims at it and the *habitus* that produces the act—which does not know the essence of the object and will never know the essence of the act that attains it. Thus it is impossible to know whether or not one possesses charity.

But to return to our analysis. We know our acts by direct awareness, and we can reflect upon them. Can the act of charity perhaps be explained in this way?

St. Thomas first notes that the act of charity does not spring from an intellectual but from an affective *habitus* (*De Ver.*, 10, 9, c). Now every intellectual *habitus* is at once the principle of an act and the principle of the knowledge of the act—it is the immediate principle of its own knowledge; and it is in this way that faith inclines the spirit towards the act of assent through which it reveals itself (*ibid.*, 8ᵐ). But an affective *habitus* is not a principle of knowledge: it is the principle of an act that supplies the intellect with the matter of knowledge. The intellect has an "idea" of the affective *habitus* and recognizes it in the acts it posits (*ibid.*, 1, *contra*). Though one must not exaggerate the gap between the two "parts" of the soul, which are not "separate in space" (3, *contra*), though it is the same soul that believes and loves, nevertheless it remains a fact that the affective reality does not manifest itself in the centre of the intellect, and before it can be known the intellect has to make a movement, has to glance away, has to "return" upon an inward act that has not sprung from itself and is not its own light. Hence, charity is not the principle of knowledge of its own act (*De Ver.*, 9, c, & 1ᵐ, 3ᵐ, & 10, 1ᵐ); and this gap between existence and knowledge, the ontological and the noetic, is of great importance when we consider the particular conditions of the object to be known.

But this is true of all affective acts: we have still not reached the particular difficulty raised by the act of charity, which is supernatural. Let us put it this way: this act can be known as an act of love, but not as an act of supernatural love—in technical terms: the act of charity can be known in its substance as an act of love, but never in its mode as a supernatural act. Let me try to explain.

Perfect virtue not only means doing good; it means doing good properly (I. II, 109, 9, c). In other words, for an act of virtue to be completely good it needs to be (I. II, 109, 9, c) both determined by the object in its substance (paying a debt, giving alms, and so on) and determined by the subject in its mode: one needs to know what one is doing, will it[18] and perform it promptly, firmly, and with joy. The substance of the act is defined by its relationship with the object, its mode by the quality of the willing. The mode is not therefore something extrinsic to the act, it is its subjective aspect,

[18] This willing includes *voluntas*, a simple act relating to the end in itself (and in so far as implied in the means), and *intentio*, an act relating to the means as ordained to the end (and to the end as attainable by the means). These two acts cover the whole course of the activity in any single concrete movement.

the sign of the concrete conditions of its esse and the inner condition of its value. And if the act, instead of being considered in itself, is grasped in its connection with the end, even its substance appears as a kind of matter, whose form is the impulse towards the end.

Applying this to the act of charity, we can say that in its substance it is an act of love of God and the neighbour, and its proper mode as a supernatural act lies in loving God as the object of beatitude and spiritual society, with a will informed by grace and with "a certain quickness and joy" (I. II, 109, 3, 1, 1^{m}; cf. *I Sent.*, d. 17, 9, 1, a. 4; & II. II, 171, 2, 3^{m}). And this indeed applies to the Christian life as a whole. For the act of charity—both in its substance and in its mode—is in the supernatural order the mode of all the acts of perfect virtue, because it ordains them to its own end[19] and thus confers upon them the mode required by their perfection. In each of them it makes the will to be willed "in the required way" and the commandments to be performed "as is necessary for salvation."[20] It does not change them in their substance, but it transforms their mode of operation: it confers upon this matter the required "form."[21] Giving alms is always an act of alms-giving (*De Ver.*, 24, 14, c, & 1^{m}, 2^{m}), but when it is performed "as a result of natural love or goodness" it is devoid of real finality and of no avail towards salvation; whereas when it is performed "as a result of the charity that unites man's spirit to God" it is "raised above human power" and carried along in the efficacious movement towards the Last End, and thus becomes of merit towards eternal life. Thus the act of charity has its own proper mode—the efficacious tending towards the Last End—and it is the proper mode of all fully supernatural acts because it ordains them to their last end, which is its proper end. The whole experience is thus involved in this problem of the mode of charity.

Now to us this mode is unknowable. It is the quality of a willing—to be precise, its relationship to a supernatural principle and object. But since we cannot know either the principle or the object, we cannot know the relationship between the willing on the one hand and the principle and the object on the other. When man is

[19] I. II, 100, 10, c.

[20] I. II, 65, 4, c (faith and hope); 109, 4, c (commandments).

[21] II. II, 23, 8, c: "It is charity which directs the acts of all other virtues to the last end, and which, consequently, also gives the form to all other acts of virtue."

preparing himself for justification, and charity is about to enter into him, we should expect the soul to be able to have a distinct experience of such a decisive ontological change. But it is not so. For the preparatory movement has to take place in accordance with the particular mode conferred by charity, and "this mode is unknowable to man, because the very gift of grace exceeds human understanding; and the mode of preparing for a form cannot be known unless the form itself is known" (*De Ver.*, 24, 15, c). When man possesses charity and is inclined towards the act of love, one would expect him to see the charity in this inclination; but again it is not so, "because it would be necessary to have perfect knowledge of the object towards which the *habitus* tends (it is thus that it is judged), and in the case of charity this cannot be known" (*De Ver.*, 10, 10, 4^m).

The connection with the object settles the question in principle, but it may be wondered whether the emergence into consciousness of an act so utterly beyond nature and so fraught with consequences is not by its newness and particularity bound to provide a clear revelation and sufficient sign of charity. Once again the answer is in the negative. Taken in itself the act of charity is never a "sufficient" or decisive sign of charity. St. Thomas seems at first sight to base this on a very commonplace fact—the similarity between the two acts—the natural and the supernatural—arising from the love of God: "*Propter similitudinem naturalis dilectionis ad gratuitam*" (*De Ver.*, 10, 10, 1^m); and again: "We know habits through acts. Now the acts of the infused virtues have the greatest resemblance to the acts of the acquired virtues, so that one cannot easily be certain of possessing grace from acts of this kind" (*De Ver.*, 6, 5, 3^m). How is one to understand this statement? The answer can only be given with reference to a series of three "resemblances," given in experience and perceived by reflection.

First, the resemblance of impulse. The act of will is an inclination or impulse. The two different kinds of acts of love—the natural and the supernatural—branch from the same original impulse—natural or supernaturalized—of the human will, to love God above all things. Both tend towards God—the first towards God as the principle and end of natural good, the second towards God as the object of beatitude and communion. Both therefore appear as though springing from the depths of ourselves, expressing our most fundamental desires, possessing the spontaneity and authenticity that characterize all our most personal acts. They are, of course, radically different from each other, for grace superelevates the natural inclination and fulfils it both in the line of its natural desire and to a point beyond its own possibilities. But for the specific difference between them to appear, it would be necessary for their cause to appear; and this cannot happen. For this cause is in fact the First Cause, which leads man forward according to natural "dilection" by the movement common to all beings, whereby each returns to God in his own way, but in charity by the special movement of grace, whereby men are made to tend towards God as the object of communion and beatitude (I. II, 109, 6, c). In the first case we do not perceive the cause; we deduce it by metaphysical reasoning; in the second case, the end of the act being unknown to us, the principle is unknown too. Psychological experience does not enable us to distinguish between the two impulses with any certainty.

Secondly, there is the resemblance in psychological structure. The act of charity is made up of two psychological reactions—one that is affective in the proper sense of the word (a union of affections, a feeling of love), the other a reaction of freedom (benevolence, or the generosity of giving). But these two things both characterize the natural love of friendship too, and grace does not change the materiality of psychological reactions even though it transfigures them inwardly. Now with regard to the first reaction, affectivity is particularly unamenable to any penetration by the intellect—feelings are as mysterious in their essence as they are easy to perceive in experience—and it is therefore difficult to see how the two feelings can be separated from each other as they exist in themselves. As for the movement of the will, its real effectiveness (its worth in the line of merit), and hence its actual quality, are literally unknown to us. Thus the psychological appearance of the two acts remains the same in both cases, and the consciousness that grasps them cannot find in its apprehension of them any sure way of distinguishing between them.

Thirdly, there is the resemblance in "substance." We cannot grasp any of our inner acts, in their immediate emergence, by their first principle. An act of will always means a will for something; it is through its relationship with the object that we grasp it directly, and any attempt to abstract this relationship means obliterating the act itself. No matter how subtle our thinking may be, it can never reveal the pure principle of the act, for that would mean a direct intuition of the soul and its powers, a thing we can never have on earth. And so at least one aspect of our inner acts must always remain wrapped in mystery. Now in the case of charity the principle of the act is unknown to us in one of its essential components. The act springs from the will informed by grace, but this "form" escapes us, and consequently the proper mode of the act escapes us too. From this it follows that the act of charity which we experience, "in so far as we can perceive it"—*secundum id de quo est perceptibile* (*De Ver.*, 10, 10, 1^m)—is not a "sufficient sign" of charity. We experience it in its substance, which is the same as the substance of natural dilection; we do not experience it in its mode—which is specific and supernatural. "What we can perceive of it" is therefore a certain psychological structure similar to the structure of natural dilection. An apprehension of a similar structure in both cases, a complete lack of knowledge of the specificity of the mode—these are the insurmountable obstacles to any strict certainty about charity.

The result is that not one of the aspects of supernatural love can deliver up its secret to us—not the inclination towards the act that normally reveals the existence of a *habitus*, because we have no "knowledge" of the object (*De Ver.*, 10, 10, 4^m) or of its source (*De Ver.*, 24, 14, c); not the delight of the act, the "privileged mode" of revelation (I, 89, 6, c), because this can spring from an acquired *habitus* (*De Ver.*, 10, 10, 2^m); not the concrete efforts of charity—brotherly love, for example (*De Ver.*, 10, 10, 3^m)—which I can experience as love but not as charity; nor the practice of the other commandments, whose acts I can only grasp according to their substance, not according to the mode "whereby their performance may be meritorious" (I. II, 109, 5, 2^m; cf. 109, 4, c).

Thus the way is closed: apart from a special revelation there can be no "sufficient sign" of charity, and the Christian can never know with certainty that he possesses it. Charity remains enveloped in the obscurity of faith—and with it all the supernatural acts of a Christian in a state of grace. We here come up against the essential obscurity of Christian experience, in which the coinherence of the mystery and the experience is a law and can never disappear. The conclusion to which all this leads is that the Christian must live in generous effort and hope (*De Ver.*, 10, 10, 7m), distrusting himself and his own masks and ruses—all the deep, subtle impurity that can insinuate itself even into his most genuine aspirations. In short, he must "watch and pray." And this explains the always rigorous and sometimes terrifying vigilance that the great ones of the spirit have always maintained against the illusions and snares of love—the vehemence of Angela of Foligno, for instance, enumerating "the falsities and dangers in good spiritual love," and saying, "Of nothing in the world—neither man, nor devil, nor any other thing—am I more wary than I am of love."[22]

Our Knowledge of Charity. Nevertheless, in this matter the Christian cannot and must not remain in pure ignorance. He cannot know charity, but he can have a knowledge of charity by way of its signs.

It must be made clear straightaway that it is necessary for him to have this knowledge. Without it the Christian life would have no meaning; it would be blind and hopeless; whereas it is in fact a life lived in light and hope. The Council of Trent, faced with the Protestant view, reminded the faithful that though a man may always feel apprehensive at the thought of his own wretchedness, he should always trust in the all-powerful mercy of God. And in those days of "controversy" St. Robert Bellarmine gave his own vigorous expression of the expostulation made by the Catholic consciousness. He quotes Chemnitz's outburst: "What is this doctrine whose effect and general sense and end are to reject these anguished consciences that in the midst of perpetual hesitation and doubt seek consolation about their reconciliation with God, their salvation and eternal life?" He recalls that ordinary Catholic doctrine holds a position that "may not remove all fear, but certainly removes all anxiety and hesitation and doubt, if 'doubt' is meant to describe the state of the man who cannot give his complete assent to either side." For between the certainty of faith on the one hand and anxiety on the other hand there is a middle term, "moral certainty with respect to the intelligence; hope and confidence with respect to the will." And he goes on: "Undoubtedly there is solid consolation and cause for

[22] *Le Livre de la bienheureuse Angèle de Foligne* (ed. Doncoeur, Paris, 1926), ch. xxxvi, pp. 311-325. This contains an extraordinary analysis of the conjoint and progressive purity and impurity of love and attention.

peace in the inner tranquillity and joy that are engendered in Catholics by a good conscience, contrition, charity, the effort to perform good works, frequent reception of the Eucharist, the visitation of the Holy Spirit, which is the hidden manna known only to him who receives it. All these things are something much better than the vain confidence and truly temerarious presumption of the Lutherans. . . . We willingly recognize the kind of certainty that is born not of the presumption of an imputed justice (that is not a Catholic certainty of faith) but of the experience of charity and good works—and which can therefore be called a conjectural moral certainty."[23]

Furthermore, statements in Scripture imply this knowledge. To keep to the passages mentioned earlier in this book—St. John, for instance, asks us to reflect on the communion between Christians and God and their fellow men and calls upon the faithful to live in the full light of this communion, providing us with the standards whereby it is to be judged; whilst St. Paul's experience of the Spirit is something that he wants all his Christians to have too, and so he describes its main features and signs and its paradoxical certainty.

Lastly, tradition witnesses to this same knowledge. Here we need only pick out passages from two Doctors of the Church and quote their own words. Discussing the need for charity if the Christian virtues are not to remain "bare" and empty, St. Leo says, as though it was the most natural thing in the world: "The faithful should scrutinize their minds and thoroughly examine their heart's inmost affections, and then, if they find any of the fruits of charity in their consciousness, let them not doubt that God is within them; and, that they may become more and more able to receive so great a guest, may they grow in works of a more assiduous compassion."[24] For St. Bernard, the Christian life is inconceivable without the living sense of security that God gives to his followers. "For when has God ever left his elect without witness?"[25] he asks, and goes on to insist

[23] Bellarmine distinguishes between evident certainties and obscure certainties: faith, human authority, and opinion. The last is based on a number of signs and conjectures, and it excludes, not all fear, but all anxiety, and so "makes man sure" (*De Justificatione*, III, c, 2). Despite the words and the ambiguity of the phrase "conjectural certainty," this means a genuine certainty—as I shall explain in more detail later.

[24] *Sermo* 48, P. L., 54, 300 A.

[25] *Sermo* 11, *post Oct. Paschae*, 3.

on both the transcendence of God's action in man and the intrinsic power of the signs that reveal it to us. To the question whether the Christian can know himself to be engendered of God and predestined, St. Bernard replies, "We cannot be certain, but the confidence that comes of hope consoles us, that we may not be absolutely at the mercy of the anguish of doubt. And that is why we have been given signs and manifest indications of salvation, that it may be a matter beyond all doubt that the man in whom these signs dwell is numbered with the elect. That is why, I say, 'those whom he has known in advance he has predestined to be conformed to the likeness of his Son,' so that those who cannot be certain, because they have cause for anxiety, may at least be given confidence by the grace of consolation. And that is why it is necessary that in care, and fear, and trembling, we humble ourselves under the mighty hand of God; because though to a small extent we can know what we are, it is absolutely impossible for us to know what we shall be. Therefore, let him who is now standing take care that he does not fall, let him persevere and progress in that way (of life) that is an index of salvation and a sign of predestination."[26] There is therefore a knowledge of grace and charity, or, to be more precise, a knowledge of their life within us. What is this knowledge?

The Experiential. First a point of the utmost importance. This knowledge is not empirical or experimental, but experiential. It does not relate to any act or state as it is in itself, or to any particular abstracted aspect of any act or state: it is not empirical. It does not relate to any acts or states that are deliberately provoked with a view to "having an experience" and so end in a list of certainties: it is not experimental. It relates to a number of signs that have been lived through, exist in a hierarchy, and are linked together; signs that are part of the body of the experience and also its adherent signs: it is experiential. That, it seems to me, is the cardinal point. Let us turn again to the First Epistle of St. John. There we find that communion with God is to be judged by a series of lived determining standards—consciousness of sin, observation of the commandments,

[26] *Sermo 1, De Septuages.*, no. 1 (cf. no. 2, & *S. 11, De Oct. Pasc.*, 3-5). Despite its different language it is the same thought as that of later theologians. No "certainty," says St. Bernard; no "knowing," says St. Thomas later; but a calming, or a conjectural certainty, by way of signs.

brotherly love, the struggle against the world, and faithfulness to the Church, Church dogma, and the Spirit. The experience is made up of communion, and of the signs that ensure and reveal the communion, joined together in an unbreakable unity. This experience is experiential in the highest degree.

If we turn to the sermons of St. Leo we find the structure of this experience described with remarkable conviction. Here are two particularly significant passages: "Where is the believer who does not know what virtues he is to pursue and what vices he must fight against? Who can be so complacent, or so incompetent a judge of his own conscience, as not to realize what he must tear up out of himself or cause to grow within himself? Is there anyone so much a stranger to reason that he cannot tell the quality of his own behaviour or know the secrets of his own heart? Then let no man please himself in everything he does, or judge of himself according to the pleasures of the flesh, but let him weigh his habits and behaviour in the balance of the divine commandments. And since we are told to do some things and not to do others, let the man who wishes to estimate the value of his habits of behaviour weigh himself justly, and see them in the light of this double obligation. For God in his mercy has given us, besides his commandments, an excellent mirror, in which we may see the face of our souls, and discover to what extent we are like or unlike the image of God; and especially so that, by gradually throwing off the cares of the flesh and all disturbing occupations, at least in the days of our redemption and reparation, we may be transported from earthly things to the things of heaven."[27]

"And now, when faithfulness to the divine commandments bears its splendid fruit in the progress of all believers, and the words 'Let your light shine before men' are fulfilled, who could fail to understand that the divinity is present where true virtue is seen to appear? For such does not exist without God, and it does not bear the mark of divinity unless it is nourished by the spirit of its author. Since the Lord said to his disciples, 'Without me you can do nothing,' it cannot be doubted that the man who does good has from God both the accomplishment of his labour and the beginning of his willing. For this reason the Apostle is never tired of exhorting his flock to work out their salvation 'with fear and trembling.' And the reason why the saints go in fear and dread is that, being exalted by the works of their

[27] *Sermo* 49, *P.L.*, 54, 304 AB.

own piety, they fear that they may be deprived of the help of grace and abandoned to the weakness of their own nature.

"Therefore, let the man who wishes to discover (*experiri*) whether God—of whom it is said that he is 'admirable in his saints'—dwells within him, examine his innermost heart sincerely, and see with exactly what humility he resists pride, with how good a will he fights against envy, whether he turns a deaf ear to flattery and rejoices in the good qualities of others; let him find out whether or not he desires to return evil for evil, or prefers to leave injustices unavenged rather than to lose the image and likeness of his Creator, who calls all men to acknowledge him in the good things he gives to all, 'making his sun to shine on the just and on the unjust.' And that he may not grow weary with his endless inquiry into all these disquieting matters, let him seek within the depths of his heart for the mother of all virtues, charity, and if he finds her turned with all her heart towards the love of God and the neighbour, so that he wishes it to be done unto his enemies as he would it were done unto himself, let him who finds himself in this condition not doubt that God is guiding him and dwells within him—God, whom he receives in a more excellent way, the more he glories not in self but in the Lord."[28]

These passages are quite clear, and they at least teach us that these three things are normal for the Christian—knowledge of self, of one's duties, one's conscience, one's conduct; judgment of self in the light of the Lord's commandments, which determine one's duties, decide one's worth and reveal as in a mirror, accusing or reassuring, the face of one's soul; and awareness of the presence of God, which in certain cases does not deceive, for since true virtue reveals the presence of God, the Christian has only to inquire rigorously into his virtues, above all his charity, and he will then soon know whether God is in his soul. Thus it is our lived, conscious relationship to the commandments that reveals to us our relationship to God, a relationship involving the likeness between the soul and God and the efficacious presence of God in the soul. This complex of interconnected relationships, whose centre is charity, defines a structure; and the awareness of it takes place in the experiential order.

We find the same lesson in St. Bernard. In his *Sermons on Canticles*—by no means concerned entirely with mystical states—he

[28] *Sermo* 38, 3-4, P.L., 54, 261-262.

returns again and again to the theme of the comings and goings of the Word and the Spirit, the essential variability of the Christian life,[29] and he also makes frequent mention of the signs that characterize this presence and should reassure the soul. The splendid passage that follows is no doubt mainly a description of a mystical state, since it is concerned with the alternations that characterized the life of the saint at a particular stage. But the criteria which it suggests are for this reason all the more significant. "I confess that I too have been visited by the Word—I speak as a fool—and more than once. And although he has often entered into me, several times I have not felt him entering. I have felt that he has been, I can remember his being there, occasionally I have even had a presentiment of his coming, but as for feeling it, never, nor his going away either. For, when he has come into my soul, whither he has gone on leaving it, and how he has come in and gone away again—again I confess that I do not know; according to the saying, 'You know not whence he cometh nor whither he goeth.' Yet this is not surprising, since of him it is said, 'No one shall see the traces of his footsteps.' Certainly it is not through the eyes that he comes, for he has no colour, nor through the ears, for he has no sound, nor through the nostrils, for he mingles with the soul, not with the air (which he does not impregnate but makes), nor through the throat, for he is not a thing to be eaten or drunk, and I have not felt him, for he is not a thing palpable. How then did he come in? Perhaps he did not even come in, perhaps he does not come from outside?—for he is not a thing outside. On the other hand, he could not have come from within me, for he is good, and I know that there is nothing good in me.

"I have also ascended above myself, but higher still rose the Word. Lower than myself I have descended also, like an inquisitive explorer, and yet he went lower still. Then I have looked outwards, and realized that he is beyond all that is outside me; I have looked within, and he was more deeply inward still. And I realized the truth of the saying, 'In him we live and move and have our being'; but blessed is the man in whom he lives, who lives for him, and is borne along by him.

"You will ask how I know he was there, if his ways are so indis-

[29] This theme is always appearing in St. Gregory, and also in Origen in the *Commentary on Canticles*, and in a passage that ought perhaps to be compared with the passage from St. Bernard. Cf. E. Gilson, *La Théologie mystique de saint Bernard* (Paris, 1934), p 28, n. 1. (English translation, *The Mystical Theology of St. Bernard* [Sheed & Ward, London and New York, 1940].)

cernible. He is alive and effective, and as soon as he came into me he awoke my sleeping soul, he moved and softened and wounded my heart, which had been as hard as rock and without health. Also he began to root up and destroy, to build and plant, to water that which was dry, to enlighten what was dark, to open what was closed, to warm what was cold, and also to make level and straight that which was crooked and uneven; and my soul did bless the Lord, everything within me blessed his holy Name. Thus, then, when the Word who is the Bridegroom has sometimes entered into me, he has never given the slightest sign of his entrance, neither by voice, nor countenance, nor by the sound of his approach. He has never revealed himself to me by any of his movements; none of my senses has perceived him slipping stealthily into my most secret parts. Only (as I have said), by the beating of my heart I have known that he was there; in the flight of vices and the dying down of passion I have recognized the might of his power; in the examination and reprobation of my most secret sins I have marvelled at the depths of his wisdom; in the peaceful progress of my life I have experienced his sweet goodness; in the renewal and re-creation of my spirit at its highest point—in my most inward being—I have had glimpses of the beauty of his countenance; and, taking in all these things at one single glance, I have begun to tremble at the thought of his overpowering majesty."[30]

It is a remarkable fact that in describing this profound penetration of the Word into his soul St. Bernard should so utterly avoid all empiricism. He insists most emphatically upon the absolute identity between the mystery and the experience; for this visit is transcendently above all sense feeling, above any imaginative "setting" or spiritual vision, and it gives no decisive evidence of itself. There are simply a number of signs revealing the presence of the Word, and these are effects produced in the soul. St. Bernard first describes them in general terms—the soul's awakening, the change of heart, the great work of destruction, purification, rectification, illumination, enkindling. He then goes back to them, pointing out the various elements in the lived and discerned experience—the affective element, the beating of the heart that reveals the presence of the Word; the voluntary element, the purification and subjugation of passion that reveals his power; the intellectual element, the dis-

[30] *In Canticum, Sermo* 74, 5-6, P.L., 183, 1141-1143.

covery and condemnation of hidden sins that reveals his wisdom; the active element, the rectification of behaviour that reveals his goodness; the spiritual element, the radical renewal of the spirit that reveals his beauty. And when he takes all this in in one glance, he is seized with a feeling of holy terror at the thought of the absolute transcendence of the Word of God. Here again, the Word escapes detection: he is only perceived through these signs, this network of relationships, linked together in a single experience. But though the soul cannot fix its eyes upon the Word, the Word can see the soul, and the soul can perceive the effects and signs of his gaze. As St. Bernard himself explains elsewhere when he is speaking of the countenance of the Word, in words whose beauty is utterly untranslatable, "His countenance is not formed (in front of the eyes), but formative; it does not strike the eyes of the body, but rejoices the face of the heart; it gives joy by giving, but not by the appearance of love."[31] If this is true of such high experiences as these, then it must be all the more so for the ordinary religious life: Christian experience is experiential or it is nothing.

Later theologians did no more than repeat this doctrine, and we can find it in St. Thomas linked with grace, charity, and contrition. St. Thomas does not seem to have spent much time on this problem, however. He insists emphatically that it is impossible for us to know that we have charity; he no less emphatically describes the knowledge that we can have of it as a knowledge by conjecture—"by means of certain signs"—and when occasion demands he mentions some of these signs, as things well known, which it is sufficient to recall. When we attempt to collect together the various data that he supplies,[32] we find that all these signs taken together lead to an awareness of three things—the purity of the soul before God, in the sense that there is no consciousness of mortal sin; the soul's movement against sin by a firm intention, and towards the good by acts of charity; and thirdly a series of likes and dislikes—sorrow for sin, contempt for the things of the world, delight in God and the things of God. Signs intellectual, voluntary, and affective, in fact.

[31] *In Canticum, Sermo* 31, 6, P.L., 183, 945 C. One is tempted to say that the countenance of the Word is never revealed, but revealed in revealing.

[32] *I Sent.*, 17, 1, 4; *III Sent.*, 27, 2, 10^{m}; *IV Sent.*, 9, 1, 3, sol. 2; *De Ver.*, X, 10, c & 1-3^{m}; I. II, 112, 5; III, 80, 4, 5^{m}; *in II Cor.*, c. 12, lect. 1, 2.

The important thing here again is that the discernment takes place within a structured experience, the signs of which are both integrating and revealing elements in it.

The Signs. Let us try, then, to make a provisional sketch of what all these signs are. Charity is an inclination of grace towards God the Last End. We know that, in themselves, object and end escape us. What remains to be investigated, then, is the orientation towards the end, which should be manifest in a general line[33] running through the various signs, which mark out the movement in so far as they reflect the rectitude (both objective and subjective) of the will, its concrete effectiveness, and its lived contact with God—in other words in so far as it manifests through these signs an experience of faithfulness.

The first sign is undoubtedly right faith. All Christian experience takes its meaning from true faith: this is the primary condition of the experience, its foundation, its necessary starting-point, its rule, its permanent standard. If all spiritual experience is "at least the lived testing of a doctrine,"[34] the Christian experience will in the first place be a loyal and generous lived testing of the Christian faith. The sign of a right faith is voluntary conformity with the Word of God in Scripture as taught by the Church. Let us recall some well-known passages in St. Thomas: "The formal object of faith is the First Truth, as manifested in Holy Writ and the teaching of the Church, which proceeds from the First Truth. Consequently, whoever does not adhere, as to an infallible and Divine rule, to the teaching of the Church, which proceeds from the First Truth manifested in Holy Writ, has not the habit of faith" (II. II, 5, 3, c). And again, the proper means to knowledge, in faith, is "the First Truth proposed to us in the Scriptures, according to the teaching of the Church who has the right understanding of them" (*ibid.*, 2^{m}). Thus the will to conform to the rule of the Church makes a man one of the faithful, as the will to avoid it makes another man a heretic.

The control exerted by faith is therefore in practice a control

[33] Cf. J. Maréchal, *Études sur la Psychologie des Mystiques, Vol. I* (Paris-Bruges, 1924), pp. 60-63.

[34] *Ibid., op. cit., Vol. II* (Paris, 1937), p. 414.

exerted by the Church at the heart of the spiritual movement. Voluntary conformity to the rule of the Church brings us into contact with her infallible teaching, and guarantees the authenticity of the formal motive of our faith and real contact with the truth of God. But in the deified soul this conformity requires a deliberate and costing preference for the Word of God as taught by the Church, and consequently a fundamental humility at the basis of our faith; and then, in adoration and obedience, we are able to pay absolute homage of mind and will to the Word of God. Finally, since this preference and conformity are voluntary, and spring from a choice and the gift of self, they are conscious, and form the fundamental sign of all genuine communion with God.

The second sign is keeping the Commandments. "Circumcision is nothing, and uncircumcision nothing: but the observance of the commandments of God" (I Cor. vii, 19). The essential commandment is charity towards God and our neighbour. This commandment presupposes faith, without which it cannot exist, and it implies all the other commandments to the extent that they radiate from the one original commandment and realize its demands.[35] Thus, in a single infinitely diversified movement there is a fulfilment of the Christian vocation, of Christian being, and of the Kingdom of God. It is thus natural that the practice of the commandments as thus understood should be for St. John the sign of true love: "If you love me, keep my commandments" (John xiv, 15); "He that hath my commandments, and keepeth them, he it is that loveth me. And he that loveth me shall be loved of my Father: and I will love him and will manifest myself to him" (*ibid.*, 21). And since everything springs from charity, charity is—for St. Paul—the fulfilment of the law (Rom. xiii, 8-10), and the only thing that has to be done is to "keep the commandment" (I Tim. vi, 14).

But keeping the commandments is usually a tragic business for the Christian. It is an obligation laid upon a being who is sinful and divided, and it brings war and the sword. One whole side of man has to die, if the soul is to be resurrected into newness of life. God's commandment to Abraham called for a faith that was heart-rending,

[35] Cf. G. Kittel, *Theologisches Wörterbuch zum Neuen Testament*, Vol. II, pp. 542-553, s.v. *Entolè* (G. Schrenk).

before it became a means to fulfilment;[36] it meant exile, hoping against hope, the sacrifice of an only son. The Father's commandment to Jesus Christ required him to preach Israel, to give testimony and surrender his life in utter abjection before he could be resurrected and save us. Sacrifice is thus at the heart of any keeping of the commandments—and this means abnegation, repentance, redemptive suffering through faith and charity, which decentralize the mind and heart and deliver them still trembling to God. Death and resurrection with Christ—that in the end is what keeping the commandments means, and here again the sign is the experience of some sort of faithfulness—the faithfulness of the "heart" being transformed into the faithfulness of action in a single movement. Speaking of the power of grace, St. Thomas once wrote, "One and the same *habitus* of grace informs the soul and produces inner and outer acts and in a certain sense leads to perseverance, in so far as this involves resistance to temptation" (*De Ver.*, 27, 5, 2^m^). One single fundamental movement, through the activity of grace and the infused virtues—that is the sign of faithfulness to the commandments, the sign of true love.

Moreover, there is one essential condition for this faithfulness—insertion within the Church, the sphere wherein the commandments are observed.[37] For faithfulness is not possible unless it is nourished, and it is nourished above all by the sacraments and the liturgy, and by the Holy Eucharist, which is necessary both to the soul for the fulfilment of its personal vocation, and to the Church for the fulfilment of its own proper function: faith and charity culminate in worship, praise, and supplication to Christ in the Eucharist. Contrariwise, the faithfulness can only be real if it leads to the apostolic activity that issues from brotherly love, according to the measure meted out to each one of us in the building up of the Kingdom of God. Faithfulness is thus rooted in the Church in its two major aspects—in the mystery of the Presence and in the mystery of the Mission. It is thus the second sign of real communion with God.

The third sign is self-judgment. It is necessary for man to descend into the depths of his conscience and take himself into his own

[36] Cf. J. Guillet, *Figure d'Abraham dans l'Ancien Testament*, in Abraham, *père des croyants* (*Cahiers sioniens*, June 1951, pp. 31 *et seq.*).

[37] *Conc. Trid.*, *De Justific.*, sess. vi, c. 10: the just grow in justice "unto sanctification, by observing the commandments of God and the Church."

hands and judge himself. And this judgment is concerned with two main objects—sin, and the gifts of God.

Every Christian experience involves an absolutely clear awareness of the fact of sin. To begin with, the Christian always sees himself as a sinner before God. The product of a sinful race, a sinner like all his forebears, unable to get rid of the traces and marks of his sins, prone to sin and susceptible to sin, sinning daily, always liable to be cutting himself off from God, never knowing whether he is justified—how can he have any real awareness of himself before God except as a creature steeped in sin, whose first motions must be humility, contrition, and supplication? "Against thee only have I sinned, I have done evil before thee": such is one's inevitable judgment upon oneself. This does not mean that the Christian may not realize that he has no mortal sin on his conscience, in those blessed hours when his conscience "does not reproach him." His insight does not forego clear-sightedness, humility, loyalty, a holy fear of God, and gratitude; but it always ends in hope, because his awareness is not complete, because spiritual awareness always lags behind spiritual being,[38] and the ultimate judgment on any human heart is always a matter for God alone: "I do not judge myself, it is the Lord who judges me."[39] To know that we are not guilty of sin implies a knowledge of the state of grace; but the transcendence involved in this experience is not a perceptible fact in the experience. Moreover, this awareness is linked for the believer with the sacrament of penance, in which, but without losing its mysteriousness, the mystery of forgiveness is truly accomplished. The living movement of the awareness arises from sorrow for past sin, joy in the forgiveness granted to it, and a firm determination to avoid it in the future—a clear, determined will, based entirely on the mystery of the grace of God and involving a conscious commitment for the future. Thus it is in humility, contrition, supplication, confidence, and gratitude that this first form of self-judgment is realized.[40]

But it should also relate to the gifts received from God. The humble man sees clearly because he seeks God's glory, and gives glory to God for all that God has done within him—given him

[38] Cf. the very fair observation by Fr. H. Dondaine, *L'attribution suffisante* (Paris, 1943), pp. 50-59 ("St. Thomas somewhere opposes *subjectum* to *conscientia*, i.e. the person's real condition to his awareness of his condition").

[39] *Cf. Conc. Trid.*, sess. vi, cap. 16 end.

[40] *Ibid.*, sess. xiv, *De Confess.*, cap. 3, end (on peace, serenity and consolation).

his Christian vocation, baptism, and the true faith, snatched him from a life of sin, kept him faithful despite all vicissitudes, allowed him to advance in the knowledge of God, in purity of heart and the service of the Lord, and given him the longing to grow increasingly in all this, to use and spend himself in the cause of God's greater glory. When the Christian can judge himself in these terms, gratitude must overflow his soul. And the judgment is made more humbly and fearfully than ever, because everything comes from God; and more trustingly and firmly than ever, because it is simply a beginning, and an earnest of better things to come. All true self-judgment is realized in the depths of prayer.

But the heart of the Christian experience is the soul's movement towards God, and the last sign of it comes from this movement itself. It has three different aspects.

First, this movement is an inclination towards God, an inclination of charity towards its Object and End, by means of its own acts and the acts of the other virtues, which it directs towards its own end. This sort of polarization of the whole soul round God, the first of all loves, is one of the normal signs of the experience. It is grasped, not so much in one act as in an interconnected group of acts that have been renewed and consciously orientated. If one admits with St. Thomas that the love of God above all things is a thing impossible to fallen nature, then, when this love that is at once affective and effective is present in any life, it becomes a sign—not an absolutely decisive sign, of course, but one that is really significant and enlightening, in so far as it reflects a general orientation that lasts, is endlessly renewed and deepened, and is effective in practice. And this sign is not an affective state, but the concrete movement of a loved faithfulness, both in its inward impulse and in its expansion outside.

Secondly, this movement is a search for God. "The generation of those who seek God"—that is a true description of Christians as they exist here on earth, a people by whom God can never be sufficiently known, loved, and served. The search is endless, because it proceeds from a faith that cannot see, and a love that can only know imperfect possession; it is also deliberate, because it is made by a soul that can realize its own position and be obedient to the call of the Spirit; it is a search that grows increasingly pure, because the soul tends increasingly towards God for his own sake and submits in love to the sovereign, unforeseeable, imperative calls of his revealed will; it is a search endlessly renewed, because each day brings a new choice, a new beginning, a new stage on the long road of the pilgrimage; and it is a search that takes on all the varying appearances of the spiritual life itself—can be dry or joyful, gay or apathetic, progressive or static, its only law the law of change.

Lastly, this movement means joy in God—"I have delighted in the Lord"—a flowering of sense affectivity, or spiritual affectivity, or both at once. In its strongest form—as illumination or consolation—it is a direct sign—though still subject to definite standards—but this does not last. On the other hand, a less striking, but deeper and surer form of it seems to form part of the essential structure of the experience. It is then a lived quality of the movement towards God, coinciding with the actual movement of the spirit in its vigour and faithfulness, revealing a sort of blessed need to be with God in the very midst of dryness and darkness, and thus being a kind of spontaneous polarization and attraction towards God, a strong, humble choice, lived, willed and loved, for God and the things of God, in spite of all temptation and hardship. It persists through the disturbances, the disgust, the anguish, that are more keenly felt because they are more superficial and perceptible: the soul finds it still there when it becomes recollected, sees in it proof of the genuineness of its movement, and so lives in the "peace that transcends all feeling." Understood in this way, this "delight" is one of the normal features of the Christian experience and is part of its very substance.[41]

Clearly, we are here at the heart of the world of the experiential. Through these signs we can perceive a close network of relationships. They are adherent, homogeneous, and immanent to the experience—are the experience itself, in fact, revealed in certain of its essential structural lines. The Christian consciousness unfolds within them, and can grasp itself in the dimensions of the personal and the ecclesiastical, in clearness of vision and faithfulness of behaviour, according to an inwardness conditioned by the soul's relationship to God, through the truths of faith, its insertion within the Church and its pure and trusting search for God. No amount of thought can

[41] Cf. the remark by Rev. Fr. A. Gardeil on "*Consolations*" in *La Structure de l'âme et l'expérience mystique* (2nd ed. Paris, 1926), Vol. II, pp. 218 *et seq.*

ever equal such a gift as this, which is, moreover, being renewed every moment in the grace of God. And the faithfulness upon which the whole experience is built is also the means whereby it can emerge fully into the light.

Our Knowledge of the Signs. How does the Christian perceive these signs? How do self-awareness and self-judgment operate?

They do not involve an act of faith, of course. Faith relates to revealed truths, and—leaving aside any special graces—the state of my conscience is not and cannot be a revealed truth. Perception is in this case, then, a matter of spiritual reason, but reason bathed in the grace of God.[42] The whole soul, in fact, is involved in the perception of self, and therefore the supernatural enlightenment that cures, comforts, and illuminates the reason plays its part in it. The theological virtues play their part too, by transfiguring the spirit from within. Faith purifies the intellect of its carnal darkness, helps it to share God's own knowledge, and reveals to it the world of divine truths. Charity brings the spirit into contact with the actual reality of God, and develops in the soul a sympathy and connaturality with the divine realities, or with realities that are linked with God. Hope gives the soul the support of God's merciful Omnipotence, and helps it to work confidently towards its salvation. Prudence leads to a right estimation of self with regard to the Last End, and enables man to judge himself. The gifts of the Holy Spirit, which are present within every soul that is in a state of grace, make it docile and sensitive to the motions of the Spirit. The result of all this is that the soul lives in a supernatural atmosphere, and the reason is prepared to perceive the signs and to decipher its experience.

[42] In the remarks that follow I refer to the curative and strengthening effect of grace on reason. However difficult this may be to explain, the fact itself is undeniable: the old theologians frequently made references to the influence of faith upon reason. John of St. Thomas, for example, insists on the purifying and perfecting function of faith with regard to philosophical investigations, and shows the vigour, the reliability, the certainty that faith adds to "science" (*De Fide*, disp. 2, art. 1, nos. 18-29). He says that this "participation in certainty is of the same species as faith, *reductive* though not formally" (26). If this is true of an investigation that in the author's view remains philosophic, it must be all the more so in the case envisaged here, in which what is involved is a normal function of the supernaturalized reason. Cf. again the distinction suggested by John of St. Thomas (on the certainty of the state of grace, in I. II, q. 112, disp. 25, art. 3, no. 2) in connection with hope, the practical certainty of which is "*regulata a fide, sed non regulata per fidem.*"

As the inner life unfolds on the natural level, a spontaneous lived awareness acompanies its development; and similarly, as the Christian life is built up consciously and freely, a direct, spontaneous, lived knowledge accompanies it as one of its normal dimensions, and flowers in a spontaneous, reflective spiritual perception.

This perception is a concrete knowledge, because it springs from a soul supernaturalized in its intelligence, its affectivity, and its freedom, and because it relates to the very life of the soul, to its conscious activities and passivities and the spiritual movements that connect it with the God it loves. It is a direct knowledge, since the signs are not something constructed, superadded, deduced, but aspects or elements of the experience itself. What is known indirectly, or inferred to exist in the mystery, is the grace or charity that the signs denote or signify; but the signs themselves are apprehended directly, not only materially, but in their significance as suggested and lived and enlightened by faith. Perception here means confrontation and recognition, not by deduction, but by a direct grasp springing from spiritual affinity.

This perception is a synthesis, as every spiritual perception must be that integrates a number of lived elements and aspects. It is rare, no doubt—perhaps impossible—for all the elements to be clearly perceived: this would need perfect natural and supernatural lucidity, accompanied by great purity and love. But the whole complex of signs is posited present and living in the consciousness, and from time to time one or other of them, thanks to the help and enlightenment of the rest, emerges more clearly, and provides a foundation for the soul's personal certainty. Moreover, inner act and outward action are usually linked together, and in a well-instructed consciousness and an upright life the inner act finds its effective expression and the proof of its genuineness in the outer action, whereas the outer action takes its spiritual value and significance from the inner act. "By their fruits you shall know them" (Matt. vii, 16, 20): sap and fruit testify to each other's existence.

This perception is "religious," and, indeed, theocentric. It relates to the signs of a life that is directed towards God through charity, and, though it cannot sort out the separate signs of this movement, it perceives them as they are borne along by it—the will to remain faithful to the actual faith in one's life, the will to be sincere in one's self-examination, the single-minded search and choice of

God in intention and in act—all these things refer to God or relate to God. But though God may be given to the Christian soul, he is not given to the soul's spiritual experience. He is, and remains, the Transcendent One, grasped in the darkness of faith. The signs are thus rooted in mystery as in their native soil, and they are aspects of the movement to discover this God of mystery; the knowledge that grasps them is all the clearer and more certain, the more it is detached from self and directed towards God. The more one looks for God, the more one finds oneself; the more one looks at God, the more clearly one sees into oneself. The worst enemy of the true understanding of these signs is a certain anxious, egoistic self-absorption, a kind of indulgence in self, that easily leads to pride and error. Only by following, in humility, detachment, and generosity of heart, the actual movement of the experience and the signs that reflect it, can one perceive the signs and judge the experience truthfully.

This perception can be reflected upon. The rudimentary sort of consciousness that usually accompanies the Christian life can and should at times become fully conscious. The Christian, in fact, is expected to inquire into the honesty of his actions and to test his faith, and thus to reflect upon his life in the light of revealed standards and in a way that will give true results: "Let a man prove himself." Here we come to the techniques of meditation that have a place in every Christian life. The simplest form is the examination of conscience that every Christian should perform daily, and especially before confession and communion: the meditation upon the uprightness of his "heart," his intentions, his behaviour, so that he may ask for forgiveness, for the rectification of his impulses, and for reunion with Christ. This effort has an intrinsic connection with the Church, for our self-judgment is not always correct and has itself to be judged. Where the saint would find matter of condemnation, the ordinary Christian is content to absolve himself—which means that he must be encouraged to condemn himself; whereas the scrupulous person tortures himself and needs to be reassured. The mystery of conscience and the requirements of the Faith come together, so that meditation on self may be submitted to the judgment of the Church in the person of the priest. Again—apart from matters of sin in the strict sense, and strictly extraordinary phenomena—in matters of consolation and desolation, inspiration and temptation, in the orientation of one's personal life, there rises the problem of the discernment of spirits.[43] A whole technique has been built up around this matter from the beginning, and developed in detail as a result of the experience of the Church and her saints through the ages. Here, more than ever, personal meditation is not enough, but needs to trust and submit itself to the judgment of an experienced guide inspired by the wisdom of the Church, who can enable a balanced judgment to be reached. This is another example of that "church government" that descends into the very depths of the most intimately personal actions—because for the Christian there is no life, no light, no security, outside Mother Church.

Finally, this perception has various degrees of acuteness, depth and certainty. It is a function of the purity and charity of the soul.[44] In the matter of discovering God's presence and action within oneself, everything depends on the degree of union between the soul and God, on God's grasp of the soul and the soul's transparency to itself before God. Now the thing that measures both the purity of the soul and the extent of the divine action upon it is the depth to which it is rooted in charity. The greater the charity, the more the gifts of the Holy Spirit that always accompany it make the soul open to the divine action, susceptible to its light and certain of its effects. In concrete terms it seems possible to make out three degrees of clarity in this perception, according to three degrees of charity.[45]

Beginners hardly manage to emerge from their sins. They remain full of attachments and impurities. They are a mixture of good and evil. They know nothing about the realities of the spiritual life and little about themselves, and have no experience of the things of God. They have eyes, but are like little children who have not really learned how to use them. They have to grow in purity, have gradually to accustom their eyes to the light, and to discover for themselves this new world into which the grace of God has so

[43] A general view and suggestions for bibliography will be found in J. DE GUIBERT, *Leçons de théologie spirituelle*, Vol. I (Toulouse, 1943), ch. xxv.

[44] H. PINARD DE LA BOULLAYE, *Expérience religieuse*, in *Dictionnaire de théologie catholique*, Vol. V, 1838 *et seq.* (on the three ways—1823 *et seq.*—the Rev. Fr. uses the most recent schema, but his remarks are excellent).

[45] Cf. *III Sent.*, d. 29, 8, 1; II. II, 24, 9. Cf. the account by Fr. J. DE GUIBERT, *Theologia spiritualis*, nos. 326 *et seq.*

recently introduced them. Progressives have been delivered from the habit of mortal sin and are beginning to tend towards the achievement of positive good and progress in virtue. They have learned a little humility and purity; they know something about the spiritual life and their own nature. Through humility and detachment their charity is growing and increasing their union with God. They are entering into the light, and their perception of the things of God is gradually becoming clearer and more habitual.[46] Lastly, the perfect have become naturalized to the things of God. Charity means that "man, having grown familiar with the good things of God, possesses them as though they come naturally to him, and finds his joy and peace in them" (*De Car.*, 11, 10^{m}). And St. Robert Bellarmine describes the certainty that the perfect feel in these words: "The man who loves God knows with certainty that he is loved by God; or rather, he knows that he loves because he is loved. And he does not merely know this as a matter of words because God has said, 'I love those who love me,' but by experience. For 'the Spirit of God itself witnesseth to our spirit that we are sons of God.' Now the man who knows himself to be God's son and friend can approach him with the highest confidence . . . People who are perfected in charity and have affective charity, whose thoughts always tend towards God, whose one wish is to please him, who show contempt for all created things for the love of him, who know from experience that they can suffer joyfully—these are so certain of loving and being loved that they have no doubts about it and can thus say with the Spouse: 'My Beloved is in me and I in him.' "[47]

There are thus three degrees or levels of charity in the soul, and to a corresponding degree the signs of charity are present within it and it has a corresponding degree of perception of these signs. It would be a tragic mistake to lump all three together and to speak of a beginner in the same way as one speaks of one of the perfect. This is the mistake made by all illuminisms, and it is a subtle revenge on pride and ignorance of the Christian life. It is essential in fact

[46] Discussing the illuminative way, Fr. PINARD writes: "Without falling into the Lutheran error of believing in one's justification as a matter of faith, it may be said that the moral evidence of good will and its fruits—unless there is a particular difficulty involved—is sufficient to remove any doubts that the soul may have about God's friendship for it" (*loc. cit.*, 1827).

[47] Quoted by E. RAITZ VON FRENTZ, *La Vie spirituelle d'après le bienheureux Robert Bellarmin*, in *Revue d'Ascétique et de Mystique*, 1926, p. 133.

to make a rigorous distinction between these stages and states. Growth in charity, growth in experience, growth in discernment—these things go together, normally at least, due regard being had for the sovereign initiatives of the grace of God. There is only one Christian experience: it is one in its principles, one in its objects, one in its structure and one in its standards. But there are degrees, ever stronger and ever clearer, of this experience, and of the awareness that goes with it. This is indeed a law of the Christian life, which goes from faith to faith and from light to light, until it reaches at last the light of eternity.

CONCLUSION

"Placing" the Experience

THE Christian experience means *grasping oneself* in relation to God; the Christian life means *being* in relation to God. To go straight to the main point, the Christian experience means knowing through faith and hope that we love God, and the Christian life means, quite simply, loving God. The life comes first; then the experience of the life. Therefore, to bring this work to an end, we must try to "place" the experience within the life; and this means, in the first place, marking its main boundaries.

The Christian life adheres to God by faith, and is united to God by charity. Its first object is not experience, but God himself. Now God always remains doubly transcendent to experience. In the first place, and quite clearly, no experience is ever exhaustive of God—not even the Beatific Vision itself. In the second place, no experience here below ever grasps God in himself, but only through the veil of faith, and consequently it unites us with him as with the unknown. An experience is certainly implied in the life of faith and charity, because this life, being spiritual, implies an awareness of the acts that are posited. But faith and charity are not in the first place an experience: they are a mysterious divine life, inserted into our souls so as to lead us to God. If they bear within them an experience of a magnificent kind, this can never be their equal, or a thing to judge them by, because it can only grasp its uncreated Object through a created mediation. It does not have perfect possession of its Object; it is a refraction of the divine Object through a spiritual impulse;

and the fruition of God which follows this incomplete possession is only a feeble foretaste of Beatitude.

This absolute transcendence of God, as Object and End of the Christian life, immediately relativizes the whole essence of the Christian experience, which can be no more than an effect and reflection of the life in God, a means adopted by this life, an early sketch of the ultimate achievement. Clearly, then, in its very texture it must include darkness, fear, and hope. "Let those who believe themselves to be keeping the faith take care not to fall, and let them work out their salvation with fear and trembling, in watchings, giving of alms, in prayers and offerings, in fasting and chastity. For they must necessarily fear, knowing that they are born again into the hope of glory, but not yet established in glory."[1] The Christian experience is the awareness of this possession, which is a magnificent thing, but it is also partial, obscure, embryonic, and subject to change.

There is no Christian life without a knowledge of self, and therefore without an experience of one's own "misery" and one's own "greatness." But it is not enough to say this: the only valid saying is "Knowing Thee, I shall know myself." This experience takes place within a relationship that is the basis of the experience and at the same time transcends it, for the knowledge of God comes first always: it comes first as End, because eternal life means knowing the one true God and Jesus Christ whom he sent, and thus sharing in the knowledge they have of themselves, which the Son came to communicate to us; it comes first as Source, because this knowledge throws light upon ourselves, on our nothingness as sinful creatures and our dignity as adopted sons, and only in Christ can we know ourselves as sinners, as redeemed, as deified; it comes first as Norm because it puts us in our proper place, and is a permanent reminder of our impurity compared with him who is All-Holy, our pride before him who is Lord God, and our powerlessness before him who is All-Merciful; and is thus continually bringing us back to an awareness of ourselves, who tend so easily to fall away. God is first, the experience second. Knowing oneself means knowing oneself before God, and—to repeat—this connection absolutely governs and relativizes our knowledge of ourselves.

By no means, therefore, is there any need for the Christian to

[1] *Conc. Trid.*, sess. vi, c. 13.

burrow into himself in search of self-knowledge, there to spread and disperse himself like water over an endless plain; or to enjoy himself as though in a world that is enchanting and self-sufficient. The Christian life is only self-knowledge as a means to the knowledge of God. Knowing oneself means discovering one's vocation—the obstacles in one's way, one's resources and responses—so as to be able to give oneself to God and serve him. Every genuine experience of self should be from this point of view a judgment on self corresponding to God's judgment, and a free decision in response to God's call. But here again experience is completely transcended: "Because we all commit many offences, every man should have mercy and goodness before his eyes as well as severity and judgment. And no one should judge himself, even though he is not conscious of any sins, because all men's lives are to be examined and judged not by any human judgment but by the judgment of God, who will bring into the light secrets hidden in darkness and reveal the designs of all men's hearts. And then praise will be given to every man by God himself, who, as it is written, will render unto each according to his works."[2]

Furthermore, the Christian experience is not its own norm. It is a structured experience, and the essential lines of its structure are its permanent norms. It is an experience in Christ, and it is from this that it derives its value and fruitfulness. But for this experience in Christ to be genuine, it must be an experience in faith and in the Church: these two essential relationships establish its constituent norms, and because faith means adhering to the Word of God as proposed by the Church, these two norms finally tend to coincide.

The norm of my experience, in fact, is in the first place faith, because faith is its living principle, its vital medium; it governs it according to the truth—negatively, because everything that is opposed to faith is *ipso facto* erroneous, and contaminates the entire experience to such a point that it becomes a mere pseudo-experience; positively, because everything that is in conformity with faith, and nothing else, is able to be integrated into a genuine experience. I say "able to be," because there is always a certain coefficient of mystery affecting the experience, and this prevents any absolute judgment from being made on it. But the clearest norm of faith is, on the

[2] *Conc. Trid.*, sess. vi, c. 16, end.

one hand, the teaching of the Church, "the mistress and guardian of the revealed Word," and, on the other, life in the Church, in conformity with the commandments of the Gospel, which define the *veritas vitae*. My faith is genuine to the extent that it is immersed in this teaching and life, and therefore to the extent that, while remaining mine, it is more than mine—"the faith with all the saints," rooted in the faith of the Church herself.

Consequently, personal experience is only safe if it is continually being re-immersed in the faith of the Church, continually referred to the Church's norms, continually judged by her infallible propositions and in ceaseless conformity with the movement of her life. It is the experience of one who is a member, and only on condition that he wills to remain such can it find its "place," and be lived authentically, and grow into the supreme experience of a person delivered, sanctified, and fulfilled by Christ. Conformity to these norms, therefore, simply means that the experience must conform to its own essential structure, the living principle of its stability, strength, and fruitfulness.

We must add, finally, that though the Christian experience is one in its specific structure, it is infinitely diverse in its personal realizations. There is a theology of the Christian experience because it has its own essential, normative structure; there is a theology of personal experiences only in so far as these verify the essential lines of this structure. For the rest, they are diversified from within and are absolutely irreducible, like the persons themselves. They exist in a spiritual universe in which, in one of its major aspects, everything is singular and incommunicable. They imply at any given moment the whole preceding spiritual history of the person who lives them. They are an aspect and an element of a process that is irreducibly individualized.

And in so far as each of these experiences descends into the mystery of the person's vocation, it is entirely a secret between the soul and God—a secret that may burst forth, when God destines some particular Christian to be a means of enlightenment to his brothers, and the depth of his singularity enables him to become a universal figure, as in the case of the great founders of the religious orders and other great spiritual leaders; but a secret hidden in humility, when God works upon a soul here on earth to reveal it only in Paradise; a unique secret in either case, because it is the result of a unique response to a unique love; a lasting secret to the soul itself, since its deified life is hidden with Christ in God, and shines here on earth only for the heart of God—it will only be revealed on the day that Christ reveals himself in all the splendour of his Sovereignty, sitting at the right hand of God, and in the unimaginable depths of his intimate life—Christ, our life—when we are revealed to ourselves and to others along with him, by him, and in his glory (Col. iii, 3-4).

These limitations, however, must not be allowed to obscure the greatness of the Christian experience; on the contrary, they should serve to bring it out. They do not limit it from outside, like walls; they form it from within, like the essential structure of a living organism. They are its constituent relationships: they only limit it in order to specify it, they define it in order to ensure it, they impose themselves on it in order to give it existence. Practically, they are a complex of living relationships to Christ in the Church—and it is this fact which lies behind both the greatness and the misery of the experience.

Of its greatness, because the experience is a relationship to Christ as one who is possessed, and here at one stroke this is strengthened and prolonged to infinity. It shares in all the goods of the Church and all the riches of Christ. What would be intolerable audacity if the experience was something self-enclosed, and sprang from pure immanence, becomes a normal affirmation when the experience is open to the mystery of Christ and exists only in this relationship which is its foundation and assurance, because it makes it depend entirely on Christ and tend entirely towards Christ. To take an extreme example, St. Augustine was not afraid to say that the Christian, in spite of his wretchedness, should repeat the words of the psalm: "*Quam sanctus sum*!" According to the line of interpretation that regards the psalms as Christ speaking to the Father, it is Christ who is speaking; thus this means that I must not separate my voice from his, but I too must say, "*Quam sanctus sum!*"—not as though referring to myself, for that would be pride and mendacity, but as referring to a "sanctified saint": "Let him, then, the body of Christ, let this unique man who cries from the ends of the earth, dare to say with his Head and under his Head, *Quam sanctus sum!*"

For the Christian has received this grace of holiness in baptism, and since the Apostle (I Cor. vi, 11) describes those who are baptized as being sanctified, then "Let all the faithful too say, 'I am holy.' This is not the pride of the man who puffs himself out, but the praise that comes from one who is not ungrateful. If you say that you are holy as a result of your own efforts, you suffer from pride, but you who are faithful in Christ, and are a member of Christ, if you say that you are not holy you are guilty of ingratitude. Recognize, then, both that you possess, and that you possess nothing of yourself, so that you may be neither proud nor ungrateful. Say then to God, 'I am holy, because you have sanctified me; because I have received, not because I had anything of my own; because you have given, not because I have deserved. . . .' If Christians have become members of the Body of Christ and say that they are not holy, they insult the head whose members are not holy. Mark well, then, where you are, and draw dignity from your Head."[3]

But this relationship to Christ as possessed is at the same time a relationship to the Christ who is hoped for and therefore not possessed; it is the Christian's "misery," with regard to full possession, and yet at the same time his "greatness" as a pilgrim far from the Lord. St. Augustine himself points out this connection at the end of the passage we have quoted: "This 'saint' is not proud, because he hopes in the Lord."[4] This is the eschatological dimension of the experience. Presence, possession, awareness, are all bathed in hope. They are stretched towards the ultimate plenitude, vision, security—"for we are saved by hope," and "we hope for that which we see not" (Rom. viii, 24-25). They do not rely on themselves, but on God, on the marvellous, all-powerful Agape. Amongst what shadows, what fears, what sorrows, we have already tried to describe; what remains perhaps to be emphasized is that when the soul is thus supported, it hopes really to possess its God, and tends towards eternal happiness—"to be with Christ"—as an end that grace has made possible, as a reward that has been promised—its personal fulfilment in beatitude. Which, according to St. Thomas, is the very act of hope.[5] The experience is underpropped, raised up and

[3] St. Augustine, *Enarratio in Psalm.*, 85, 4, P.L., 37, 1084-1085.

[4] *Ibid.*, 1085.

[5] *III Sent.*, d. 26, q. 2, a. 3, sol. 1: "This inclination of the will tending to the eternal good, as a thing possible to itself through grace, is the act of hope."

carried along entirely by this movement; it is thus based entirely on God's faithfulness to his promises—"I am a just God and I save men" (Isaias xl, 21). But, once again, it is the relationship to Christ, in whom are all the promises of God, in Christ our living hope, that the experience is founded and its paradoxical certainty founded.

Being thus a relationship to Christ as possessed and hoped for, the Christian experience is betwixt and between—like the pilgrim Church, like the Christian who is himself a pilgrim. It expresses the Christian being and situation;[6] and that is why it includes absence as well as presence, promise as well as possession, fear as well as confidence.[7] But the contact which it makes possible with Christ is irreplaceable and absolutely necessary to the growth of the son of God. The Christian experience, in fact, interiorizes the truths of faith, awakens desire and aspiration, sustains and nourishes faithfulness; it enables us to see,[8] touch, and taste God. As it develops, it detaches man from himself and plunges him into God, and thus realizes the paradox of going deeper into oneself by centring oneself on God, going beyond oneself by building oneself up, going outside oneself by enriching oneself. In this sense it is co-extensive with the Christian life, while always remaining subordinate to it: it represents at once, on the level of consciousness, an efflorescence of its richness, a growth (painful or pleasurable) of its mystery, a point of emergence of its living force. And because it is inserted entirely within the movement of hope, it helps to join earth and heaven, today and tomorrow, the eternal heaven and the way that leads there.

The profoundest remark on the subject of the Christian experience was made by St. Bernard when he described it as being situated between Christ's first and second coming. The Incarnation and the Parousia are comings of light; between them is the coming of grace—all the comings and goings and returns of Christ within the soul: a hidden coming always, glimpsed in mystery through those personal signs whose coherent but unpredictable totality forms the experi-

[6] Cf. L. MALAVEZ, *L'Église, Corps du Christ* (*Recherches de Science religieuse*, 1944), p. 59 (Commentary on "saved in hope").

[7] St. AUGUSTINE, *in Psalm* 85, 16: "If there is no joy, there is defect in us; if we feel wholly safe, we exult wrongly"; P.L., 37, 1090.

[8] "The life of faith gives to the eyes of faith a clarity that is almost sight," H. PINARD DE LA BOULLAYE, *L'expérience, la raison, les normes, dans le Catholicisme*, in *Revue de philosophie*, 1912, p. 526.

ence itself and enables the "elect" to "see Christ in themselves"—in the dark mirrors which they will always be to themselves. But this mysterious coming is the link between the first and the second coming, the means of going from the one to the other; rest and comfort during the pilgrimage,[9] during our life on earth, "this hour between spring and summer."

Christ is the traveller's bread; and the Christian experience is a little of this bread, which he gives to his own, to prevent them from falling by the wayside.

[9] *De advendu Domini, Sermo* 5, no. 1; P.L., 183, 50: "This intermediate coming is a kind of way leading us to the final coming. In his first coming, Christ was our redemption; in the last, he will appear as our life; in this . . . is our rest and consolation."